The Scientist Practitioner
(PGPS-128)

Pergamon Titles of Related Interest

Bellack/Hersen RESEARCH METHODS IN CLINICAL PSYCHOLOGY
Hersen/Barlow SINGLE CASE EXPERIMENTAL DESIGNS:
Strategies for Studying Behavior Change
Hersen/Bellack BEHAVIORAL ASSESSMENT:
A Practical Handbook, Second Edition
Ollendick/Hersen CHILD BEHAVIORAL ASSESSMENT:
Principles and Procedures

Related Journals*

BEHAVIORAL ASSESSMENT
PERSONALITY AND INDIVIDUAL DIFFERENCES

*Free specimen copies available upon request.

PERGAMON GENERAL PSYCHOLOGY SERIES
EDITORS
Arnold P. Goldstein, *Syracuse University*
Leonard Krasner, *SUNY at Stony Brook*

The Scientist Practitioner
Research and Accountability
in Clinical and Educational Settings

David H. Barlow
SUNY at Albany

Steven C. Hayes
University of North Carolina at Greensboro

Rosemery O. Nelson
University of North Carolina at Greensboro

PERGAMON PRESS
New York   Oxford   Beijing   Frankfurt
São Paulo   Sydney   Tokyo   Toronto

Pergamon Press Offices:

U.S.A.   Pergamon Press, Maxwell House, Fairview Park, Elmsford, New York 10523, U.S.A.

U.K.   Pergamon Press, Headington Hill Hall, Oxford OX3 0BW, England

PEOPLE'S REPUBLIC OF CHINA   Pergamon Press, Qianmen Hotel, Beijing, People's Republic of China

FEDERAL REPUBLIC OF GERMANY   Pergamon Press, Hammerweg 6, D-6242 Kronberg, Federal Republic of Germany

BRAZIL   Pergamon Editora, Rua Eça de Queiros, 346, CEP 04011, São Paulo, Brazil

AUSTRALIA   Pergamon Press (Aust.) Pty., P.O. Box 544, Potts Point, NSW 2011, Australia

JAPAN   Pergamon Press, 8th Floor, Matsuoka Central Building, 1-7-1 Nishishinjuku, Shinjuku-ku, Tokyo 160, Japan

CANADA   Pergamon Press Canada, Suite 104, 150 Consumers Road, Willowdale, Ontario M2J 1P9, Canada

Copyright © 1984 Pergamon Press Inc.

Second printing 1985

Third printing 1986

Fourth printing 1990

Library of Congress Cataloging in Publication Data

Barlow, David H.
  The scientist practitioner.

  (Pergamon general psychology series ; 128)
  Bibliography: p.
  Includes index.
  1. Clinical psychologists – Training of.   2. Clinical psychology – Practice.   3. Clinical psychology – Research.   I. Hayes, Steven C.   II. Nelson, Rosemery O.
III. Title.   IV. Series.
RC467.B36 1983   150'.23   83-12187
ISBN 0-08-027217-7
ISBN 0-08-027216-9 (pbk.)

Printed in the United States of America

For Joseph R. Cautela

Contents

Section III: Realistic Research Strategies

Preface

Throughout the human service professions, the term *scientist-practitioner* and its variants has been seen as an ideal seldom fulfilled. This ideal refers to a clinician or practitioner who can not only directly assist people with their problems, based on knowledge developed within his or her profession, but also contribute to our collective knowledge, thereby improving our practice. Recent developments in the human service professions, in particular the increasing emphasis on greater accountability in the human services, makes the ability to be empirical and scientific in one's professional activities all the more important. Within the last several years, scientific methodologies have been developed that are more compatible with the activities of practitioners and clinicians in applied settings. However, articles and books describing these methodologies continue to be written primarily for practicing scientists. But implementation of these methods in research settings often entails a level of sophistication in terms of measures and strategies neither possible nor desirable in applied settings. This book is directed at those practitioners and scientists who wish to be more accountable in their practice and who wish to contribute to advancing our knowledge through science within the practical and realistic confines of their human service activities.

The book is organized into three sections. The first section provides a historical perspective, including recent developments, on various approaches proposed in the past for integrating science and practice. Based on this analysis, a specific model of research in which the practitioner can be accountable and contribute to science within an applied setting is outlined. The second section describes realistic and practical measures of behavior change that are feasible and particularly suitable for use in applied settings. These measures are, of course, the sine qua non of accountability. The third section describes, in some detail, realistic research strategies that can be integrated into the work of full-time practitioners. Ethical and other issues that arise in this endeavor are also discussed. Finally, at the end of this section, the process of clinical replication in which a practitioner can accumulate a series of treated cases and thereby make important contributions to science is described and examples are given.

The terms *clinician* and *practitioner* are used interchangeably in this book. *Clinician* tends to be used more often when referring to examples that are appropriate to clinical settings, whereas the more generic term *practitioner* may refer to activities in any human service setting concerned with behavior assessment and change. While the origins of the term *scientist-practitioner* are found in the profession of clinical psychology, the basic principles of accountability and contributions to science are germane to a number of diverse professions, such as rehabilitation therapy, social work in all of its professional settings, the field of education and, of course, the core mental health professions of psychiatric nursing, social work, psychiatry, and clinical psychology. Thus, we attempted to write the book so that the basic concepts and their implementation would be clear to professionals from these diverse professional backgrounds. To the extent that we have been successful in this effort, we can only express our deepest appreciation to Sallie Morgan, who literally produced this book from start to finish, and to our editor, Jerry Frank, for his patience. To David Sakheim, who worked for days setting up and monitoring the electronic transmittal of this book to Pergamon, our sincere gratitude and admiration for helping us cross another technical frontier. We would like to thank Susan Cohen and Janet Klosko who worked long and hard to produce a readable and hopefully useful index, as well as Adam Lipson for reviewing sections of the book. Any scholar who reads this book will also recognize our intellectual debt to David Shakow, who first conceptualized the role of the scientist-practitioner, and B. F. Skinner, who pioneered methods allowing practitioners to work scientifically with individuals.

Finally, it is with the deepest respect that we dedicate this book to Joseph R. Cautela, a true scientist-practitioner who modeled the essential values of this approach at a time when many professionals had foresworn any hope of its realization. The perseverance of Joe Cautela and some of his colleagues deeply influenced the next generation of scientist-practitioners, making this book possible.

SECTION I
A REINTEGRATION
OF SCIENCE AND
PRACTICE

Chapter 1
The Scientist-Practitioner:
Origins and Current Status

INTRODUCTION

From the perspective of the 1980s, one must wonder why anyone thought that practitioners in the general area of behavior change would be scientists? Why did those who formulated the lofty ideals of training programs imagine that we could turn out, in a wholesale fashion, full- or even part-time practitioners and clinicians who would do research and earn the title *scientist-practitioner?*

As applications of basic behavioral science and biology emerged in clinical and educational settings, philosophies abounded on how best to train practitioners from various fields of human behavior change in the use of these applications. While these debates and controversies have continued over the decades, a unifying feature of training in these areas has been the desirability of including a broad acquaintance with research methodology, including data collection and analysis, as well as actual participation in the process of applied research. Whether the field was psychiatry, social work, clinical psychology, education, or other health professions, the expectation was that practitioners finishing these programs would, at the very least, bring an analytical mind to their professional practices and actively participate in, if not actually initiate, experimental inquiries in the context of their applied work. In this way the area of human behavior change would progress, and our collective knowledge increase. This training approach would also produce a professional who was empirical and therefore accountable for the results of his or her intervention through awareness of those behavior-change procedures showing evidence of effectiveness and objective measurement of the process of change. Thus, the practitioner would be an active consumer of research, using the latest procedures developed in research centers and observing the effects of these procedures in individuals by careful measurement of change.

Therefore, the scientific side of practice, as it has evolved, describes three primary and interrelated activities or roles for practitioners. In the first role

3

the practitioner is a consumer of new research findings from research centers, usually new assessment or treatment techniques that he or she will put into practice. In the second role, the practitioner is an evaluator of his or her own interventions using empirical methods that would increase accountability. The third role describes the practitioner as researcher, producing new data from his or her own setting and reporting these data to the scientific community.

What was the origin of the idea underlying the scientist-practitioner model of training? What were the goals that the founders of clinical psychology were attempting to reach and why were leaders in all of the mental health professions as concerned as they were, even in the early 1960s when it seemed that a split between science and practice was developing? Why is the model of a scientist-practitioner or clinician who will remain in the mainstream of scientific research in our fields still the most popular and highly revered model of training for clinical psychologists (Leitenberg, 1974; Shakow, 1976) and increasingly popular in such fields as social work (Jayaratne & Levy, 1979), despite the seeming failures of this model over the years? To find answers to these questions, one must examine some of the original documents espousing the scientist-practitioner as a model for training. The history of the movement is found largely in clinical psychology and closely allied educational fields, although the issues are equally relevant to other practitioners in applied settings.

The remainder of this chapter will trace the origin of the scientist-practitioner model of training as it evolved in clinical psychology and the experiences of all of the behavior-change professions in the ensuing decades that forced reconsideration of this model by some. Practical and philosophical differences that prevent practitioners from doing research will be described as well as the more important discovery that research findings have had little impact on practice; that is, practitioners stopped "consuming" research. Reasons for the development of this scientist-practitioner split, with the consequence that many practitioners are not empirical and therefore not accountable, are suggested, as well as the seemingly contradictory notion that the scientific-empirical approach is more highly valued than ever.

DEVELOPMENT OF THE SCIENTIST-PRACTITIONER MODEL

David Shakow and F.C. Thorne

The idea that a psychologist should be trained both as a scientist and a professional became the policy of the American Psychological Association following a report of an influential committee chaired by David Shakow in

1947 (Shakow, Hilgard, Kelly, Luckey, Sanford, & Shaffer, 1947). While Shakow would go on to make many important contributions during his distinquished career, he remained the foremost spokesman for this model of training (e.g., Shakow, 1969).

But the ideals of the scientist-practitioner were never more clearly laid out than in a paper published in *American Psychologist* in 1947 by Frederick C. Thorne, entitled "The clinical method in science." Stating what could well be the thesis of this book, Thorne made the following observations on the conduct of clinical practice:

> Formerly, clinical technology was mainly empirical, i.e., based on study and "experience" rather than experiment. To a certain degree therapy must always be empirical since the primary consideration is the welfare of the patient rather than the conduct of a scientific experiment. Perhaps the most significant development, however, is the increasing application of the experimental approach to the individual case and to the clinician's own "experience." Ideally, diagnosis (description) and treatment of each individual case may be regarded as a single and well-controlled experiment. The treatment may be carefully controlled by utilizing single therapeutic factors, observing and recording results systematically, and checking through the use of appropriate quantitative laboratory studies. In addition to the general scientific orientation to the individual case there are frequent opportunities in clinical practice to conduct actual experiments to determine the validity of diagnosis or the efficacy of treatment. For example, a simple experiment may be set up in which a placebo and a specific drug may be administered according to a definite pattern, such as A/B/B/A, with careful recording and mathematical analysis of results. . . . Individual clinicians are encouraged to apply experimental and statistical methods in the analysis of case results and larger scale analyses are made of the experience of the whole clinic over a period of years. Thus the clinician comes to regard each individual case as part of a larger sample. (p. 159-160)

Unfortunately, Thorne was wrong. This did not represent the development of the practice of clinical psychology or any of the human service professions. Clinical practice was to remain intuitive and based on experience for many years yet to come. But perhaps Thorne's writings, at the very least, would influence an important group of professionals meeting two years later.

The Boulder Conference

Although clinical psychology has a long history (e.g., Garfield, 1966), it is not an exaggeration to say that the birth of clinical psychology, as we know it today, occurred in August of 1949 in Boulder, Colorado. At that time, a total of 71 representatives from training universities, mental health service agencies, and allied professions met daily for the unusually long period of two weeks. This conference was sponsored by the National Institute of Mental Health and the American Psychological Association to arrive at a consensus on the content of training of clinical psychologists. Although a committee of the American Psychological Association, chaired by David Shakow, had recommended a training model emphasizing both science and practice two years earlier (Shakow et al., 1947), the Boulder conference, representing as it did all of the clinical psychology training programs existing at that time as well as representatives from numerous clinical and governmental agencies, was in a position to have an enormous impact. But even its participants were most likely unaware that the words *Boulder conference* would be mentioned during the ensuing 30 years every time psychologists convened to discuss training and that any innovations in training suggested subsequently would always be discussed in the context of conclusions reached during those two weeks in August of 1949. Furthermore, the close interrelationship of the professions comprising the original "mental health team," specifically psychiatric nurses, psychiatric social workers, psychiatrists, and clinical psychologists, was recognized even then. In view of their overriding interest in what was basically the same problem, it was inevitable that considerations of training, and particularly the role of research in training, would be seriously considered by all of these professions. These considerations have had some impact on all professions producing mental health practitioners as well as other clinical and educational professions, despite the very different history and traditions of these other professions.

The unanimous recommendation at the end of this conference — the validity of the scientist-practitioner model for training — did not reflect the attitudes of participants when the conference began. In the oft-cited report on this conference (Raimy, 1950), it was observed that the role of research in the training of the clinical psychologist was perhaps the most challenging issue debated there. This was true since "neither tradition nor the definition of clinical psychology provides much guidance," (Raimy, 1950, p. 79) because clinical psychology, even at that time, functioned in many different fields, from research planning to full-time psychotherapeutic intervention. Training emphasis then, as now, varied from producing statistically sophisticated therapists to service-oriented practitioners. These opinions were reflected initially by factions who questioned sincerely whether graduate students could be trained in both areas. Then, as now, one faction suggested that emphasis on research training might dilute and weaken the necessary training for competence in diagnosis and treatment. An equally strong faction, less in evidence today, pointed out that as much damage might be done by diluting a good research training with time spent on applied diagnostics and therapy. In retrospect, the underlying rationale for the latter position was quite valid, in that this faction questioned whether anything clinicians did as service workers at the time was effective, or at least had been proven effective. This position was best represented by a quote which has run down through the decades, "Psychotherapy is an undefined technique, applied to unspecified problems, with unpredictable outcome. For this technique we recommend rigorous training" (Raimy, 1950, p. 93). Eysenck's more serious and better documented statement on the effects of psychotherapy three years later was to have a more profound impact (Eysenck, 1952), but the same feeling prevailed in 1949.

Five Reasons for "Joint" Training.

Against this background, it is very surprising to see that the decision of the conference to recommend the training of clinical psychologists for research and practice, with equal emphasis on both, was not a compromise to resolve a dilemma, but was an almost unanimous consensus of the participants. This unanimity occurred despite the realization that there were considerable risks involved in deciding to train students in both areas and that this model of training was an almost unique experiment in professional training.

The basis for this unanimous recommendation rests on five important considerations, many of which are still relevant today. First, it was decided that students should receive training in both research and practice in order to develop an interest and background in both areas, despite the fact that some might only concentrate on one area during their careers. Thus, every clinical psychologist receiving the doctor of philosophy degree was seen as unique, in that combined training in practice and research enabled one to engage in either research, training, or preferably a combination of the two. Underlying this reason was a further assumption that specialization by a large group of individuals, in this case specialization in either research or practice, had certain well-known tendencies to produce narrowness of thinking and rigidity of action. But, as the conferees noted:

> When, however, persons within the same general field specialize in different aspects, as inevitably happens, cross-fertilization and breadth of approach are likely to characterize such a profession. Whether the four-year doctoral training program, which emphasizes both research and service, will achieve the desired result is a question to be settled by the future. (Raimy, 1950, p. 81)

Second, with a rationale that would find many sympathizers today, the conferees stated, "The manifest lack of dependable knowledge in clinical psychology and personality demands that research be considered a vital part of the field of clinical psychology. Participants at the conference displayed considerable humility with respect to confidence in present techniques" (Raimy, 1950, p. 80). Today it seems we have made considerable progress in identifying specific techniques that are effective with specific problems (e.g., Barlow, l98l; Rachman & Wilson, 1980), but few would disagree that we still have much to be humble about.

Third, the participants believed that there was no reason that clinical psychology could not find people capable of carrying out both roles. It was noted, even then, that applicants far exceeded the number of slots for training and that preference should be given to the student who showed some potential for combining both functions.

Fourth, it was observed that direct involvement in the clinical process by researchers would bring them into intimate contact with important research issues. This rationale is widely accepted today. Finally, effectively delivered service may provide some of the much needed financial support for the initiation and continuation of research projects. This is still true to a large extent, although the conferees did not anticipate fully the important role that government funding was to play in supporting large clinical research centers in the coming decades.

There is no question that the experimental nature of this very different training experience did not escape the conference participants:

> The development of the profession of clinical psychology constitutes something of an educational experiment in that clinical psychologists are being trained both as scientists and as practitioners. Most professions base their practices on one or more sciences and train their future members in a separate professional school. In contrast, clinical psychologists are trained concurrently in both the theoretical (scientific) and applied (clinical) aspects of psychology. This training occurs not in professional schools but in graduate schools of our colleges and universities. (Raimy, 1950, p. v)

What is particularly interesting to note from a perspective of over 30 years is that the conference participants were not a bit naive about the difficulties inherent in combining both roles or the types of research skills which should comprise the major part of the training effort. A section of the conference report was devoted to enumerating methods whereby research could be made more meaningful and relevant to the trainee. Among the most important was a recommendation that research methodology be taught in the context of significant clinical problems. Indeed, specific clinical research skills suitable for training were suggested that were different in many ways from the research skills suitable for an experimental psychologist. This recognition is best exemplified in the following conclusion:

> Research training for "rat" psychology is probably most efficiently accomplished by lengthy exposure to problems in which rats are the objects of observation and discussion. . . . Nonetheless, the problems

of human beings may demand approaches other than those used in studying the lower animals. If rigorous thinking can produce good research in animal psychology, equally rigorous thinking should be possible where humans are concerned. Proper methodology and crucial issues in the field of personality may be more difficult to establish and define; the problems faced by one field of science are rarely if ever solved by a simple carryover of techniques and concepts from another field. (Raimy, 1950, p. 87)

The conference participants were aware not only of the importance of developing a science that would be particularly applicable to clinical problems, but also were well aware of the dangers of not developing this approach, as illustrated in the following passage:

> Too often, however, clinical psychologists have been trained in rigorous thinking about nonclinical subject matter and clinical problems have been dismissed as lacking in "scientific" respectability. As a result, many clinicians have been unable to bridge the gap between their formal training and scientific thinking on the one hand, and the demands of practice on the other. As time passes and their skills become more satisfying to themselves and to others, the task of thinking systematically and impartially becomes more difficult. (Raimy, 1950, p. 86)

Here the scientist-practitioner gap was clearly anticipated. Fears that this gap would bring about the overspecialization, rigidity, and narrowness of thinking mentioned above were important considerations in producing specific recommendations for dual training.

The type of research that the participants thought would be suitable for training and even for dissertation requirements was much broader than one would think after reading reports on the recommendations of this conference in later years. It was thought that one of the important skills forthcoming from this training effort would be an empirical approach to clinical phenomena, where observation and analysis would remain the most important tools for understanding what problems were in need of further investigation and what answers were likely to be permitted by the facts observed. Training in the skills of empirical observation would help the clinician to separate preconceptions and inferences from observations. This resembles what we have termed the *evaluative* scientific activity of practitioners. While it was stressed that training in statistics and the writing of experimental reports would be an important part of this training, it was recognized that there would be a great deal of variability in the need for statistics and that a minimal, rather than an optimal degree of competence was desirable.

There is little question that the Boulder conference did not intend the clinical psychologist to do his or her research in an animal laboratory or even to confine research to the traditional hypothetico-deductive strategy so popular at that time. Indeed, evaluation research and policy research were noted as being particularly important for clinical psychologists. Even the study of individual cases, a procedure deeply rooted in the case-study method of psychoanalysis (Hersen & Barlow, 1976), was thought to be a legitimate exercise, as noted in the following passage:

> Intensive studies of individual cases might well reveal the significant variables required for an adequate scientific account of personality dynamics and change. The value of the individual case study as legitimate research for an advanced degree has been debated for a number of years. One cannot, however, question the case study as a means of making intimate observations, for getting "close to the data," or "securing clinical phenomena" that demand explanation, and for making dramatically evident our present lack of understanding. (Raimy, 1950, p. 85)

The participants did doubt that a single case study, no matter how brilliantly executed, could satisfy the requirements of a doctoral dissertation, but noted, "However, this question deserves further study before a categorical denial of the suitability of this form of research enterprise is made" (Raimy, 1950, p. 89). This seems a particularly "liberal" position in view of the fact that single-case experimental designs, as opposed to clinical case studies, had not yet appeared.

In summary, the recommendations of the Boulder conference did not constitute an overly narrow and rigid set of restrictions on the training of clinical psychologists wherein every clinician would spend equal amounts of time on practice and the production of research, whether they were related or not. Rather, what was recommended was a well-trained clinician, who would combine clinical practice with an empiricism and a research methodology particularly suited for clinical work. Many of these empirical clinicians, but not all, would make substantive contributions to answering the important questions concerning assessment and treatment that would benefit the profession as a whole. The unquestionable rationality of this approach may be one reason for the persistence of this training model in the face of numerous alternatives proposed in recent years, which have not yet impacted to a significant degree on the majority of clinical training programs. The more important question left unanswered is, Why has this model failed?

Subsequent Conferences

The Boulder conference was followed by numerous conferences, varying in size and scope, and occurring at a frequency of approximately every 2 years. This process was punctuated occasionally by other large conferences, often convened to review the recommendations of the Boulder conference as they applied at that time. Such conferences occurred in Miami Beach in 1958, in Chicago in 1965, and in Vail in 1974. At Miami Beach the scientist-practitioner was strongly reaffirmed as the optimal model for training clinical psychologists:

> In the research and evaluation area, probably lies psychology's greatest and most singular opportunity for contributing to mental health. By improving the scientific basis for mental health programs and participating in the evaluation of the results of the wide range of mental health services and activities, psychology, along with other disciplines, not only can render the widest possible public health service by investing and sharpening the tools of mental health, but provide administrators, legislators, and the public with the information they need to implement program development. As usually the only members of the mental health team with research training, the clinical psychologist, counseling psychologist, school, and other psychologist, all have a special responsibility in this area for not only utilizing their own research knowledge and skills but for bringing other psychologists and other scientists in on the many problems that lie beyond the competencies of any one psychologist. (Roe, Gustad, Moore, Ross, & Skodak, 1959, p. 38)

Later on it was noted:

> It was, however, agreed that the defining characteristic of the psychologist is his research training. The conference approved the broad definition of research to include a continuum of research methodologies from the most rigid hypothesis testing to the use of clinical and naturalistic devices for the formulation of communicable and testable generalizations. It approved an early and extensive experience with research for all doctoral candidates. (Roe et al., 1959, p. 88)

These characteristics apply to the practitioner as researcher and evaluator, rather than consumer. Throughout these conferences it is assumed that the clinician would be a consumer of research. Nevertheless, some problems were noted at this time, such as the fact that the Boulder conference had dealt with dual training only as a generality and had not provided guidance on the specifics of implementing this role. At Miami Beach the broad definition of research was reaffirmed, which may have reflected an early realization that the more basic "hypothesis-testing" research strategy was not being integrated successfully with the clinical aspects of training.

What was noteworthy about the next major conference in Chicago in 1965 was the almost defensive reaffirmation of the scientist-practitioner model in terms far stronger than had been used before, accompanied by a dramatic relaxing of the definition of science. This position was accompanied by a frank statement on the difficulties of doing meaningful clinical research. To quote the proceedings:

> The conferees particularly deplored the view, often implicit in the organization of clinical training programs, that clinical psychology is comprised of two separate elements: science and practice. They went on record as viewing science and practice as two facets of the same fundamental entity, declaring that a systematic search for truth can occur in a clinical setting as readily as in a laboratory. The premise leads to the conclusion that training necessarily involves an ongoing, continuous integration of science and practice and that where such integration is achieved, the relative proportions in which the two aspects are present in any particular training program are of secondary importance. (Hoch, Ross, & Winder, 1966, p. 75)

The conferees did conclude, however, that collecting empirical data is only one possible interpretation of research, even within the context of the dissertation. Other examples would be theoretical, historical, evaluative, or scholarly contributions that might not include the collection of data.

Throughout this conference an undercurrent of dissension on the adequacy of the scientist-practitioner model was obvious. Warning signals were beginning to appear that the model was not working as hoped and that the model, to once again quote the conference, was not being implemented "with sincere investment and enthusiasm." Opinions to appear in print in the next several years would confirm this suspicion. Bergin, Garfield, and Thompson (1967) were to point out that these recommendations for loosening of the guidelines for dissertation research, contained in the Chicago conference, were startling and an "unambiguous challenge to a tradition which has tended to stultify research in clinical psychology and which has produced many trifling dissertations" (p. 314). They noted that this declaration of independence was a clear expression of the long frustration endured in clinical psychology training, resulting from an exclusive reliance on the experimental model for clinical research. They confessed, however, that they had not been successful in providing greater integration between research and practical training at Columbia University, widely considered a model program at the time.

Disillusionment

In retrospect, these sentiments of frustration and dissatisfaction had really been there all along. The Boulder conference affirmed the logic and integrity of the scientist-practitioner model, but expressed some question whether it could be implemented, noting that the answer was somewhere in the future. At Miami Beach in 1958, the conferees lamented the fact that the Boulder conference had not told them in what specific ways clinicians could do research or researchers could do clinical practice. And Chicago, despite the strongest defense of the model to date, deftly did away with the collection of data as one of the functions of the clinical scientist. Without question, this was shocking!

But the Chicago conference, with its glossy prose and optimistic views of the future, communicated only through its inherent contradictions the frustration and pessimism evident at that time. In fact, science and practice were not integrated, and some thought this would never happen. As early as 1961, the Joint Commission on Mental Illness and Health published a report on its alarm over the developing scientist-practitioner split, particularly in view of the growing necessity for the development of new assessment and treatment procedures at that time. For, if there was one thing that most empirical clinicians and researchers agreed upon, it was that therapeutic procedures were still largely unproven (Eysenck, 1965). In a landmark book on psychotherapy research, Bergin and Strupp (1972) concluded, after interviewing leading researchers in the field of behavior change, that traditional hypothesis-testing, group-comparison research was simply not applicable to clinical problems. Their major criticism of this approach was the exaggerated importance accorded to problems of methodology and a lack of emphasis on socially important behavior change. As they observed, the kinds of effects interesting to clinicians should be so readily observable that resorting to statistical significance should not be necessary. And yet, this was an essential component of traditional research at that time.

Thus, despite some lip service to the model, it was no surprise that clinicians did little or no research themselves. This assumption, of course, was supported by data indicating that the modal number of publications of clinical psychologists was zero (cf. Barlow, 1980) and by a survey of clinical psychologists published by Garfield and Kurtz (1976) indicating that most clinicians would have preferred a deemphasis on research training in their curriculum. Against this background, it is not surprising that the next move was a suggestion to drop research training from the curriculum altogether and to proceed with a recommendation that really had its roots in the Boulder conference, and possibly before: the training of clinical psychologists in professional schools.

Professional Training in Professional Schools

Vague concerns arose from time to time in the report of the Boulder conference (Raimy, 1950). These concerns revolved around potential problems with training in the methods of science when so much time had to be devoted to professional training itself, particularly since many students were not interested in science. Ten years later, in Miami Beach in 1958, the conferees observed that the notion of a professional degree was brought up from time to time, but generally evoked little interest. Nevertheless, within 10 years of that conference the first professional degree in psychology, the doctor of psychology program at the University of Illinois, was established (Peterson, 1968). This program, and others that followed, including independent or "free-standing" professional schools of psychology, were based on multiple sources of dissatisfaction with traditional training. Among these dissatisfactions were political and logistical issues, as articulated so clearly by Albee (1970). Albee noted that psychology did not have its own captive training sites, such as hospitals for medical schools or schools for colleges of education, and therefore had to rely on other professions for practical training. Furthermore, the political control of training programs was often in the hands of experimental psychologists. Nevertheless, topping the list of reasons put forth by the founders of this movement was the incompatibility of the scientist and the professional. In a controversial but highly regarded article on the uncertain future of clinical psychology, Albee (1970) observed that one of the most serious problems for the scientist-practitioner psychologist "has been the requirement that he play the incompatible game of science" (p. 1075). Albee then detailed his view of the essentially conflicting types of research that are relevant to science and clinical work: "The clinician, including the clinical psychologist, often must engage in life history research rather than experimentation" (p. 1076). This statement reflected Albee's belief, at the time, that the causes and maintaining factors of most psychological problems lay in childhood and only longitudinal study could elucidate these causes.

In his proclamation of the first doctor of psychology program at the University of Illinois, Donald Peterson, one of the most eloquent defenders of this alternative training model, noted that the number of clinical psychologists generally interested in both research and service appeared to be very small and that the professional degree recognized the reality that most students wanted to be professionals rather than scientists. To do this properly and to teach the abundance of knowledge and skills required of the thoroughly trained professional in the 1970s, the competing activity of research training would have to be sharply curtailed or eliminated. As Peterson observed, "Our students now spend three-sevenths of their time doing dissertation research and studying languages. That is an intolerably ineffective use of expensive resources for people who are planning to enter careers of professional service." (Peterson, 1968, p. 511). The clear implication of this statement is that research training has no more relevance for the professional than learning foreign languages.

Continuing a tradition begun in Chicago in 1965, the doctoral dissertation became the primary target for those questioning the relevance of research. Adler (1972) observed that the research techniques utilized in most dissertations "are those of obsolete research methodology essentially inapplicable to the illumination of meaningful social and clinical issues" (p. 72). Adler proposed that any research in the new doctor of psychology program would be submitted to the test of relevance for practice regardless of the methodology. Stricker (1973), echoing a broad consensus of the times, reiterated Bergin and Strupp's observations on the peripheral and trivial nature of most dissertations that were making little or no contribution to knowledge. In 1973 Stricker remembered the recommendations for a dramatic broadening of the definitions of research made in Chicago in 1965, but observed that these recommended changes had no parallel in the halls of our universities where "business appears to go as usual."

Yet another major conference on training in clinical psychology, the Vail conference, took place for a week during July of 1973. Recommendations from this conference (Korman, 1974) went far beyond previous conferences in explicitly endorsing the creation of doctor of psychology degrees and downplaying the scientist-practitioner model as the one appropriate model for training clinical psychologists. While noting that some programs may wish to retain the PhD and, by implication, the traditional scientist-practitioner model, recommendations for research training included a reaffirmation and extension of those recommendations made in Chicago 8 years earlier calling for greatly increased flexibility in dissertation research criteria. This included a wider range of possible dissertation chairs, persons presumably with less "traditional" research interests. For the first time in the history of these conferences on psychology training, no section describing recommended research training was included. Remarks on research are confined to those that advocate greatly increased flexibility and relevance in doctoral dissertation research. As Stricker (1975) observed, "The recommendations emanating from this conference were often contradictory and inconsistent, making rejection by mainstream psychology seem inevitable and perhaps throwing out a few promising babies along with the bathwater" (p. 1063), but the devaluation of the scientist-practitioner role during this conference was the culmination of a train of thought stretching back years.

It was left for Peterson to summarize and defend logically this line of thinking in a series of articles in 1976 (Peterson, 1976a, 1976b). While others have continued to make these arguments, no one has been as clear in pointing out that there is no need for the word *scientist,* or for that matter any other word, such as *scholar,* to be attached to the word *professional* in describing the optimal training model for clinical psychologists. Reflecting on the fact that professional psychologists have not done research despite their training as scientist-practitioners, Peterson concludes that the primary role of the professional psychologist is the delivery of human services, specifically those of a psychological nature concerned with assessment and behavior change. This does not require extensive training in, or the production of, empirical research. If one goal of the scientist-practitioner model is familiarity with findings from the science of psychology as well as the capability of critically evaluating those findings as they appear, then this does not necessarily require research productivity or even the process of dissertation research. To continue with our terms, one does not need to produce new data to be a consumer of research. Rather, it simply requires that the profession of psychology, much as any profession, adopt a scholarly attitude towards training that should be based on the scientific findings underlying that particular professional field. In this way psychology is really no different than professions such as medicine, social work, or education in that all of these professions should be equally dependent on advances in science, and, in that sense, scholarly, for the practice of their professions. Following this line of thinking, the scientist-practitioner model is dead, and given the lackluster performance over the decades, perhaps was never even born. Therefore there should be nothing unusual or unique about clinical psychology relative to other health professions, since all would be scholars only in the sense that scholarly activity is necessary to become a capable professional; that is, a good consumer.

But traditions die hard, and despite the difficulties in countering this very logical set of arguments, most clinical psychologists were not ready to give up an idea whose basic integrity was in large part responsible for its longevity, despite the absence of hard data indicating that the model was viable. While arguments brought up in opposition to Peterson's ideas ranged from administrative (i.e., doctor of philosophy versus doctor of psychology) to the optimal location for training in clinical psychology, at the heart of most of these arguments was a continuing struggle in conceptualizing the proper place of research training and research productivity in the training programs of clinical psychology, including those of the new professional schools.

The Elimination of Research Training

But is this really the issue? Is the meaningful and fruitful integration of science and practice really a function of where one's professional skills are learned? Are the goals, if not the implementation, of the scientist-practitioner model, as formulated down through the decades of clinical psychology, really in question? Despite the rhetoric and the tendency to see the establishment of professional schools in psychology as a refutation of the importance of basic grounding in the theory and practice of science as part of professional training, most proponents of professional schools do not take this view (Peterson, 1976a, 1976b; Stricker, 1975). Rather than deemphasizing the importance of science, these authors emphasize the importance of clinical training and question activities that are not directly relevant to, or that compete with, those experiences enabling one to practice professionally. This is quite a different emphasis, which is not always clear in the dialogue of the last 10 years. As Stricker notes (1975), the assumed attack on science posed by the professional schools has appeared to be the most critical issue in the ongoing debate. Indeed, he concludes that the call for changes in the research requirements by those who advocate professional schools is seen by many as "a camouflage for anti-research, anti-intellectual attitude that does not befit a doctoral level practitioner of any orientation" (p. 1064). However, as has been characteristic in this dialogue, Stricker himself says later on that it is "impossible to provide high level professional and research training simultaneously" (p. 1065).

Nevertheless, Stricker's clear message is that what is needed is a reaffirmation of the flexibility in research training endorsed by the Chicago conference. This conference, of course, only reiterated recommendations made in the original Boulder conference calling for research training to be provided in the proper context and be relevant to the subject matter at hand. While Stricker (1975) goes no further than any of his predecessors in outlining the specifics of how this could be implemented in a professional school, he does mention the desirability of courses in the usual areas such as statistics, research design, and methodology to make students informed research consumers. He also mentions the possibility of additional training in *evaluation research,* which had been suggested quite frequently in the previous conferences. Of course, Peterson (1976a, 1976b) also endorses this sort of acquaintance with research methodology as one of the bases of the scholarly foundation of professional practice. But, along with Stricker (1975), he concludes that since psychologists are not going to do research, it makes no sense to require years of direct, on-line research experience, because this competes with opportunities for additional clinical course work and training. Here, Peterson seems to be referring to the practitioner as researcher rather than consumer or evaluator. One obvious implication is that research activity that does not compete with clinical training, or is perhaps even relevant to clinical training, would be quite compatible in professional schools; although only vague examples were ever given, such as Stricker's *evaluation research.* But this possibility was overlooked as the large majority of organized psychology thundered to the defense of the scientist-practitioner model.

The Scientist-Practitioner Model Reaffirmed

Few psychologists reconsidering the role of research in the training process over the decades have held any illusions concerning the success of the scientist-practitioner model as it has been implemented. In a very insightful and personal statement on the issue in 1966, Garfield concluded that all of the major discontents and confusions within clinical psychology could be traced to the uniqueness of the "Boulder experiment" as opposed to failure of the model as implemented.

Garfield attributed this failure to a lack of adequate role models for psychologists in training. "Unfortunately, they are not given an integrated model with which to identify, but are confronted instead by two apparently conflicting models — the scientific research model and the clinical practitioner model. As I see it, the Boulder model is really not available to them . . ." (Garfield, 1966, p. 357). The biggest disappointment of this failure, according to Garfield, was the observation that practicing psychologists "have contributed so little to a better understanding of what is involved in modifying personality and behavior and in contributing to newer and more efficient ways of helping people with problems of adjustment" (p. 358).

But far from seeking alternative models or abandoning research training, Garfield concluded at that time that it was more important than ever that this be made workable. Echoing the Joint Commission on Mental Illness and Health (1961), where the dimensions of our ignorance about assessment, therapy, prevention, and other aspects of psychological intervention were observed, Garfield concluded that there are few fields that need research as badly as clinical psychology. In this respect, the lack of research activity by PhD psychologists was a social and professional tragedy. What was most needed to temper this tragedy was the production of a clinical psychologist who could solve significant problems, devise new techniques, and evaluate both these new procedures as well as adaptations of older ones. This could only be accomplished through a true integration of research and practice and the devising of clinical research procedures that would be fully appropriate to the clinical situation.

It is significant that the need for research, despite progress in recent years, and the need for clinically relevant methods to enable the professional to do research are as vital now as they were in 1966 when Garfield observed that most clinical psychologists saw their doctoral program, and particularly the dissertation, solely as hurdles to overcome before they hung up their shingle and practiced psychotherapy. And yet, as we have seen, the recommendations for developing a research methodology uniquely applicable to the clinic was made with equal intensity at Boulder in 1949 and at every conference since, without any discernible change in the products of the graduate schools of clinical psychology.

Garfield was not the only one who strongly reaffirmed the scientist-practitioner model during this period and after (e.g., Proshansky, 1972; Schover, 1980; Tyler & Speisman, 1967; Wollersheim, 1974). Surveys of practicing psychologists conducted during this period overwhelmingly reaffirmed the scientist-practitioner model of training as unique and appropriate (Thelen & Ewing, 1970). In 1979, Perry pointed out that the number of APA clinical programs training clinical psychologists in university-based graduate departments leading to a PhD increased from 67 in 1975 to 102 in 1977, and noted that this could hardly be construed as a rejection of the Boulder model. He also cited recent surveys discovering greater satisfaction among psychologists with their training in contrast to similar surveys conducted in earlier decades.

The growth of alternative models, particularly the professional model with an implied reduction of emphasis on research training, was viewed as a very small development in the overall context of the growth of clinical psychology, and yet one receiving much attention in print through the efforts of a "vociferous minority." With research training as the unique difference and asset that clinical psychology brings to the public, Perry (1979) warned against relying on others for the production of new knowledge that would form the basis of any further advance in the practice of clinical psychology. Perry quoted Ericksen (1966), "Insofar as professional psychology becomes pinched off from scientific psychology, it will be taking one clear backward step toward becoming a second-class service technology" (Ericksen, 1966, p. 953). Professional schools of psychology, particularly those with no university affiliation, were seen as a move in this direction. The same situation in medicine in 1910 provoked a radical restructuring of medical education from a varied series of "free-standing" schools to a strong affirmation that medical education could only be administered properly in the context of the university (Flexner, 1910).

While many others defended the scientist-practitioner model, none did it better than the chair of the committee that put forth the original recommendation for this model in 1947. Approaching the end of his distinguished career as a clinical psychologist, David Shakow (1976) concluded that the viability of the scientist-practitioner model "derives fundamentally from the recognition by clinical psychologists that in the scientist-practitioner model they have captured most adequately the underlying motivation that led them to select psychology as a life work which is other-understanding through self-understanding by way of science" (p. 554). Shakow challenges training programs to ask themselves, "How well do the programs develop persons who can examine evidence critically, who are concerned with the advancement of knowledge, and who, if necessary, can carry on activities directed at the acquisition of this knowledge?" (p. 560)

In the face of an overwhelming reaffirmation of the importance of producing scientist-practitioners, the practical issues basic to this deeply philosophical confrontation were often overlooked. As noted above, for example, there is nothing in the arguments of those advocating professional schools of psychology that would preclude scientific training and practice as an integral part of clinical work. Even those advocating the abandonment of the scientist-practitioner model in favor of a professional model (e.g., Peterson, 1976b), do not advocate a lack of acquaintance with research methodology. Others (e.g., Stricker, 1975) emphasize more frequent and intensive clinical learning experiences rather than a deemphasis on research. Naturally, research that competes with these clinical practice would have a lower priority. But, ever since the Boulder conference, everyone writing about ideal training has advocated a clinical research methodology that does not compete with clinical work, but rather is directly related to clinical work and the acquisition of new knowledge about clinical procedures.

Research and Empiricism in Human Service Professions

Clinical psychology, of course, is not alone in espousing the lofty ideals of science and research as cherished activities for its members. Indeed, all of Western culture has long viewed rational inquiry and the scientific method as the primary means of solving man's problems and advancing our culture (e.g., Ehrenfeld, 1978). Those who carry out applied research in the area of human behavior change, as well as other health-related or educational fields, are held in high esteem. Their activities are valued, at least in an abstract way.

Thus, in the midst of this reaffirmation of the scientist-practitioner model in clinical psychology, other professions outside of the context of psychology, with its tradition of production of knowledge in both basic and applied areas, had begun to advocate very strongly the need to train personnel in appropriate research methodology in order to advance the field. For example, in social work Reid (1979) observes a growing trend toward what he calls *evaluation research*. Since the profession of social work is involved in so many types of human service programs, such as child welfare, family services, public assistance, corrections, aging and health care, as well as mental health, homogeneous trends or developments in the area of evaluation research would be impossible to identify. Nevertheless, a review of all articles published in major social work journals in the mid-1970s revealed that research with the aim of determining the basic effectiveness of human service program intervention was "a growth industry in social work." Reid (1979) attributes this growth to the demands on human services generally for better accountability and for more systematic evidence of program impact.

As part of this trend, social workers have advocated training all practitioners in methodology that would enable them to evaluate more effectively their intervention efforts (Bloom & Block, 1977). Reid (1979) observes that such case-by-case testing by "practitioner-researchers" would enable social workers to identify and build upon effective approaches. But Reid concludes that social workers to date have not been trained in the methodologies of evaluation research suitable for more productive efforts in program evaluation and research. Nevertheless, in line with the "growth industry" perception of evaluation research in social work, a considerable expansion of training in the necessary methodologies is seen as an important step in the building of a more empirically based service technology. A major step in this direction within the field of social work was the appearance of an important book by Jayaratne and Levy (1979) which constituted the first training manual for social workers and others who wished to integrate an empirical approach and a research orientation into their practice.

These efforts in the profession of social work are particularly interesting in the context of this discussion, because social work has many more practitioners than psychology working in a far greater number of human service areas. And yet, unlike psychology and to some extent medicine, social work is not closely allied with its own idiosyncratic traditions of research methodology accompanying these basic sciences. Because of this, the focus in social work is solely on utilizing a methodology that will be totally appropriate to the human service subject matter at hand without consideration of traditional approaches growing out of basic science. Thus, there are no arguments in social work on what is appropriate and inappropriate in the way of science as one finds in psychology. Consistent with the recommendations of the Boulder model, and with all of the major conferences on the training of psychologists since then, work is proceeding on adapting science to make it directly applicable to the human service arena rather than somehow integrating the methodology and questions of experimental psychology with clinical practice (e.g., Jayaratne & Levy, 1979).

A similar situation exists in medicine, where the basic biological sciences or, in the case of psychiatry, the basic biological and behavioral sciences underlying clinical practice are, for the most part, distinctly separate in their approaches and methodologies from clinical practice. Thus basic research is left to the medical research centers, usually comprised of scientists located full-time in medical school or laboratory settings. And yet, the same pressures evident in social work for accountability and evidence of effectiveness are also evident in psychiatry, particularly in the area of psychotherapy. Although the government mandates thorough evaluations of pharmacological agents for safety and effectiveness through such agencies as the FDA, there is an increased emphasis on greater accountability for all interventions in psychiatry, including psychosocial interventions. This has produced a growing realization of the necessity of a more thorough empirical approach on the part of psychiatric practitioners through more accurate and reliable classification (DSM-III) (APA, 1980). Equally important is objective evidence of the effectiveness of any intervention. Much as in psychology and social work, however, the realization of this goal requires, in an ideal world, that psychiatrists do more than consume the latest research developments, whether in biological or psychosocial areas. Rather they should become active participants in determining the efficiency and effectiveness of their treatments in a manner that will be readily apparent to those who seek this information, such as consumer groups and government and third-party agencies. In other words, psychiatrists should become, at least, evaluators of their own work and preferably researchers providing new data to the professional community interested in behavior change.

While social work and psychiatry have been concerned with accountability and research for many of the same reasons as clinical psychology because of their mutual concern with mental health, other professions have also been grasping for a way to develop a more empirical approach to their subject matter. In many cases these professions are dealing with populations and techniques that are rather distinctive and therefore have difficulty "borrowing" research findings. For example, rehabilitation medicine requires a large number of physical therapists to carry out necessary procedures with patients, many of them involving behavioral or attitudinal change. And yet there is only a very limited body of research relevant to this field. Schindele (1981), the editor of the *International Journal of Rehabilitation Research,* points out the need for more relevant research in both the area of program evaluation as well as more basic research on the efficacy of new procedures in this area.

The field of education is continually crying out for more empirical, objective evaluation and research by those working in the front lines of educational enterprise. The plea for increased criterion-referenced testing, which refers to the use of objective, behavioral indices of change, reflects the gap between the necessity for evaluation and the methods available for evaluating learning and behavior change (see chapter 3). Most of the behavior-change or behavior-management procedures employed in the classroom, of course, emanate from the science and practice of psychology (e.g., O'Leary & O'Leary, 1977). Therefore, the course of research and development of procedures and the role of practitioners such as school psychologists in this course is indistinguishable in many ways from that of clinical psychology. This scientist-practitioner "split" in school psychology has been described by Kratochwill (1977). There are some examples in the field of education, however, of substantial progress in adapting research methodology to the classroom settings in which educational practitioners work. The best evidence for this is found in the program evaluation work of Tharp and Gallimore (1975) and Walker, Hops and Greenwood, in press. The relevance of these efforts to the training of practitioners will be described more fully in chapter 2.

THE SCIENTIST-PRACTITIONER SPLIT

Ideal Model: Inadequate Methods

For the most part, professionals are not disillusioned with the need for research and the necessity of training people to do research. In fact, there seems to be a growing realization that research is critical to the continued advancement and the very existence of the basic clinical and educational professions. In addition, few would deny that the scientist-practitioner model of training should ensure that, at the very least, those who become interested in research during their training or shortly thereafter will have the skills to conduct meaningful research and advance our knowledge, while those who choose not to do research will have had the opportunity to make this choice. But the high ideal so often espoused, that all practitioners will participate in the research process and advance our knowledge, cannot happen at this time. The appropriate research methodology to reach this ideal, recommended in the Boulder conference, and in every conference and paper on the subject since that time, has not been forthcoming. The true integration of research and practice so long envisioned as a solution to the scientist-practitioner split has not occurred due to the almost universally acknowledged inadequacies of our research methodology to address issues important to practice. Every recommendation that has been made since 1949, while endorsing greater integration of research and practice, and development of new research methodology, has been unable to outline specifically what this would entail. And each training conference or each well-thought-out observation published individually has lamented previous efforts for not specifying how research could be accomplished in practice. Leitenberg (1974) observed, as did Garfield in 1966, that the scientist-practitioner model had never really been tested in clinical psychology because the research methodology taught to our students involved an approach that had been developed in laboratories of experimental psychology and was inappropriate to the subject at hand.

The overriding consequence of the lack of an appropriate research methodology for practice has been a disillusionment with research on the part of professionals in training in all health and educational fields. The oft-noted observation that research is viewed as a hurdle to be circumvented, if possible, on the way to the professional degree, and the observation that relatively few trained practitioners with the inclination or skills to do research are doing any research at all, confirms the general disillusionment. It is not the idea that was wrong, but rather the inability to develop the tools to implement the idea.

Nowhere is this issue better described than in the now well-known survey of leading psychologists and psychiatrists conducted by Bergin and Strupp in the early 1970s (Bergin & Strupp, 1972). This survey substantiated the comments from individual leaders in the field that the research approach itself was the major reason that students in the behavior-change field did not have a scientific methodology that was appropriate to applied problems. Bergin and Strupp concluded:

> Among researchers as well as statisticians, there is a growing disaffection from traditional experimental designs and statistical procedures which are held inappropriate to the subject matter under study. This judgment applies with particular force to research in the area of therapeutic change, and our emphasis on the value of experimental case studies underscores this point. We strongly agree that most of the stand-

ard experimental designs and statistical procedures have exerted, and
are continuing to exert, a constricting effect on fruitful inquiry, and
they serve to perpetuate an unwarranted overemphasis on methodology.
More accurately, the exaggerated importance accorded experimental
and statistical dicta cannot be blamed on the techniques proper — after
all, they are merely tools — but their veneration mirrors a prevailing
philosophy among behavioral scientists which subordinates problems
to methodology. The insidious effects of this trend are tellingly illustrated by the typical graduate student who is often more interested
in the details of a factorial design than in the problem he sets out to
study; worse, the selection of a problem is dictated by the experimental design. Needless to say, the student's approach faithfully reflects
the convictions and teachings of his mentors. (Bergin & Strupp, 1972,
p. 440)

Other leading clinicians, working within a different perspective, drew
similar conclusions, "The failure of integration between practice and traditional psychological research methods is due to fundamental inadequacies
of those research methods for tackling issues open to the practitioner" (Raush,
1974, p. 679). These conclusions, of course, were not new. Throughout the
1960s, particularly at the major conferences, there is an undercurrent of disaf-
fection with traditional research methodology emanating from the experimental laboratories. In fact, as we have seen, as far back as 1949 the participants
at the Boulder conference also recognized that traditional experimental
research approaches were probably not adequate for use by the majority of
clinicians in studying clinical problems. But with the emphasis on pro-
mulgating the scientist-practitioner role, little attention was paid to the specific
deficiencies of traditional research models which made them inappropriate
for applied problems, nor were detailed suggestions forthcoming on what
alternatives were available. But, with the widespread realization that traditional research methodology was inappropriate, an analysis of the specific
inadequacies of these procedures as applied to clinical and educational problems began (Bergin & Strupp, 1972; Hersen & Barlow, 1976). Among these
were practical and ethical limitations to doing research on the part of practitioners, as well as other characteristics of traditional research methodology
that limited the relevance of traditional research findings to practice.

Why Practitioners Do Not Do Research

With few exceptions, traditional research methodology emanating from
the laboratories of experimental psychology emphasized data collected from
large groups of subjects, usually animals, which would then be analyzed either
within or between large groups. The historical origins of this approach have
been described in Hersen and Barlow (1976), but applying this approach to

applied problems poses enormous practical problems for erstwhile applied researchers. This strategy requires, among other things, the matching of large numbers of clients who are relatively homogeneous. For example, if one were studying the effects of a particular intervention on generalized anxiety disorder, one would need a minimum of 20 such clients matched on relevant background variables such as severity of the problem as well as other variables thought to be pertinent in the particular experiment, such as age, sex, personality characteristics, history of previous treatment, and the like. Ideally, these clients would be treated at approximately the same time. The simplest type of experiment would involve treating one group of 10 of these clients and examining the effects in comparison to a second untreated group of 10. More sophisticated factorial experiments looking at the interaction of treatments with organismic variables thought to interact with treatment, such as ages of clients or severity of problems, would require in some cases far more than these two basic groups, greatly increasing the number of subjects required. Following tradition, the minimum number of subjects per group is approximately 10, although methodologists generally prefer a far greater number to allow one to determine the effects of a given intervention over and above the considerable intersubject variability that inevitably occurs in such an effort. As many young researchers have discovered, the activities associated with this type of effort, such as gathering and analyzing data, following clients, paying experimental therapists, and simply recruiting the clients, may take years. This is one reason why much of this research, particularly in the context of doctoral dissertations, has been carried out with readily available, large pools of subjects such as college sophomores. But the effects of these interventions on college sophomores will not necessarily be the same as the effects on clinical populations (e.g., Mathews, 1978), making the relevance of such efforts questionable in many cases.

This is further complicated by tremendous advances in the technology of assessing specific behavioral problems in recent years. As noted earlier in this chapter, an applied researcher must spend much of his or her time keeping up with sophisticated advances in measurement procedures, often requiring intimate knowledge of physiological monitoring equipment and computer technology. For example, clinical research on sexual problems now requires a sophisticated laboratory, expensive physiological monitoring equipment, the potential for assaying biochemical samples in some instances, and data-reduction procedures that have become so complex that computer technology is desirable. To set up such a laboratory, taking advantage of the recent advances in objective measurement of sexual arousal, takes the better part of a year and costs many thousands of dollars. Similarly, in the field of anxiety disorders, rather complex verifiable behavioral observations of the consequences of anxiety, along with portable physiological equipment capable of measuring the physiological component of anxiety in the client's natural environment, have become very important parts of the assessment of anxiety in clinical research centers dealing with this problem. In addition, new assessment procedures and strategies are developing continually, and meaningful clinical research efforts must incorporate these advances in assessment to ensure the greatest relevance of the data from these studies. In clinical practice, on the other hand, where the emphasis is on dealing with an individual, a family, or a small group of individuals, these sorts of efforts are very difficult to mount, even if one had the necessary funds, equipment, and space to carry them out.

Practitioners must be concerned also with the ethical implications of any research efforts. In applied research settings, most of which are connected with large universities or medical schools, committees exist to determine if risks are inherent in the research procedures and, if so, whether the benefits of the research to the individuals participating and to society at large outweigh the risks. This problem is most apparent in withholding treatment from clients in the control group when one is dealing with therapy-outcome research. This cannot be done without careful consideration of the risks involved. Of course, in most instances there is no evidence that the treatment works in the first place, which forms the basis for conducting research on its effectiveness. Therefore, one could argue that withholding an unproven treatment from a control group might be less of a risk than applying this same treatment to the experimental group. But, in the area of clinical practice, where the goal is always to relieve human suffering in the individual, intervening with some treatment, however inadequate or unproven, will always be preferable to leaving a distressed client to his or her own resources.

In addition to these marked practical differences, there are obvious procedural and philosophical differences between practice and research. The goal of the practitioner necessarily must be to get clients better as quickly as possible. The nature, length, and intensity of any intervention is tailored to the individual client and his or her individual problem. But in research on behavior-change procedures, clients are randomly assigned to fixed treatment conditions, most often in the absence of any individual behavioral analysis that might result in variations of the treatment offered. In addition, practitioners will alter therapeutic strategies as soon as it seems reasonable and beneficial to the client, based on some ongoing monitoring of the program, however informal. In research, on the other hand, treatment must continue irrespective of individual progress, since the comparisons made at a posttest will examine data from those who do not improve as a result of the fixed-treatment protocol, and average the results in with those who improve in order to look at overall differences among the treated and control groups. In most cases, if this research using traditional methodology is conducted properly, those evaluating the therapy and in a position to make changes in the therapeutic protocol will not even be aware of a specific individual's success or failure, because they will be blind to the assignment of clients to conditions. For these reasons, professionals seldom act as scientists in the sense of researchers or evaluators.

Why Practitioners Do Not Consume Research Findings

These practical and strategic issues are not the only factors inhibiting practitioners from an involvement with science. If this were the case, practitioners would certainly participate where possible and where resources allowed with enthusiasm, for the results at least would be directly applicable to their work. Furthermore, practitioners would eagerly await research findings from major research centers that would help them improve their individual practice. But other more important limitations exist that diminish the relevance of research to practitioners. In the last analysis, it is these issues, more than any other factors, that have accounted for the scientist-practitioner split and led to a lack of interest among professional students in research and research methodology a subsequent deemphasis on research training in graduate and professional schools.

Statistical Significance

One of the strongest and most pervasive traditions accompanying traditional experimental methodology has been a reliance on statistical significance to determine the existence of the effects of various interventions. This reliance on statistical significance has come under sweeping attack, even in basic research where investigators have been concerned that statistical determinations hide important sources of variability and lead investigators to assume that experimental effects are important if they reach statistical significance; even though they may, in fact, be very weak. This is particularly true if the number of organisms or observations within the experiment are very large. For example, Meehl (1978) considers that this approach to the basic science of psychology has produced "low grade ore" or very weak and unreliable findings that are often difficult to replicate, given the large intersubject variability inherent in psychological experiments. In some cases an experimental effect will reach statistical significance, most often defined as the .05 level of probability that the results are due to chance, while attempts at replication might indicate that there is a .25 probability that the results are due to chance. Meehl (1978) concluded that this reliance on statistical significance was one of the "worst things that ever happened in the history of psychology" (p. 817).

The important issue in this controversy is the size of the experimental effect with which one is dealing, since statistical significance, even when properly interpreted, bears no relation to the importance of or the size of the effect. The noted experimentalist S.S. Stevens observed, "Can no one recognize a decisive result without a significance test?" (1958, p. 853). These arguments have been elaborated over the years by many leading experimental theorists such as Bakan (1966), Cronbach (1975), Cronbach and Snow (1977), and Tyler (1931). In the most recent, and also one of the more comprehensive discussions of this issue, Carver (1978) recommends abandoning all statistical significance testing and reverting to alternative ways of evaluating research results. These strategies would involve more direct observation of the data, including strength of effect and replication. Using educational research as his starting point, Carver suggests that researchers should ignore statistical significance testing when designing research since a study with results that cannot be meaningfully interpreted without looking at the *p* values is a poorly designed study.

One of the problems lies in the word *significant.* A statistically significant result can be very trivial indeed and be very far from the usual meaning of the word *significant.* And yet, once one achieves statistical significance, typically it is simply reported in a journal or book, with most consumers of research assuming that the result is truly significant or clinically important.

When these procedures are used in applied research, particularly to determine if the results of an intervention are effective, the problems are multiplied and compounded. As Bergin and Strupp (1972) pointed out:

> With respect to inquiry in the area of psychotherapy, the kinds of effects we need to demonstrate at this point in time should be significant enough so that they are readily observable by inspection or descriptive statistics. If this cannot be done, no fixation upon statistical and mathematical niceties will generate fruitful insights, which obviously can come only from the researcher's understanding of the subject matter and the descriptive data under scrutiny. (p. 440)

The major issue here is that the practitioner is always concerned with the individual; and, statistical significance says nothing about improvement in an individual client undergoing that treatment (Barlow, 1981).

This is best illustrated by referring once again to our simple, between-group, experimental comparison of a treatment for clients with generalized anxiety disorder. For example, if anxiety were reliably measured on a 0 to 100 scale, with 100 representing *severe anxiety,* a treatment that improved each client in a group of anxiety neurotics from 80 to 75 would be statistically significant if all anxiety neurotics in the control group remained at 80. But this improvement would be of little use to the clinician, since the clients in the treatment group would probably not notice the improvement themselves and would certainly still be very anxious. An improvement of 40 or 50 points might be necessary before both the clinician and the client considered the change clinically important (Chassan, 1960; Hersen & Barlow, 1976). Statisticians will quickly point out, of course, that this problem is easily correctable by setting a different criterion for "effectiveness." Nevertheless, examination of applied research in the major journals of the human service professions shows that this practice is not followed and probably could not be followed in view of the enormous variability among clients or intersubject variability present in any effort such as this.

In fact, this intersubject variability can also account for a tendency to underestimate clinical effectiveness of a given treatment when relying on statistical significance to determine the presence of an effect. For example, a given treatment might be quite effective for a few clients, while the remaining clients do not show substantial improvement, or even deteriorate somewhat. Statistically, then, the experimental group does not differ from the control group, whose members are relatively unchanged. When broad divergence such as this occurs among clients in response to an intervention, as is often the case in clinical research (Bergin & Garfield, 1978), statistical treatments will average out the clinical effect along with changes due to unwanted sources of variability. This problem is referred to generally as *clinical* versus *statistical* significance (Hersen & Barlow, 1976).

Some have attempted to correct for the problem in determining the size of effect statistically by using such techniques as *percentage of variance accounted for* (Hays, 1963). But, as Yeaton and Sechrest (1981) point out, these procedures do little to help the clinician attempting to interpret clinical research, because even procedures shown to account for a large percentage of the variance in the group as a whole may be quite ineffective for some specific clients in the group.

Garfield (1980, 1981) concludes that the failure to attend to extent of therapeutic change in an individual or a group of clients has obscured perhaps the most important findings in all of psychotherapy-outcome studies. In his well-taken argument, surveys over the years, which make available this information, generally indicate that a small percentage of clients show major changes from any one of a number of therapeutic interventions undergoing evaluation in a particular study, to the point where they could be called cured, while a larger number show small to medium changes, with yet another group showing no improvement at all, and a few who actually show deterioration. Attending more closely to the factors present in those subjects showing major systematic changes in their behavioral or emotional problems, rather than statistically significant differences between the group as a whole and some control group, would contribute far more to uncovering the active processes in effective psychotherapy than has been possible using traditional statistical significance testing. Thus, both very major changes as well as deterioration may well be represented in a group of treated clients. And although the group average might be significantly different statistically than the control group, practitioners can infer little or nothing about the extent of change.

The Average Client

In 1865 one of the first great scientist-practitioners, the physician and researcher Claude Bernard, castigated a colleague interested in studying the properties of urine. This colleague proposed collecting specimens, from urinals in a centrally located train station, to determine properties of the average European urine. Bernard countered that this would tell us very little about urine or the individuals providing the samples. Despite Bernard's warning, this tradition has continued in research, limiting the relevance of this type of research to practitioners interested in an individual client (Hersen & Barlow, 1976; Sidman, 1960). This critical issue is the averaging of results. To take our example again, 10 clients homogeneous with generalized anxiety disorder would bring very different histories, personality variables, and environmental situations to the treatment setting and will respond in varying ways to treatment. That is, some clients will improve and others will not. This is because any group of clients chosen for an experimental investigation will very seldom reach the degree of homogeneity that would lead to a relatively uniform response among all members of the group. In fact, as Kiesler (1966, 1971) has pointed out in what he calls the *patient uniformity myth,* clients are most often heterogeneous, as described above. This makes it very difficult, if not impossible, to generalize results obtained from the average response of the group as a whole to an individual client walking into the therapist's office. Therefore, the practitioner cannot know if a treatment that reached statistical significance will be effective with his client.

In fact, there is a wealth of evidence showing that response to our treatments is quite variable; with some people improving, others staying the same, and some people getting worse (Bergin, 1966; Bergin & Garfield, 1978; Garfield, 1980; Hersen & Barlow, 1976). Practitioners, always concerned with the individual person in their office, may use one of these new therapeutic procedures with a client who is likely to get worse and be quite unimpressed with the results from the research study, demonstrating once again to the practitioner that research is unlikely to tell him or her much about treating clients.

These problems, of course, have their origins in traditional research methodology and, in particular, the improper use of sampling theory (Fisher, 1925; Hays, 1963). Sampling theory dictates that if one is going to make adequate inferences about the population with which one is working, then one should randomly sample this population and then apply a particular therapeutic technique to the random sample. Any effects that one then achieves could be said to apply to the population as a whole. Translating this into applied research, one would have to determine all of the relevant characteristics of the disorder that may or may not be present in all clients. One would then have to draw a sample representing all of these characteristics, which, of course, would be likely to be a fairly large sample. If one treated this sample with the latest procedure, and found a statistically significant effect compared to a control group not receiving the treatment, then theoretically one would conclude that the treatment would be effective with all people having this disorder. But applied researchers discovered long ago that it was impossible to obtain a random sample of clients with a given disorder, because even if one were able to overcome the practical problems involved, the sample would be so heterogeneous that few treatments would be likely to show a statistically significant effect.

Therefore, applied researchers opted for the strategy of trying to obtain a homogeneous sample; that is, 10 to 20 clients who would be very much alike on all relevant characteristics (Hersen & Barlow, 1976). The thinking was that the large differences in responding among the clients in the group would be reduced somewhat and the effects of the treatment, if they existed, would become more clear. The difficulty here, of course, is that even if one were able to obtain a uniformly, clinically significant result with these clients, one could only infer that the treatment would be effective for other individuals possessing roughly the same characteristics. Thus, one infers that treatment would be successful only for other clients resembling the specific group of clients in the experiment. But, as research experience has shown (Hersen & Barlow, 1976), even these small groups of homogeneous clients vary greatly in their responses to treatment, producing a large amount of intersubject variability which necessitates statistical determination of an effect. And, since the next client walking into a practitioner's office is unlikely to be identical to anybody in the homogeneous sample, the relevance of the effects for the practitioner are greatly diminished.

In view of our inability to collect random samples, the only method available to the practitioner to determine if results from one experiment would be relevant to the next client walking into a therapist's office, is the process of *logical generalization* (Edgington, 1966, 1967; Hersen & Barlow, 1976). In this procedure, the practitioner judges similarity of his or her clients to those experimental clients showing varying degrees of improvement and determines which of his or her clients are most like those that showed marked improvement among the experimental clients. These clients would be the ones in his or her office most likely to benefit from the specific treatment package. This procedure will be discussed in greater detail below. (See chapters 2 and 12.)

RESEARCH HAS LITTLE INFLUENCE ON PRACTICE

Thus, the prevailing experimental strategy growing out of the traditional research methodology of treating large groups of subjects, determining the average results, calculating statistical significance in comparison to some control group, and then inferring that these results indicate that a treatment may be effective for any individual client seen by a practitioner, has served to widen the scientist-practitioner gap. Practitioners have been disillusioned as to the relevance of traditional research in contributing to their effectiveness with individual clients with complex human problems.

If practitioners at least consumed research, this would fulfill Peterson's (1976a, 1976b) definition of the professional who has been trained to evaluate and sift through the various research findings in order to glean from these findings the latest advances that will assist in the relief of human suffering. But the most important consideration mentioned above is that practitioners do not consume research findings, and that clinical research does not influence clinical practice. As Goldfried and Padawer (in press) observe, it is no secret that practicing clinicians are often reluctant to alter what they do as a function of reported research findings. This is most evident in comments from leading clinicians surveyed by Bergin and Strupp (1972), and most prominent among these comments is the oft-noted quote from Matarazzo, ". . . even after 15 years, few of my research findings affect my practice. Psychological science per se doesn't guide me one bit. I still read avidly, but this is of little direct practical help. My clinical experience is the only thing that has helped me in my practice to date . . . " (Bergin & Strupp, 1972, p. 340). People were less surprised with Carl Rogers, who took the same position; but erstwhile scientist-practitioners were still a bit shaken when, in 1969, he advocated abandoning formal research in psychotherapy altogether. It is not a large inferential leap to assume that many clinicians who have not achieved this prominence, but are nevertheless trained in the scientist-professional model, suffer an equal lack of influence from research. Other investigators support this view (Cohen, 1976; Fairweather, Sanders, Tornatsky, & Harris, 1974; Larsen & Nichols, 1972). Fairweather et al. conclude: "New mental health programs have more often than not been instituted on the basis of the authority of the advocate for that program rather than upon any careful longitudinal exploration of the outcomes of the new technique, particularly as it is contrasted with other treatment programs" (p. 2).

Cohen (1976) reviews surveys of educational and mental health professionals indicating the belief that fewer than 20% of research articles have some applicability to professional educational settings, while 40% of professionals in mental health think that no research exists that is relevant to practice. Cohen (1979), in an interesting survey on factors that influence clinicians' judgments of the adequacy of clinical research, notes that clinicians are more critical of research methodology in studies reporting that psychotherapy was not effective, undoubtedly since this runs counter to their own experience. In a later, very thoughtful paper, Cohen (1981) describes the difficulty of defining research utilization, noting that it is possible that studies that are widely publicized might have delayed effects (see Strupp, 1981). But, as Cohen notes, there are no data one way or the other on this issue.

Strupp observed as early as 1968 that the lack of influence of research on practice had progressed to the point where in many quarters a disdain between researchers and clinicians existed: He observed that it was a common finding that clinical observations were totally disregarded by researchers, while research efforts were considered inappropriate or trivial. He also noted (Strupp, 1968) that practicing clinicians typically make judgments about the efficacy of their procedures on the basis of their own personal experience, not empirical findings. More recently, Lehrer (1981) accused clinical researchers on the whole of being insensitive to the clinical process, noting that research in psychotherapy is not possible unless one views the entire enterprise "in the mechanical way that is so fashionable among many of our colleagues who are too frightened and too inept to establish an interpersonal relationship of a therapeutic variety with a patient" (p. 42). Some experienced clinicians who have also been involved in the research process, such as Goldfried, admit to a certain "schizophrenia," in that the manner in which therapeutic techniques are applied in clinical research bears only a passing resemblance to their own clinical practice (Goldfried & Padawer, in press).

This lack of influence of research on practitioners, and even hints of growing animosity, is clearly a more dangerous and difficult state of affairs than the observation that few are likely to do research, the more typical issue raised in discussions of the scientist-practitioner split. Indeed, Wollersheim (1974) arguing for the continuation of research training in clinical psychology programs, observed that this would at least ensure that clinical psychologists were sophisticated consumers of psychological research rather than "crystal ball gazing practitioners." But it seems clear at this point in time that the majority of practitioners are not inclined to be empirical to the point where they will look to clinical research findings for guidance in their practice (Cohen, 1976), a problem understandably of great concern to government officials (NIMH, 1971).

As noted throughout this chapter, this state of affairs is not unique to the human service field or the area of behavior change in particular. For example, in the field of rehabilitation medicine, Schindele (1981) describes in some detail how the same limitations in experimental research methodology, described above, severely limit the usefulness and applicability of research in rehabilitation to the practice of rehabilitation medicine.

WHERE DO PRACTITIONERS GET THEIR TECHNIQUES?

Since it seems clear that applied research has little influence on practice, the question arises, where do practitioners get their techniques and procedures? Every day thousands of people enter professional settings with a variety of complaints representing the full range of psychological, educational, social, or medical problems. These problems are assessed, the problem is formulated, and the intervention is conceptualized and delivered. In the area of mental health, the latest estimate indicates more than 250 different varieties of psychotherapy are in use today (Herink, 1980) and the number seems to be multiplying exponentially. These procedures clearly do not come from systematic research.

As did Matarazzo when he was in training (Bergin & Strupp, 1972), most practitioners report learning their procedures from watching their teachers. Subsequently, these practitioners may alter the therapeutic procedures learned in professional school, based on their own trial-and-error experience. Very often these procedures are described in the context of systems or theories that in turn arise out of the trial-and-error experience of previous practitioners who had elaborated their approach into a system. Since some clients always get better, no matter what one does, there is ample opportunity for all practitioners to attribute their success to their particular procedure and to discount failures for one reason or another, usually lack of motivation of the client (Barlow, 1981). Those early practitioners who could communicate their theories clearly, or who presented new and exciting principles, tended to attract many followers. If these same people wrote prolifically and/or gave numerous workshops, then their procedures would be far more likely to be adopted through sheer exposure than would procedures of those who gave fewer workshops or wrote very little about what they were doing. That practitioners are more influenced by workshops, conversations with colleagues, and manuscripts describing clinical innovations, than by research, has been verified in a recent survey by Cohen (1979). But it seems that these procedures would be rarely applied in quite the same way as they were demonstrated. The same trial-and-error experience engaged in continuously by practitioners, as well as conversations with colleagues, would ensure that new variations or twists of the original procedures would be implemented and would vary from practitioner to practitioner. Thus, any client with some psychopathology, for example, walking into a therapist's office today, might receive a variety of treatments for exactly the same condition, ranging from primal scream therapy through long-term daily sessions of psychoanalysis or short-term rational emotive therapy, depending on which office the client enters. Unfortunately, the client would be unlikely to benefit from many of the more radical versions of the 250 different types of psychotherapy developed over the years if they are practiced with theoretical purity.

But few procedures are practiced with theoretical purity, to the great advantage of millions seeking help from psychotherapy. Fortunately, given our inadequate data base, therapists continue to innovate and often do hit upon successful procedures. For example, therapists from psychoanalytic, behavioral, and rational emotive schools, treating agoraphobia, would all recommend *in vivo* exposure as part of the treatment, albeit for different theoretical reasons, and in the context of a variety of additional procedures. And chances are that the clients experiencing all of these treatments would benefit (Mavissakalian & Barlow, 1981). Similar statements could be made about educational or rehabilitation practices, and the like.

Thus, despite the seemingly strict adherence to theoretical constructs and the allegiance to psychotherapeutic schools verbalized by most psychotherapists, there is a growing feeling among observers of clinical practice that most therapists are more similar then they are different in their practice. This is particularly true within the context of the 50-minute hour, which continues to prevail, most likely for reasons of economics and convenience, as the modal psychotherapeutic practice (Goldfried, 1980). In view of this process, with its frequent successes, a number of clinicians have espoused an intuitive, eclectic approach as the most efficient and effective path to the common goal, shared by all therapists, of relieving human suffering (Lazarus, 1967). This is certainly a positive step in view of the present need to deal with the immediate problems presented by clients who are requesting immediate treatment, because adherence to rigid but unproven theoretical doctrines is loosened. But strict adherence to this approach, or what Wollersheim calls "crystal ball gazing" practice, will, in the long run, realize the worst fears of the participants of the Boulder conference, in that psychotherapists will be little more than glorified technicians switching from procedure to procedure, depending on what is in vogue or what new charismatic leader in the field of psychotherapy happens to be most visible or is giving the most workshops. Most people, of course, will continue to get better depending on the skill of the therapist, the circumstances of the client, and the particular mix of procedures used by the therapist. But neither the therapist nor the client nor, more importantly, the thousands of other therapists trying to treat the same types of clients, will ever know why that particular client got better. Operating on intermittent schedules of reinforcement, most therapists will continue to use the procedure or variations of it, ignoring the fact that many treated in a similar fashion will either improve very little, not at all, or even deteriorate. There will be no truly cumulative growth of knowledge. No therapeutic advances that, resting firmly on a data base, will enjoy widespread dissemination to relieve the suffering of the many rather than the few. The overriding question, What procedures work for what clients under what conditions? will go unanswered.

The type of intuitive eclecticism practiced by clinicians, of course, depending as it does on clinical trial and error, bears little relation to a data-based eclecticism espoused recently by several leaders in the field of psychotherapy (e.g., Garfield, 1980; Goldfried, 1980). Here a truly cumulative body of knowledge of therapeutic techniques could develop, free of current theoretical constraints which so often dictate the direction of our research efforts. Of course, theorizing at some stage will always be necessary to organize newly emerging data, but the eclecticism currently employed by many practitioners is not data based but intuitive, and does not seem to be altered by advances in science.

On the surface, these conclusions and the survey data supporting them (e.g., Bergin & Strupp, 1972; Cohen, 1976) may seem contradictory, because several procedures popular with clinicians of late, such as biofeedback or cognitive behavioral therapy, have been associated with major research or theoretical efforts (Bandura, 1979). A closer examination, however, indicates that the popularity of these procedures with clinicians, to the extent that it exists, is most often due to convincing clinical demonstrations or persuasive communication, rather than data. For example, cognitive therapies were developed and popularized by Ellis (1962) and later by Beck (1967), Mahoney (1974), and Meichenbaum (1977) and widely adopted before any convincing data appeared on effectiveness of these procedures with clinical populations (e.g, Rush, Beck, Kovacs, & Hollon, 1977). In many ways, Ellis is a good example of the charismatic communicator able to influence large numbers of clinicians through workshops, writings, and clinical demonstrations. Similarly, little or no evidence existed, until lately (see chapter 12), for the effectiveness of biofeedback as a technique separate from relaxation (Silver & Blanchard, 1978), but early clinical demonstrations (e.g., Budzynski, Stoyva, & Adler, 1970) and wide publicity convinced thousands of clinicians (and scores of equipment manufacturers) that this procedure would be helpful. Even in the case of agoraphobia, where exposure-based treatments have received overriding experimental support during the last 20 years (e.g., Mavissakalian & Barlow, 1981), the director of the largest phobia clinic in North America, TERRAP, located in California with branches around the country, is reported to have devised his exposure-based treatment without any knowledge of data emanating from research centers. A former agoraphobic patient, desperate for relief, decided to risk what he thought was his life by exposing himself to his most feared situations. His subsequent "cure" formed the basis for the establishment of this new clinic. Thus, research data and clinical improvisation or idiosyncratic observation happened to merge, although the route to this merger for each approach was very different indeed. There are far more examples, of course, where this merger has not occurred and where empirical evidence and practice coexist without any mutual contact. Once again, this type of creative clinical effort has had little relation to, and has not been influenced by, science.

The successful experiences of practitioners must be observed, verified, and accumulated through empirical practice and accountability. The theoretical and research developments in applied research centers that hold out so much promise for dealing with the variety of severe behavioral and emotional problems must be tested in ways that will influence and be relevant to practitioners. Attention must be paid to the absolute amount of improvement or the size of effect, with an emphasis on changes within the individual in his or her own particular environment. Without the development of a cumulative body of knowledge on the effects of various interventions in the human services, we are doomed to a series of never-ending fads and promises. Traditional scientific methodology alone is not appropriate to answer the major questions relevant to applied settings. An alternative scientific and empirical approach is needed.

Chapter 2
Research Strategies
and the Role of the Practitioner

INTRODUCTION

Before examining alternative models of research and the role of the practitioner in this process, it is important to put these alternative models in perspective by considering the contributions made to the field of behavior change by traditional research methodology. We have seen in chapter 1 that practitioners neither do research nor evaluate their procedures and that applied research has little or no influence on usual and customary practice; that is, practitioners do not consume research findings. Nevertheless, in the light of recent advances in what has become one of the most exciting periods in the development of behavior change procedures, few would state that applied research has made no contribution whatsoever. It is possible to draw a distinction between the contribution of research to knowledge and the influence of research findings on practitioners.

Progress in applied research, specifically on the development and evaluation of new and more effective behavior-change procedures, is a very young field that began gaining momentum only in the 1960s. During this time, systematic research has progressed on a number of problems across the health, mental health, and educational fields. Often this research has been carried out by closely knit groups of investigators in applied research centers around the world who meet and communicate frequently to compare notes. These are the research "specialists" who have made a career of applied investigation. Of course, we have discovered more about dealing with some problems, such as phobia or behavioral problems in the classroom, than we have with other problems. But the more important issue is that, regardless of the effectiveness of our procedure, progress has been uneven with certain problems. Only certain questions have been answered while others have been largely ignored. We are answering some questions, and these answers are contributing to our knowledge, but we are leaving unanswered the questions that would make this knowledge relevant to practitioners.

There are many problem areas that are appropriate examples with which to examine the strengths and weaknesses of current research efforts and the critical role that could be played in the research process by practitioners. Problems such as depression, marital disorders, or classroom management could serve as examples, because research has progressed in a similar fashion in many of these areas. One area that is particularly appropriate, however, is the problem of clinical phobia, both because research is reasonably well advanced and because a number of new intervention techniques have recently emerged.

This chapter will review briefly the progression of research in clinical phobia, looking at advances that have been made that have contributed to our fund of knowledge, questions that have been answered, and also questions that traditional applied research methods have not answered. One major question that has not been answered concerns the generality of effectiveness of new treatments across clients in applied settings. One aspect of this question has also been termed *client-treatment interactions* or *client-treatment matching* (e.g., Garfield & Bergin, 1978; Kendall & Butcher, 1982). We will suggest that difficulties with this question and its many corollaries have contributed to the weak influence of research on practice and the relative lack of interest of practitioners in the research process. This thorny issue will be illustrated in some detail in the context of clinical phobia.

Previous attempts to make research more relevant to the practitioner will be reviewed briefly. A model of research is then presented that attempts to answer questions relevant to practitioners, including the generalizability of research findings to practice, by including practitioners directly in the research process. This model emphasizes *time-series methodology,* a method that concentrates on collection of data from individual clients in empirical case-study and single-case experiment format. This model also emphasizes *clinical replication* (Hersen & Barlow, 1976), which refers to a process wherein practitioners accumulate a series of cases in a particular problem area, treated with a specific intervention, while observing individual successes and failures and analyzing, where possible, the reasons for this individual variation. This process relies heavily on time-series methodology carried out by practitioners in the course of their daily activities. The contribution of this strategy to the research process and ways in which time-series methodology and clinical replication can answer important questions not covered by traditional research methodology is outlined. We suggest that this strategy may assist in closing the scientist-practitioner gap by designating important roles for both the practitioner and the full-time researcher in the research process.

RESEARCH ON CLINICAL PHOBIA

The Development of Systematic Desensitization

One area where the strengths and weaknesses of traditional clinical research are readily apparent is clinical phobia. Radically new treatments for fear, phobia, and anxiety have been developed during the last 25 years. The emergence of these treatments has influenced practice and also, quite independently, stimulated research. This research has contributed to our basic knowledge about treatments for phobia but has left important questions unanswered.

These developments stem from the pioneering work of Wolpe (1958), who devised a new treatment for fear and anxiety in general, and phobia in particular, called *systematic desensitization.* His influential work, *Psychotherapy by Reciprocal Inhibition,* published in 1958, was unique in that it contained both the rationale for the development of this treatment as well as descriptions of the treatment of a very impressive series of 210 cases.

Several years earlier, Wolpe had become dissatisfied with the results of psychotherapy, which in those days was predominantly psychoanalytic. Looking for alternative techniques that would be more successful, he began reading Pavlov and was impressed with the way in which behaviors and emotions were precisely described and quantified. Working with animals, Wolpe produced experimental analogues of neuroses in cats, using some of the terminology and methodology of conditioning suggested by Pavlov. Specifically, cats would be subjected to strong and inescapable shock in the presence of specific compartments or cages. The resulting fear response was then reduced by feeding the cats in situations gradually approximating the cage in which the shock had been originally delivered until they could enter the original cage with few, if any, behavioral signs of fear. These experiments led Wolpe to formulate a general theoretical principle of fear reduction; "If a response antagonistic to anxiety can be made to occur in the presence of anxiety-evoking stimuli so that it is accompanied by a complete or partial suppression of the anxiety responses, the bond between these stimuli and the anxiety responses will be weakened" (Wolpe, 1958, p. 71). At this point, Wolpe demonstrated the creativity of an experienced and competent clinician by substantially altering the basic paradigm from the animal laboratories and applying the principle to people suffering from clinical phobia. Since exposure to the feared situation was impractical for many people, Wolpe substituted imagined scenes of the feared situation. And, because there was a limit to the amount clients could eat, even for such a good cause, Wolpe introduced deep muscle relaxation, as originally described by Jacobson (1929), as a response thought to be equally capable of inhibiting anxiety. This was the origination of one of the most widely utilized and most often tested psychotherapeutic techniques, and Wolpe called it *systematic desensitization.*

The Importance of the Clinical Series

The animal experiments alone, or an experimental exposition of the basic principle involved in humans would not, of course, have influenced practicing clinicians. In fact, somewhat similar laboratory exercises had been carried out numerous times before, with perhaps the most famous being the early work of Mary Cover Jones (1924) who, under the supervision of Watson, demonstrated that a fear of furry rabbits in a young boy named Peter could be reduced and eliminated through a carefully orchestrated, gradual exposure to a rabbit. What distinguished Wolpe's work from that of his predecessors was his description of the treatment of 210 cases with this procedure. His report that 90% of these cases were cured or much improved— after treatment, and at follow-ups of up to 7 years in some cases—attracted wide attention among practicing clinicians always on the lookout for new and more effective procedures to use with their clients. Another advantage was that it was a rather straightforward procedure that could be easily incorporated into the armamentarium of practicing therapists. It required minimal training or, as was most often the case in the early years, simply reading Wolpe's description of the procedure along with examples of its use. Naturally, it was not long before numerous workshops and other practical guides were available for clinicians interested in learning more about the procedure. The importance of this series, which was an early example of clinical replication, will be discussed later in this chapter and again in chapter 12.

The Beginning of Research

Simultaneously, an unprecedented development occurred in the field of psychotherapy in that systematic desensitization as a psychotherapeutic technique was subjected to an enormous amount of research, testing both its efficacy and, later on, its mechanisms of therapeutic action. Historically, this was a turning point in psychotherapy research, because it redirected the attention of many clinical researchers at this time. From an emphasis on either process research, which was the intensive study of the process of psychotherapy without regard to outcome, or large-scale outcome research testing the effects of a vaguely defined procedure (psychotherapy) using global and unreliable measures, researchers turned to a clearly specified procedure easily replicable in other settings. Agras, Kazdin, and Wilson (1979) list other factors contributing to the surge of research on this procedure. Foremost among these was the development of an objective measure of fear, the behavioral avoidance test, in which the ability to approach a feared object or situation was quantified, directly observed, and measured. This objective behavioral measure was a major advance in clinical research and set the stage for the development of similar behavioral measures for the variety of clinical phobias, including agoraphobia, as well as for other emotional and behavioral problems.

Questions Answered by Research

In the ensuing 20 years, this research has increased our knowledge in several areas. First, considerable knowledge has accumulated on the general effectiveness of systematic desensitization, or alternative procedures subsequently introduced for reducing fear and phobia. Second, component analyses of the necessary and sufficient conditions for fear-reduction procedures to be effective have been undertaken. Third, the mechanism of action present in these various procedures has been explicated to a large extent. And, finally, research into the nature of fear itself, utilizing both laboratory and clinical research settings, has advanced. All of this research is summarized in detail (e.g., Mavissakalian & Barlow, 1981), but brief summaries of our knowledge will be reviewed here to illustrate what questions traditional research can answer and what questions concerning the application of these procedures are difficult or impossible to answer using these research strategies. While these four categories of research did not proceed in a clear-cut, sequential fashion, they will be summarized as such for ease of description.

Effectiveness and Component Analysis

The first wave of research was directed at the rather straightforward question: Is systematic desensitization more effective than other more popular treatments at the time, such as traditional psychotherapy? Rather crude comparisons were carried out, both in the consulting room (Lazarus, 1961) and in the laboratory, using an analogue of clinical phobia, snake fears (e.g., Lang & Lazovik 1963). The overwhelming evidence from this early series of studies was that systematic desensitization was significantly more effective (statistically) than no treatment or alternative forms of treatment in reducing simple fears and phobias. Put more precisely, using the .05 level of probability, there were less than 5 chances in 100 that the differences attained in these studies were due to chance.

Subsequently, a detailed analysis of the various components of systematic desensitization were explored. The rather surprising finding from a long series of studies (cf. Mavissakalian & Barlow, 1981) was that systematic desensitization was a rather flexible procedure that could be altered in a number of ways without reducing its effectiveness. For example, it was determined that the order of hierarchy presentation from *least fearful* to *most fearful* did not seem to be critical to progress in therapy. The presence or absence of a therapist did not seem to be critical to the procedure since there were examples of successful self-administered desensitization. A great deal of research explored the necessity of therapeutic instructions and found that, in general, these instructions were important ingredients in fear reduction. However, later evidence from research with clinical phobics indicated that instructions or expectancy effects might become less important with increasing severity of fear (Mathews, 1978). Most interesting, perhaps, was the finding that one of the two major components of systematic desensitization, specifically deep-muscle relaxation, did not seem to be critical to therapeutic effectiveness because introducing it or removing it from a therapeutic package during treatment did not affect the rate of progress (e.g., Agras, Leitenberg, Barlow, Curtis, Edwards, & Wright, 1971). When this was confirmed in other studies (cf. Mavissakalian & Barlow, 1981), the stage was set for major questions concerning the mechanisms of action of systematic desensitization since, of course, deep-muscle relaxation, which was hypothesized to be an anxiety-inhibiting agent, was critical to the Wolpian formulation of reciprocal inhibition.

Alternative Procedures and Mechanisms of Action

At the same time, research was progressing on a number of fronts examining the effectiveness of alternative fear-reduction procedures. Among the major procedures were *implosion,* originated by Stampfl (1967), *reinforced practice,* first described by Agras, Leitenberg, and Barlow (1968), and the general procedure of *modeling* (Bandura, 1969) as applied to fears and phobias.

Implosion, involving, as it did, high-intensity imagination of the feared situation and its concomitants, was not far removed from systematic desensitization in imagination and was also attended by early studies showing its (statistically significant) effectiveness when compared to no treatments or alternative treatments (cf. Mavissakalian & Barlow, 1981). Similar results were obtained for modeling both in imagination (covert modeling) as well as in the real situation, or *in vivo.*

At about this point, what was in retrospect a very nonproductive research strategy began, consisting of a long series of studies directly comparing two or more treatments, such as implosion and systematic desensitization. Predictably, some studies showed slight advantages for systematic desensitization, others for implosion, while the vast majority of studies indicated no statistically significant differences (cf. Mavissakalian & Barlow, 1981). But these comparisons took place before it was known why any of these treatments worked in the first place. The more productive research strategy examined mechanisms of action of the various treatments.

One important series of experiments, from the point of view of the mechanism of action involved, occurred during testing of an operant approach to fear reduction. In this procedure, gradual approaches to the feared object or situation were reinforced by, for example, verbal praise from the therapist. Precise feedback of progress was also given. This procedure, which later became known as *reinforced practice,* initially was reported as successful in 1968 (Agras, Leitenberg, & Barlow, 1968), but further component analyses using time series methodology (see chapter 7) indicated that praise was not a necessary condition of the procedure. Since this was a very simple, straightforward procedure, there were not many components left. In one series of studies, feedback of progress, specifically knowledge of precisely how well one was doing as one approached the feared object or situation, was demonstrated an effective ingredient, but could not alone account for the major part of success. Finally, careful comparisons of systematic exposure *in vivo* to the feared situation *versus* nonexposure demonstrated the extremely powerful contribution of this factor to fear reduction after controlling for the presence or absence of other hypothetical therapeutic ingredients. It is interesting to note that this series of studies, conducted over several years, utilized individual clients, in a series of single-case experimental designs particularly appropriate for teasing out effective components of treatment and ultimately mechanisms of action of change.

These findings on the importance of exposure were accompanied by analogue studies in laboratory situations, using primarily snake fears, demonstrating that exposure to the feared situation *in vivo,* or in reality, was at least twice as effective as exactly the same procedure carried out under exactly the same conditions in imagination. This was due, presumably, to some inefficiency in representing all of the feared cues in imagination (Bandura, 1969; Barlow, Leitenberg, Agras, & Wincze, 1969; see Mavissakalian & Barlow, 1981)

Researchers then concluded that perhaps a variety of techniques existed to facilitate exposure to feared situations, exposure that clients or fearful subjects were unlikely to carry out on their own. These techniques included relaxation, presence of a therapist during exposure, modeling by the therapist of entrance into or interaction with the feared situation or object, and precise feedback on gradual progress. Nevertheless, the central therapeutic ingredient was exposure.

This hypothesis was tested in a variety of clinical situations and, indeed, direct exposure was found to be more effective than systematic desensitization in imagination or other alternative forms of fear reduction, particularly those using imagination. What was most impressive is that direct exposure was also effective with the most severely disabling phobia encountered: agoraphobia (Agras, 1978; Marks, 1978; Mathews, 1978; Mavissakalian & Barlow, 1981).

As with any dramatic discovery in science, it was no surprise that this was a relatively simple concept that had been utilized in a variety of contexts, such as other schools of psychotherapy, or other cultures, to reduce fear (Marks, 1978; Mathews, Gelder, & Johnston, 1981; Mavissakalian & Barlow, 1981). This was due most likely to serendipitous clinical discoveries of the effectiveness of this procedure in various settings. One good example was psychoanalysis, where the now-famous quote from Freud himself indicated that all the analysis in the world would not be useful without some direct experience in encountering the feared object or situation (Freud, 1919/1959). It is also interesting to observe that among the numerous phobia clinics now in existence in this country and abroad, many of these were more heavily influenced by clinical innovation and accidental discovery than the research findings mentioned above. The example of TERRAP is described in chapter 1. In addition, Claire Weekes, the Australian family practitioner, without substantial background in psychiatry, originated a treatment based on direct exposure to feared situations along with procedures for managing anxiety that have been widely distributed throughout the world through books, audio-tapes, and records (of. Weekes, 1972). Thus, clinical and research innovations and discoveries seem to progress as much in parallel as in interaction. Nevertheless, despite the well-advanced conclusions of this progression of research, and despite numerous examples of successful clinical innovation, it is probably safe to say that the majority of fears and phobias are still treated by non-exposure-based methods around the world. Some of the reasons for this will be described below.

The Nature of Fear

Perhaps more important for the long run is the last category of research stimulated by these developments: research into the very nature of fears and phobia. This research goes on both in laboratories and clinical settings and is stimulated by the advancement in measurement techniques and theory occasioned by research into component analysis and mechanism of action. To take one example in the case of fear, Lang, in 1968, observed that traditional definitions of anxiety were probably inadequate because anxiety, as observed in his laboratory over the previous 10 years, seemed to be comprised of three loosely connected response systems: verbal report or cognitive representations of fear, physiological responses, and behavioral avoidance responses. Subsequent research (Barlow & Mavissakalian, 1981; Rachman, 1978) indicated that this finding was equally and dramatically true for clients with severe phobias, such as agoraphobia, as well as for those with mild fears. This, in turn, raised the very basic question of what response or combination of responses was being modified during the administration of fear-reduction procedures. In other words, what does it mean to be better? It has been observed, for example, that some people report that they are completely recovered from severe phobias despite maintaining extremely high physiological responding (Barlow, Mavissakalian & Schofield, 1980). Other patterns have also been observed. Further exploration of the nature of fear and the meaning of these patterns of responding in individuals should have direct implications for making treatment more efficient and effective, perhaps by helping therapists to assess phobia individually in their clients. They can then tailor an exposure-based treatment to each individual client to achieve maximum response (e.g., Norton, DiNardo, & Barlow, 1983). How to do this, or whether it is even necessary, awaits further experimental inquiry.

This is a very impressive body of programmatic research findings that, in and of itself, gives one confidence in the research process. From a theory proposed by one man, based loosely on findings from the animal laboratories, we have progressed to the point where we seem to have determined the active ingredient in a variety of fear-reducing procedures. Furthermore, we are making progress in understanding the very nature of fear itself, which in turn will benefit treatment. In short, we have begun to answer basic questions such as, What procedures reduce fear and why do they work?

Unanswered Questions: How Effective Is Treatment?

Nevertheless, this leaves us well short of our goal of answering what are by far the most important questions for practitioners: How effective are these procedures, for whom will they work, and with whom will they fail? Related questions involve the generalizability and maintenance of the effects of these treatments. The reason we do not know the answers to these questions now is that our traditional research methodology is not capable of addressing these important issues, for reasons mentioned in the first chapter. These reasons include the somewhat "artificial" administration of therapy in research settings, an overreliance on statistical rather than clinical significance, and a necessity of averaging findings across a somewhat heterogeneous group of clients to determine overall effects. This prevents us from finding out what works in each individual case and why.

Problems with Percentage-of-Success Strategies

At the most basic level, it would seem one might answer the question, How effective is a treatment? by looking at percentages of success based on some clearly specified criterion of success in between-group comparison studies. But even this question is very difficult to answer from research that has been reported thus far; although, as mentioned above, the progression of research in the treatment of phobia is as advanced as any other problem area at this time. To estimate the percentage of individuals improved, one must look at those groups within a controlled study that have received a relatively unadulterated form of the treatment within an experimental design; that is, the treatment should have been delivered in roughly the same fashion as one would expect it to be delivered clinically. This precludes, for example, crossover designs where clients receive one treatment for half of the experiment and then "cross over" to receive another treatment for the second half of the experiment. This also precludes, to some extent, designs where there are groups of clients receiving only one component of the treatment. To take one example, a therapist might administer intensive *in vivo* exposure to an agoraphobic *without* instructions to practice between sessions, an ingredient that seems very important in the context of these treatments (e.g., Mathews, Teasdale, Munby, Johnston, & Shaw, 1977). Of course, interventions administered in research settings are often delivered in an ideal fashion, with many experimental assistants ensuring that the details of treatment are delivered precisely. These conditions do not obtain in typical applied settings.

For these reasons, there are very few instances where interventions have been delivered to large enough groups of clients, in the manner described above, such that determination of percentage of success would be useful (other difficulties with this approach notwithstanding for the moment). For example, one widely cited and important study on outcome has been reported by Emmelkamp & Kuipers (1979), who lumped together a number of their experiments in which agoraphobics received different versions of exposure-based procedures, depending on what experiment they were in. These versions included imaginal exposure, instructions to practice, supervised practice, cognitive restructuring, and the like. Some clients received only one component, others received different components or a combination of components, depending on the purpose of the experiment. All were treated, of course, in a predetermined number of sessions and in accordance with other experimental design requirements in force at the time. Those clients who responded to a letter asking for follow-up information from these experiments 4 years after they finished their particular experiment were included in this analysis. The criterion for "success" was movement of 2 points on a 9-point, self-rated, global rating scale of improvement on the "main phobia." Naturally, these reports are subject to the usual distortions of self-report of progress. The data indicate that 75% of the respondents had met the criteria of achieving and maintaining at least a 2-point improvement after 4 years.

Obviously, some clients must have improved more than 2 points, but from this study, and most reports of its kind, it is not clear who improved, with what particular characteristics and, more important, who failed. Furthermore, as Garfield (1981) points out, improvement of 2 points on a 9-point scale, vague as this criterion is, can mean relatively little improvement for at least some clients. For example, in one follow-up study where these data were reported, only 18% of a group of 56 were "symptom-free" at follow-up, although 83% had met the criteria for "improvement" (McPherson, Brougham, & McLaren, 1980).

There are other limitations to the interpretation of these data. For example, the Emmelkamp and Kuipers (1979) data were concerned solely with clients seen in the Netherlands by either Emmelkamp or one of his colleagues. Similarly, those data reported by McPherson, Brougham, and McLaren (1980) were all locally seen and followed up only by telephone. Thus, the generality of these findings across clinical centers remains in question until many more centers report in. Finally, to reiterate, these figures are gleaned, for the most part, from controlled experiments where treatment was delivered in an artificial manner to conform to experimental requirements (e.g., a specific number of sessions, exposure only during sessions rather than between, no imaginal exposure, etc.). This is quite different from the usual delivery of these treatments in clinical settings. Furthermore, as noted above, reports of individual clinical success and failure are not reported.

Effects of Treatment on the Individual

All of this raises serious questions about the effectiveness of these procedures with an individual client walking into an individual therapist's office. Will this particular client be one of the approximately 12% who drop out (Jansson & Ost, 1982), or perhaps one of the 30% who not only fail to improve, but perhaps deteriorate a bit? What are the client characteristics that are associated with improvement, with no improvement, or with deterioration? Perhaps just as important, what are the client characteristics and the characteristics of the client's situation that predict marked improvement to the point of "cure," versus minimal to moderate improvement in the neighborhood of 2 points on a 9-point scale? As noted in the first chapter, traditional research is not designed to provide answers to these questions despite the overriding importance of these answers to practitioners.

As a result, even with the major contribution to knowledge of research in the area of anxiety-based disorders, practitioners still know little about the effectiveness of these procedures with their own individual clients. It is very likely that if clinicians experience two or three failures in a row they will very quickly give up an innovative procedure, such as exposure-based therapy, in favor of some other recent innovation. Thus, research and practice continue in parallel.

A concern with these unanswered questions in this otherwise relatively successful area of clinical research led a National Institute of Mental Health sponsored conference of 20 leading investigators from around the world to recommend against further conventional comparative outcome research unless significant process questions, particularly in regard to basic mechanisms of action of these treatments in individuals, were included (Barlow & Wolfe, 1981). This group also recommended that any future research efforts report data for individual clients and pay close attention to successes, failures, and the reason for these outcomes during follow-up.

This, of course, is not a new recommendation. It has been made many times in many contexts. For example, both Kiesler (1971) and Paul (1969), from the standpoint of traditional comparative outcome research, have called for much greater attention to organismic variables (i.e., individual differences and their interaction with the effects of various treatments). But, as evidence from the current status of clinical research on phobia suggests, traditional research strategies will seldom accomplish this particular goal.

The major questions left unanswered can be summarized as follows: (a) How effective is a therapeutic procedure? That is, how many people with a specific problem will improve to what extent? (b) What causes greater, as opposed to lesser, degrees of success, and what causes failure? (c) Will an otherwise successful intervention in a research setting generalize to individuals in a practice setting? This individual analysis is a missing link in our research that is of vital importance to practitioners. It is unlikely that practitioners will be seriously influenced by research, despite impressive contributions to our knowledge, until answers to these questions are forthcoming.

Alternative Models of Research

Recognizing the lack of influence of traditional research on practice, many skilled theorists and investigators have attempted to adapt research methodology or research practices to applied settings so that the data produced from the research efforts will be more meaningful and relevant. Sechrest (1975) suggested that practitioners become more involved in research in an administrative and participatory way. For example, clinicians could assist in planning or could make clinical records available. Also, clinicians could act as judges in clinical research projects. But, Sechrest does not suggest how the unanswered questions might be answered. In 1971, Kiesler described a series of questions of more interest to "artisans" (practitioners) than to scientists, such as who gets chosen for therapy, who drops out, and who succeeds or fails, recognizing, even then, the narrow focus of traditional research. But Kiesler did not propose new strategies to answer these questions, suggesting instead that client and therapist variables thought to be important by clinicians could be plugged into grand factorial designs.

Program Development and Evaluation

More elaborate models for making research relevant, at least in the area of program development, can be found in the recommendations of Thomas (1978) and Reid (1979) from the field of social work, Tharp and Gallimore (1975) working in an educational setting, and Gottman and Markman (1978). Thomas's term *developmental research,* or Gottman and Markman's term *program development model,* are each appropriate descriptions for this type of effort. Each of these investigators noted the lack of influence of research on practice (Reid, 1979) or the inability of traditional research to give us a "full understanding" of the effects of the intervention and suggest a different or more comprehensive approach. Each group of authors, citing Scriven (1967), among others, advocates a step-by-step developmental or *formulative* research strategy. In this strategy, an intervention is constructed based on clinical trial-and-error or research data and tested bit by bit in the applied setting in which it is relevant. At each step the program is modified based on input or feedback from previous steps. Research may include studies of feasibility as well as effectiveness of different strategies or treatment components. Perhaps the best description of this type of effort has been offered by Tharp and Gallimore (1975).

These authors, in a very informative paper, describe a number of steps in this process in the context of developing a model reading program in the classroom for children in Hawaii from different ethnic backgrounds. In addition to more traditional experimentation and program evaluation, a step or stage of qualitative/personal knowing is suggested which involves, for example, incorporating various clinical intuitions into new program components that are added from time to time. Another suggested step is termed *data guidance.* During this stage, observations are made and data are collected on a program in progress to determine if it needs alteration or "tinkering." Any necessary changes can then be combined with clinical intuitions from the process of *qualitative knowing,* and these new program components may be included. The end result is a full operating program that can be evaluated against alternative programs in a more typical program-evaluation fashion.

Reid (1979) notes that this type of research results in a fuller integration between program innovation and evaluation, and certainly between research and practice. As such it seems a particularly useful model for research in other settings where similar program development efforts are ongoing. This would include programs within an agency, hospital, or school system where a relatively well-defined, coexisting group of clients is found. Of course, in any program-development effort there is less emphasis on the individual client *per se.* But, the model, particularly with its emphasis on accountability of practitioners through procedures such as data guidance, does not preclude determination of individual effectiveness, individual predictors of success, or generality of effectiveness over clients, settings, and practitioners. In fact, the emphasis on collecting data on effectiveness as one proceeds, attending closely, in an almost intuitive way, to changes *as they are occurring,* is similar to the emphasis found in clinical replication procedures described below. One of the best examples of this effort is the program developed over a period of years by Hill Walker and his associates for use in regular classrooms (e.g., Walker et al., in press). In this effort, Walker and his colleagues made extensive use of single-case experimental designs in determining the effects of various components of their intervention during the development of their comprehensive program packages.

Quasi-Experimental Designs

Realizing that traditional experimental designs were often impractical in applied settings, Campbell and his associates originated quasi-experimental designs (Campbell & Stanley, 1963; Cook & Campbell, 1979). This strategy, developed particularly in the context of social policy research, involves an adaptation of traditional research designs such that causal inferences are still possible, albeit with an explicit recognition of those factors that pose threats to the validity of the causal inferences. The major difference between quasi-experiments and more traditional experimental methodology is that the quasi-experiments do not use random assignment to groups to create the comparisons from which treatment-caused change is inferred. Instead, " . . . the comparisons depend on non-equivalent groups that differ from each other in many ways other than the presence of a treatment whose effects are being tested. The task confronting persons who try to interpret the results from quasi-experiments is basically one of separating the effects of a treatment from those due to the initial non-comparability between the average units in each treatment group; only the effects of the treatment are of research interest" (Cook & Campbell, 1979, p. 6).

Basically, there are two kinds of quasi-experimental designs. One is a variation of the more traditional randomized, between-group comparison, termed *nonequivalent group design.* In this design the assignment to groups is not randomized, and therefore the groups are not directly comparable in one or more ways (in addition to the administration of the independent variable or treatment). The second is an interrupted time-series design in which the effects of a treatment are inferred by comparing measures taken at several points before the introduction of a treatment with measures taken at several points afterward. In a well-known example, the effects of a new tough crackdown on speeding in one state was evaluated by looking at traffic fatalities for a lengthy period before and after the introduction of the law. As noted in Hersen and Barlow (1976), this latter quasi-experimental design has much in common logically with some of the single-case experimental designs used in studying the effects of interventions on behavior change, particularly the withdrawal design (see chapter 8). Nevertheless, although power analyses and confidence limits are strongly advocated in the context of quasi-experimental designs, this approach was designed for, and is most useful in, the context of evaluation research or policy research. Therefore, this approach maintains the necessary feature of statistical significance testing, statistical control of variability, and a resulting deemphasis on the individual, which is often appropriate for evaluation and policy research. However, when the focus is on individual behavior change, this strategy poses all of the difficulties mentioned above.

A monumental contribution of this work to research in any context, however, is the elucidation and specification of the specific threats to internal and external validity proposed originally by Campbell (1957) and elaborated by Campbell and Stanley (1963) and Cook and Campbell (1979). What becomes clear from this analysis is that levels of inference or conclusions from an experiment are on a continuum, with increasing threats to the inferences or conclusions one can draw as one moves further away from tightly controlled experimental designs. For example, in research on behavioral intervention, as one moves from the traditional randomized group-comparison or single-case experimental design toward the uncontrolled case study, one will be less and less confident about the cause of any effects one observes.

Nevertheless, with these threats in mind, well-specified conclusions can be drawn, even from the individual case study, when properly conducted, and there are many strategies available to reduce the threats to internal validity occurring in the typical uncontrolled case studies or series of cases (e.g., Kazdin, 1981). It is this fact that makes it possible for practitioners to be at least empirical, and at best true scientists, in the context of their own professional activity (see chapter 7). Recommendations emanating from Cook and Campbell's (1979) analysis of causality contribute to guidelines, suggested later in this book, outlining the steps necessary for practitioners to be empirical and scientific in their practice.

Highlighting the Individual

Kiesler (1971) has cogently observed that the science of behavior change looks for laws applying to individuals generally. We have pointed out that traditional research has concentrated on the *general,* while practitioners continue to see *individuals,* either singly or in groups. The unanswered questions, concerning individual differences or intersubject variability in response to intervention, will continue to puzzle the individual practitioner as he or she works with whomever happens to appear in his or her setting. This problem has so concerned some prominent professionals, that serious proposals have been made to abandon the scientific method altogether in favor of total concentration on the individual. This concentration would highlight the individual client's interaction with the behavior-change agent in a phenomenological or naturalistic sense (Raush, 1974).

Few would agree with this position; but, consideration of the state of our knowledge in the area of clinical phobia, discussed above, would seem to point to the necessity for a new emphasis on the individual in applied research in order to address some of the unanswered questions. This emphasis would highlight the effects of various interventions on individual clients, examining client-treatment interaction, client-treatment matching, and other aspects of a particular individual's response to treatment and what this response can tell us about other individuals who will experience the same treatment. It is the importance of this issue that distinguishes the area of human services from other areas of science. This is the one single factor that requires substantial alterations in, and additions to, the way we do science. But a methodology that highlights the individual and, at the same time, maintains the integrity of an empirical and scientific approach to the study of human behavior has been slow in developing.

Deviant Case Analysis

One creative approach, proposed by Alan Ross in 1963, is called *deviant-case analysis.* As expanded in a later important article (Ross, 1981), the essential feature of this method is the intensive study of individuals (participating in research employing traditional randomized group designs) who differ markedly from the group average. Ross proposes that this be done immediately after the experiment is finished, preferably by the experimenter or a collaborating clinician, so as not to lose contact with the clients participating in the experiment. Ross notes that this would be a much less expensive strategy than gathering detailed information on every single subject participating in a traditional experiment. Yet, this strategy would yield a great deal of data and, ultimately, knowledge, on the variety of patterns of individual responses to a given fixed intervention. In this way, at least within the context of traditional research, some information on the generalizability of findings from experimental clients to clients entering the practitioner's office would be available through the process of *logical generalization* (Edgington, 1966; Hersen & Barlow, 1976). This simply refers to the process of deciding, on logical grounds, how similar the experimental subjects are to the ones seen by the practitioner (see chapter 12). Thus, practitioners reading reports on deviant-case analyses, subsequent to reports of the major research findings, could decide when to use the procedures and with whom, depending on the similarity of the client they are seeing to those in the deviant case analyses. Deviant-case analyses, then, would not involve practitioners in the research process as researchers or evaluators, but should ensure, at the very least, that they would consume research findings. This strategy will form an important part of our recommendations outlined below.

Single Case Designs for Practitioners

Within the area of applied research, a methodology capable of determining the effects of interventions in individuals and the reasons for these effects has evolved (e.g., Hersen & Barlow, 1976; Kazdin, 1982; Kratochwill, 1978). For example, much of the research in the problem area of clinical phobia, discussed above, has utilized this methodology, most often termed *single-case experimental design.* This methodology has been helpful in determining effective and efficient components of intervention procedures in those experiments where component analysis is the goal, as well as ascertaining basic mechanisms of action of given intervention techniques. Usually this is done through careful introduction and withdrawal of various components of a given intervention procedure in the manner described in Hersen and Barlow (1976) and in chapters 7 through 11 of this book. A major advance in our applied research efforts has been practitioners' increasing use of single-case experimental designs in applied settings to determine the effectiveness of treatment across a small series of clients or, on occasion, of active ingredients within a treatment.

Nevertheless, the overwhelming majority of research activity involving single-case experimental designs to date continues to be carried out in applied research centers rather than in the offices of practitioners, due to the relative newness of this experimental approach and some of the perceived practical difficulties thought to conflict with the implementation of research of any kind in an applied setting (Agras, Kazdin, & Wilson, 1979; Kratochwill & Piersel, in press; Thomas, 1978). Among many limitations, often mentioned are ethical and practical difficulties. These include, but are not limited to, imposing baseline phases on clients who may require immediate treatment or withdrawing presumably active ingredients from the treatment package of a client who has been doing better. This, of course, is a common characteristic of the withdrawal type of single-case experimental design often reported in the literature (Hersen & Barlow, 1976; also see chapter 8). Single-case experimentation shares other difficulties with more traditional between-group comparisons when used by practitioners, including the increasing complexity of necessary dependent variables, such as sophisticated physiological measures of clinical phobia. Few practitioners would be expected to have on hand this state-of-the-art measurement instrumentation (Agras et al., 1979; Kratochwill & Piersel, in press).

These cogent and reasonable observations have resulted in increasing recognition that the major obstacles to practitioners doing research with individuals in their settings have been practical and ethical. Thus, modifications in single-case experimental designs have been proposed that make it possible for practitioners to use these tools to establish functionally analytic relationships and participate in the research process as researchers and evaluators (Barlow, 1981; Hayes, 1981). These developments include the use of practical and realistic measures easily employed in the offices or settings of most practitioners, and the modification of experimental strategies or the organization of new strategies so that ethical and practical problems preventing their use in applied settings are overcome (see chapter 11). A description of these strategies, along with the presentation of realistic and practical measures easily employed by practitioners, will form the major part of this book.

We believe utilization of this research methodology by practitioners will greatly increase the amount of data available, multiplying by an enormous factor the number of replications of findings initially discovered in either applied research centers or other clinical settings. This development should also provide us more quickly with answers to basic, important questions such as: How effective is treatment compared to no treatment? Why do treatments work? What are the active ingredients? and How effective is one treatment compared to another?

If this were the major outcome of a widespread adoption of single-case experimental designs in the human services area, it would be a very satisfying one indeed. For the way would be open for practitioners, who so choose, to become scientists and fulfill the long-held ideal of the scientist-practitioner. But the major questions referred to above would remain unanswered; that is, we would still know little about client-treatment interaction or individual successes and failures. This information is necessary in order to establish a set of facts about interventions that will be applicable to all individuals. To accomplish this goal, a somewhat different strategy seems needed, combining data collected by practitioners and applied researchers from empirical case studies and single-case experiments. This strategy, relying heavily on the contribution of practitioners treating cases and experimentally analyzing successes and failures, has been termed *clinical replication* (Hersen & Barlow, 1976).

CLINICAL REPLICATION

Clinical replication is a procedure, more properly termed a model or a framework, that can incorporate the findings of practitioners gleaned from both single case experimental designs as well as from empirical case studies if measures are carefully taken. These observations are then arranged in a series. As noted above, the purpose of this series would be to direct attention to both successes and failures, defined clinically rather than statistically, in a series of individual clients receiving a given treatment, as well as to test the generalizability of an intervention delivered in a research setting to a practice setting. Chapter 12 is devoted to a full description of this procedure. One important part of the clinical replication strategy is a procedure called *intensive local observation* (Cronbach, 1975).

Intensive Local Observation

Describing this now well-known recommendation, Cronbach (1975) noted:

> An observer collecting data in one particular situation is in a position to appraise a practice or proposition in that setting, observing effects in context. In trying to describe and account for what happened, he will give attention to whatever variables were controlled. But he will give equally careful attention to uncontrolled conditions, to personal characteristics, and to events that occurred during treatment and measurement. As he goes from situation to situation, his first task is to describe and interpret the effect anew in each locale, perhaps taking into account factors unique to that locale. . . . As results accumulate, a person who seeks understanding will do his best to trace how the uncontrolled factors could have caused local departures from the modal effect. That is, generalization comes late and the exception is taken as seriously as the rule. (pp. 124-125)

At the heart of this process, of course, is a full realization by practitioners and researchers alike of the types of inferences that can be made from data such as these and of the specific threats to internal and external validity accompanying these efforts.

Cronbach's thinking emerges out of an intellectual history in social science, and particularly in educational research, which adheres to the notion that the tightly controlled, fixed-condition, traditional experimentation borrowed from the physical sciences cannot answer all of the questions important to us in social science (e.g., Campbell, 1959; McGuire, 1973; Snow, 1974). While this position, of course, has had its champions in psychology, who would like to do away with experimentation altogether (e.g., Gadlin & Ingle, 1975), Cronbach (1975) makes the very specific observation that our science is incapable of determining the generalizability of laws established in our research centers to practice settings, for reasons mentioned above. One important reason is the inability to detect client-treatment interactions.

The experimental strategy dominant in psychology since 1950 has only limited ability to detect interactions. Typically, the investigator delimits the range of situations considered in his research program by fixing many aspects of the conditions under which the subject is observed. The interactions of any fixed aspect are thereby concealed, being pulled into the main effect or into the interactions of other variables. (Cronbach, 1975, p. 123)

And again,

The investigator who employs a factorial design can detect some interactions of those conditions he allows to vary, but sizable interactions are likely to be suppressed just because any interaction that does not produce a significant F ratio is treated as non-existent. (p. 124)

To take our typical example once again in applied research, we may wish to conduct a 2 × 2 factorial experiment on anxiety disorders where, for example, two levels of intensity of the same treatment are administered to either male or female clients with anxiety. It is possible that we may be able to say, after this experiment, that there is a good (statistically significant) chance that while more intense treatment is not significantly different (better) for males than less intense treatment, more intense treatment is better for females. This might give us a hint of the importance of one rather low-level interaction: intensity of treatment with gender. But, as any practitioner knows, this would be merely scratching the surface of individual differences. Other important variables that might interact with treatment include the gender of the therapist, the age of the client, the social class of the client, the client's method of coping with the experience of anxiety, such as persevering in the presence of the anxiety response versus seeking support from others for a period of time, and, perhaps most important, the nature of the family support system and the role this plays in the anxiety response. And we have not even mentioned occupation, number and intensity of stressors in the environment, and so on.

Mischel (1973) has argued that research in personality must become the study of higher order interactions, and Campbell (1973) points out further the need to reflect on what it means to establish empirical generalizations in a world in which most effects are interactive. Within this context, testing only for the null hypothesis, as Cronbach points out, encourages a disregard for all other individual observations made in the course of the experiment. Depending on the particular applied situation, an applied investigator might observe a very marked interaction between response to treatment and level of support within the family of the client, but if this were not being tested specifically, it would be unlikely to be reported in any journal article.

Returning to our example of clinical phobia, it now becomes clear why the answers to the questions so important to practitioners, such as how effective is the procedure and with whom will it work, have not been answered. These questions cannot be answered using traditional research methodology. The complexity of the human condition will preclude any attempt at experimentally establishing generalization. The number of person/treatment interactions present in an applied setting can never be tested adequately in clinical research centers through the use of factorial designs, even if other weaknesses, such as sampling deficiencies, reliance on statistical significance, averaging, and differences between research and practice settings were not present. Results from the applied research centers on the whys and hows of treatment, so evident in our well-advanced series on clinical phobia, will advance our understanding very little without information on the applicability of these procedures. In applied research the answers to the unanswered questions must come from the practitioners themselves in collaboration with the research centers. It is, in fact, the unique ability of practitioners to observe extent of effect, successes, failures, and interactions, that makes them the focal point in the process of intensive local observation as well as, in the last analysis, full-fledged partners in the scientific process. If properly developed, this process could be the way in which practitioners fulfill the role of scientist-practitioner so long envisioned in our training centers.

The Process of Clinical Replication

As noted above, when translated into the general area of behavior change, intensive local observation has been termed clinical replication (Hersen & Barlow, 1976). Clinical replication has been defined as ". . . the administration of a treatment package (containing two or more distinct treatment procedures) by the same investigator or group of investigators. These procedures would be administered in a specific setting to a series of clients presenting similar combinations of multiple behavioral and emotional problems, which usually cluster together" (Hersen & Barlow, 1976, p. 336). In retrospect, this definition is a bit stiff. It is enough to say that clinical replication is a process wherein practitioners using a clearly defined set of procedures or "treatment" intervene with a series of cases that have a well-specified and measured problem often encountered in applied settings such as depression in adults or attention deficit disorder in children. In the course of this series, the practitioner observes and records successes and failures, analyzing, where possible, the reasons for these individual variations (or intersubject variability). This process embodies all of the functions of intensive local observation, as Cronbach (1975) described it, and takes advantage of the strength of practitioners, specifically their observational skills, in the most important context of all: the treatment setting.

This process, of course, is not new to our clinics and educational centers. It goes on continually, and occasionally the results of such an effort are published. When series are published, they often have an enormous impact on practitioners, although most typically these reports are held in low regard by applied researchers and other scientists, because they do not usually contain the customary experimental controls. But the fact that these series have been influential, at least to practitioners, suggests that they are providing information not obtainable elsewhere. In fact, recent analyses (e.g., Kazdin, 1981) have determined that case-study strategies that comprise a large part of clinical replication series can be as powerful as a well-controlled experiment in contributing to causal statements on the effectiveness of an intervention in some instances. But this section will emphasize clinical replication as a strategy to answer the unanswered questions concerning generality of effectiveness of a given procedure.

Masters and Johnson Series

An example of one of the more famous clinical replication series of recent years was published by Masters and Johnson (1970). This series led to the wide adoption of sex therapy by practitioners. Despite many inadequacies outlined below, this effort is a good example of the potential of the intensive local observation process within a clinical replication series to answer the unanswered questions on client-treatment interactions and generalizability of the effects of treatment. In this series, Masters and Johnson described uncontrolled conditions occurring during treatment and client characteristics that seemed to have had some influence on outcome. Furthermore, detailed accounts of reasons for failures were described, and therefore made available to practitioners for comparison with their own clients presenting with sexual dysfunction. Finally, answers to the general question concerning the extent of effectiveness of these procedures were provided in a preliminary way, subject to several serious limitations that resulted in an overstatement of the effectiveness of these procedures.

This series, of course, has many drawbacks and limitations that decrease its usefulness in communicating to practitioners answers to the unanswered questions. For example, Masters and Johnson report failure rates rather than success rates, which tends to obscure the degree of clinical improvement obtained in those cases where improvement was noted, a problem not far removed from the issue of clinical versus statistical significance. Furthermore, intervention procedures are not always as clearly outlined as it might seem. Numerous departures from the standard program are apparently a common tactic (Wincze & Lange, 1981; Zilbergeld & Evans, 1980), but not well described. In addition, assessment of change is not always carried out by methods that would receive wide agreement from practicing clinicians. Many more measures that are practical and therefore easily used by clinicians are now available. Because of the importance of this series, a detailed description of limitations as well as suggestions on how this series could have been improved will be presented in chapter 12.

In view of the enormous influence of this series, it must be noted that its publication seems to have had at least two unintended deleterious effects. First, other practitioners adopting these procedures, and therefore in a position to provide numerous additional data on their generalizability as well as client-treatment interactions, have either failed to report their results in a useful way or have failed to obtain results at all. For example, Hartmann and Fithian (1972) observed that they did not wish to get into a "horse race" with Masters and Johnson, and therefore did not publish either their results, their criteria for determining success, or detailed descriptions of their numerous clients. Kaplan (1974), another experienced sex therapist who has written widely and seen numerous cases, also does not report results on her series, nor does she describe in any detail client-treatment interactions or the extent of success or failure among clients (Rachman & Wilson, 1980).

Second, a more intriguing deleterious effect seems to be the inhibition of further scientific exploration of why treatment is effective and how treatment is effective. The rationale seems to be that this series was so successful that major research efforts would be wasted, since it is difficult to improve on the therapy as practiced. This may account, in large part, for the fact that our knowledge of the nature and treatment of sexual dysfunction is not nearly as far along as our knowledge of other problem areas such as clinical phobia and depression (Marks, 1981; Rachman & Wilson, 1980). For example, while there are several studies demonstrating that sex therapy is more effective than no treatment (e.g., Obler, 1973), there are few, if any, studies indicating that Masters and Johnson-style sex therapy is better than some other reasonable alternative (Crowe, Gillan, & Golombok, 1981; Marks, 1981; Wright, Perreault, & Mathieu, 1977). Even within the Masters and Johnson series, different rates of success and failure are reported for specific problems. For example, the treatment of premature ejaculation is substantially more successful than the treatment for primary erectile dysfunction, where there is considerable room for improvement. In summary, these procedures seem successful for some forms of sexual dysfunction, but we need more research into the mechanisms of action of these treatments, a component analysis of the treatment package, and a better understanding of the nature of sexual dysfunction.

These deleterious effects, described above, seem directly tied to the enormous influence of this clinical replication series on both practitioners and researchers. This influence, in turn, is caused by the ability of this series to answer important questions for practitioners.

Other Series

Other examples of extremely influential series of this type can be found in the very beginnings of the development of the newly effective procedures for clinical phobia described above. As noted in chapter 1, Wolpe's 1958 series of 210 phobics and other anxiety-based disorders, reporting success rates approaching 90%, had a large impact on clinical practice, which in turn contributed to the illuminating and extremely useful course of clinical research during the subsequent 20 years. What is now needed in the anxiety disorders is a number of clinical replication series from around the world looking at extent of successes and failures as well as client-treatment interactions that might account for these successes and failures, so that further research can proceed on maximizing the efficiency of these treatment procedures. It is somewhat ironic that an area of clinical research beginning with an impressive clinical replication series now suffers from the lack of data that only this effort can provide.

As indicated earlier, other important and new clinical procedures, widely adopted by practitioners, have been largely influenced by clinical replication series. Biofeedback, which originated in the laboratories of experimental psychology, became popular with practitioners for treating psychophysiological disorders after early clinical reports, many of which were unsystematic case studies. In one instance, thermal biofeedback enjoyed wide application in the late 1960s and early 1970s after reports of its use by Elmer Green, who only later published an uncontrolled clinical trial (Sargent, Green, & Walters, 1972). The use of thermal biofeedback then increased substantially, to the point where it became a standard tool of many practitioners. This is a good example of the power and influence of this type of effort, since years of subsequent research failed to demonstrate the effectiveness of thermal biofeedback or biofeedback, in general, over and above relaxation procedures (e.g., Katkin, Fitzgerald, & Shapiro, 1978; Silver & Blanchard, 1978) and yet the field continued to grow. (However, see Blanchard, Andrasik, Neff, Arena, Ahles, Jurish, Pallmeyer, Saunders, Teders, Barron, & Rodichok, 1982, and chapter 12 for new discoveries concerning biofeedback.)

Once again, the power of clinical replication series, in terms of their influence on practitioners, is due in large part to the ability of these series to answer questions relevant to practitioners. But experimental analysis of other, more basic questions, as illustrated in the series on clinical phobia, must occur simultaneously with, or in the context of, clinical replication series. These efforts are best carried out in clinical research centers or through the judicious use of single-case experiments by practitioners within clinical replication series. Attempts to address, simultaneously, all of the important scientific questions concerning behavior-change procedures should help to check unbridled acceptance of unproven procedures, a problem that has plagued the human services down through the years.

The overriding emphasis of this strategy is a return to the paramount importance of the individual in any research process concerned with developing techniques or procedures in the general area of behavior change. Nor, as recommendations in subsequent chapters of this book will make clear, is this process of clinical replication a return to the type of percentage-outcome study often reported in the 1950s. In these efforts, ill-defined techniques such as psychotherapy were applied to diffuse, heterogeneous populations, and progress was assessed by some overall global judgment of outcome, usually on some general personality measures. The strategy envisioned here will be quite different, particularly in its specificity and the inclusion of functional analyses through single-case experiments. In what appears to be the beginning of research on the process of clinical replication, Boice (1983) has demonstrated the power of this strategy to produce effects in a relatively uncontrolled clinical situation that are equivalent to results in a rigidly controlled experimental context. Employing well-specified procedures and flexible single-case designs in the treatment of writer's block, Boice provides important new information on the generalizability of this particular set of procedures. This clinical process, with a strong underlying awareness of the threats to internal and external validity, and the level of inferences that can be drawn, can bring the practitioner back into a position of true partnership with the researcher, and ensure a contribution by the practitioner to science.

AN INTEGRATED MODEL OF APPLIED RESEARCH

It is now possible to suggest an integrated model of applied research that will highlight not only the important and necessary advances emanating from applied research centers, but also the critical role played by full-time practitioners in the scientific enterprise. Models of applied research, listing the essential components of the process, are plentiful. Recent descriptions include updated analyses of both the framework of the research endeavor as well as the specific types of research efforts that contribute to this framework (e.g., Kendall & Norton-Ford, 1982; Wilson, 1981).

Agras and Berkowitz (1980) present an updated model of clinical research that was originally published in Agras, Kazdin, and Wilson (1979) and is one of the more comprehensive and well-thought-out descriptions. This model describes the progression of specific research activities involved in originating, developing, and testing an effective behavior change procedure (see Figure 2.1).

The first stage involves an assessment of the current status of the intervention field and a look at the various sources from whence new techniques may emerge, such as clinical innovation, basic research, or new theoretical developments. Once a suitable procedure is discovered, the next logical step

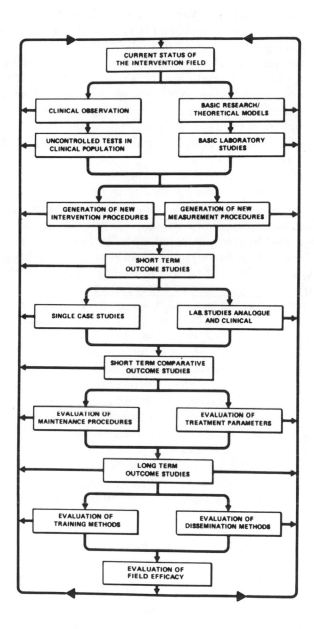

Figure 2.1. - A progressive model of clinical research. (Reprinted from Agras, W.S., & Berkowitz, R. Clinical research in behavior therapy: Halfway there? *Behavior Therapy,* 1980, *11,* 472-487.)

involves short-term outcome studies on the effectiveness of the procedure as compared to no treatment. Agras and Berkowitz then conceptualize this process as continuing with a component analysis of the treatment approach, followed by short-term comparative outcome studies comparing the treatment to other alternative interventions for a specific problem. If the short-term effectiveness is established, questions on the most efficient way of delivering the treatment, as well as issues involving the long-term effects of treatment, become relevant. Long-term outcome studies should then occur as a further test of efficacy concurrent with an examination of such factors as cost effectiveness.

After evaluating methods of disseminating these new procedures, Agras and Berkowitz propose tests of what they term *field effectiveness* so as to compare "efficacy between the clinic and clinical trial" or the relationship between findings in a typical clinical setting versus the clinical research center. As Agras and Berkowitz (1980) point out, very few procedures have reached the point of long-term outcome studies, and none (that we know of) has undergone systematic field testing. An intriguing exception is the clinical replication series on the treatment of writer's block (Boice, 1983) described above. In this series a direct comparability was established between the clinical application of the procedure and its more rigid laboratory version. This model of the progression of research is, of course, ideal rather than realistic at this point in time, because no procedures or interventions have undergone the course of systematic development outlined in the model, nor are any likely to undergo this process in view of the scientist-practitioner split. As we have seen in chapter 1, the identification and development of procedures through research is often a separate and parallel effort to the development and use of procedures in applied situations. However, examination of the several clinical replication series, described above, as well as the important study by Boice (1983), suggests a way in which all of the major questions at the various levels of analysis proposed by Agras and Berkowitz (1980) could be addressed through close cooperation and integration of the work of scientists and professionals.

There is little question that some research can only be carried out in well-developed, advanced, applied research centers. This will be research that is somewhat further removed from the applied situation, involving such issues as the development of suitable measures of change and basic questions on the nature of the problem at hand. Often this type of research will require sophisticated equipment, such as physiological monitoring devices in the case of anxiety disorders or sexual disorders, or expensive observational procedures in the educational setting. But subsequent to these developments, practitioners can and should join the research process. Utilizing single-case experimental designs and practical and realistic measures of change, practitioners can join full-time, applied researchers in providing important knowledge on the effectiveness of an intervention and its components. But, for reasons outlined above, questions concerning the extent of effectiveness and the generalizability of this effectiveness, as well as of field effectiveness, are unlikely to be answered at all in applied research centers due to the nature of the questions asked. The fact that these questions have not been answered for any procedure or intervention is further evidence to support this contention.

Therefore, these questions can only be answered in a meaningful way by practitioners treating large numbers of clients in diverse settings. Essential to this process would be the careful examination of successes and failures as this series progresses, and preferably subsequent experimental analyses of the reasons for failures or lack of substantial success. This, of course, would be followed by the very natural clinical process of attempting alterations or additions to an intervention that did not work in a particular case, to the ultimate benefit of the client; for this is the practitioner's first responsibility. This process, of course, mirrors the normal clinical process. If an intervention does not work with an individual, the practitioner will, typically, tinker with that intervention until it does work, sometimes adding or subtracting wholly new interventions (see chapter 7). If realistic measures are taken during this process, and some attention paid to the essentials of single-case experimental design (see chapters 8-10), then important statements can be made about not only those who do not respond to treatment, but the reasons why, and factors that will ensure a good response. It would be important just to identify those who fail (or respond minimally) through the process of clinical replication. To then discover why they failed and analyze factors that ensure a good response would be an extremely important scientific contribution by practitioners. If done systematically, all of this information would then be published in journals that are now making room for efforts of this type (Barlow, 1983). This information, then, would be fed back to the major research centers where examination, in a more intensive fashion, of these reasons for individual failure or limited success could be undertaken with an eye to the implication of these findings for the very nature of the problem at hand.

GENERALIZABILITY THROUGH INDIVIDUAL ANALYSIS

Single-case designs and an emphasis on the individual have been called a good way to begin the research process, but not necessarily a good way to end it (Leitenberg, 1973). In view of the development of our knowledge of the progression of research during the last decade, it seems possible to ensure that research is applicable to practitioners, without a return to the intensive study of the individual by those very practitioners. At some point, knowledge developed in applied research centers must be integrated into applied situations in such a way that this knowledge is relevant to practitioners. The most efficient, fruitful, and economical way to answer these questions is to collect data directly from practitioners.

Once again, the advantage of using time-series methodology to answer these questions is that variability due to sources other than treatment can be identified at the level of the individual, and thus more reliable rules can be generated that relate particular client or therapist characteristics to outcome. It may at first be surprising to see a recommendation that single-subject designs should be used with many individuals so that rules of generality can be identified. This is due to a misunderstanding about the nature of time-series methodology in general and single-subject designs in particular. This strategy is applicable to the analysis of the individual. It is not intended to restrict the numbers of individuals analyzed.

Group-comparison designs are commonly said to have more external validity than single-subject designs. This is due to a confusion of numerosity (few/many) with the level of analysis employed (group/individual). In fact, because the level of analysis is the group, we have argued that group-comparison designs have inherent limitations in the ability of practitioners to apply their results to individuals. The use of time-series methodology with similar numbers of individuals will offer far more possibilities for applicability. Furthermore, practitioners can participate in this enterprise. It is only through the work of many practitioners that the development of rules of generalizability, based on the analysis of the individual, becomes practical.

It has been suggested occasionally that alternative strategies, such as multicenter clinical trials or meta-analysis (e.g., Smith & Glass, 1977) might shed some light on these issues. But the purposes of meta-analysis, of course, are quite different from those of clinical replication. Clinical replication concentrates on an individual analysis of clients treated with similar procedures across settings, with particular emphasis on individual successes, extent of success, failures, and the reasons for failure. Meta-analysis, on the other hand, seeks to determine overall size of effect of an intervention in statistical terms (usually standard deviation) when compared to some alternative intervention or no treatment. This is accomplished through determining an average of averages based on multiple, between-group comparison studies with little or no regard for individual response. However, statisticians are now raising serious questions concerning methods used to calculate effect sizes (Kraemer, 1982). This particular process, of course, is very controversial (Rachman & Wilson, 1980; Shapiro & Shapiro, 1982, 1983; Wilson & Rachman, 1983). As Rachman and Wilson (1980) point out, this type of effort averages good studies with bad, reasonably valid conclusions (albeit of a statistical nature) with faulty conclusions, and hopelessly loses the effects of a specific procedure on a specific client in the context of hundreds of studies containing possibly thousands of clients. Others would have a different view (Shapiro

& Shapiro, 1983). But, in any case, this procedure is not capable of ascertaining generality of effectiveness although it may, with refinements, help to answer the more preliminary question of whether the treatment, on the average, is effective or not.

Large-scale, multicenter, clinical collaborative studies have potential for yielding a great deal of information on the disorder being treated and the nature of the intervention. Typically, these studies look at comparisons of treatment with no treatment, or with some good alternative treatment, conducted simultaneously in many different applied research centers by a large number of therapists. However, since this method is essentially traditional, between-group experimental methodology where the same comparison is conducted across several research centers, all of the problems for determining generality of effectiveness of the technique across individuals, described above, remain. Particularly salient are the issues of adhering to a rather rigid treatment protocol that precludes attempts to analyze the reasons for failure or limited success, when this occurs. Naturally, some tinkering with the protocol usually goes on in these studies as variations in the treatment protocol initiated by individual therapists creeps into the process in different settings. But these variations, as well as the effects of these variations, would not be reported, but rather buried in the group averages of the overall report. Of course, it would be possible to learn a great deal about client-treatment interactions in such a study by utilizing the procedure of clinical replication and at least identifying failures and minimal responders if not analyzing the reasons why. But this, after all, is not the primary purpose of this effort, which is determining if treatment is effective compared to some comparison group. Furthermore, the large bureaucracy and rigid centralized planning necessary for this effort would probably discourage the type of decentralized, locally managed approach necessary for the process of clinical replication. Therefore, although the most recent effort undertaken by the National Institute of Mental Health, evaluation of cognitive behavioral treatment for depression, will undoubtedly be very useful (NIMH, 1980b), it has evoked predictable reactions from individual practitioners. To quote one (Ostow, 1981):

> The NIMH project, as described, fails to distinguish among the varieties of depression, the differing functions of psychotherapy in each of these varieties and at the several stages in the treatment and recovery process. The conception of the project reflects the view of the institutional psychiatrist who deals with patients in statistically significant numbers, with correspondingly insignificant personal attention to individuals. This contrasts with the understanding of the private practitioner who, intensively and laboriously, and using all of the tools available, helps the individual patient escape from illness (p. 984).

The remainder of this book will attempt to provide the researcher and practitioner with tools that emphasize analysis within the individual client in order to answer all of the important questions posed above, and thereby advance our science and profession in an integrated, cooperative fashion.

THE EMPIRICAL PRACTITIONER
AND ACCOUNTABILITY

The practitioner, of course, is not only concerned with research, despite the important role that he or she can play in the investigative process as a researcher. There is little question that one of the clearest trends in the decade of the 1980s is a concerted movement towards greater accountability in the delivery of human services at all levels, from hospital care through community mental health and educational centers, and individual providers. This trend seems to be due in large part to the greatly increased costs of health and educational services in general and mental health services in particular, as well as the much increased federal role in reimbursing, either directly or indirectly, health and mental health services. The best example of this trend can be seen in the United States, in legislation introduced into the Senate in both 1980 and 1981 requiring the clear demonstration of safety, efficacy, and appropriateness of various forms of psychotherapy before reimbursement would be forthcoming. While various mechanisms have been proposed within the context of these bills to determine which treatments are safe, as well as the more difficult question of which treatments are efficacious, the procedure most often mentioned is a decision by a panel of clinical researchers and clinicians on the effectiveness of an intervention. This decision would be made after an examination of the experimental and clinical evidence.

The model for this newly developing policy is the Food and Drug Administration, which uses similar criteria, along with numerous data from clinical research laboratories, to determine the safety and efficacy of pharmacological agents before allowing their prescription in the United States. This agency is known as being one of the toughest regulatory agencies on pharmacological agents in the world. Most other countries with well-established mental health services already have in place a variety of cost-containment procedures possible only with the degree of control present in a national health service, but few seem to have gone so far as to "approve" specific psychotherapeutic intervention. This move on a national level towards approval of specific procedures is complimented by quickly expanding programs, termed *quality assurance* programs, which have, as at least an equally important goal, cost containment. Many of these programs are now in place and the reviews of individual service providers administered by these programs are required for reimbursement of services by either national or independent third-party payers.

One of the most comprehensive experiments in quality assurance for individual provision of mental health services is being carried out by the Civilian Health and Medical Program of the Uniformed Services (CHAMPUS). This program, which is a very large one, covering as it does all personnel connected with the armed services, contracted with the American Psychiatric Association and the American Psychological Association to set up a mechanism to provide peer review of services provided either individually or in clinics. This process was based on professional standards review organizations (PSROS) and committees set up earlier in the decade. PSROS consist of groups of professionals who determine such things as the appropriateness of the treatment, factors associated with the delivery of the treatment, and, most important, adequacy of progress or improvement given the particular problem for which treatment is indicated at selected points in time (Claiborn & Zaro, 1979). These initiatives have stimulated major interest among third-party payers. There is little question that this program may act as a model for other programs concerned with patient improvements and systemwide quality assurance activities.

Nevertheless, one of the major stumbling blocks has been the lack of practical and realistic measures of behavior change for use by practitioners. Clinical replication, of course, presumes adequate practical and widely agreed upon measures of change. It would seem that for many behavioral problems confronted by practitioners, there now exist reasonable measures on which practitioners could widely agree (see chapters 3-6). Many of these measures, originating in clinical research centers, have only recently been developed. Accountability, of the type described above, which will be required of all behavior change agents in the near future, will necessitate, at the very least, demonstration of efficacy on every client or group of clients for whom reimbursement is sought. But the activities involved are little different from those required for a basic clinical replication series. Essentially, it necessitates the creative use of practical and realistic measures of change, along with clear descriptions of behavior-change procedures employed with each individual client. Based on the early experience of such programs as CHAMPUS, demonstration of change on standard behavioral and questionnaire measures of clinical phobia or depression, for example, would be welcome indicators of progress and would more than fulfill the current requirements for accountability and subsequent reimbursement for treatment. The practitioner who is aware of those realistic measures of change will be accountable and will become an evaluator of his or her efforts. And yet, the requirement to be accountable should also assist the practitioner in his or her scientific and empirical activities by providing an incentive to collect data on clients with similar problems that will form the basis for clinical replication series. This, in turn, will greatly add to our data base on the generality of treatment effectiveness of given interventions. It will also increase our knowledge of client-treatment interactions and the all-important factors associated with failure. Accountability and empiricism go hand in hand and it would seem these goals are now within the practitioner's reach.

SECTION II
PRACTICAL AND
REALISTIC MEASURES
OF CHANGE

Chapter 3
General Strategies in Assessment

INTRODUCTION

Being an effective scientist-practitioner requires knowledge of time-series methodology and of measures of behavior change, the latter often referred to as dependent variables. While other sections of this book focus on time-series methodology, this section focuses on measures.

The measures of special interest to scientist-practitioners are clients' problems, expressed in quantifiable, measurable terms. In other words, the specific presenting problems and/or treatment goals for each individual client should be measured and expressed quantitatively. In addition, measures of certain aspects of treatments themselves are often important (Yeaton & Sechrest, 1981).

Quantification of clients' problems is no small task. Such quantification requires conceptual and practical ingenuity. The task of problem measurement may be especially challenging for nonbehavioral therapists, who tend to formulate treatment goals in terms of changes in clients' intrapsychic functioning or in self-perception (Nelsen, 1981). While goal specification and measurement are more conceptually compatible with behavior therapy, even behavior therapists report practical difficulty with this task. Nearly half of the behavior therapists (43.87%) who responded to a survey indicated that a disadvantage of behavioral assessment techniques was their impracticality in applied settings (Wade, Baker, & Hartmann, 1979), even though such techniques do lead to quantified data. Similarly, respondents to a survey by Ford and Kendall (1979) rated several barriers to naturalistic observations (often cited as the *criterion* measure in behavioral assessment with which the accuracy of all other measures are compared): time and expense (mean of 3.6 on a 5-point scale, where 5 equals the most formidable barrier); lack of cooperation from clients (3.0); and unavailability or unfeasibility of requisite assessment methods (2.9).

While the quantified measurement of clients' problems is a prerequisite for scientific clinical practice, this task seems to present some difficulties for both nonbehavioral and behavioral clinicians. This and following chapters attempt to resolve the difficulties. This chapter discusses the need for quantified measures of clients' problems and guidelines to accomplish this measurement. These guidelines are also useful in measuring parameters of treatment for purposes of determining treatment "integrity." This will be discussed below. Subsequent chapters present alternative practical measures, useful in clinical settings.

REASONS FOR COLLECTING MEASURES

There are several good reasons for practitioners to collect quantified measures of their clients' problems and progress. Three reasons are elaborated below.

Improve Treatment

By Measuring Problems

The first reason for practitioners to collect quantified measures of their clients' problems and progress is to improve treatment. Measures of clients' problem(s) should be taken before treatment begins, several times during the course of treatment, and at short- and long-term follow-up when treatment ceases. When measures are collected at regular temporal intervals, they provide feedback to the therapist about the client's progress. If the treatment procedures are not producing desired results, then the procedures can be modified. Frequent measurement allows timely revision in unproductive therapeutic strategies. Client and therapist time and effort and client fees are not wasted on ineffective techniques. If the treatment procedures are producing desired results, the therapist can continue the procedures with renewed confidence.

While the above statements may seem obvious, experimental verification is needed to corroborate them. In other words, it makes sense that the collection of objective measures can improve clinical efficacy. But applied science has yet to provide experimental support for this claim. To remedy the situation, a between-subjects design might be employed, with two groups of clinicians: An assessor collects repeated measures on all client-subjects. Half of the clinicians view the results during treatment, while the other half do not. The relative improvement in the clients treated by the two groups of clinicians is determined. Alternatively, and more in keeping with the spirit of this book, a single-subject research design might be used to determine if the collection of objective measures produces improved treatment, for example, a multiple baseline across several problems in an individual client. An assessor collects measures on all problems each week. The quantified measures are revealed to the therapist, however, at successive weeks in a multiple-baseline format. The hypothesis would be that each client problem would receive better treatment, as evidenced by improvements in measures of his or her problem, when the data about the problem was shared with the therapist.

Until such experiments are performed, it is a common sense statement that the collection of repeated measures improves therapeutic efficacy. The measures provide feedback to the therapist on the effectiveness of the treatment, so that the current treatment can be altered or maintained.

By Measuring Aspects of Treatment and Treatment Integrity

Treatment may also be improved when aspects of treatment are measured. Clinicians and clinical researchers are recognizing that measuring certain aspects of treatment can be very important in clinical practice. Two aspects of particular importance are the strength and integrity of treatment (see Yeaton & Sechrest, 1981, for a detailed discussion). In most instances, practitioners choose treatments because they think these treatments will be effective. As our technology improves, it is necessary to pay some attention to the particular "dosage" of treatment that should be used. For example, in treating a medical problem by pharmacological means, a physician generally recommends a particular dosage of a given drug. This decision is based on some prior knowledge of what dosage is usually effective with the particular type of patient presenting with a given problem. Strength or "dosage" of psychological treatment, then, would have to do with the intensity of the treatment (e.g., verbal reprimands versus contingent electric shock for self-destructive behavior) and the frequency of administration (seven times a week versus one time a week).

A more important concept emerging in the clinical literature is termed *treatment integrity*. Treatment integrity refers to the degree to which treatment is delivered as intended. For example, someone could be prescribed the right dosage of medication, but through "cheeking" the medication, not actually receive the treatment as intended. Similarly, one might deliver cognitive therapy in order to change severe depression or anxiety. But unless one monitors changes in cognitions, one cannot be sure if a treatment failure is due to the ineffectiveness of a cognitive therapy approach that was properly delivered or to the fact that the client did not receive enough of a "dosage" of cognitive therapy to change the cognitions in the first place, which in turn should affect the depression or the anxiety.

To take another example that occurred recently in our clinic, two agoraphobics were administered a treatment package consisting of cognitive restructuring and detailed instructions on gradually approaching a hierarchy of feared situations. These clients self-monitored a variety of items, including the amount of "practice" exposing themselves to feared situations that occurred between sessions. In many cases, this self-monitoring was corroborated by a spouse. Measures of the problem, specifically the avoidance behavior and amount of subjectively reported anxiety, indicated that one client improved, while one client did not. Measures of treatment integrity, that is, how much treatment was actually experienced by each patient based on the amount of practice between sessions, revealed that the client who got better had practiced, while the other client did not. In this case, one can conclude that the treatment is effective, but one client simply did not receive it in its intended form. Alterations may then be made in the treatment approach that will improve treatment and make it more effective.

Thus, many of the strategies suggested in subsequent chapters (chapters 4, 5, and 6) can be used not only to measure problems, but also to measure the integrity of treatment. In each instance, this should improve treatment. In most cases, measures of treatment integrity are different from measures of treatment outcome. In the example above, measuring amount of practice in feared situations is not the final outcome that one desires, which is reduction of subjective and behavioral aspects of fear. Taking blood levels to determine if a patient with bipolar affective disorder has reached an adequate level of lithium is not the same as observing changes in the client's manic behavior. Monitoring the implementation of a contingency contract between a disruptive adolescent and his parents is different from decreasing the disruptive behavior itself. Practitioners can monitor depth of relaxation through portable physiological monitoring equipment as a measure of treatment integrity when using relaxation or biofeedback as a treatment for headaches, hypertension, or some other stress-related physiological syndrome. Other measures would be used, however, to assess desired changes, such as self-monitoring of headache pain.

Most practitioners check integrity of treatment in an informal way. Formalizing this procedure should improve treatment and increase accountability.

Enhance Clinical Science

The second reason for practitioners to collect quantified measures of their clients' problems and progress is to enhance clinical science. The thesis of this book is that data collection and experimentation by practitioners who bridge the scientist-practitioner gap expand our armamentarium of effective techniques and our knowledge of therapeutic processes (Azrin, 1977; Barlow, 1980; Hersen & Barlow, 1976; Jayaratne & Levy, 1979; Meehl, 1978).

In order to draw valid conclusions from the work of the scientist-practitioner, the work must have internal and external validity. Internal validity allows the reasonable conclusion that the treatment (independent variable) produced the results seen in the measure of change (dependent variable). Alternative hypotheses about the causes of treatment outcome must be ruled out.

There are many threats to internal validity. These threats are events other than the independent variable that occur within or outside the experiment and that may account for the results (Kazdin, 1980). One of the threats to internal validity is changes in the measuring instrument or measurement procedure over time. An example might be a practitioner's rating of the severity of a client's depression. On the first visit, the therapist rates the client's depression as severe. Several visits later, while the client's depressed symptomatology may, in fact, not have changed, the demand characteristics may be such that the therapist rates the client's depression as moderate. To do otherwise may endanger the therapist's self-esteem, continued access to third-party payments, and so on. This change in the way the therapist is making the rating is a threat to internal validity. It endangers the validity of conclusions that the scientist-practitioner may draw between the therapy (the independent variable) and the depression (the dependent variable).

Accurate measurement of the problem is a prerequisite for internal validity. Hence, the scientist-practitioner, in contributing to clinical science, must utilize accurate measures. Of course, accurate measurement by itself does not ensure internal validity.

Provide Accountability

The third reason for practitioners to collect quantified measures of their clients' problems and progress is to enhance accountability. As noted in chapter 2, there is increasing pressure from a variety of sources for evidence that therapy is actually helping clients. One source is from insurance companies and third-party payers. Stricker (1979) cites Dörken and Webb (1978) as saying that approximately half of all outpatients seen by psychologists are covered, at least in part, by some form of insurance, and approximately one of every three dollars earned in private practice by psychologists comes from a third-party payer. These figures would be somewhat greater for psychiatrists; and somewhat less for social workers. But the trend is toward increasing coverage of services by all mental health professionals. Thus, accountability demands by insurance companies and other third-party payers are sure to have far-reaching impact.

As described in chapter 2, the American Psychological Association and others recently contracted with the Civilian Health and Medical Program of the Uniformed Services (CHAMPUS) to devise an internal and national peer review system to evaluate outpatient psychological services provided under its coverage. It is generally believed that the CHAMPUS system will be widely accepted among insurance companies making third-party payments (Craighead, 1978).

As part of the review process, each provider is asked to submit at designated review points (after 8, 24, 40, and 60 sessions) a CHAMPUS Out-Patient Psychological Treatment Report. This form asks for information about the patient's problem, the therapist's goals and planned intervention, and an estimate of progress since the last form was submitted. As noted by Stricker (1979, p. 121), "The progress report on the (form) must relate to the specific treatment goals and must contain a clear justification when progress is not of a reasonable magnitude. Both the therapist and the patient will make independent judgments as to the extent of the progress since the last review point."

It is evident that objective measures collected by the therapist will facilitate estimates of client progress required by CHAMPUS. If measures of both the problem and the integrity of treatment are taken, so much the better. Again, the CHAMPUS requirements are presented in detail because this project is thought to be a prototype of the type of accountability to be required by other insurance companies and third-party payers.

In summary, there are at least three good reasons for scientist-practitioners to collect repeated measures on clients' problems: (a) to improve treatment offered to clients, (b) to enhance clinical research, and (c) to provide accountability. The remainder of this chapter focuses on guidelines for quantifying clients' problems and progress as well as for measuring treatment. While most guidelines will be provided in the context of measuring problems, these guidelines are equally applicable to assessing the integrity of treatment as illustrated in examples given above.

GUIDELINES FOR COLLECTING MEASURES

The following suggestions may help practitioners in implementing data-collection procedures in their settings.

State Client's Problems in Specific Terms

The presenting problems of each individual client must be stated in specific terms. Clients' problem behaviors and desired therapeutic objectives should be defined with clear behavioral referents (Mischel, 1968). Clients and some therapists may initially conceptualize presenting problems in global terms, such as *the reduction of nervousness* or *improvement in self-concept*. The following questions have been useful in intake sessions to help concretize presenting problems and to establish treatment objectives. One example is to ask the client for "acceptable evidence" of having attained the desired global goal.

For example, if the client wants to improve his self-concept, acceptable evidence of that improved self-concept might include: being able to speak in front of groups without one's voice faltering, saying fewer negative statements to oneself (e.g., "I'm such a bore."), and being able to decline invitations that are momentarily not appealing.

A second useful question to help define client problems in specific terms is to ask the client for his or her "three wishes." In other words, if any three of the client's wishes could be granted, what would they be? For example, a schizophrenic in remission might wish that he could have a girlfriend, be able to study without intrusive fantasies, and be able to obtain a part-time job.

Another strategy in specifying client problems is to ask the client about a "typical day or week." Describing a *current* typical day or week helps to specify current problems. Describing an *ideal* typical day or week helps to establish therapeutic goals. For example, an ideal typical week for a currently depressed female client might be to get up and go to work in the mornings, to go out with a male partner a few evenings a week, and to receive calls or visits from her grown children on the weekends.

It may be especially challenging to nonbehavioral practitioners to describe clients' problems or therapeutic objectives in specific terms. The long-term goals may be rather global and distant. Nelsen (1981) suggests that nonbehavioral clinicians specify partial or instrumental goals. Partial goals involve part of a final goal or doing something that builds up the skills needed to accomplish the final goal. Nelsen provides the following example of a partial goal. A woman's long-term final goal is being less socially isolated. Partial goals may be saying hello to a stranger, speaking briefly to a neighbor, and calling up a friend. Instrumental goals lead indirectly to a final goal. Nelsen provides the following example of an instrumental goal. A client's final goal is experiencing higher self-esteem. Her instrumental goal may be getting a raise at work.

Another source of suggestions for specific behaviors or goals for both behavioral and nonbehavioral clinicians is the operational criteria of the current *Diagnostic and Statistical Manual of Mental Disorders* (DSM-III) (American Psychiatric Association, 1980; Liberman & Wong, 1980). The diagnostic labels in DSM-III are, of course, useful for a wide variety of purposes, including communicating with other professionals, identifying homogeneous populations for group research, and compiling summary statistics. The labels themselves, however, are too global to serve as the targets of therapeutic intervention. The operational criteria or diagnostic criteria that define each diagnostic category, however, may provide useful suggestions for specific therapeutic goals.

Practitioners who have been using the Problem-Oriented Record (POR) (Katz & Wooley, 1975; Weed, 1968) have a headstart in specifying client problems. The problem list of the POR generally requires a specification of problems to be treated. Strategies or techniques to measure progress in treating these problems can serve as measures and can be reported in the "subjective" and "objective" portions of the SOAP notes. The SOAP notes are the portion of the POR in which progress is recorded under the format of subjective data (S), objective data (O), assessment (A), and plan (P).

Another rather well-known strategy by which problem behaviors and treatment goals are specified is *goal-attainment scaling* (Kiresuk & Sherman, 1968). Individual goals for each client are selected, goals which will ameliorate his or her problems. For each goal, a scale is created, composed of a series of likely treatment outcomes varying from *least favorable* (-2) to *most likely* (0), to *most favorable* (+2). An objective event is tied to each scale point. In an example provided by Kiresuk and Sherman (1968), a goal was "dependency on mother." The least favorable outcome (-2) was "lives at home; does nothing without mother's approval." The most likely outcome (0) was "chooses own friends, activities, without checking with mother; returns to school." The most favorable outcome (+2) was "establishes own way of life; chooses when to consult mother."

In summary, the first guideline in creating measures is to specify the client's problem and treatment objective in terms of specific behaviors. This specification can be accomplished with the help of particular interview questions, partial or instrumental goals, DSM-III, Problem-Oriented Record, and goal-attainment scaling.

Specify Several Problem Behaviors

This guideline, of measuring multiple problem behaviors per client, is implicit in the preceding discussion. Most cases are sufficiently complex that several intervention goals can readily be identified.

In some cases, these various intervention goals comprise a recognizable syndrome. To illustrate, a client may display several of the diagnostic or operational criteria outlined in DSM-III as typical of a particular disorder. A depressed woman, for example, may cry as she describes her situation; she may report that she has difficulty sleeping through the night, has recurrent thoughts of suicide, has difficulty concentrating on a task, and has lost interest in usual pastimes. It would be useful to take quantified measures of each of these problems. Even though these problems are characteristic of the depressive syndrome, it is not certain that they covary or change at the same rate in any individual client.

In other cases, the combination of intervention goals is more idiosyncratic. For example, Humphreys and Beiman (1975) describe a case in which six problem areas were specified: uncertain vocational goals, inadequate social skills, unassertiveness, marital difficulties, fear of crowded places, and public speaking phobia. Quantified measures should be obtained for each of these problems.

At times, several therapeutic goals may be established that are all final or terminal goals, to use Nelsen's terminology (1981). At other times, some of the multiple goals may be partial or instrumental goals. In other words, when listing several therapeutic goals, it is not critical that they be comparable in importance.

Upon occasion, it may be critical to measure some behaviors that will not be subjected to treatment. An example might be a pedophiliac who showed normal sexual arousal toward his wife. Pedophiliac arousal would, of course, be measured to demonstrate that treatment was effective in reducing deviant arousal. In this case, however, it would also be advisable to measure heterosexual arousal to determine that it was not adversely affected by the treatment. Although Brownell, Hayes, and Barlow (1977) demonstrated a functional independence among these types of arousal, it is nevertheless a useful precaution to measure both deviant and normal arousal during the course of treatment.

Obtain Multiple Measures For Each Problem Behavior

In addition to measuring several different problem behaviors or treatment goals per client, it is also advisable to obtain several different measures for each problem or goal. One reason for multiple measurement is that there is no one true measure of the client's problem.

Let us suppose that a clinician was treating a person with deviant sexual arousal. The clinician obtains measures of physiological arousal, a self-report measure of arousal, and a self-report measure of deviant sexual activity. The various measures may not agree (Barlow, 1977). Since there is no prior basis on which to decide which is the "best" or "true" measure, the various types of measures should continue to be collected. Similarly, a clinician treating a phobic client might measure avoidance or approach behavior, might obtain a physiological measure of fear (e.g., heart rate or galvanic skin response), and might obtain a self-report of fear. Again, the measures might not agree (Rachman & Hodgson, 1974). But, since there is no basis on which to select the one true or best measure, the various types of measures may all be true measures that together are useful in painting a broad picture of the client's status.

Moreover, even if synchrony (or agreement) were found among various measures for a particular client at a particular point in time, there is no guarantee that this synchrony would be maintained as treatment progressed. The relationship between simultaneous measures of heart rate and approach behavior was examined during treatment of nine phobic cases by Leitenberg, Agras, Butz, and Wincze (1971). In some cases, heart rate increased as phobic avoidance behavior decreased. In other cases, there was a parallel decline. In still others, there was a decline in phobic behavior without any accompanying change in heart rate; and, finally, in several cases heart rate decreased only after phobic behavior had declined. The point is that inaccurate conclusions would have been drawn about at least some clients's progress if either heart rate or avoidance had been selected as the sole measure. Similar asynchrony (lack of agreement) among behavioral measures, heart rate, and self-reports of anxiety was reported in three agoraphobic women, over the course of therapy, by Barlow, Mavissakalian, and Schofield (1980). Again, all three measures were needed to form a complete picture of client progress.

Inconsistency among different measures of the same problem is generally attributed to method variance; that is, to different methods of measurement being used to measure the same problem (Campbell & Fiske, 1959; Cone, 1979). In Hartshorne and May's classic research (1928) on children's moral behavior, for example, there was substantial inconsistency in children's honesty as measured in actual situations and on questionnaires. This inconsistency can be attributed to method variance.

Not only is method of measurement frequently varied, but so is the content of what is measured. Cone (1979) argued that the frequently reported asynchrony among motoric, physiological, and self-report measures is due to a confound between the method of measurement and the content being measured. In other words, self-report methods are used to measure cognitive content ("Tell me what you are thinking"), but direct observation methods are used to assess motor or physiological content. Cone (1979) proposed that if only method and not content were varied, more consistent relationships might be obtained across physiological, motor, and self-report responses. Typically, self-reports of *fear* would be compared with direct observation of a physiological response, like perspiring during a behavioral avoidance test, with resultant asynchrony. If Cone's suggestion were followed, self-reports of *perspiring* would be compared with direct observations of perspiring during a behavioral avoidance test. Indeed, as Cone would have predicted, when subjects are asked to report what they would do and then are asked to perform those tasks, the correlations between self-report and overt behavior are often very high (Bandura & Adams, 1977; McReynolds & Stegman, 1976).

Relationships are frequently inconsistent, however, not only across different response systems, but also in measures taken from the same response system. Different measures of change in obesity status produced by weight loss treatment, for example, are imperfectly correlated (Rogers, Mahoney, Mahoney, Straw, & Kenigsberg, 1980). Also, inconsistent responding on different questionnaires purporting to measure depression or assertiveness would not be surprising.

In light of these data, consistency among different measures of the same problem behavior or treatment goal cannot be assumed. Multiple measures are, therefore, recommended to obtain converging evidence of the client's progress or lack thereof.

Select Measures That Are Both Sensitive and Meaningful

Measures can vary on a molecular-molar dimension as related to the presenting problem. Some measures may be very molecular, very precise, and very sensitive to weekly therapeutic change. These measures, however, may be weak in construct validity; that is, they may not provide a meaningful measure of the presenting problem. To illustrate, assume that the presenting problem is a deficiency in social skills ("I can't get along with anybody; nobody seems to like me"). Molecular, precise measures might be selected, such as smiles displayed or percentage of eye contact made during weekly role-playing sessions in the clinic. If the client is taught through behavioral rehearsal to smile more and to increase eye contact, these measures may show weekly improvements. It is unclear, however, in what ways smiles and eye contact relate to social skills. These precise, molecular measures might change, and the presenting problems remain intact. Thus, it may not be sufficient to rely on molecular measures as the sole criterion of client improvement.

Conversely, if only molar measures are taken, they may have good construct validity; but they may be difficult to measure precisely and may be insensitive to weekly therapeutic progress. To continue with the social skills example, a molar measure might be to ask significant others in the client's environment to rate his or her social skills on a 1-7 rating scale. Such ratings may have good construct validity, but may be insensitive to small therapeutic changes.

The ideal, then, may be to take both types of measures, molecular measures that can be measured with precision and that are sensitive to gradual therapeutic progress, and molar measures that relate to the presenting problems in a meaningful way. Since it is not likely that a single measure can fulfill both roles, it may be necessary to rely on multiple measures for each presenting problem.

In another example, a child may be referred because of academic achievement that is below grade level. A global achievement test like the Wide Range Achievement Test (Jastak, Bijou, & Jastak, 1965) or the Peabody Individual Achievement Test (Dunn & Markwardt, 1970) may have good construct validity, but such tests may be insensitive to small, gradual therapeutic changes. As a solution, such tests might be given two to four times per year, or at the beginning and end of treatment; but other more sensitive, more molecular measures might be more frequently administered. Examples of the latter might be daily homework assignments that are completed correctly or grades on weekly in-class quizzes.

Another example relates to the presenting problem of depression. Molar measures like the Depression scale of the Minnesota Multiphasic Personality Inventory (MMPI) (Hathaway & McKinley, 1951) or the Beck Depression Inventory (Beck, Ward, Mendelson, Mock, & Erbaugh, 1961) may have good construct validity. In other words, if a client's scores on these measures improve dramatically, it is believable that the client is truly less depressed. These measures, however, may be insensitive to gradual therapeutic improvement. A client's depression may be related to problems in several different response classes (Craighead, 1980); for example, an unfavorable ratio of pleasant and unpleasant events, a deficiency in social skills, or an excess of irrational cognitions (Lewinsohn & Arconad, 1981). More molecular measures may be selected that are sensitive to changes in these individual response classes, for example, role play measures of social skills, or questionnaire responses on the Pleasant Events Schedule (MacPhillamy & Lewinsohn, 1975). The molecular measures may be administered weekly or biweekly, while the more molar measures may be administered monthly or bimonthly.

In addition to good construct validity, another advantage of some molar measures is the normative data available for them. In other words, for some molar measures, there are published means and standard deviations of how particular samples of subjects scored on these molar measures. Such normative data are useful as a standard of comparison against which to measure a particular client's score. Before treatment, the comparison helps to gauge the severity of the client's complaint; after treatment, the comparison helps to gauge the degree of improvement, relative to a "normal" sample (Kazdin, 1977; Nelson & Bowles, 1975).

Thus, both molar and molecular measures have their advantages and disadvantages. Molar measures generally have good construct validity and frequently have normative data; molecular measures generally are more sensitive to gradual therapeutic improvement.

The terms *molar* and *molecular* in this chapter relate to some current distinctions made in measurement or testing. Carver (1974) distinguished two dimensions of tests. The *psychometric* dimension of tests focuses on measuring between-individual differences. The *edumetric* dimension of tests focuses on within-individual growth. Carver concluded that both dimensions are important, but for different purposes, for example, "the danger . . . is that the psychometrically developed tests may not be sensitive to gain when, in fact, there is gain" (1974, p. 518). Glaser (1963) distinguished between *criterion-referenced* testing and *norm-referenced* testing. Criterion-referenced testing measures whether a student can satisfactorily attain a criterion performance; it depends upon an absolute standard of quality. Norm-referenced testing provides a relative ordering of individuals with respect to their test performance; it depends upon a relative standard of quality.

The point of these distinctions (molar-molecular; psychometric-edumetric; norm-referenced, criterion-referenced) does not seem to be which type of testing is better, but which type of testing is better for which purpose. They may both be useful, for different reasons.

Collect Measures Early in the Course of Treatment

In most cases, a reasonable hypothesis about the nature of the problem behaviors can be constructed during the initial, or intake, interview. Thus, some measures can begin to be collected immediately. For example, a depressed client may cry and complain during the intake interview, and report weight loss, inability to sleep, and inability to complete routine duties. As measures, the assessor may count the number of crying episodes and of complaints during a portion of the intake session (e.g., the last 30 minutes), and weigh the client before he or she leaves. The client may also be given a weekly activity schedule to complete for homework. The schedule lists the days of the week and the times of the day. The client is asked to record sleeping and waking times and duties completed during the forthcoming week.

If data collection has begun early enough, as in the above example, the assessment phase may be concluded with a substantial baseline in hand (Hayes, 1981). Baseline, of course, consists of measures of the problem behaviors prior to intervention. Early collection of measures precludes unnecessary delays prior to treatment implementation, delays that are sometimes cited as an objection against the collection of baseline data.

It is advisable to collect data initially on a rather large number of possible measures of the client's problems. As assessment and intervention proceed, irrelevant measures can be discarded and relevant measures retained. Further strategies for collecting data in baseline will be presented in chapter 7.

Take the Same Measures Repeatedly, Prior to, During, and Following Treatment

The bare minimum to determine if the client changed during the course of treatment is to measure the client's problems before and after treatment. Even if an improvement is noted by such pre-post measurement, the causal efficacy of the treatment has not been established, unless proper experimental controls have been employed. This is discussed more fully in chapter 7. Nonetheless, a pre-post objective measure of client change is, of course, superior to no measure, especially for accountability purposes.

Repeated measurement prior to, during, and following treatment is better than pre-post measurement for two reasons. First, repeated measurement provides feedback to the therapist about the effectiveness of the treatment strategy at an opportune time. If the treatment is effective, it should continue to be employed. If the treatment is not effective, however, the therapist has received feedback at a time when the treatment can be changed. The ineffective treatment can be replaced with one that is potentially more effective. If repeated measurement is continued, the validity of that promise can be determined.

The second advantage of repeated measurement over pre-post measurement is in enhancing clinical science. If repeated measures are obtained, marked changes or variability in the data may be noted. The scientist-practitioner uses such variability to formulate hypotheses about the independent variables or factors that are controlling the dependent variables or the client's problems. As an example, let us say that a client keeps daily records of the duration and severity of his or her tension headaches. These headaches seem to be worse on some days more than others. The clinician can explore with the client the factors that make these particular days different from other days. Identification of those factors may provide suggestions for more effective treatment. In this example, let us say that headache severity and duration is related to increased job demands. Depending on the circumstances, the clinician may intervene by teaching the client better organizational skills, or appropriate assertiveness toward the boss, or relaxation coupled with coping statements. If headache severity and duration now change, assuming appropriate experimental controls have been utilized, then the causal link has been established with greater certainty between job demands and worsening of headaches and between a particular treatment and improvements in headaches.

In summary, pre-post objective measures of client problem behaviors are helpful in determining whether or not a client changed during the course of treatment. Repeated measures, prior to, during, and after treatment are superior to pre-post measures for two reasons. First, timely feedback is provided to the therapist so that the treatment strategies may be altered or maintained. Second, variability in the data can be explored to help identify the factors or independent variables contributing to the client's problems or dependent variables.

Make Comparisons Within a Specific Measure Only If Data Are Collected Under Similar Conditions

Repeated measures should be obtained under similar stimulus conditions if valid comparisons are to be made across the measurements. As an example, let us say that the therapist is counting the number of complaints that a depressed client makes in each therapy session. Obviously, the number of complaints could be influenced by the content of the therapy session or by how much the therapist talks in relation to how much the client talks. In this example, the therapist may attempt to keep such factors constant by beginning each session with the same instruction: "Tell me about your week," and by counting client complaints made in the first 10 minutes. In other words, the therapist attempts to keep "irrelevant" factors constant, like the content of the conversation or therapist talk time, so that the number of client complaints can be controlled by "relevant" factors, like the actual events of the week or the client's reactions to those events.

As another example, a mother brings her adolescent daughter to the clinic, complaining that the daughter is overly dependent on the mother and shows no initiative of her own. One way that lack of initiative is operationalized is that the daughter will do household chores only if the mother instructs her to do so and will not initiate those chores herself. As a measure, the therapist and mother draw up a list of chores; the mother is to mark each chore daily if the daughter undertakes the chore at her own initiative. Obviously, these daily measures of chores undertaken can be compared only if the stimulus situation is relatively constant. In this example, if the family goes on vacation, or if the daughter is ill, or if relatives come to visit for several days, the data may be altered by these factors. Thus, the daily data will not accurately reflect therapeutic progress or lack thereof. In this instance, the "atypical" days' data may either be discarded or be noted as atypical.

The main point is that the measures should be influenced by relevant independent variables, like treatment or life events. The influence of irrelevant independent variables, such as alterations in the measurement conditions, should be minimized or at least noted, so that the influence of the relevant independent variables can be better detected.

The underlying principle here is that behavior tends to be situation-specific (Mischel, 1968). In other words, the immediate stimulus situation has some influence on the observed behavior. For example, in the classic Hartshorne and May research (1928) on children's moral behavior, children's honesty varied depending on the stimulus situation, for example, home, party games, classroom, athletic contests. The more the situations changed, the lower became the correlations of moral behavior as measured in the different situations.

The measures of interest to a scientist-practitioner are also subject to situation-specificity. To be useful, these measures should reflect relevant situational changes due to treatment or to life events, rather than irrelevant situational changes such as alterations in the measurement circumstances. The latter has been conceptualized as measurement error, variance that should be minimized if accurate measurement is to be obtained.

Graph the Data

As a scientist-practitioner collects repeated measurements for a particular client, it becomes necessary to synthesize and to store the data. This is especially true when each of several different client problems are measured in several different ways. It is necessary to synthesize the data not only for practical storage reasons, but also for purposes of meaningfully interpreting the data.

A convenient way to store and interpret repeated measurement is by graphing the data (Hersen & Barlow, 1976; Parsonson & Baer, 1978). Time from baseline through treatment and follow-up is indexed on the abscissa.

Depending on the type of data being collected, the time on the abscissa may be in terms of weeks or days. For example, if observations of a particular behavior are made in the clinic at a weekly therapy session, the abscissa for such data would be in weekly temporal units. Conversely, if a client conscientiously recorded on a daily basis the duration of time spent in compulsive rituals, the abscissa for such data would be in daily temporal units.

The measure is indexed on the ordinate. The unit of measurement must be appropriate to the type of measure taken. For example, if a questionnaire is administered on a weekly basis in the clinic, the unit of measurement on the ordinate is possible scores on the questionnaire. For another example, if sex role motor behavior is observed weekly in the clinic waiting room using an appropriate checklist (Barlow, Hayes, Nelson, Steele, Meeler, & Mills, 1979), then the unit of measurement on the ordinate is possible checklist scores.

If several types of measures are taken for the same problem behavior, as is recommended, it is usually desirable to store the different measures of the same problem on the same graph. The same abscissa can be used for all types of measurement, although entries may be on a daily or a weekly basis for different measures. Different ordinates will probably be necessary, since the different types of measures will probably have different units of measurement. The purpose of storing the different measures of the same problem on the same graph is to determine how and if the different measures covary. In other words, do the measures respond in a similar or dissimilar fashion to the same intervention? Dissimilar responding, asynchronous responding, or lack of covariation implies that the different types of measures are functionally controlled by different independent variables, or respond to the same independent variables in a different manner.

Another item to enter on the data graphs is any significant event that might account for alterations in or variability in the measures. The beginning of a new treatment program is an example of a significant event that is expected to produce a change in the data. Other significant events may not be planned, but may nonetheless markedly alter the data. Examples might include a visit by a relative or an unpleasant change in job status.

In summary, as the data accumulate for several different measures of several different problems, it is necessary to store the data, for practical reasons and for purposes of understanding the data. Graphs provide a convenient means of storage. On these graphs, time is quantified on the abscissa and the measures are quantified on the ordinate.

Record Inconvenient Measures Less Frequently Than More Convenient Measures

Although it is recommended that several different types of measures be taken of several different client problems, it is not necessary to obtain all these measures with the same frequency. Measures that are inconvenient to record may be taken on a less frequent basis than more convenient methods. It is better to take the inconvenient measures on an infrequent basis than not at all, because these measures may provide different or additional information about the client's problems. Recall that there is no one "true" measure of a specific problem, but rather that different measures provide converging evidence about different aspects of the problem.

To illustrate, self-ratings of sexual arousal and physiological measures of sexual arousal do not necessarily covary (Barlow, 1977). Since self-ratings are more convenient to obtain than physiological measures, self-ratings of sexual arousal to deviant and heterosexual stimuli could be taken at every treatment session, whereas physiological measures of arousal could be taken on a monthly basis.

As another example, self-monitored data and direct observation by a trained observer need not always agree (Lipinski & Nelson, 1974). In naturalistic settings, self-monitored data are more convenient to obtain, given a cooperative client, than are data taken by a trained observer. Hence, the client may be asked to self-monitor on a daily basis, whereas a trained observer may enter the naturalistic setting only occasionally. For example, in a case study reported by Katell, Callahan, Fremouw, and Zitter (1979), the overweight client completed a daily food diary in which she recorded the antecedents of eating and facts about her eating. On a *weekly* basis, the client was asked to eat a meal in a small on-campus dining area while being videotaped; her eating behaviors were subsequently coded from the videotapes. Also on a *weekly* basis, an observer entered the home and coded her eating behavior during a family supper. Presumably, self-monitoring was a more convenient measure and hence was undertaken on a daily basis. Since the direct observations of eating in both the analogue and naturalistic settings were probably more inconvenient, these measures were obtained on a weekly basis.

In a similar example, Eyberg and Johnson (1974) requested that parents keep daily data on their children's behavior problems. Home observation data by trained observers were collected for five days during baseline and for five days at the conclusion of treatment. Again, the more convenient measure was obtained on a more frequent basis.

Select "Good" And Accurate Measures

So far, a broad recommendation has been made that multiple methods of measurement should be employed for several problems of each client. There are, however, a great many available methods of measurement. How is the scientist-practitioner to select among them? By what criteria are "good" and accurate measures to be selected?

One criterion is the measure's psychometric properties (i.e., its reliability and validity). The scientist-practitioner encounters two problems when employing psychometric properties as central criteria in selecting measures. The first problem is that psychometric calculations are nomothetic, that is, they depend on data from groups of individuals. Psychometric data do not provide idiographic information about individuals. For example, even if the concurrent validity between role playing in the clinic and observed behavior in the natural environment were determined to be high or low, such information would not indicate whether or not a particular client's role-playing and naturalistic behavior were similar. Psychometric data may provide some "good guesses" for the scientist-practitioner about which measures to use or to avoid, but some idiographic validation would be needed to determine if these are reliable and valid measures for the individual client.

A second problem with psychometric criteria for the scientist-practitioner is the assumption underlying psychometric procedures. Among these assumptions is that there is a true score or a universe score for an individual on a particular test or assessment device that is somewhat difficult to detect because of measurement error. Consistency of measurement is thought to be a desirable quality of tests or of assessment devices because consistent scores indicate that more of the true score is being assessed than error variance. Consistency of measurement is demonstrated by high correlation coefficients in investigations of reliability and validity.

The problem here is that inconsistency may be a characteristic of client behavior, rather than an indicator of an inferior assessment device. Client behavior may be inconsistent due to therapeutic change, due to different situations (Mischel, 1968), due to different response modes being measured (e.g., verbal, motor, physiological; Lang, 1968), or due to different methods of measurement (e.g., self-report, direct observation, physiological measures; Campbell & Fiske, 1959). Thus, inconsistent measurement may nonetheless be very accurate measurement. The measurement may be inconsistent not due to a poor measuring device, but rather due to actual changes in client behavior.

The yardstick of concurrent validity presents another problem in selecting measures because there is no universally accepted criterion measure against which to evaluate other measures. Some assessors may believe that the criterion measure is motor behavior in the naturalistic setting. In other words, the "real" measure of behavior is what the client *does* in the natural setting, as measured by trained observers. Exceptions are apparent. To illustrate, take the case of a sexual deviant who has not committed an actual sexual offense in several months. The question facing the courts and the therapist is not only what the client is doing *now* in the natural setting, but what he is likely to do in the future. McReynolds pointed out a limitation of direct observation of client motor behavior in naturalistic settings: "...the fact that the method is applicable only to situations that the subject is *in,* and cannot directly be employed to predict how he or she would behave in novel situations" (1979, p. 245). In the case of the sexual deviant, physiological measures of arousal *may* more accurately predict what the client will do in the future when faced with a provocative stimulus than do measures of current motor behavior.

Another example of the limitations of direct observation of motor behavior in the natural environment as the criterion in concurrent validity is the case of depression. According to DSM-III, the chief characteristic or operational criterion of depression is: "Dysphoric mood or loss of interest or pleasure in all or almost all usual activities and pastimes. The dysphoric mood is characterized by symptoms such as the following: depressed, sad, blue, hopeless, low, down in the dumps, irritable" (1980, p. 213). The point is that this chief characteristic of depression may be better assessed by self-report methods than by direct observations of client motor behavior.

What alternatives to psychometric criteria are available to the scientist-practitioner in selecting a "good" or accurate assessment device? One alternative is to use some psychometric procedures without their underlying assumptions (Cone, 1977; Jones, 1977). For example, consistency or reliability of measurement should be expected of a good assessment device under certain circumstances. These circumstances are when the behavior under examination is somehow "captured" or "frozen." To be more specific, let us say that two observers are coding the same videotape or the same live interaction. Since the observers are watching the same behaviors, any inconsistency in coding would be due to measurement error rather than to actual changes in behavior.

Another useful extrapolation from psychometric procedures is to use the multitrait-multimethod approach (Campbell & Fiske, 1959), as suggested by Cone (1977). For example, a group of subjects could be assessed by two questionnaires and by two observational coding systems. These comprise two different *methods* or measurements. One questionnaire and one observational coding system, in this example, are purported to measure depression, while the other questionnaire and the other observational coding system are purported to measure social skills. These comprise two different *traits* or sets of behaviors to be measured. It should be expected that if the questionnaires and the observational coding systems really measure depression and social skills, respectively, then the trait correlations should be higher than the method correlations. The point is that construct validity is a reasonable expectation for the measures that are to be employed — the measures should measure *something.* Construct validity can be established by the convergent and discriminant validity that can be assessed by the multitrait-multimethod matrix. Again, no one measure is the "true" measure. Several measures must be taken to provide converging evidence about the client's problems or progress.

In addition to limited use of psychometric procedures, the quality of measures can be assured by monitoring the circumstances in which the measures are employed. Previous research has discovered at least some of the controlling variables that contribute to the quality of data produced by different assessment devices. For example, the quality of self-monitored data is improved if the self-recorder is aware that his or her reliability can be determined (Lipinski & Nelson, 1974). Thus, if a practitioner chooses to use self-monitoring as a measure, it is wise to arrange occasional reliability checks for the self-recorder. As another example, it is known that performance on the behavioral avoidance test is influenced by the amount of "demand" in the approach instructions (Bernstein & Nietzel, 1973). Therefore, in order to compare a client's performance across different points in time, the amounts of demand in the approach instructions must remain constant. In other words, questions such as "Is self-monitoring a good assessment device?" or "Is the behavioral avoidance test a good assessment device?" have no generic answer. Instead, there are certain circumstances, established in part by past research, that make the data collected by the assessment device of higher or lower quality. The practitioner who employs the device should employ the optimal circumstances possible to ensure data of high quality.

Finally, one criterion that the scientist-practitioner can use in selecting an assessment device is its functional utility (Nelson & Hayes, 1979). Initially, the assessment device should help to determine the treatment that should be provided for the client. That is, a better treatment should be selected by utilizing the assessment information than by not utilizing it. Later, the assessment device should help to determine if the treatment is effective. That is, use of the assessment device should provide better feedback to the therapist about client progress or lack thereof than not using the assessment device.

In summary, it is desirable for scientist-practitioners to use "good" or accurate measures. Psychometric criteria cannot be used alone to make this determination because of the nomothetic nature of psychometric data and because of the psychometric assumption that inconsistent measurement implies poor assessment. As alternatives, the scientist-practitioner can employ as criteria in selecting good measures: psychometric procedures under limited circumstances, particularly reliability and multitrait-multimethod matrices; modification of controlling variables so as to optimize the quality of data produced by a particular assessment device; and evaluation of the functional utility of the assessment device and the data that it produces.

Obtain Clients' Informed Consent When Necessary

With most methods of measurement, client awareness of and cooperation with the measurement procedure is essential. As examples, a client is provided with questionnaire instructions and is asked to complete the questionnaire; or a client is provided with role-playing instructions and is asked to participate in role-playing.

Many such obtrusive methods of measurement are, however, reactive. *Reactivity* refers to changes in the client's behavior that are due to the measurement process per se. The problem with reactivity is that it interferes with external validity; that is, it is difficult to generalize from measurement to nonmeasurement circumstances. In other words, the client's behavior while he or she is being assessed may not be the same as when he or she is not being assessed.

One proposed solution to the problem of reactivity is the use of unobtrusive measures (Kazdin, 1979). For example, let us say that a transsexual is coming to a clinic to help make a male-to-female adjustment. In one aspect of treatment, the therapist is teaching the client more feminine motor movements. The therapist asks the receptionist to code the client's motor behavior unobtrusively, while the client is in the waiting room, using a sex role motor behavior checklist (Barlow et al., 1979). In a second example, the husband of a depressed woman is asked to record unobtrusively her crying episodes and her complaints in their home.

While these unobtrusive measurement methods may reduce the problem of reactivity, they introduce ethical concerns about the client's informed consent (Kazdin, 1979). One solution might be to explain to the client beforehand the need for unobtrusive assessment and to ask the client's permission to obtain some unobtrusive, unspecified measures. In the above examples, releases of information to the clinic staff and to the husband would have to be assumed or procured.

Institutions Can Encourage the Collection of Measures

As noted earlier in this chapter, even behavior therapists, for whom the collection of quantitative measures is conceptually compatible, complain of the impracticality of the task. There are some steps that institutions can take to facilitate or encourage this understanding.

First, the scientist-practitioner model can be taught in university and internship training programs (Conte & Levy, 1979). Of course, many training programs claim to espouse the scientist-practitioner model. In reality, as noted in chapter 1, this all too often means that the same staff who see clients on the weekends do research on the weekdays. Or different types of students are required to complete internships and dissertations. A true integration of research and practice, in the manner described in this book, is too seldom taught.

Second, the national movement toward accountability by third-party payers may require clinicians to collect quantified measures, as noted earlier in this chapter and in chapter 2. While such requirements would be looked upon with alarm by some clinicians, the requirements would certainly increase the use of such measures.

Third, clinic administrators can arrange the clinic setting to encourage the collection of measures. One way to do this is to provide necessary assessment materials, such as a file of questionnaires, self-monitoring devices, video equipment to tape role-played interactions, or physiological recording equipment. Another way to do this is to require that case staffings be data-based and to reward practitioners who comply. Another way is to provide in-service training workshops on the collection of measures for scientist-practitioners.

Subsequent chapters present descriptions of specific, realistic measurement strategies for practitioners. Each of these strategies incorporates the guidelines described above.

Chapter 4
Self-Monitoring

INTRODUCTION

One of the most popular and useful techniques for obtaining measures of client progress is self-monitoring. Prior to the initiation of self-monitoring, specific target behaviors must be selected. During self-monitoring, or self-recording, the client then records the occurrences of the selected problems or behaviors as they happen. Self-monitoring can be prescribed in either an inpatient or outpatient setting. In addition, it can be used to measure either problems or aspects of treatment necessary to ascertain treatment integrity (see chapter 3).

Self-monitoring is a popular means of data collection for several reasons. One reason is that self-recording can be used with a wide range of clients, including clients who live alone, as well as single parents not living with another adult. For these clients, no "participant observer," such as a spouse or parent, is readily available to collect data. Similarly, paid and/or trained observers who could enter the home, school, or work environment to collect data on the client's behavior are generally available only in conjunction with research projects that have their own source of funding. Even clients who cohabit with another adult are sometimes alone. Self-recorders, then, may be able to provide more complete data than observers because they are aware of the full range of their target behaviors, as compared with the sample that an observer might witness (Kazdin, 1974a).

A second reason for the popularity of self-recording is that it can be used with a wide range of problems. Some targets are cognitive or covert, and hence are inaccessible to external observers. To illustrate, self-monitoring has been used successfully to provide records of paranoid thoughts (Williams, 1976) and obsessional thoughts (Emmelkamp & Kwee, 1977). Other target behaviors are private by societal convention. As examples, self-monitoring has successfully been used to keep measures of domestic sexual behavior (Lobitz & LoPiccolo, 1972) and sleeping (Borkovec, Kaloupek, & Slama,

1975). When external observers are used, they frequently are reactive; that is, the very presence of the external observer alters the occurrence of the behaviors being observed (Haynes & Horn, 1982). This reactivity would presumably be even greater with behaviors that are typically private.

Self-monitoring or self-recording is a two-stage process. First, the client must notice or discriminate aspects of his or her own behavior; that is, determine that the target behavior has indeed occurred. Second, the client must make the self-recording response; that is, use the procedure that records the occurrence of the target behavior. The self-recorder must perform both of these behaviors if the self-recorded data are to be accurate. Obviously, clients' compliance with self-monitoring instructions and the resultant accuracy of self-recorded data are important issues. Major decisions, such as determining whether or not to continue the same treatment strategy, are frequently made, based on self-monitored data. Therefore, the availability and accuracy of these data are very important. A subsequent portion of this chapter describes strategies to enhance clients' compliance with self-recording instructions as well as the accuracy of their self-monitored data.

WHAT AND HOW TO SELF-MONITOR: BEHAVIORS AND DEVICES

This section provides many examples of the types of problems that have been successfully self-monitored and of the devices used for self-monitoring, as reported in the research and clinical literature. The purpose of these multiple exemplars is to provide a broad perspective. Hopefully, either the particular examples or their derivations will prove useful to individual practitioners in their own work.

Frequency Counts

A frequency count is an appropriate recording procedure when the target is discrete; that is, when the duration of separate instances of the target behavior do not vary a great deal. The same unit of time must be used to record frequencies of any specific behavior so that one frequency count can be compared to another.

One common way of self-recording frequency counts is to make tallies on a piece of paper; for example, a paper tucked into the cellophane of a cigarette package on which to record the number of cigarettes smoked per day. Some novel but simple self-recording procedures were suggested by Watson and Tharp (1972). One client moved a toothpick from one compartment of her purse to another each time her target behavior occurred. Another client transferred pennies from one pocket to another, each penny representing one occurrence of the target behavior. Behavioral frequencies have also been self-recorded on a variety of counters: Lindsley's (1968) wrist golf counter; Mahoney's (1974) handcrafted leather jewelry that disguises counting devices; Sheehan and Casey's (1974) knit tally; and Mattos's (1968) hand-held digital counter for recording the frequency of several target behaviors.

As noted above, self-recording is especially useful for recording cognitive or private behaviors. Along these lines, the frequency of obsessive-compulsive behaviors has been self-monitored. On a daily log sheet, a 34-year-old female recorded the type and frequency of each obsessive thought and of each compulsive ritual (handwashing, checking ashtrays and stove), along with the discomfort each produced on a 1-100 scale (Milby, Meredith, & Rice, 1981). Various aspects of paraphiliac sexual behavior were self-monitored in notebooks by Callahan and Leitenberg's (1973) clients: daily sexual urges, sexual fantasies, masturbation, and overt sexual acts with other people. Similarly, sexual urges and fantasies defined as a thought, image, or fantasy of a given sexual behavior, whether it occurred in the presence of the arousing object (urge) or not (fantasy), were self-monitored in small notebooks by two exhibitionists and a pedophiliac treated by Brownell, Hayes, and Barlow (1977). Likewise, Maletzky's (1974; 1980) exhibitionists self-recorded covert exhibitionistic behavior, including urges (wishing to expose oneself in a situation not allowing it), fantasies (extensive daydreaming about exposing oneself), and dreams, as well as overt exhibitionistic behavior.

Other types of behaviors have also been self-monitored by frequency counts. Following a car accident, a woman was treated for pronounced startle responses while driving her car; she was asked to self-record these startle responses about every 15 minutes on an index card positioned on the car's instrument panel (Fairbank, DeGood, & Jenkins, 1981). A compulsive gambler self-recorded the amount of money he wagered each week (Rankin, 1982).

Several medically related problems have been monitored by self-recording. A bulimic college student self-recorded the number of episodes in which she overate and vomited (Linden, 1980). A patient with daytime bruxism self-recorded each instance of teeth-jaw clenching on a response counter; she telephoned the clinic every other day to report these self-recorded frequencies (Rosen, 1981). A patient, who was the victim of bladder cancer, and his wife both recorded the frequency of days in bed that the patient spent due to gastrointestinal pain; perfect agreement was found between the patient's and wife's recordings (Hamberger, 1982). Clients with muscle-contraction headaches were asked to record on index cards each day the frequency of headaches; in addition, the clients self-recorded the duration of each headache and its severity on a 0-100 subjective pain scale (Chesney & Shelton, 1976). Self-monitoring of this type is, of course, the main measure used with headache sufferers.

Children have been instructed to self-monitor the frequency of specific target behaviors. A 10-year-old girl self-recorded each episode of stomach pain on a Girl Scout calendar; her mother also recorded each episode of her daughter's pain complaints on a different calendar. The agreement between the daughter's and mother's frequency counts was 96% (Miller & Kratochwill, 1979). Children with a mean age of 6.8 years were taught to telephone the therapist's office daily to report whether or not they had wet the bed the previous night (Azrin, Hontos, & Besalel-Azrin, 1979). Two boys, one aged 9 years and one aged 11, self-monitored the frequency of facial tics; their mothers and teachers simultaneously recorded these instances in the home and school settings, respectively, with resultant agreement scores of correlations in the .80s (Ollendick, 1981).

Examples of forms used by self-recorders to record the frequencies of problem behaviors are shown in Figures 4.1 and 4.2. In Figure 4.1, the client records the number of cigarettes smoked in the indicated time period of each day. In Figure 4.2, the idiosyncratic obsessive-thoughts or compulsive acts of the client are noted. The client records the frequency of those thoughts or acts, preferably by making a slash mark in the appropriate space, immediately after the thought or act has occurred. The average daily intensity of the obsessive-compulsive urges is entered in the bottom row.

	SAT.	SUN.	MON.	TUE.	WED.	THUR.	FRI.
MIDNIGHT- 6:00 A.M.							
6:00 - 8:00 A.M.							
8:00 -10:00 A.M.							
10:00 A.M. - NOON							
NOON - 2:00 P.M.							
2:00 - 4:00 P.M.							
4:00 - 6:00 P.M.							
6:00 - 8:00 P.M.							
8:00 -10:00 P.M.							
10:00 - MIDNIGHT							
DAILY TOTAL							

Figure 4.1. Log of cigarettes smoked

Obsessive Thoughts – Compulsive Acts	Week of: _____ Client:_____						
	MON.	TUE.	WED.	THUR.	FRI.	SAT.	SUN.
1.							
2.							
3.							
4.							
Intensity (rate daily) 1 = not at all; 100 = extremely							

Figure 4.2.

Duration

The cases described above provide examples of measuring discrete target behaviors by self-recording the frequency of their occurrence. When each occurrence of a behavior can vary considerably in duration, the behavior is more appropriately measured by self-recording the duration of each occurrence.

Duration may be self-recorded by means of a stopwatch. Several types of wristwatches have a stopwatch accessory, called an *elapsed time indicator,* which is useful for self-monitoring duration. Mahoney and Thoresen (1974) describe a switch that may be used with an electric clock to facilitate the self-recording of duration. When the target behavior is occurring, the switch remains in the "on" position, permitting the self-recording clock to accumulate the duration measure.

The following cases exemplify appropriate uses of self-recorded duration. A time meter, which cumulatively recorded hours studied, was activated by a freshman for as long as she studied (Spurr & Stevens, 1980). Compulsive patients with washing rituals were instructed to self-record on forms the duration of each washing episode (Foa, Steketee, & Milby, 1980). A 63-year-old man with ritualistic checking was asked to self-record the beginning and ending time of each checking episode, and also to self-record its duration with a stopwatch (Melamed & Siegel, 1975).

An example of a form used to self-record duration is shown in Figure 4.3. The form may be useful with a depressed person or with a disorganized person, both of whom complain of not accomplishing desired goals. The task attempted is noted in the first column, with times begun and ended in the second and third columns respectively. In the last column, the client rates his or her satisfaction with the performance.

	Task	Time Begun	Time Ended	Rating of Satisfaction (1 - 10)
Monday				
Tuesday				
Wednesday				
Thursday				
Friday				
Saturday				
Sunday				

Figure 4.3. Daily record of accomplishments

Self-Ratings

Self-monitoring can be used to provide a measure of subjective states, as they are occurring in the client's natural environment. In practice, this is one of the more frequent uses of self-monitoring. The general procedure is to have the client provide a rating of his or her subjective state at some predesignated time. In this way, the client's feelings can be quantified. Some examples follow.

The severity of clients' headaches has been self-recorded using several different procedures. The procedures differ primarily in the number of units in the subjective rating scale and in the event that triggers the self-recorded rating. Clients were asked to self-record not only the frequency and duration of each muscle-contraction headache, but also the severity of the pain from each headache; a 0 (*barely noticeable headache*) to 100 (*extremely painful headache*) scale was used (Chesney & Shelton, 1976). Naturally occurring events, rather than the occurrences of headaches, were used to trigger headache ratings by Epstein and Abel (1977); clients were asked to record headache ratings in small notebooks at mealtimes and at bedtime, using a 6-point scale where 0 meant *no headache,* and 5 meant *very severe headache.* This latter type of self-rating was compared to more frequent self-rating by Collins and Martin (1980). They found that self-ratings cued by mealtimes and bedtime (what they termed *reduced demand self-monitoring*) were satisfactorily representative of more frequent self-ratings cued temporally on a bihourly basis (what they termed *intensive self-monitoring*).

Temporal cues for self-ratings of subjective states were used in some cases described below. Following a car accident, a woman exerienced unpleasant startle responses while driving (Fairbank et al., 1981). In addition to recording the frequency of the startle responses, she also self-rated her anxiety while driving on a 1 (*state of relaxation*) to 5 (*extreme anxiety*) scale. About every 15 minutes, marked by the clock on the instrument panel, she was to make a self-rating on an index card kept on the panel. Depressed subjects carried portable timing devices that cued self-ratings on a variable-interval 1-hour schedule; during different phases of this single-subject experiment, clients self-rated on a 1-5 scale the pleasantness of either their present mood or their ongoing current activity (Harmon, Nelson, & Hayes, 1980). An asthmatic client set a parking meter timer on a 30-minute schedule; when the timer signaled, she rated her level of muscle tension (Sirota & Mahoney, 1974).

A commercially available timing device that emits a tone is described by McNamara and Bechtel (1975). The occurrence of the tone can be programmed for either a fixed or variable interval, and an earphone jack is available so that the tone is audible only to the self-rater. A much less expensive timing device is described by Foxx and Martin (1971). Other readily available devices, such as parking meter timers, cooking timers, or elapsed time indicators on wristwatches, are also adequate for cuing purposes. A device that generates a tactile instead of an auditory cue is described by Hart and McCrady (1977). This device could be carried in a pocket or affixed to a belt to provide a more private cue for self-rating.

Finally, another naturally occurring event, the end of the day, has been used to cue self-ratings. Patients with duodenal ulcers were asked to self-rate at the end of each day the severity of that day's ulcer distress, using a 1 (*no pain*) to 5 (*pain sometime during the day, severe enough to require antacid, pain not relieved by antacid, a significant interruption of planned daily activities necessitated*) scale (Brooks & Richardson, 1980). Two patients with morbid ruminations were asked to self-rate, at the end of each day, the distress that they had experienced that day associated with each recurrent morbid thought, using a 1-8 scale (Farkas & Beck, 1981). Six couples who were in marital counseling self-rated at the end of each day their general marital happiness, using a 1-10 scale (Wolf & Etzel, 1982).

An example of a form for self-ratings is provided in Figure 4.4. The form was designed for a client who was both anxious and depressed. The cue to self-rate anxiety and depression could be either predesignated times of the day, or particularly intense emotional experiences.

NAME: _____   DATE: _____

TIME: _____

NERVOUS	0 CALM	20	40	60	80	100 PANIC
DEPRESSED	0 NOT DEPRESSED	20	40	60	80	100 VERY DEPRESSED

TIME: _____

NERVOUS	0 CALM	20	40	60	80	100 PANIC
DEPRESSED	0 NOT DEPRESSED	20	40	60	80	100 VERY DEPRESSED

TIME: _____

NERVOUS	0 CALM	20	40	60	80	100 PANIC
DEPRESSED	0 NOT DEPRESSED	20	40	60	80	100 VERY DEPRESSED

TIME: _____

NERVOUS	0 CALM	20	40	60	80	100 PANIC
DEPRESSED	0 NOT DEPRESSED	20	40	60	80	100 VERY DEPRESSED

Figure 4.4. Self-ratings of anxiety and depression

Diaries

In the examples described above, the self-recorded information was limited to the target behavior, either its frequency, duration, or self-rating. Sometimes it is helpful to the practitioner if additional information is also self-recorded by the client. Additional information is especially useful during the gathering of intake information, early in assessment, prior to the development of a treatment program. Here, it might be helpful to the therapist if the client self-recorded the antecedents or consequences that precede or follow the occurrence of the problem behavior, or if the client self-recorded several response parameters, such as the cognitions or feelings that accompany the problem behavior. When such additional information is requested, self-recording may be accomplished by means of a diary format. A general diary format is columns labeled *A* (antecedents), *B* (behavior), and *C* (consequences). Sometimes, the behavior column is expanded to include several response parameters. Some examples follow.

The form used in Figure 4.5 can be used to provide diary-like information about assertive behavior. The client records the antecedents in the first two columns, labelled "date and time" and "situation." The third and fourth columns are used to self-record motoric and cognitive behaviors or responses to those situations. The fifth and sixth columns are used to self-record consequences, and the last column is used to record behavioral alternatives.

DATE AND TIME	SITUATION	WHAT DID YOU DO?	WHAT WERE YOU THINKING?	HOW DID THE SITUATION END?	HOW DID YOU FEEL ABOUT THE OUTCOME? (0 = VERY DISSATISFIED; 10 = VERY SATISFIED)	WHAT SHOULD YOU HAVE DONE?

Figure 4.5. Assertiveness situations

Agoraphobic patients were asked to keep a diary of the time spent away from home, the nature and number of journeys made, whether they were accompanied or not, the distance traveled, and the number of times they practiced going into feared situations (Figure 4.6).

NAME: _____   WEEKLY RECORD: (_____TO_____)

* PLEASE PUT A "✓ " BY ANY ACTIVITY THAT WAS AN ASSIGNED PRACTICE FOR THIS WEEK.

DATE	TIME LEFT HOME	TIME RET'D. HOME	LIST EACH ACTIVITY (INCLUDING TRANSPORTATION) AND PLACE TRAVELED TO WHILE AWAY FROM HOME *	TOTAL TIME SPENT	TIME ALONE	ANXIETY RATING (0-8)	
						MAXIMUM	AVERAGE

Figure 4.6. Agoraphobic clients' Weekly Record form.

While this diary is probably more detailed than needed for most clinical purposes, it provides a variety of information that is important to clinicians. For example, an examination of the number of practices that clients engaged in provided the clinician with an estimate of treatment integrity, described in chapter 3. In this case, clients were instructed to practice entering difficult situations as one step in overcoming agoraphobia. Examination of the number of practices provides the clinician with an estimate of the extent to which the treatment is in effect. If the client is not improving, one can determine if a change in treatment is needed, or simply more vigorous application of the treatment currently in effect.

In another example, college students self-recorded in a diary their different social interactions (that progressed beyond a mere greeting); from these diaries, the frequency and range (number of different people) of same-sex and opposite-sex interactions could be tabulated (Royce & Arkowitz, 1978). During the initial assessment phase, a 68-year-old cancer patient who was experiencing gastric pain attacks was asked to self-monitor situational variables related to attacks, including physical setting, interpersonal interactions, and cognitions, and the frequency and duration of each gastric attack (Hamberger, 1982).

Sometimes it is useful for the therapist if several response parameters are self-monitored, as in the following illustrations. During the early phases of assessment, a bulimic college student self-monitored her thoughts in the binge-eating situations, her food intake, physical exercise, and binging-vomiting episodes (Linden, 1980). Relatedly, overweight adolescents were asked to keep a diary of food requested and exercise undertaken; the diary was later quantified by rating from 1 to 5 the portion size and caloric content of each food item, and the level of energy expenditure per exercise activity (Cohen, Gelfand, Dodd, Jensen, & Turner, 1980). Couples complaining of sexual dysfunction were asked to complete a daily record form detailing their sexual behavior; for each activity, the client specified its duration, numerical ratings of the pleasure and arousal that he or she obtained, numerical ratings of the pleasure and arousal that the partner appeared to have obtained, and any subjective comments about the activity (Lobitz & LoPiccolo, 1972). Sleep-disturbed clients completed daily sleep questionnaires that requested information on five response parameters: latency to sleep onset on the previous night (number of minutes prior to falling asleep), number of times the person awoke during the night, number of times the person woke during the night and had difficulty returning to sleep, a 5-point rating of difficulty falling asleep, and a 4-point rating of of restfulness upon awakening (Borkovec, Kaloupek, & Slama, 1975). Similar response parameters were self-monitored by Turner and Ascher's clients (1979); in addition, however, a spouse-roommate also monitored, with the client's knowledge and consent, the client's latency to sleep onset for at least one night.

STRATEGIES TO ENHANCE COMPLIANCE AND ACCURACY

Self-monitored data can provide useful feedback to the therapist on client progress, as well as serve as measures of outcome and treatment integrity. Finally, self-monitored data can be used for accountability purposes. If self-monitored data are to serve these functions, it is critical that clients comply with self-recording instructions and generate accurate data.

The following suggestions are intended to enhance the likelihood that clients will comply with self-monitoring instructions and produce accurate self-recordings. Many of the suggestions are based on research findings. The typical research strategy that generated these findings was to manipulate an independent variable (e.g., training in self-recording) and to examine the effects of the independent variable on the accuracy of self-monitoring. Accuracy was typically determined by comparing the self-recorder's data with some criterion. Frequently, the criterion was data collected by two independent trained observers. Two observers were used to determine the extent of their agreement, an index of the quality or reliability of the observational data. For example, Lipinski and Nelson (1974) compared self-recorded counts of students' face touching in a classroom situation with counts made by two independent trained observers. Another criterion used to assess the accuracy of self-recorded data was recordings made by mechanical recording devices. For example, a teaching machine used by Mahoney, Moore, Wade, and Moura (1973) automatically recorded the students' answers while the students were also self-recording their correct answers. The accuracy of the students' self-monitoring was determined by comparing their self-recorded responses with the machine's recordings. A third, less frequently used and less precise criterion was a by-product that was believed to be related to the self-monitoring behavior. For example, hair length can be used as a measure of accuracy of self-monitored hair pulling (McLaughlin & Nay, 1975), or body weight as a measure of accuracy of self-monitored caloric consumption (McGlynn, 1980).

Establish a Commitment to Self-Monitoring

Several procedures have been shown to increase the probability that people will actually do what they verbally agree to do. One procedure is to have the person agree overtly to perform the promised behavior. The overt agreement can be oral or written. Levy (1977) found that an oral plus written agreement produced more compliance with an assigned task than an oral agreement alone; but the oral agreement produced more compliance than no overt agreement. Similarly, Kanfer, Cox, Greiner, and Karoly (1974) found that a written contract which specified the nature of the task and the performance criterion produced more compliance with an assigned task than an implicit commitment to perform the task.

Another procedure that has been found to increase the probability of self-monitored data collection is the refundable monetary deposit. Subjects who were required to render a refundable deposit were more likely to return self-monitored data (94%) than subjects who were not required to render a deposit (84%) (Ersner-Hershfield, Connors, & Maisto, 1981).

Applying these ideas to self-monitoring, then, the probability that a client will collect self-monitored data is enhanced if he or she makes a verbal and/or written commitment to collect such data, and if he or she provides a monetary deposit that is refunded contingent on self-monitoring.

Arrange Antecedents to Enhance Compliance

Clients' compliance with self-recording is, in part, a therapist responsibility. The therapist must select a self-recording response and device that is suitable to the problem at hand. To illustrate, it is not appropriate to measure continuous behaviors by means of frequency counts. A client is more likely to self-record sleeping, television watching, exercise, or other continuous behaviors if a duration is requested, rather than a frequency count. Similarly, the self-recording device must be appropriate for the type of self-recording; that is, counting devices for frequency, timing devices for duration, diaries for antecedents-behaviors-consequences. The self-monitoring device should be sufficiently obtrusive to remind the client to self-record and sufficiently unobtrusive to save the client from public questions (Nelson, 1977).

Modification can be made in self-monitoring procedures to suit particular clients. For example, a client who refrains from self-monitoring each occurrence of a high-frequency behavior over an entire day may successfully self-record when asked to do so for selected shorter daily intervals. For clients who cannot or will not write, alternative self-recording methods include talking into a tape recorder or telephoning the clinic (Mahoney, 1977). To illustrate, a child was instructed to telephone the clinic to report bed-wetting instances or a lack thereof from the previous night (Azrin et al., 1979), as noted above. If a client does not self-monitor in the natural environment, perhaps he or she could self-monitor in the clinic, if the target behavior were suitable. For example, clients with ruminative thoughts were asked to count the frequency of the thoughts' occurrence within therapy sessions (Leger, 1979).

Self-monitoring assignments can be given in gradually increasing steps. The client is first asked to comply with a small request, such as self-monitoring on only one day, or a portion of a day, or self-monitoring only one behavior. If the client complies with the small request and is rewarded for doing so, then he or she is more likely to comply subsequently with a larger task (Shelton & Levy, 1981).

The therapist should provide the self-recording device, rather than asking the client to procure or to design a device. The rationale is that one less behavior is being requested of the client, thereby increasing the probability of compliance. Also, the device itself will serve as a cue, reminding the client to self-record. Thus, it is better for the therapist to have available some counting or timing devices and some small notebooks to sell or to give to clients, rather than asking clients to obtain these devices or notebooks from a store. Similarly, it is fair for the therapist to design a self-monitoring format (for example, a form suited to the self-monitoring of antecedents-behaviors-consequences, or to the self-monitoring of several response parameters), rather than expecting the client to do so.

Provide Training in Self-Monitoring

Before he or she leaves the office, the client should be taught how to self-monitor. An easy error is to think that the task is self-explanatory. Mahoney

(1977) provided some explicit suggestions for training in self-monitoring: (a) give explicit definitions and examples of target behaviors; (b) give explicit self-monitoring instructions; (c) model the appropriate use of the self-monitoring device; (d) ask the client to repeat the target definitions and self-monitoring instructions; and (e) have the client self-monitor several occurrences of the target behavior as described by the therapist.

Using this procedure, plus videotaped practice and practice in the criterion classroom situation, Nelson, Lipinski, and Boykin (1978) trained four retarded adolescents to self-record their appropriate classroom verbalizations. The self-recording accuracy of the trained adolescents (.914) was significantly higher than that of less trained adolescents (.784). Similarly, Bornstein, Mungas, Quevillon, Kniivila, Miller, and Holombo (1978) found that training self-recorders (by having them either self-monitor specific aspects of their own tape-recorded speeches or monitor specific aspects of others' tape-recorded speeches) produced more accurate self-monitored data than not training self-recorders (by having them listen to and rate general dimensions of their own or others' tape-recorded speeches). Attempts have even been made in training self-recorders to self-monitor their cognitive responses (Meyers, Mercatoris, & Artz, 1976); but there are obvious difficulties in determining the accuracy of self-monitored cognitions (Nelson, 1977).

Awareness of Accuracy Assessment

One variable that has been repeatedly shown to influence the accuracy of self-recording is awareness of accuracy assessment. Self-recording is more accurate when self-observers are aware that their accuracy is being monitored than when their accuracy is monitored covertly.

This finding has been replicated in three analogue studies in which the target behavior was classroom face touching. Lipinski and Nelson (1974) found that agreement between self-recorders and trained observers was .86 when the subjects were aware of reliability checks, as compared with .52 when accuracy checks were made covertly. In two similar studies, Nelson, Lipinski, and Black (1975) found that awareness of reliability checks increased the accuracy of self-recorded face touches from .554 to .810, and Lipinski, Black, Nelson, and Ciminero (1975) reported a comparable increase from .46 to .67.

In day-to-day clinical work, the accuracy of self-monitored data can be evaluated against concurrent data collected by another person. For example, the accuracy of adolescents' self-monitored eating and exercising was evaluated against parental data that was collected one day per week (Cohen et al., 1980). Likewise, the frequency of the daughter's stomachache complaints were recorded each day by both the mother and the daughter (Miller & Kratochwill, 1979).

The observers do not have to collect data as often as the self-recorders to enhance the accuracy of self-recording, given the proviso that the self-recorder knows that his or her accuracy can be checked on a random basis. For example, a spouse-roommate monitored the self-recorder's latency to sleep onset, with the client's knowledge and consent, for at least one night (Turner & Ascher, 1979).

Self-recorders can also be informed that their accuracy can be checked against mechanical devices or behavioral by-products. For example, the accuracy of self-monitored food consumption could be assessed against weight for obese, anorexic, or bulimic clients. Similarly, the accuracy of self-monitored study time could be assessed against grades. Obviously, there is not a one-to-one correspondence between the self-monitored behavior and its by-product; but perhaps the awareness of this potential accuracy check may enhance the accuracy of self-recording.

Reinforcement for Accurate Self-Recorded Data

Another variable that has consistently been found to influence the accuracy of self-recorded data is reinforcement for accuracy. Risley and Hart (1968) found that the initially low correspondence between the children's verbal and nonverbal behavior could be improved when reinforcement was made contingent on correspondence, as evaluated by external observers. Fixsen, Phillips, and Wolf (1972) found that the .76 level of agreement between peer and self-reports of room cleanliness could be enhanced to .86 through contingent reinforcement. Just as positive reinforcement has been demonstrated to increase the accuracy of self-recorded data, punishment or threats of punishment have also been reported to minimize discrepant ratings (Hundert & Batstone, 1978; Seymour & Stokes, 1976).

Such reinforcement or punishment need not occur on a continuous basis to maintain accurate self-recording. For a group of children in a classroom situation, high levels of self-recorded accuracy were maintained when the accuracy of only one child per group was checked per day (Hundert & Bucher, 1978). Similarly, for a group of children in a camp, high levels of self-recorded accuracy were maintained when the accuracy of the group was checked on the average of every third day (Layne, Rickard, Jones, & Lyman, 1976).

Rewards for accurate self-recorded data that are available to therapists include praise and reduction in session fees. Monetary deposits can also be refunded contingently.

Minimize Concurrent Response Requirements

The accuracy of self-recording diminishes when clients perform other tasks in addition to self-recording. The detrimental effects of concurrent responding on self-recording accuracy were confirmed in experiments by Epstein, Webster, and Miller (1975) and by Epstein, Miller, and Webster (1976). Subjects made fewer errors in their self-monitoring of respiration when they engaged in self-recording alone (respective error rates of .28, .23, and .4%), than when they engaged in a concurrent operant task of lever pressing in addition to self-monitoring (respective error rates of .72, .49, and 9.5%).

Although it is impractical for clients to limit their other ongoing activities completely, perhaps overly busy clients could be asked to clear their calendars or to refuse new commitments for the duration of therapy. Alternatively, self-monitoring could be limited to less rushed times of the day, with the proviso that the target behavior occur at those times in a typical manner.

Schedule Self-Monitoring for Each Response

Frederiksen, Epstein, and Kosevsky (1975) reported that when subjects self-recorded each cigarette that was smoked, their accuracy of self-recording was greater (93.6%) than when they self-recorded the number of cigarettes smoked at the end of each day (85.8%) or at the end of each week (87.3%). To increase the likelihood that clients will self-monitor ongoing occurrences of the target behavior, clients can be asked to mail their self-monitored data to the clinic on a daily basis (Harmon et al., 1980), or the therapist may make telephone calls to the client at random times to obtain self-monitored data (Christensen, Johnson, Phillips, & Glasgow, 1980).

Self-Monitor One Behavior Only

In an investigation of the effects of self-monitoring one, two, or three target behaviors concurrently, Hayes and Cavior (1980) reported that the accuracy of self-monitoring was significantly higher when only only target behavior was self-monitored than when either two or three behaviors were self-monitored. Based on this investigation, it seems advisable to ask clients to self-monitor only one target behavior to attain maximal accuracy. Perhaps good accuracy could be maintained if other behaviors to be self-monitored were gradually introduced.

Types of Clients Who Self-Record Accurately

Very little data exist on the question of who makes a good self-recorder. It is likely that children generally do not produce accurate self-recorded data (Kazdin, 1974a). This hypothesis was verified in three experiments reported by Nelson, Hay, Devany, and Koslow-Green (1980). Many of the studies described above, however, found that under certain conditions, children were accurate self-recorders. Generally, these conditions included being checked and rewarded or punished for accuracy.

In a study that differentiated subjects based on the Marlowe-Crowne Social Desirability Scale, Kiecolt-Glaser and Murray (1980) found that subjects high on this social desirability measure seemed to inflate positive consequences that they reported in their self-recording diaries, as compared with subjects who scored low on the Marlowe-Crowne measure.

Again, however, there is very little research to determine what type of clients self-record accurately. Instead, most of the research has focused on environmental variables that contribute to accurate self-recording.

Duration of Self-Recording

One reasonable question is that of how long clients can be asked to self-monitor without decreasing their accuracy. The answer seems to be for a reasonably long duration of time, given favorable conditions.

Subjects were asked to self-record the frequency of their face touching in a classroom situation for either 2 weeks or 9 weeks (Nelson, Boykin, & Hayes, 1982). The accuracy of their self-recording was comparable for both groups. The long-term group did not display decreases in accuracy across time. These subjects were aware that they were participating in an experiment, and they turned in their self-recorded data at the end of each class period.

Conversely, Boren and Jagodzinski's subjects (1975), who were all parents, were left to self-record on their own. In a follow-up interview 8 months after the cessation of weekly contacts with the therapists, only one parent out of 20 was collecting data of any kind. Most had stopped data recording soon after the cessation of regular monitoring.

Probably, under normal circumstances, clients would continue to self-record accurately for fairly long durations. The therapist must, however, show interest in the self-recorded data and reward the client's efforts.

What to Do if Clients Do Not Self-Monitor

The first step if a client is not complying with self-monitoring instructions is to explore possible reasons for the noncompliance. Shelton and Levy (1981) suggest three possible reasons for noncompliance: (a) the client lacks the necessary skills and knowledge to complete some or all of the tasks in the assignment; (b) the client has cognitions that interfere with the completion of the assignment; and (c) the client's environment elicits noncompliance. Each of these hypotheses can be explored, and appropriate remedial action taken.

Similarly, Shelton and Ackerman (1974) suggest two common reasons for noncompliance: (a) lack of explicit instructions and (b) lack of relevance of the assignment to the client's needs. Appropriate remediation in the latter case is to reemphasize the rationale for the task and to reassign it.

Haley (1978) believes that once a task has been assigned, the therapist should challenge the client if he or she has not completed the task, regardless of the reasons given for noncompliance. Haley (1978) stresses that the client has failed him or herself, rather than failing the therapist.

In a similar vein, Mahoney (1977) outlines four steps that he follows if a client fails to comply with self-monitoring instructions. First, he makes the importance of self-monitoring more obvious by asking the client retrospective questions. In other words, the therapist asks the client questions about his or her activities or behaviors during the previous week that the client is unlikely to be able to answer without consulting written self-monitored data. Second, Mahoney reports that he tries to shape self-recording by first assigning self-monitoring tasks that place minimal demands on the client, and then by gradually increasing those demands. The third step is to confront the client with the fact that the success of the treatment may be jeopardized if the therapist is receiving insufficient feedback about the client's progress. Mahoney's last resort is to threaten termination of professional services unless self-monitored data are forthcoming.

If these suggestions prove futile, the scientist-practitioner should recall that many other sources of data are available, apart from self-monitoring. Alternative or additional measures are described in chapters 5 and 6 of this book.

THE REACTIVITY OF SELF-MONITORING

When clients self-record, the behavior that is being self-recorded changes in frequency. This phenomenon is well established and has been termed the *reactivity of self-monitoring* (Kazdin, 1974a; Nelson, 1977). Generally, this reactivity is therapeutic. The direction of the reactive behavior change is in a desirable direction. In other words, through self-monitoring, desirable behaviors increase in frequency and undesirable behaviors decrease in frequency (Cavior & Marabotto, 1976; Kazdin, 1974a; Sieck & McFall, 1976).

This reactivity is also independent of the accuracy of self-recording. This notion was suggested by Nelson and McReynolds (1971) and has been experimentally confirmed (Nelson, 1977). In other words, even if the self-recorded data are not accurate, the phenomenon of reactivity occurs.

For the clinical goals of scientist-practitioners, the reactivity of self-monitoring is generally desirable. The reactivity enhances therapeutic effectiveness. For the research goals of scientist-practitioners, the reactivity of self-monitoring must be considered in making appropriate interpretations of results. If a scientist-practitioner is conducting single-subject research in which one measure is self-monitored data, any changes from A (baseline) conditions to B (treatment) conditions must be interpreted as due to an interaction between self-monitoring and any other treatment ingredient. If self-monitoring is used, changes cannot be solely attributed to other treatment ingredients.

Chapter 5
Self-Report and
Psychophysiological Measures

INTRODUCTION

The first part of this chapter focuses on measures that can be provided through client self-report. Typical self-report measures include questionnaires, self-ratings, and card sorts. A somewhat arbitrary distinction is made here between self-report and self-monitoring. In self-monitoring, the client observes his or her own behavior and records the behavior at the time of its occurrence in a fairly molecular fashion. For example, the frequency or duration of specific behaviors is self-recorded on an ongoing basis as the specific behaviors occur.

In self-report, the client also observes his or her own behavior; but, in contrast with self-monitoring, records the behavior in a more retrospective and global fashion. To illustrate, in a self-report questionnaire, a client may be asked to reflect on his or her own behavior and to record how he or she might generally act or feel, using global, summative responses such as ratings or true-false. Self-report measures are discussed in this chapter, whereas self-monitoring is described in another chapter of this book.

RELATIONSHIP BETWEEN SELF-REPORT AND OTHER MEASURES OF BEHAVIOR

A distinction has been made between direct and indirect measures of behavior (Cone, 1978). Self-report is said to fall at the more indirect end of the continuum because self-report frequently provides a filtered account of clinically relevant activities. Cone (1978) emphasized that self-report measures can be provided for any of the three behavioral content systems. To elaborate, a person can provide reports of his or her motoric activity (motor content, such as "I left my house only once last week"), physiological activity (physiological content, such as "My heart races when I'm driving "), and cognitive activity (cognitive content, such as "I think that I am worthless").

The main point here is that self-report is a method of assessment that can be used to measure motoric, physiological, or cognitive content. A client can recount his or her objective states; that is, activities that could be subjected to independent, direct measurement, as well as his or her subjective states, for which no independent, direct measurement is possible.

An important question that has been raised over and over again is the relationship between self-report measures and other measures of the same behavior: the degree of correspondence among people's verbal reports of behavior and their actual (more directly measured) motoric or physiological responses. This question is often posed within the rubric of concurrent validity; that is, How well do verbal measures of behavior relate to other measures of the same behavior?

Several investigations have shown that there is imperfect and sometimes poor correspondence among verbal, motor, and physiological activity. This result has been demonstrated when multiple measures are taken on a single measurement occasion. To illustrate, Lang and Lazovik (1963) reported that motoric responses on a behavioral avoidance test measuring approach to or avoidance of snakes and verbal responses on a fear thermometer (in which subjects rate their fear on a 10-point scale) correlated only +.40.

The same result has been observed when multiple measures are taken on repeated measurement occasions; for example, over the course of treatment. To illustrate, different relationships between change in heart rate and motoric behavior change occurred over time in phobics as they were treated by reinforced practice (Leitenberg et al., 1971). Similarly, over the course of treatment, individual agoraphobics showed different relationships between heart rate and self-ratings of anxiety (Barlow, Mavissakalian, & Schofield, 1980; Mavissakalian & Michelson, 1982).

This frequent asynchrony, or lack of agreement, among verbal, motoric, and physiological measures has resulted in a concept labeled the *triple-response system* (Lang, 1968, 1971). In other words, the three aspects (verbal, motoric, and physiological) of the same behavior need not always agree. This concept of the triple-response system has been elaborated and/or criticized by Hodgson and Rachman (1974), Hugdahl (1981), and Rachman and Hodgson (1974).

One variable that has been demonstrated to increase the correspondence between verbal and motoric measures, and between verbal and physiological measures is the phrasing of the questions requiring verbal replies. For example, motoric measures of snake avoidance (in a behavioral avoidance test) were correctly predicted 95% of the time by specific questions (where subjects verbally predicted their own degree of approach-avoidance in a laboratory situation), but only 61% of the time by more general questions (where subjects self-rated their degree of fear of snakes) (McReynolds & Stegman, 1976). Cone (1979) believed that the generally low correspondence among verbal, motor, and physiological measures was frequently due to a methodological confound. To illustrate, indirect measures of cognitive content (e.g., "I feel anxious") were often compared to direct measures of physiological content (e.g., galvanic skin response). Cone (1979) predicted that the low correlations produced by this measure by content confound could be improved if, for example, indirect measures of physiological content (e.g., "I perspire") were compared to the related direct measures of physiological content (e.g., galvanic skin response). Cone (1979) cited the results of McReynolds and Stegman (1976) to buttress his point. Thus, the correspondence between verbal reports and motoric or physiological measures increases if the verbal report is specifically about those motoric or physiological activities.

Even when verbal reports of behavior correspond in a less than perfect fashion with motoric and physiological measures of behavior, verbal reports are nonetheless important. Verbal reports simply provide *different* measures of behavior, and *not inferior* measures of behavior. There is no other means of measurement than self-report for cognitive and subjective experiences. Even for motoric and physiological activity, for which direct measurement is possible, the client's perception of the activity is also important. On a practical level, clients voluntarily seek treatment when they think that they have a problem, and they terminate treatment when they think that they do not have a problem (Tasto, 1977) (excluding court-referred or involuntarily committed patients). On a philosophical level, Wolf (1978) has quoted Levi and Anderson (1975): "We believe that each individual can be assumed to be the best judge of his [sic] own situation and state of well-being. The alternative is some type of 'big brother' who makes the evaluation for groups and nations. World history provides many examples of such 'expert' or 'elitist' opinions being at variance with what was expected by the man in the street" (p. 213). What people think — about their cognitive, motoric, and physiological behavior — does matter, practically and philosophically.

QUESTIONNAIRES

Probably the most frequently used self-report measure is the questionnaire. Typically, the client is given a paper-and-pencil questionnaire and is asked to complete it, either in the clinic or at home. To serve as a measure of change, the questionnaire must be administered at least on a pretreatment and posttreatment basis. It is recommended that the questionnaire be administered much more frequently if it is the sole or major measure of change, if the questionnaire is brief, and if the client is cooperative in completing the questionnaire (Bloom & Fischer, 1982).

The thousands of extant questionnaires can be subdivided into broad questionnaires that seek to survey several life areas or to assess degree of general life adjustment, and more specific questionnaires that seek to identify client responses in particular life areas or in particular situations. Since there are such a very large number of questionnaires, this chapter mentions some as exemplars and cites sources to obtain more complete listings. For example, an excellent reference from which to select broad questionnaires is Buros's *Mental Measurements Yearbook* (1978). Some examples of broad questionnaires follow.

Broad Questionnaires

One broad questionnaire is the SCL-90 which stands for Symptom Checklist with 90 items (Derogatis, cited by Hargreaves, Atkinson, and Sorensen, 1977, and by Clifford, 1981). This broad-based questionnaire evolved from the earlier Hopkins Symptom Checklist and is intended for outpatient use. For each of the 90 items, the respondent is instructed to rate "How much that problem has bothered and/or distressed you during the past including today," on a 5-point scale, from 0 (*not at all*) to 4 (*extremely*). The checklist has nine factors: somatization, obsessive-compulsive, interpersonal sensitivity, depression, anxiety, hostility, phobic anxiety, paranoid, and psychoticism. Sample items include: "Feeling afraid to go out of your house alone," "Pains in heart or chest," "Sleep that is restless or disturbed," and "Feelings of guilt."

Another broad questionnaire is the Denver Community Mental Health Questionnaire (Ciarlo & Reihman, cited by Hargreaves et al., 1977, and by Clifford, 1981). It consists of 71 items that focus on personal and social adjustment, contact with other human service agencies, and client's satisfaction with present services. The areas of adjustment include social roles, social relationships, leisure time activities, personal feelings and thoughts, alcohol and drug abuse, and police contact. Many of the items are answered on a frequency basis, from 0 (*never*) to 3 (*almost always*, or *constantly*, or *all the time*). Sample items of this type include the following: "In the last couple of days, have you had trouble with *headaches*? "When you are with your *family*, how often do you argue with them?" "If you use alcohol or drugs, does it cause any problem with your *employer* or job?"

Of course, a very well known broad questionnaire is the Minnesota Multiphasic Personality Inventory (Hathaway & McKinley, 1951). While any of these broad questionnaires can be used as pre-post treatment measures, an example of using the MMPI in this capacity was provided by Harmon

et al. (1980). The Depression scale of the MMPI was administered pretreatment to select depressed subjects. It was readministered to both the experimental and control subjects on a posttreatment basis to assess the effects of the
treatment procedures provided for the experimental subjects.

One major problem with the use of broad questionnaires on a pre-post
treatment basis is that they provide a relatively insensitive measure of change.
Treatment generally focuses on a few patient problems, whereas, by definition, the broad questionnaires assess many life areas as well as general adjustment. Therefore, even though the client may improve in the areas that
were the focus of treatment, the changes may not be reflected in the broad
questionnaires. Conversely, any change that is detected by using broad questionnaires adds to the credibility that treatment "really" was effective. In other
words, the treatment resulted in broad-based clinical effects. The most
desirable practice may be to use both specific questionnaires (to provide maximal sensitivity to treatment change) and broad questionnaires (to examine
broad-based changes) on a pre-post treatment basis.

Specific Questionnaires

Whereas broad questionnaires assess many different problem areas and
general life adjustment, specific questionnaires assess more focused areas.
Resources that list large numbers of specific questionnaires include the following: Bellack and Hersen (1977), Cautela (1981), Cautela and Upper (1976),
Haynes (1978), Haynes and Wilson (1979), and Tasto (1977). Actual copies
of some specific questionnaires appear in Cautela (1981), in Cautela and Upper (1976), and in Mash and Terdal (1976).

A convenient way to classify the specific questionnaires is by the functional unit that they attempt to assess. Some focus on stimulus variables,
others on response parameters, and still others on different consequences.
By way of illustration, a widely known specific questionnaire that focuses
on stimulus or situational variables is the Fear Survey Schedule-II (Geer,
1965), which is reprinted in Mash and Terdal (1976). A large number (51)
of stimulus items are listed, such as spiders, auto accidents, speaking before
a group, being with a member of the opposite sex, and not being a success.
For each item, the respondent is instructed to rate the amount of fear that
they feel toward the object or situation noted in the item, from 1 (*none*) to
7 (*terror*).

Another specific questionnaire that focuses on stimulus or situational
variables is the Social Avoidance and Distress Scale (Watson & Friend, 1969,
reprinted in Mash & Terdal, 1976). The purpose of the scale is to determine
the range of social situations that the client avoids or that distresses the client.
The client is instructed to mark each of the 28 items as either true or false.

Some of the items are subsequently "reverse scored" by the assessor to determine degree of social avoidance or distress. Items include: "Even though a room is full of strangers, I may enter it anyway," "I am usually nervous with people unless I know them well," and "I try to avoid situations which force me to be very sociable."

Other specific questionnaires assess consequences rather than antecedent stimulus conditions. The consequence of interest is usually potential reinforcers that can be used in a behavior-management program. Technically, reinforcers can only be identified empirically; that is, by observing their effect in increasing the rate of preceding behaviors. Some specific questionnaires, however, assist in the identification of potential reinforcers that can then be tested in an empirical manner. Typical of a specific questionnaire that assesses consequences is the Reinforcement Survey Schedule (Cautela & Kastenbaum, 1967, reprinted in Mash & Terdal, 1976). A large number of potentially desirable consequences or activities are listed. The client is instructed to rate each activity on a 5-point scale from *not at all* to *very much,* with the rating describing how much pleasure the activity gives to the client nowadays. Sample items include a variety of beverages, different types of music, participation in various sports, shopping for different types of merchandise, and receiving praise for various attributes.

The final and by far the largest category of specific questionnaires is designed to assess responses comprising different problem areas. These questionnaires are generally used in the following manner. A client complains of problems in a particular life area. The therapist administers a questionnaire that is intended to specify the responses within that life area that cause difficulties for the client. If normative data are provided for the questionnaire, the client's pretreatment score can be compared to the norms to determine if his or her responses are atypical in relation to the standardization group. Also, this initial administration can be used to identify specific target responses to be treated. The questionnaire can be administered repetitively as a measure of client improvement. Finally, if normative data are available, the client's posttreatment score can be compared to the standardization group to ascertain if the client's score is now in the "normal" range. This latter comparison helps to determine the substantive or clinical significance of any treatment changes.

The sources listed earlier describe many of the specific questionnaires that assess particular problem areas. For example, some of these questionnaires assess depressed responses. The therapist makes the judgment that the client may be depressed, and then asks the client to complete a questionnaire that further assesses depression. As noted above, the purposes would be (a) to compare the client's pretreatment score to the normative data to determine his or her degree of depression in relation to the standardization sample, (b) to identify particular responses within the depressed cluster that are problematic for this client, (c) to provide pretreatment and posttreatment data to measure any therapeutic improvement in depression, and (d) to compare the client's posttreatment score to the normative data to evaluate the substantive or clinical significance of any therapeutic change. One questionnaire that assesses depression is the Beck Depression Inventory (Beck et al., 1961, reprinted in Beck, Rush, Shaw, & Emery, 1980). This inventory consists of 21 items that focus on responses typical of depression. Each item contains four statements, and the client is instructed to pick out the one statement from each group that best describes the way that he or she has been feeling the past week, including today. For example, one item contains these four statements: "0 = I can work about as well as before; 1 = It takes an extra effort to get started at doing something; 2 = I have to push myself very hard to do anything; 3 = I can't do any work at all." Another item contains these four statements: "0 = I don't have any thoughts of killing myself; 1 = I have thoughts of killing myself, but I would not carry them out; 2 = I would like to kill myself; 3 = I would kill myself if I had the chance."

One group of specific questionnaires focus on the problem area of marital distress. Typical of this group is the Marital Pre-Counseling Inventory (Stuart & Stuart, 1972). Different portions of this inventory deal with congruence of partners' priorities, power distribution, communication effectiveness, sexual satisfaction, congruence in child management, and general satisfaction. For example, within the communication effectiveness area, each spouse is asked to rate on a 5-point scale, from *almost never* (1) to *almost always* (5), how frequently various statements correctly refer to interactions with the other spouse. Such statements include: "I express appreciation for the things which my spouse does for me"; "I enjoy just sitting and talking with my spouse"; and "My spouse listens to and expresses interest in the things which I say, think, feel, and do." In another example, within the general satisfaction area, each spouse is asked to rate on a 5-point scale (95%+ to 5%-) his or her general commitment to and optimism about the marriage by responding to such questions as: "Everything considered, how happy are you in your marriage?" "How committed are you to remain in your marriage?" and "What proportion of the time spent with your spouse is happy for you?"

Another group of specific questionnaires focus on the problem area of assertiveness. An example here is the College Self-Expression Scale (Galassi, DeLo, Galassi, & Bastien, 1974, reprinted in Mash & Terdal, 1976). This scale consists of 50 items. Some items are subsequently reverse-scored by the assessor to determine the client's degree of assertiveness. Each item is rated on a 5-point scale from *almost always or always* (0) to *never or rarely* (4), depending on the way in which the client expresses him- or herself. Items include: "Do you find it difficult to ask a friend to do a favor for you?" "If a friend makes what you consider to be an unreasonable request, are you able to refuse?" and "Do you freely volunteer information or opinions in class discussions?"

To summarize, specific questionnaires assess stimulus situations, problem areas, or consequences. Most specific questionnaires assess problem areas such as depression, marital distress, or assertiveness. Some examples follow of using these specific questionnaires in clinical cases.

The Beck Depression Inventory (Beck et al., 1961) was used by Rush, Khatami, and Beck (1975) with three patients. Their scores on the inventory were used to demonstrate (a) that the patients were initially depressed (by comparing their scores with normative data) and (b) that the patients improved during the course of 14 weeks of cognitive-behavioral therapy for depression (by weekly readministration of the inventory).

Two couples who were maritally distressed were treated by Bornstein, Bach, Heider, and Ernst (1981). One measure of change was weekly direct observations of client behavior in the clinic to assess communication patterns. Other measures included two specific questionnaires. The Locke-Wallace Marital Adjustment Test (Locke & Wallace, 1957) was administered at pre-post and follow-up assessment sessions as a measure of general marital satisfaction. The Marital Happiness Scale (Azrin, Naster, & Jones, 1973) was administered weekly in the clinic as an index of week-to-week fluctuations in marital satisfaction as a function of the spouse's behavior in 11 areas of common marital concern (e.g., household responsibility, affection). In recent years, the Dyadic Adjustment Scale (Spanier, 1976) has largely replaced the Locke-Wallace as an excellent measure of marital adjustment.

A distressed parents-adolescent triad received treatment consisting of problem-solving training for resolving specific disputes and of communication training for modifying negative family interactions (Bright & Robin, 1981). Several pre, post, and follow-up measures were used to assess therapeutic change: direct observation in the clinic of communication patterns during discussion of problematic topics, the Issues Checklist to assess frequency and intensity of discussions of specific issues in the home during the previous 2 weeks, and the Conflict Behavior Questionnaire to obtain evaluations of parents-adolescent communication during the previous 2 weeks. These latter two specific questionnaires are further described by Prinz, Foster, Kent, and O'Leary (1979) and by Robin and Weiss (1980), and additional examples of their use in clinical situations can be found in Barlow and Seidner (in press).

SELF-RATINGS

In addition to broad and specific questionnaires, another available form of self-report is self-ratings. In self-ratings, the client is asked to rate him or herself on some specific dimension. The rating can be made in the presence of a particular stimulus in the clinic, or a more summative and retrospective rating can be made in the absence of a particular stimulus. Examples follow.

Self-ratings have frequently been used to assess the subjective components of fear or anxiety. A behavioral avoidance test is often arranged in which the fearful stimulus is presented, either *in vivo* or representationally (slides, audio or videotapes, etc.). During the behavioral avoidance test, all three aspects of the triple-response system can be assessed: motoric responses are assessed by directly observing the client's degree of approach or avoidance; physiological responses are directly assessed by physiological recording devices (to measure, for example, heart rate or galvanic skin response); and subjective responses are indirectly assessed by self-ratings. Self-ratings in the context of a behavioral avoidance test were introduced by Wolpe (1969), who devised a 1-100 self-rating scale to assess SUDs (subjective units of disturbance). A similar 1-10 Fear Thermometer had been designed by Walk (1956). An example of self-ratings used in the context of a behavioral avoidance test is provided by Ost (1978). Storm phobics were subjected to a simulated storm, produced by slides of thunderhead clouds, audiotapes of an actual thunderstorm, and electronic flashes that resembled lightning. During the simulated storm, clients were asked to self-rate their anxiety on a 0-10 scale. The storm and self-ratings were repeatedly readministered during the course of therapy to detect any client improvement.

Subjective ratings of fear were obtained by Liberman and Smith (1972), apart from presentation of the phobic object. About every 10 days, a client with multiple phobias (of being alone, menstruation, chewing hard foods, and dental work) self-rated her amount of fear for each phobia, using 12-point rating scales from *none* to *couldn't be worse.*

Subjective ratings of distress have also been obtained from obsessive-compulsive clients. At times, the ratings are obtained in the presence of the stimulus that is related to the obsessions or compulsions. To illustrate, patients with washing rituals were presented with their individualized contaminants (Foa et al., 1980). They were then asked to rate their subjective levels of discomfort on a 1-100 scale while they approached from a distance of 8 feet, or maintained contact with the contaminant with gloves, towels, or bare hands. Stimuli that were related to obsessions or compulsions were presented to a client by means of videotapes by Milby et al. (1981). A videotape was made of a client while she obsessed aloud about her concerns about ashtrays, the stove, and cooking (all related to a fear of burning the house, injuring herself or her family, and/or leaving her destitute) and about fear of contamination by saliva from rabid dogs (related to a fear of illness and dying). While watching the videotape, the client rated herself every 5 minutes on three dimensions, using 0-100-point scales: (a) level of emotional arousal, (b) urge to perform the compulsive ritual, and (c) distractibility while watching the videotape.

No specific stimuli were presented to assess the discomfort of obsessive-compulsive patients treated by Foa and Goldstein (1978). Instead, at pre, post, and follow-up intervals, the patients were asked to self-rate, using 0-6 or 0-8 scales, their five main fears for anxiety and avoidance: free-floating anxiety, panic, depression, depersonalization, and severity of obsessive-compulsive symptoms.

Self-ratings have also been used to assess clients' degree of sexual arousal. To illustrate, a pedophiliac observed slides of girls and of women (Levin, Barry, Gambaro, Wolfinsohn, & Smith, 1977). In addition to physiological measures of penile erection, he was asked to self-rate on a 1-7 scale his sexual attraction to the person depicted in the slide. Repeated measures were taken to assess his response to treatment. A similar procedure was used by Lande (1980) to assess the relative attraction of nude women and of fire in a man with a fire fetish. While slides of nude women and of fires were shown, physiological measures of penile erection and self-ratings (0-4 scale) of sexual arousal were obtained. These measures were repeated at pretreatment, posttreatment, and at 4- and 9-month follow-ups.

As a final example of self-ratings, Royce and Arkowitz (1978) had socially isolated college students participate in a 10-minute conversation with another subject in a research setting, and then rate themselves on 7-point scales of social anxiety and of social skill. The conversation and ratings were repeated at pretreatment, posttreatment, and follow-ups to assess any treatment-related changes.

CARD SORTS

The card sort is another self-report measure useful in applied settings because of its ease of administration and individualized nature. The procedure was first described by Barlow et al. (1969). Different brief descriptions of sexual interaction are created in conjunction with the client, some containing stimuli related to appropriate sexual arousal (i.e., nude women) and some containing stimuli related to inappropriate sexual arousal (e.g., girls, sadistic scenes, exhibitionistic scenes). Each description or scene is typed on its own index card. The client is asked to sort the cards into five envelopes, using these instructions: "The numbers on the envelopes represent amount of sexual arousal, 0 equals no arousal, 1 equals a little arousal, 2 a fair amount, 3 much, and 4 very much arousal. I would like you to read the description of each scene and place a card in the envelope that comes closest to how arousing the scene is to you at this moment"(Barlow et al., 1969, p. 598). For example, one scene for a pedophile might read, "You are alone in a room with a cute, blond, 6-year-old girl who is smiling at you." Since these scenes are constructed individually with each client, the scenes will differ from client to client and are designed to assess what is maximally arousing for each client.

The card-sort procedure is not limited to the assessment of sexual arousal. Any set of idiosyncratic stimulus situations could be assessed, such as phobic situations or social situations where assertiveness might be an issue. Typically 5 to 10 scenes would be constructed. The client then sorts the scenes into five envelopes or piles. If the client put one scene in the number 2 envelope (labeled, let us say, *a fair amount*) and a second in the number 3 envelope (labeled *much anxiety*), his or her score to that point would be 5. This measure can be taken repeatedly, as often as once a day, and should take less than a minute.

Returning to the case of the sexual deviant, in addition to the card-sort measure, the client is generally also asked to self-monitor sexual urges on a day-to-day basis. Moreover, physiological measures of penile erection are taken in the clinic setting while sexually arousing appropriate and inappropriate stimuli are presented. This cluster of measures is taken repeatedly to assess whether appropriate sexual arousal is maintained or increased and whether inappropriate sexual arousal has decreased during the course of therapy. The card-sort procedure, as used to measure sexual arousal, was also employed with sexual deviants treated by Brownell et al. (1977), by Brownell and Barlow (1976), and by Hayes, Brownell, and Barlow (1978).

ISSUES IN THE USE OF SELF-REPORT MEASURES

This chapter has described three main types of self-report measures: broad and specific questionnaires, self-ratings, and card sorts. Because of their convenience, self-report measures tend to be quite popular. Nonetheless, the following issues must be considered in their use.

The first issue, discussed early in this chapter, is the relationship between self-report and other measures of the same behavior. As has been outlined, frequently there is asynchrony in the triple-response system. Self-reports of cognitive, motoric, or physiological activity do not always coincide with more direct measures of the motoric or physiological activity. The conclusion, however, is not that self-report is an *inferior* measure, but rather that it is a *different* measure. Self-report assesses what the client *says* about what he or she is thinking, feeling, or doing. Self-report is important because it is our *only* measure of cognitive activity (such as obsessions or negative self-statements) or of subjective experience (such as pain or sexual arousal). Even though physiological and motoric activity can be observed directly (at least with the assistance of instrumentation), self-report provides the client with a forum for his or her views about those physiological and motoric behaviors. The critical advice here is to obtain multiple measures to produce a complete assessment of the client's progress. It is especially important to use multiple measures, because the measures might produce different results.

Self-report has sometimes been criticized on the grounds that self-report responses are subject to response bias, demand or expectancy, and social desirability (Haynes, 1978; Haynes & Wilson, 1979; Jayaratne & Levy, 1979). *Response* bias refers to the serial dependency of responses to questionnaire items (e.g., marking several items in a row as "true," or giving several items in a row a rating of "4"). *Demand or expectancy* refers to responding to "extraneous" variables, such as "faking bad" prior to treatment and "faking good" following treatment. *Social desirability* refers to the social value that is perceived to be associated with particular items.

One point to be noted here is that all behavior has multiple determinants. The nominal and functional stimuli controlling behavior can sometimes differ. In the case of questionnaires, even though the questionnaire item is the nominal stimulus, the client may also be reacting to other functional stimuli, such as a therapeutic program that is expected to be helpful or a therapist who seems like a pleasant person. Shifting functional stimuli contribute to response differences across time and across different measurement devices. The argument can again be made that multiple measurement is desirable to help filter out the *signal* (measures of the client's problem behavior in response to the nominal stimulus of the questionnaire item) from the *noise* (the client's reply to other functional but "irrelevant" stimuli, like wanting to please the therapist or to avoid jail).

A related point is that it is not only self-report measures that are subject to demand characteristics. It has been shown that clients' approach or avoidance behavior on a behavioral avoidance test (in this instance, for claustrophobia) can be influenced by *high-demand* instructions ("If you should become fearful, please control it as best you can so you can remain for the full period. . . . Remember that it is extremely important that we get the full 10 min.") versus *low-demand* instructions ("You should stop the process at any point where you become fairly uncomfortable. . . . You should remain in the situation as long as you feel reasonably at ease") (Miller & Bernstein, 1972, p. 207).

Similarly, heart rate during a behavioral avoidance test was also shown to be influenced by high-demand versus low-demand instructions (Odom & Nelson, 1977), although this is not a consistent finding (Miller & Bernstein, 1972). Thus, there are no "pure" measures in which only the nominal or "relevant" stimulus controls the client's responses. Other types of assessment, as well as self-report, can be influenced by "extraneous" stimuli.

One extraneous variable that can influence a client's response on self-report measures is the client's reading skills. This is especially true for questionnaires which often require a fairly sophisticated reading ability. Manuals or instructions that accompany some questionnaires sometimes give the minimum grade level of skills needed to read the questionnaire effectively. The readability of various specific questionnaires used to assess marital distress was examined by Dentch, O'Farrell, and Cutter (1980). Their conclusion was that all nine of the specific questionnaires that they examined required greater reading capability than tests such as the MMPI.

A final issue regarding self-report measures is the relative importance of their psychometric properties. Psychometric examinations, especially of self-report questionnaires, are popular. Usually assessed are split-half reliability, test-retest reliability, and concurrent validity with other measures of the same behavior. These properties of the Social Anxiety Questionnaire were examined by Heimberg, Harrison, Montgomery, Madsen, and Sherfey (1980). The internal consistency and test-retest reliability of the Social Anxiety Inventory were reported by Curran, Corriveau, Monti, and Hagerman (1980). It is our opinion that only particular types of psychometric investigations produce useful data. Of utility are investigations of content validity and those which result in normative data. Content validity is important to determine if the problem area purported to be assessed by the questionnaire is, in fact, adequately represented. Regretfully, the content of many questionnaires has been determined on a logical basis (speculation about what items are appropriate or not) rather than on an empirical basis (generation of items by means of data collection) (Haynes, 1978). Normative data are important for two reasons (Kazdin, 1977a; Nelson & Bowles, 1975): First, normative data can be used in the selection of target behaviors. The client's score on a particular questionnaire can be compared against the norms to determine if the score is "ab-normal." Second, normative data can be used to assess clinical or substantive significance of any treatment changes. If the client's score falls in the "normal" range following treatment, he or she can be said to have "really" improved.

Other types of psychometric investigations may have less utility. If assumptions are accepted that behavior is situation-specific, that behavior may be inconsistent across the three response systems, and that behavior can change over time, then low correlations found in psychometric investigations may reflect real differences in behavior rather than an inferior assessment device (Nelson, 1983; Nelson, Hay, & Hay, 1977). Given the assumption that behavior is situation-specific, split-half reliability across different items should not necessarily be expected. Given the assumption that behavior is changeable, test-retest reliability should not always be expected. Given the assumption that behavior frequently varies across the response sytems, concurrent validity across different assessment methods should not be anticipated.

A final problem with psychometric criteria is that they are based on group data (Bellack & Hersen, 1977; Bloom & Fischer, 1982; Nelson, 1983). The nomothetic conclusions are not always generalizable to individual clients. For example, even if the concurrent validity between a particular questionnaire and more direct observation of motor behavior were high for a group of subjects, the relationship between these two measures would be unknown for any individual client.

In conclusion, despite, or perhaps because of, the inconsistent relationship between self-report and other measures of behavior, self-report measures are frequently indispensable. Self-report is the *only* available measure of subjective experiences or of cognitive activity. It is also the only available measure of clients' opinions about their motoric or physiological behavior. As one of several measures that are repeatedly administered over the course of treatment, self-report provides a unique assessment of client change.

PSYCHOPHYSIOLOGICAL MEASURES

The second portion of this chapter focuses on the direct assessment of clients' psychophysiological processes. These processes are measured generally with the aid of instrumentation; for example, a sphygmomanometer to measure blood pressure or a polygraph to measure electromyographic activity (EMG related to muscle tension). Physiological processes can be measured in less direct ways as well. For example, a client could self-monitor each occurrence of migraine headaches, or a client could self-report the frequency of inappropriate sexual arousal during the previous week, or a significant other could observe the number of asthmatic attacks suffered by the client. In contrast with these less direct measures of physiological events (Cone, 1978), this portion of the chapter focuses on direct measures of psychophysiological events.

The discussion provided here is, of necessity, brief. More complete discussions of the use of psychophysiological measures are provided by Epstein (1976), Geer (1977), Haynes (1978), Haynes and Wilson (1979), Kallman and Feuerstein (1977), Lang (1977), Ray and Kimmel (1979), and Ray and Raczynski (1981).

Typical Uses of Psychophysiological Measures

Clinically, psychophysiological measures are most frequently used for these three categories of disorders: (a) anxiety disorders, (b) psychophysiological disorders, and (c) sexual disorders. Examples follow.

Anxiety Disorders

An early example of the use of psychophysiological measures in the assessment of anxiety was provided by Leitenberg et al. (1971). Both heart rate and approach behavior in the feared situation were measured during the treatment of nine phobic cases. A number of different relationships were observed: in some cases, heart rate increased as avoidance behavior decreased; in other cases, there was a parallel decline; in still others, there was a decline in phobic behavior without any accompanying change in heart rate; and, finally, in several cases heart rate decreased only after phobic behavior had declined. Heart rate was measured by using a portable electrocardiogram machine.

Two obsessive-compulsive patients were treated by real-life exposure to their ritual-evoking situations by Shahar and Marks (1980). Heart rate was recorded during the exposure by an earlobe photoplethysmograph and amplified by a Grass DC amplifier. The raw data were transformed by a Devices instantaneous rate meter which samples every two consecutive beats. Exposure was followed by reduction of tachycardia associated with that item from the beginning to the end of the session. Heart rate habituated before clinical ratings showed major improvement.

Similarly, exposure, both imaginal and real-life, was used by Boulougouris, Rabavilas, and Stefanis (1977) to treat 12 obsessive-compulsive patients. Both heart rate and skin conductance were recorded on a Beckman Type-R Dynograph. Heart rate showed less decrement after treatment than measures of skin conductance or of subjective anxiety.

Pulse rate was recorded manually in clinical research with socially anxious clients by Kanter and Goldfried (1979). Pulse rate was taken before and after treatment at three times: baseline, immediately before a role-played interaction with a confederate, and after the role-played interaction.

Finally, a different methodology to record changes in the circulatory system was used by Kolko and Milan (1980). Blood-flow changes in the index finger of the client's nondominant hand were assessed by a finger thermistor and a two-channel chart recorder. The client was a diabetic with a self-injection phobia.

As this book goes to press, numerous technological advances are occurring that will ensure the availability of relatively inexpensive portable physiological monitoring equipment for practitioners who do not necessarily need to become involved with sophisticated polygraphs. For example, a number of phobia clinics are now recording heart-rate changes directly in feared situations with a lightweight Exersentry produced by Respironics, Inc. The practitioner may want to keep abreast of new developments in portable physiological monitoring equipment.

Psychophysiological Disorders

In addition to measuring psychophysiological processes directly as an indicant of anxiety, these processes have also been measured directly in relation to the treatment of psychophysiological disorders. An example is hypertension or high blood pressure. A first-time pregnant, 35-year-old woman with suspected essential hypertension was treated by anxiety management training by Bloom and Cantrell (1978). Her blood pressure was measured before, during, and after each treatment session by using a standard mercury sphygmomanometer.

Similarly, the blood pressure of two clients suffering from essential hypertension was measured within the therapy session by Beiman, Graham, and Ciminero (1978). In addition, however, the clients also recorded their own blood pressure once each morning and once each afternoon in their natural environments. They purchased their own sphygmomanometers and stethoscopes to obtain these recordings. The treatment sessions focused on progressive relaxation training.

Another psychophysiological disorder in which psychophysiological processes are often measured directly is tension or muscular contraction headaches. In a clinical research example, Haynes, Griffin, Mooney, and Parise (1975) had subjects self-record headache activity (frequency, intensity, and duration of headaches). In addition, electromyographic activity (EMG) from the frontalis muscle was monitored during each treatment session. Both biofeedback and relaxation instructions decreased subjects' self-reported headache activity. Subjects demonstrated a higher average frontalis EMG when they reported having a headache during the session than when they reported having no headache. Several subjects, however, did not demonstrate this relationship between headache occurrence and EMG level.

In a final example using a psychophysiological disorder, a patient with Raynaud's Phenomenon secondary to diagnosed collagen vascular disease was treated with biofeedback by Keefe, Surwit, and Pilon (1981). Her self-recorded vasospastic attacks dropped markedly over a year of training. Over the course of training, the patient was intermittently administered a laboratory cold-stress test. While she was dressed in a standardized fashion, the temperature of the experimental chamber was slowly dropped from 26 degrees to 20 degrees Centigrade. She was instructed to keep her hands as warm as possible throughout the session. Thermistors were secured to the middle finger of both hands. The patient displayed a gradual improvement in her ability to maintain digital skin temperature in the presence of the cold stress.

Journals and mailings available to practitioners list literally hundreds of portable, inexpensive biofeedback devices that are basically physiological monitoring devices. Many of these are quite good and perfectly suitable for clinical use. With the rapid technological advances, however, any recommendation made at this time would soon be outdated.

Sexual Disorders

Along with anxiety and psychophysiological disorders, the variety of sexual disorders are also assessed usefully by direct psychophysiological measures. Male genital arousal is generally measured by a strain gauge that assesses changes in penile circumference (e.g., Barlow, 1977; Barlow, Becker, Leitenberg, & Agras, 1970). Another more sophisticated device is available that measures changes in penile volume (Freund, Sedlacek, & Knob, 1965).

Female genital arousal is generally measured by a vaginal photoplethysmograph (Hoon, Wincze, & Hoon, l976; Sintchak & Geer, 1975). In typical uses of this procedure in clinical situations, male sexual deviants (paraphiliacs) are exposed to both appropriate and inappropriate sexual stimuli. Measures of genital arousal are obtained, as well as self-report measures of sexual arousal (self-ratings or card sorts). The client is also asked to self-monitor sexual urges and activities that occur between therapy sessions.

Representative here is the work of Barlow and his associates. Five clients, each with two patterns of deviant arousal, were treated with covert sensitization by Brownell et al. (1977). In addition to a card-sort measure and self-recording of urges and fantasies, measures of penile circumference were obtained. Each client selected three groups of slides: slides depicting heterosexual scenes that he found arousing, and slides depicting each of the clients' two deviations. Changes in penile circumference were measured as clients observed the slides. Each pattern of deviant arousal did not decline until sequentially treated with covert sensitization, and heterosexual and deviant arousal were generally independent.

In a similar example, Lande (1980) obtained both physiological measures of heart rate and of penile circumference change and self-reported measures of arousal (ratings from 0 to 4) from a male client with a fire fetish. The client was shown slides of nude females and of fire scenes. Treatment included orgasmic reconditioning to increase heterosexual arousal and covert sensitization to reduce deviant arousal.

In recent years, this type of assessment has been used to measure arousal in sexually dysfunctional men and women, as well as in sexual deviants. Such measures of sexual arousal not only assess changes during treatment, but also differentiate organic from functionally based male impotence (Sakheim, Barlow, & Beck, in press). Since this procedure is relatively easy to administer, with equipment that is inexpensive and readily available to practitioners, it may replace the more expensive and time-consuming nocturnal penile tumescence (NPT) studies that require spending two or three nights in a sleep laboratory.

ISSUES IN DIRECT
PSYCHOPHYSIOLOGICAL ASSESSMENT

As indicated above, psychophysiological measures are frequently taken with anxiety disorders, psychophysiological disorders, and sexual disorders. The following issues must be considered when using these measures.

Cost

The use of direct psychophysiological measures generally requires money and expertise. Hence, suitable instrumentation is not available in many clinical situations. As noted above, however, low-cost devices are becoming more available. Manual recording of pulse, as performed by Kanter and Goldfried (1979), costs nothing. Other devices, like the sphygmomanometer, are readily accessible. The current interest in biofeedback has fostered the development of instruments that can be used for both biofeedback and for psychophysiological measurement, as mentioned above.

Organism Variables

Organisms usually work to maintain homeostasis. Hence, for each new stimulus, the organism responds and readjusts itself. The implications of homeostasis for psychophysiological measurement are twofold (Epstein, 1976). First, after the client is prepared for the measurement, an adaptation period must follow so that the client may become accustomed to the measuring device. Second, initial presentation of the stimuli of interest may produce not only expected physiological changes, but also an orienting reflex. The latter should diminish upon repeated presentation of the stimuli.

Another type of organism variable is that individuals have different resting levels in various physiological systems. The changes that are possible within any individual physiological system are constrained by the initial resting level within that system. This phenomenon is called the *law of initial values* (Wilder, 1950). As an example, if a client's resting heart rate is quite high (e.g., 90 beats per minute), then there is a limited ceiling for an increase in heart rate in the presence of a phobic stimulus.

Importance of Stimulus Situations

The psychophysiological responses of interest occur in the presence of particular stimuli. Thus, it is critical to introduce the relevant stimulus into the measurement situation. In the clinic setting, the relevant stimulus can be presented in an analogue fashion. Numerous illustrations are described above; for example, the use of slides to present appropriate and deviant sexual stimuli or the use of real-life contaminants to assess obsessive-compulsive anxiety.

Psychophysiological measurements can also be taken in the natural environment in which the relevant stimuli are freely occurring. An example here would be the two clients with hypertension treated by Beiman et al. (1978) who recorded their own blood pressure twice daily in the natural environment.

Sometimes psychophysiological measurements can be influenced by subtle changes in the stimulus situation. To illustrate, Abel, Blanchard, and Barlow (1981) found that greater sexual arousal, as measured by the penile plethysmograph, was obtained by the presentation of sexual stimuli on videotapes than by the presentation of sexual stimuli on audiotapes, slides, or free fantasy.

RELATIONSHIP BETWEEN PHYSIOLOGICAL
AND OTHER MEASURES OF BEHAVIOR

As discussed earlier in this chapter, asynchrony is frequently found among verbal, motoric, and physiological response systems. An illustration is the work with phobics by Leitenberg et al. (1971), where a number of different relationships were found in individual phobics between heart rate and approach behavior over the course of treatment. Another example is the work with tension headache patients by Haynes et al. (1975). Whereas the group of subjects demonstrated a higher average frontalis EMG when they reported having a headache during the recording session than when they reported having no headache, several subjects did not show this pattern.

The most useful conceptualization of this asynchrony seems to be the triple-response system (Lang, 1968, 1971) in which motoric, physiological, and verbal responses are viewed as "separate but equal." Historically, some facets of society, like law enforcement officials with the lie detector test, have felt that truth rests with the physiological response system. Alternative advice is to obtain multiple measures from all relevant response systems and to emphasize one response system over another, depending on the particular circumstances. In the work with headache patients by Haynes et al. (1975), it seems that self-reports of pain must be respected, regardless of EMG readings. While this illustration is related to the ageless mind-body problem, it is generally concluded that there is no one-to-one correspondence between perceptions of pain and actual tissue damage or stress. A different conclusion, however, might be reached with sexual deviants. Especially if they are court-referred, their verbal reports of deviant sexual arousal may be less trustworthy than measures of genital arousal in the presence of inappropriate stimuli. Indeed, Abel et al. (1981) reported that paraphiliacs could suppress their penile arousal by only 15-20%, even when explicitly instructed to suppress their erections to the inappropriate stimulus by mental means.

RELATIONSHIP AMONG DIFFERENT
PHYSIOLOGICAL MEASURES

It is clear that physiological measures are not always in synchrony with motoric and self-report measures. Moreover, there is not always synchrony among different psychophysiological measures purporting to assess the same construct. An illustration is a study by Prigatano and Johnson (1974) to assess anxiety. Spider-phobic and non-spider-phobic subjects viewed spider, seascape, and surgical slides while several physiological responses were continuously recorded. Results indicated that, during spider-slide presentations, spider phobics showed significantly faster heart rate, greater heart-rate variability, and vasoconstriction as compared to non-spider phobics. Spider phobics also showed more frequent phasic skin responses, but not larger skin-response amplitudes, to spider slides. Respiration rates and respiration amplitude were not significantly different for the two groups. An illustration using a different construct is a study by Henson, Rubin, and Henson (1979) with female sexual arousal. While eight adult women volunteers viewed the same erotic film in two different sessions, their genital responses were recorded by three different measures: vaginal pressure pulse, vaginal blood volume, and labial temperature change. There were imperfect correlations among the three measures for individual subjects at each session, as well as imperfect correlations for the same measure across sessions. Labial temperature was the most consistent response.

This phenomenon of intersubject inconsistency in physiological responding has been labeled *response specificity* (Lacey, Bateman, & Van Lehn, 1953). In other words, for each individual, one particular system may reliably show a maximal response to various stimuli. The implication of this finding is that group research using a single physiological measure across subjects is often imprecise because the most sensitive measures for individual subjects may not be included. Another implication is that in single-subject clinical research, the most sensitive physiological measure for the client should be identified and utilized.

Chapter 6
Direct Observation

INTRODUCTION

This chapter describes measures that are based on direct and indirect observations of the client's behavior. Unlike self-monitoring or self-report, which rely on the client to provide the data, other people provide the data resulting from direct and indirect observations. These people may include the therapist or other staff, and significant others who frequently interact with the client in the natural environment.

The first portion of this chapter provides examples of measures that are based on direct observation of the client's behavior. These observations may occur in the therapeutic environment, that is, in the clinic or hospital, or they may occur in the client's natural environment, that is, in home, work, or educational settings. The measures that result from such direct observations may either be molar measures (particularly, global ratings on rating scales), or molecular measures (particularly, quantification of the occurrences of particular behaviors). Sometimes, by-products of behaviors or archival records of behavior are measured, rather than the behaviors directly. These and other examples of indirect observation will be described more fully in a second section of this chapter. The last section deals with issues related to the accuracy of these observational measures.

DIRECT OBSERVATION IN THERAPEUTIC SETTINGS

Molar Measures: Global Rating Scales

A wide variety of standardized rating scales can be used to evaluate client behavior in inpatient or outpatient settings. Typically, these rating scales are used on a pretreatment basis to help arrive at a diagnosis. The rating scales are then used again intermittently during treatment and especially at posttreatment to help determine the client's progress and status at termination. Generally, the client is observed for an intensive time period, and then a staff member who is trained in the use of the rating scale provides global ratings of behavior on several dimensions.

Two well-known rating scales that are used in psychiatric settings are described by Nathan and Harris (1980). One of these is the Inpatient Multidimensional Psychiatric Scale (Lorr & Klett, 1966), composed of 90 items. A typical item to measure "paranoid projection" is: Compared to the normal person of the same sex and age, does he or she manifest a hostile, sullen, or morose attitude towards others by tone of voice, demeanor, or facial expression? The staff member is to assign a rating to the item, ranging from 1 (*not at all*) to 9 (*extremely*). The other device is the Wittenborn Psychiatric Rating Scales (Wittenborn, 1955), composed of 72 items. A typical item to measure "acute anxiety" requests that the staff person select one of the following four alternatives that best describes the client: (a) no complaint of subjectively experienced anxiety, (b) experiences at least minor feelings of anxiety, (c) experiences anxiety which is strong enough to make him or her express acutely uncomfortable feelings, and (d) is desperately distressed by his or her anxiety and considers it to be intolerable.

Other global rating scales that are completed by staff members include the following. The Brief Psychiatric Rating Scale (Overall & Gorham, cited in Hargreaves et al., 1977) consists of 18 symptom constructs, each rated on a 7-point scale, ranging from 1 (*not present*) to 7 (*extremely severe*). An example, using tension, is: "physical and motor manifestations of tension, 'nervousness,' and heightened activation level. Tension should be rated solely on the basis of physical signs and motor behavior and not on the basis of subjective experiences of tension reported by the patient." The Periodic Evaluation Record—Community Version was developed by Spitzer and Endicott (cited in Hargreaves et al., 1977) to provide global ratings of the behavior of outpatients. It is comprised of several items, each rated on a 5-point scale. As examples, an item labeled *physical health* has as rating anchor points *very good* to *very poor,* and an item labeled *good friends* has as rating anchor points *many* to *none.*

Some of these staff global rating scales depend upon a structured interview with the client. An interview outline is provided; after the staff member interviews the client, he or she completes the rating scales based on the client's behavior and responses during the interview. One such scale that is based on an interview is the Psychiatric Status Schedule (Spitzer, Endicott, & Cohen, 1968, cited in Hargreaves et al., 1977). The staff member then rates over 300 items as true or false. Examples of items include: "Indicates his conviction in some important personal belief which is almost certainly not true (delusion)," an item from the "False Beliefs" category; and "Hair is unkempt, tangled, or matted," an item from the "Grooming" category. Another rating scale that is based on a structured interview with the client is the Social Adjustment Scale II (Schooler, Hogarty, & Weissman, 1974, cited in Hargreaves et al., 1977). An example of a question addressed to an employed person is: "Have you missed any time from work in the last two months? How many days did you miss? Was that a vacation?" The rater is then to include time lost due to physical or mental illness, due to being laid off or unemployed, but not due to paid vacation, in rating this item on a 4-point scale, from 0 (*less than half a week*) to 4 (*over 4 weeks*).

Other rating scales require that a staff member provide only a single or very few overall rating(s) of the client's status. One example is the Global Assessment Scale (Spitzer, Gibbon, & Endicott, cited in Hargreaves et al., 1977), on which the staff rates a client's overall functioning on a 1-100 continuum of psychological-psychiatric health or sickness. Narrative descriptions are provided for each 10-point range; for example, the 61-70 range has this description: "Some mild symptoms (e.g., depressive mood and mild insomnia) *or* some difficulty in several areas of functioning, but generally functioning pretty well, has some meaningful interpersonal relationships, and most untrained people would not consider him 'sick.' Another scale, Clinical Global Impressions (National Institute of Mental Health, cited in Hargreaves et al., 1977), contains only three general scales: (a) how mentally ill the patient is at this time; (b) how much has he changed since admission; and (c) the therapeutic and side effects of the patient's drug regimen.

Some other rating scales are intended for a significant other (someone who interacts frequently with the client in the natural environment) to complete, rather than a staff member. One of these is the Katz Adjustment Scales (Katz & Lyerly, cited in Hargreaves et al., 1977), which consists of five parts. Part 1 is a symptom scale. Particular symptoms, like "looks worn out" or "gets nervous easily," are rated on a 1 (*almost never*) to 4 (*almost always*) scale. Parts 2 and 3 deal with the client's social roles, Part 2 dealing with the client's actual performance of social roles and Part 3 dealing with his or her expected role performance. Particular social behaviors are listed, like "entertains friends at home" and "helps with family shopping," and are rated on 3-point scales, from 1 (*is not doing*) to 3 (*is doing regularly*) in Part 2, and from 1 (*did not expect him to be doing*) to 3 (*expected him to be doing regularly*) in Part 3. Parts 4 and 5 deal with the client's leisure time activities, Part 4 dealing with the client's actual performance of these activities and Part 5 dealing with his or her expected performance. Particular leisure-time activities are listed, like "works in the garden or yard" and "goes to the movies," and are rated on 3-point scales, from 1 (*frequently*) to 3 (*practically never*) in Part 4; and 1 (*satisfied with what he does here*), 2 (*would like to see him do more of this*), or 3 (*would like to see him do less*) in Part 5. Another rating scale that is to be completed by a significant other of the client is the Personal Adjustment and Role Skills Scale (Ellsworth, cited in Hargreaves et al., 1977). It consists of 57 items, purporting to measure the community adjustment of the client. Items include, "had a drinking problem that upset her relationship with family members," "needed supervision or guidance from the family," and "prepared the evening meal for members of the household." Items are rated on a 5-point scale, from 1 (*never*) to 5 (*usually or always*).

If the reader is interested in actually examining the complete scales described above or in ordering copies of these scales, an excellent reference is Hargreaves et al. (1977). Other scales are described but not actually reprinted by Newman (1979) and by Clifford (1981). Bloom and Fischer (1982) provide information about several reference books that abstract or review large numbers of rating scales. Among these are Comrey, Backer, and Glaser's *Sourcebook for Mental Health Measures* (1973) and Waskow and Parloff's *Psychotherapy Change Measures* (1975).

The above-described checklists seem to be particularly suitable for adults in psychiatric settings. Another wide array of rating scales is available for use with children, in clinic, home, or school settings. These rating scales and checklists are reviewed by Spivack and Swift (1973) and by Walls, Werner, Bacon, and Zane (1977). Only a few are noted here. The Behavior Problem Checklist (Quay, 1977) consists of 55 problematic behaviors that are rated on a 3-point scale. A factor analysis revealed four behavior clusters: conduct problems (aggression, acting out), personality problems (anxiety, withdrawal), inadequacy-immaturity, and subcultural (socialized) delinquency. The Devereux Elementary School Behavior Rating Scale (Spivack & Swift, 1967) revealed 11 clusters: classroom disturbance, impatience, disrespect-defiance, external blame, achievement anxiety, external reliance, comprehension, inattentive-withdrawn, irrelevant responsiveness, creative initiative, and closeness to the teacher. The Conners' Teacher Rating Scale (Conners, 1969) consists of 39 behaviors which the teacher rates on a 4-point scale. A factor analysis revealed five factors: hyperactivity, conduct problems, inattentive-passive, tension-anxiety, and sociability. The psychometric properties of the Behavior Problem Checklist, the Devereux, and the Conners have been reviewed by O'Leary and Johnson (1979).

The rating scales described above are global scales that encompass a wide range of possible abnormal behaviors or of life adjustment. It is also possible to use rating scales in clinical settings that are tailored to the presenting problems of a particular client. Along these lines, an assessor first interviewed obsessive-compulsive patients and then rated them, using a 6-point scale, on three dimensions: severity of compulsions, severity of obsessions, and urges to perform rituals (Foa & Goldstein, 1978). Likewise, an independent assessor (as well as the patients and their therapists) rated phobic patients, using 9-point scales, on several pertinent dimensions: free-floating anxiety, panic attacks, obsessions, depression, depersonalization, work adjustment, leisure adjustment, sexual adjustment, family relationships, and other relationships

(Watson & Marks, 1971). These 9-point rating scales have come to be widely used in assessing change in phobic symptomatology (Mavissakalian & Barlow, 1981).

Molecular Measures: Specific Behaviors

Within the clinic or hospital setting, staff members can collect data by directly observing the client and by quantifying the observed behavior. The client's behavior can be quantified into molecular measures immediately as it is occurring, or the client's behavior can be audio- or videotaped for later quantification into molecular measures. In order to obtain direct molecular measures of specific behaviors within the clinic or hospital setting, it is essential that the client's target behavior occur in that setting. Sometimes this happens naturally. At other times, conditions must be arranged so that the target behavior does occur. In this latter case, either role playing is used or the critical stimulus that elicits the target behavior is deliberately introduced. Specific examples follow later in this section.

Types of Observational Methods

There are at least seven alternative ways of quantifying observed behavior into molecular measures. Many of these methods are illustrated in more detail in the examples described below, but each is here briefly described. First is a *frequency count* in which each occurrence of the target behavior during a specific interval of time is recorded. This method is most suited to discrete behaviors of fairly low rate. Discrete behaviors are those for which (a) the initiation and termination of the behavior are quite obvious, and (b) the durations of separate occurrences of the target behavior do not widely vary. The same unit of time must be used to record frequencies of any specific behavior so that one frequency count can be compared with another. Some examples include: a child calling out three times before falling asleep at night, an inpatient approaching the nurses' station six times per hour, and an outpatient paranoid complaining suspiciously eight times per therapy session.

One of the easiest ways to record frequency is to make marks on a readily accessible piece of paper. Alternative devices to record frequency include a wrist counter, a pocket counter, or a hand-held counter. Such devices are widely available, for example, in sporting goods departments, to count golf strokes, or in variety stores, to count money spent while shopping. Lindsley (1968) describes a wrist-type golf counter; Mahoney (1974) describes hand-crafted leather jewelry which disguises counting devices; and Mattos (1968) describes a hand-held digital counter for recording frequencies of several target behaviors.

A second method of observation is the *discriminated operant*. Some behaviors do not occur at a "free" rate, but instead occur only in the presence of clearly specified antecedents. In such cases, a frequency count would be inappropriate because the occurrence of the behavior depends on the occurrence of the antecedent. Discriminated operants are reported as percentages: the number of response occurrences divided by the number of response opportunities. Browning and Stover (1971) use compliance as an example of a discriminated operant. Compliance can be recorded as a percentage: the number of obediences divided by the number of requests made.

The discriminated operant method might also be used in the following marital interaction. The husband complains that when he initiates conversations with his wife about the family budget, she typically changes the topic of conversation or busies herself with household chores. In this case, the denominator of the percentage would be the number of times per week that the husband initiates conversations about finances with his wife. The numerator would be the number of times in which she responds constructively and appropriately, by discussing finances. If he initiated this topic six times in one week, and she responded appropriately two times, the weekly quantified observation measure would be 33%.

A third observational measure is a *finite response* class, which is also expressed as a percentages. In this case, complex behaviors are subdivided into a number of response components. The percentage is the number of components successfully completed divided by the total possible number of components. An example here might be the assessment of social skills. To illustrate, a finite list might be constructed, for observational purposes, of socially skilled responses that occur during encounters with acquaintances. Some items on the list might be: greeting the acquaintance, making eye contact, smiling, using the acquaintance's name, and asking a question of the acquaintance. The client who is working on social skills might be asked to role play several scenes that portrayed meeting acquaintances. Each scene would be observed for the presence or absence of each socially skilled behavior comprising the finite list. A percentage could be determined by dividing the numerator, the number of responses which the client was observed to make, by the denominator, the total number of responses on the list. If several role-playing scenes are used, the percentages from each scene can be averaged to produce a single observational measure of the client's social skills for that therapy session.

Another example of the observational measure of the finite response class is teaching a young child or a retarded person to make his or her bed. All of the component behaviors necessary to make a bed successfully comprise the denominator. Such behaviors might include: spreading a bottom sheet on the mattress, tucking in the bottom sheet, spreading a top sheet, tucking in the bottom and sides of the top sheet, and so forth. The numerator would be the number of component behaviors successfully completed by the client on that particular bed-making attempt.

A fourth observational method is a *latency* measure. Here, the time between a particular event or stimulus and the onset of a particular behavior is recorded. An example would be the number of minutes that it takes a child to get into bed, after being instructed to do so by his or her parent. Another example would be the number of minutes late that an adolescent is for his midnight curfew. Another example would be the number of minutes that it takes a class to become quiet after the bell has rung.

A fifth observational measure is *duration,* which is especially useful for continuous behaviors. Duration, best measured by a stopwatch, is frequently expressed as a percentage. The numerator is the amount of time that the target behavior occurred, and the denominator is the total amount of observation time. It can readily be seen that duration would provide a more sensitive observational measure than would a frequency count for such continuous behaviors as compulsive hand washing, time spent studying, time spent on outings away from home, a child's tantrums, or daytime sleeping.

Duration is generally measured by a stopwatch and a clock. In this example, a mother decides to observe her child's tantrums from 4:00 to 7:00 p.m. (indicated by the clock). At the onset of the first tantrum, the mother begins the stopwatch. When the first tantrum ceases, she stops the stopwatch. The stopwatch is permitted to accumulate additional time during the second and third tantrums, and so on. The final observational measure is a percentage: the total time the child spent in tantrums (say, 45 minutes) divided by the total observational time (in this example, 3 hours), or 25%.

As an alternative to a regular stopwatch, several commercially available wristwatches have a stopwatch accessory called an *elapsed time indicator.* Katz (1973) describes a single watchband on which is mounted both a wrist counter and a watch with an elapsed time indicator. Mahoney and Thoresen (1974) describe a switch that may be utilized with an electric clock. Setting the switch in the "on" position allows the electric clock to run, whereas setting the switch in the "off" position stops the clock. Thus, the ordinary electric clock can be used as a stopwatch. Kubany, Weiss, and Sloggett (1971) report a Good Behavior Clock, an electric timer which the teacher permitted to run only when the target child was quiet and in his seat. Elapsed time earned rewards for the child and for his classmates.

The main problem with the use of the duration measure to observe continuous behaviors is that it requires near-continuous attention from the observer in order to accumulate duration properly. The seventh method, the spot-checking method, described below, provides a more convenient way to observe continuous behaviors.

A sixth observational measure, which is also used for continuous or high-frequency behaviors, is *time sampling.* In time sampling, a longer unit of time, for example, 10 minutes, is subdivided into smaller units of time, for example, 40, 15-second intervals. Within each short interval, the occurrence of one or more preselected target behaviors is recorded, usually in an all-or-none fashion. Duration of the target behavior or its multiple occurrences within the interval are not recorded. Time sampling is usually recorded as a percentage: the number of intervals in which the target behavior occurs, divided by the total number of observation intervals.

In time sampling, data sheets are routinely divided into a number of intervals with coded symbols within each interval, the coded symbols representing the preselected target behaviors. Since this time-sampling method requires a great deal of concentration on the part of the observers, generally observers who are not normally part of the observational setting are trained in the use of the observation system. They then mark the coded symbols as the behaviors occur in the observational setting. To facilitate observation, the elapse of the short intervals can be indicated to the observers by means of an auditory signal received through headphones (Horan, 1974; Quilitch, 1972). Thus, the observer can concentrate on the behaviors being observed, rather than on a stopwatch. Also, two or more observers can record behaviors during these synchronized intervals, which is useful for continuous or high-frequency behaviors.

Two representative time-sampling codes are those devised by Patterson for home observation, and by O'Leary for classroom observation. The Patterson code (Patterson, Ray, Shaw, & Cobb, 1969) consists of 29 behavioral categories which characterize family interactions. Each category is represented by a letter abbreviation, and each family member is identified with a number. The trained observer is provided with a clipboard and an interval-timing device. The observer focuses on each family member for a period of 5 minutes, broken into 30-second intervals. During each 30 seconds, the observer writes the symbols which represent the behaviors of the target person and of other family members interacting with the target person. Each family member is observed for two non-consecutive 5-minute intervals. The family is requested to remain in two adjoining rooms and not to watch television; the observations are made during the hour prior to dinner. This procedure is described by Patterson, Cobb, and Ray (1973), by Patterson and Reid (1970), and by Jones, Reid, and Patterson (1975). Jones et al. (1975) present an exemplary analysis of the reliability and validity of their code.

While the Patterson code was devised for observations in the home, O'Leary's code was designed for classroom observatons. O'Leary's code consists of 9 categories of disruptive child behavior (summarized by Romanczyk, Kent, Diament, & O'Leary, 1973) and 11 categories of teacher behavior. Precoded data sheets are provided to the trained observers so that they can circle the symbol for each child or teacher behavior that occurs within a 20-second interval. At the present time, the O'Leary code does not permit the recording of behavioral interactions between students and teacher.

The seventh and last observational method to be described here is *spot checking,* also known as *momentary time sampling.* This method is used for continuous or high-frequency behaviors. It is a more convenient method for this purpose than either duration or time sampling. In spot checking, at predesignated moments, usually cued by a timer, the observer notes whether or not the client is displaying the target behavior *at that instant.* Thus, spot checking does not require the observer's continuous attention, as does duration or time sampling. Spot checking is usually expressed as a percentage: the number of spot checks at which the target behavior was occurring divided by the total number of spot checks made.

The method, as first described by Kubany and Sloggett (1973), was for a teacher to set a timer on a predetermined variable-interval (VI) schedule, for example, either a 4-, 8-, or 16-minute VI schedule. Each time the timer rang, it was reset with the next number of minutes on the predetermined schedule. Each time the timer went off, the teacher glanced at the target child and noted at that instant if the child was displaying on-task behavior, passive behavior (not engaging in appropriate behavior, but not disrupting others), or disruptive behavior. Either an ordinary kitchen timer may be used or a portable Memo-Timer (Foxx & Martin, 1971). This procedure can obviously be adapted for other situations and other target behaviors, for example, a parent could set the timer and then check to see if the child at that instant is thumbsucking.

Naturally Occurring Behaviors

Some target behaviors may occur spontaneously in the clinical setting. These behaviors may thus be observed with no special arrangements needed to prompt their occurrence. Some examples follow.

In an inpatient setting, nursing aides used the fifth method (described above) and recorded the duration of time in which a patient engaged them in conversation about an inappropriate topic (Sanders, 1971). Also in an inpatient setting, two correlated measures were used over a 3 1/2-year period to record a patient's persistent hiccuping (Van Heuven & Smeets, 1981). The first measure was a duration measure, the total time that the patient spent hiccuping, while the second measure was a frequency measure, the number of hiccup attacks per day.

In an outpatient setting, during the first 10 minutes of each therapy session, the therapist can ask, "How are things going?" and make only reflective comments while using the frequency method to count the number of client complaints, negative self-statements, delusional references, or similar behaviors (Hayes, 1978). Appropriate problem responses can also be counted by the therapist throughout the therapy session; for example, patient crying episodes, tics, stutters, or incoherent statements. In one of our cases (R.N.), the number of words spoken per session was used as a frequency count measure for an elective mute teenager. To take such frequency counts, the therapist can keep a counting device in his or her pocket, or simply make slash marks on the same paper used to take session notes. As another example, during the therapy sessions themselves, an observer behind a one-way mirror counted the number of words per 30-second interval used by a depressed man with a very slow speaking rate (Robinson & Lewinsohn, 1973). To further illustrate, Leonard (1981) described the case of a 28-year-old male whose complaint, among others, was that people made derogatory comments about his feminine appearance. The therapist recorded the number of effeminate behaviors occurring at the beginning of each therapy session, using the checklist for sex-related motor behavior developed by Barlow et al. (1979). As another example of observing naturally occurring behaviors in an outpatient setting, the number of marathon group members appearing for a follow-up session was used as a measure of group cohesion (Shadish, 1980). As a final example, in group therapy for depressed women, at the beginning of the first therapy session and at the end of the last therapy session, each woman was videotaped while she spoke individually about her current level of functioning (Rehm, Fuchs, Roth, Kornblith, & Romano, 1979). The tapes were subsequently scored on several measures related to depression.

Role-Play Situations

Some target behaviors may not occur in the clinic unless some special arrangements are made to prompt their occurrence. When the target behaviors involve interactions with another person, a convenient way to prompt their occurrence is through role-playing. The client and a significant other may be instructed to interact with a staff member who is pretending to have another role; for example, an employer conducting a job interview or a prospective date. Of course, both the client and the staff member are aware of the role-played nature of the interactions.

Following are several illustrations where a client and a significant other were instructed to interact as if they were in their home setting. Maritally distressed couples were asked to discuss in the clinic topics that had been selected as idiosyncratically problematic for that couple (Bornstein et al. 1981; Jacobson, 1979). These role-played interactions occurred on a pre- and post-treatment basis. To produce a measure of change, the interactions were videotaped and coded using variations of the Marital Interaction Coding System (Hops, Wills, Patterson, & Weiss, 1971). To assess the nature of mother-child interactions, mothers and their children were instructed to play in the clinic playroom; various aspects of mother and child behavior were coded during these interactions (Eyberg & Johnson, 1974; Roberts, McMahon, Forehand, & Humphreys, 1978). To assess difficulties in mother-adolescent dyads, such dyads were requested to discuss, in the clinic, topics that typically generated conflict between them (Bright & Robin, 1981; Robin, Kent, O'Leary, Foster, & Prinz, 1977). Audiotapes of these conversations were subsequently scored for various types of verbal behavior.

As an alternative to a client's role-playing in the clinic with a significant other, the client may be asked to role-play with a staff member who is assuming a role. As an example, a staff person role-played an employer and conducted job interviews with formerly hospitalized patients (Kelly, Laughlin, Claiborne, & Patterson, 1979). In another example, staff members role-played potential conflict situations with convicted offenders within a state correctional institution (Kirchner, Kennedy, & Draguns, 1979). Situations included: dealing with a critical boss, responding to insults from an acquaintance, and asking for proper car repairs from a service manager. The videotaped role plays were subsequently rated on various interpersonal measures. To further illustrate, to assess the conversational skills of some unmarried male clients who were enrolled in a marital health center's aftercare program, a female staff member engaged the clients in brief conversations; tapes of these conversations were scored to determine the clients' skills in asking questions, in paying compliments, and in self-disclosure (Kelly, Urey, & Patterson, 1980). As a final example, staff members role-played typical scenes from home or hospital life with a depressed 10-year-old inpatient boy; the child's body position, eye contact, speech quality, and affect were assessed during these role-played scenes (Frame, Matson, Sonis, Fialkov, & Kazdin, 1982).

Contrived Situations

In the above examples, role-playing was used to prompt the occurrence of target behaviors in the therapeutic settings. Sometimes, other stimuli must deliberately be presented so that the target behavior will occur.

One well-known type of contrived situation is the behavioral avoidance test. The phobic or fearful stimulus is deliberately presented to the client so that his or her fearful behavior can be measured. During the behavioral avoidance test, all three aspects of the triple-response system may be assessed; that is, the client's motoric approach or avoidance, the client's self-report of fear, and the client's physiological responses. To illustrate, the following materials were prepared to assess storm phobics: tape recordings of thunder, slides of storm clouds, and neon lights or electronic flashes to resemble lightning (Ost, 1978). The measures were the duration for which the client endured this simulated storm and her self-ratings of anxiety. In another example of a behavioral avoidance test, a university dental school attempted to reduce patients' dental fears. Fears were assessed by making progressively stronger requests of patients: to observe a dentist handling dental tools, to sit in a dental chair, to allow the dentist to look in the mouth, to telephone for an appointment for dental work (Wroblewski, Jacob, & Rehm, 1977). A behavioral avoidance test was used to assess a mannequin phobia in an adult retarded client. The phobia prevented shopping trips or trips to restaurants, both for fear of encountering mannequins. Three mannequins were obtained and the client's approach or avoidance responses were measured (Waranch, Iwata, Wohl, & Nidiffer, 1981).

Other contrived situations to prompt target behaviors in therapeutic settings have involved the use of special physical arrangements and/or instructions. To illustrate, to assess two patients with writer's cramp, the patient was seated in front of a writing surface, holding a pen in his dominant hand; the measure was the latency (the fourth method described above) until a hand cramp occurred (Sanavio, 1982). As another example, patients with obsessional slowness were asked to perform three tasks: a real-life task that ordinarily took the patient a long time to complete (e.g., shaving, combing hair), a standard cancellation task (cross out all fours on a page of digits), and a series of arithmetic problems. The time to completion (a duration measure) and subjective discomfort experienced were the measures (Rachman, 1974). As another example, a schizophrenic patient with a history of fire setting was deliberately given sheets of tissue and matches; the measure was the latency to set each sheet afire (Royer, Flynn, & Osadca, 1971). In a similar fashion, depressed patients were asked to count from one to ten; the time taken to complete the count has been shown to correlate with self-rated depression in some patients (Teasdale & Fennell, 1982).

In conclusion, useful measures of target behaviors can be obtained within the therapeutic setting by directly observing clients. Some measures are molar; that is, are ratings of adjustment or difficulties. Other measures are more molecular and involve the quantification of specific behaviors. At times, target behaviors may spontaneously occur in therapeutic settings. At other times, special arrangements, like role-playing or the introduction of particular stimuli, are needed to prompt the occurrence of the target behavior so that it may be quantified.

DIRECT OBSERVATION IN NATURAL ENVIRONMENTS

The observational procedures illustrated above took place in therapeutic settings. Similar observational procedures are also suitable for natural environments. Typical observers that can be employed in natural environments include the client's significant others, mechanical recording devices, and clinic staff members.

Molar Measures: Global Rating Scales

In the description provided above of molar measures of behavior, two rating scales were mentioned that are completed by significant others of the client, the Katz Adjustment Scales (Katz & Tyerly, cited in Hargreaves et al., 1977) and the Personal Adjustment and Role Skills Scale (Ellsworth, cited in Hargreaves et al., 1977). These scales were described in a previous section because the significant other typically completes the scale in the therapeutic setting.

Sometimes, significant others are asked to produce a global rating of a specific aspect of a client's behavior. The rating is presumably based on the significant other's direct observations of the client in his or her natural environment. To illustrate, two male and two female acquaintances of each client were asked to rate the client on several 1-100 point scales, assessing the client's dating frequency, social activity, and skill and anxiety in same- and opposite-sex social interactions (Himadi, Arkowitz, Hinton, & Perl, 1980). In a similar fashion, a significant other for each sexual offender treated by Maletzky (1980b) was asked to rate the client on two scales, ranging from 0 (*not at all*) to 4 (*very much*): (a) how much has the patient progressed, and (b) how well does the patient follow through with the treatment program? In a final example of a molar rating provided by a significant other, someone living with each headache patient was asked to rate the degree of change in the patient's headaches since he or she entered the treatment program. These ratings were made on a 100-mm visual analogue scale which was anchored by *unchanged or worse* and *markedly improved or cured*. The ratings made by significant others correlated significantly ($r = .44$) with patients' daily headache self-monitoring (Blanchard, Andrasik, Neff, Jurish, & O'Keefe, 1981).

Molecular Measures: Specific Behaviors

In addition to molar measures of behavior described above, direct observations of the client in the natural environment can also result in molecular measures. The various types of observational measures described above as appropriate to therapeutic settings are also suitable for natural environments; for example, frequency counts, duration, or time-sampling.

Recorded by Significant Others

Significant others may be requested to record the occurrences of specific target behaviors that the client might emit in the natural environment. To illustrate, parents kept frequency counts of the occurrence of their child's behavior problems (Christensen et al., 1980); in an effort to keep parents' data current, data were collected by telephone calls made on a randomly selected day each week. Another parent kept a duration measure of the time required for her child to complete household chores after she requested him to do so (Resick, Forehand, & McWhorter, 1976). The granddaughter of an 82-year-old heart patient monitored his compliance with a regimen consisting of exercise, diet, and medication; another family member also recorded these data on occasion so that interobserver agreement could be calculated (Dapcich-Miura & Hovell, 1979). The wife, parents, and attorney of an exhibitionistic client who also made obscene telephone calls were asked to report any suspicious or deviant behavior (Alford, Webster, & Sanders, 1980). In a final example of a molecular measure taken by a significant other in the natural environment, a mother made a spot check of her 10-year-old son's nocturnal thumbsucking four times each night. The father or older brother occasionally made simultaneous observations with the mother to provide reliability checks. The measure was expressed as a percentage: the number of checks in which the boy's thumb was in his mouth divided by the total number of checks (Lewis, Shilton, & Fuqua, 1981).

Recorded by Staff Members

The therapist or another staff member may occasionally observe the client in the natural environment. For example, agoraphobics were instructed to leave their homes and remain outside until feelings of tenseness or discomfort occurred; the therapist remained in the house and recorded the duration of time that the client spent outside (Emmelkamp, 1974). Relatedly, a therapist followed in his own car a patient with a fear of solo driving and recorded the distance that she drove before stopping due to anxiety (Wellman, 1978). One of us (R.N.) has taken an adult retarded client to a restaurant to record behaviors that embarrassed her parents: approaching strangers to make conversation and/or to touch them.

Contrived Situations

Even though target behaviors are generally much more likely to occur in the natural environment than in the clinic setting, sometimes it is more convenient for the observer if stimulus conditions are arranged so that the target behavior is likely to occur during time set aside for observation. Otherwise, an unduly long period of observation time might be needed to observe the target behavior as it spontaneously occurs. As an illustration of such a contrived situation, exhibitionists underwent a temptation test in which an attractive female confederate purposely placed herself in situations that had a high probability of eliciting exposing behavior (Maletzky, 1974). The method used here was the discriminated operant method. The numerator would be the number of times the client exposed himself. The denominator would be the number of temptation tests. Similarly, the frequency of a verbal tic was obtained during telephone calls made to the client by a confederate (Lamontagne, 1978). In a final example, an assessor accompanied a shoplifting client into two stores that she typically frequented and where stealing had previously occurred. The client agreed to put her hand on her purse whenever she had an urge to steal and for as long as the urge was present, making feasible a duration measure (Gauthier & Pellerin, 1982).

Obtaining Observations with Mechanical Assistance

Mechanical instruments may be used to help collect molecular data in the natural environment. A time-activated audio recording system can be used to monitor family or marital interactions in the home (Christensen, 1979). A device to measure the sleep duration of insomniacs at home is useful for particular clients. The device emits a tone at specified time intervals. If the client hears the tone, he or she is to reply "I'm awake," which is tape recorded (Kelley & Lichstein, 1980).

INDIRECT MEASURES

The measures described above rely on direct observations of the client's behavior. Indirect measures may also be useful, either as measures in their own right or as ancillary measures to validate more direct response measurement. There are at least two types of indirect measures of behavior, behavioral by-products and archival records.

Behavioral By-Products

Behavioral by-products are measures, not directly of the target behavior as it is occurring, but rather of by-products produced by the target behavior. For example, weight as a by-product of eating is a useful measure for problems of obesity (Mahoney, Moura, & Wade, 1973), vomiting (Cunningham & Linscheid, 1976), and anorexia nervosa (Monti, McCrady, & Barlow, 1977). Compliance with a medical regimen by an elderly heart patient was assessed by measuring behavioral by-products. The amount of orange juice remaining in a special calibrated container was measured to infer the amount of orange juice consumed by the patient. The number of pills remaining in a prescription bottle was determined to indicate the number of pills consumed by the patient (Dapcich-Miura & Hovell, 1979). Similarly, the size of bald spots was a behavioral by-product used to measure hair pulling in a trichotillomanic client (Bornstein & Rychtarik, 1978). Another behavioral by-product was the number of body sores which were self-inflicted by a self-injurious 10-year-old who scratched himself (Carr & McDowell, 1980). In one of our own cases (R.N.), one target behavior for a retarded adult client was nail biting. Instead of counting episodes of nail biting, the client's hands were photocopied each week. The length of her nails was measured on the photocopies. At times, special instrumentation may be required to measure behavioral by-products; for example, a carbon monoxide analyzer for measurement of smoking (Hughes, Frederiksen, & Frazier, 1978).

Archival Records

Another indirect measure of behavior is archival records, which are collected routinely for some behaviors. Generally, these archival records are used as ancillary measures. To illustrate, all municipal, county, and state police records were examined during treatment and follow-up to determine if any charges were filed or convictions obtained against sexual offender clients (Maletzky, 1980a or b). Relatedly, to validate the self-report of alcoholics, official records were examined to determine driving violations, arrests, and inpatient hospitalizations (Sobell & Sobell, 1978).

ISSUES IN OBSERVATIONAL MEASURES OF BEHAVIOR

Pros and Cons of Global Rating Scales

Global rating scales require a staff member or a significant other to rate the client on one or more scales, based on direct observations of the client's behavior. Among the benefits or positive attributes of global rating scales are the following. First, such scales are relatively easy to use. Once an appropriate scale has been selected and obtained (not always a simple task), and once staff members have been trained in the use of the scale, it is relatively straightforward to apply the scale to multiple clients. Second, because many of these global rating scales are standardized, they can be used as a common measure by different therapists, clinics, hospitals, or clinical research projects (Newman, 1979). This standardization benefits clinical research, because the results of different treatment approaches by different therapists and with different clients can be compared. Third, because these rating scales are so "broad-spectrum," they can be used with heterogeneous clients. Thus, they would provide suitable measures for program evaluation in hospitals, clinics, or educational settings that serve a wide variety of clients. Thus, "broadband" questions could be answered; for example, what percentage of the clients that are served by this clinic improve? Fourth, many of these rating scales have demonstrated reliability and validity. Before selecting a particular rating scale for ongoing use, the reliability and validity of that particular scale should be evaluated. The reliability of rating scales is most commonly determined by interrater reliability procedures (Newman, 1979). In other words, two or more raters independently apply the same rating scale to the same clients. Their ratings are then compared. Consistent ratings are taken to mean that the scale can be applied reliably. The validity of rating scales is most commonly determined by comparing clients' scores on other concurrent measures of psychiatric functioning (concurrent validity) or with other measures of psychopathology or adjustment (e.g., readmission to the hospital in the future, which would determine the predictive validity of the scale) (Newman, 1979). Fifth, global ratings are a way to provide a social validation for more molecular measures of change (Kazdin, 1976; Wolf, 1977). In other words, the merits of some molecular measures of change might be open to question. For example, someone might say, "Yes, I know that he can now leave conspicuous dirt on his hands for five minutes without washing, but is he *really* less anxious?" Or someone might say, "Yes, I know that his eye contact during conversations has increased, but do people now like him more?" These global ratings help to provide social validation that the client has changed in noticeable and meaningful ways.

While global ratings have several positive features, as noted above, there are also some disadvantages to their use. First, a relatively high degree of inference is frequently required to complete a rating. The rater must observe the client and, through inference, determine which rating is most appropriate for the client. Second, and relatedly, rating scales have been shown to be more susceptible to observer bias than are more molecular measures of behavior. In the following studies, molecular observational data were more robust and less subject to bias effects than were rating scales. Kent, O'Leary, Diament, and Dietz (1974) found that global ratings were biased by expectancies that children's disruptive behavior had either decreased or not changed from a baseline to a treatment phase. Shuller and McNamara (1976) found that global ratings were biased by giving different trait labels (hyperactive, aggressive, and normal) to the same videotaped child. Fogel and Nelson (in press) showed that questionnaire responses by teachers were biased by giving different special education labels (learning disabled, emotionally disturbed, educable mentally retarded, normal, or no label) to the same videotaped child. Cunningham and Tharpe (1981) demonstrated that global ratings were influenced by the amount and type of off-task behavior evidenced by peers sitting adjacent to the target child. Two variables, however, have been found to reduce bias effects on rating scales: using very specific items in the rating scale (Siegel, Dragovich, & Marholin, 1976), and explicit training in the use of the rating scale (Madle, Neisworth, & Kurtz, 1980). Third, another negative aspect of global ratings is that they may be relatively insensitive as a measure of client progress (Bloom & Fischer, 1982). Since, by definition, the measure is global, some smaller improvements may have occurred in the client's behavior that are yet to be detected by using a global rating scale. Fourth, the data needed to use rating scales and to interpret scores on these scales come from groups of subjects. Reliability, validity, and norms are all derived nomothetically; that is, from groups. The generalizability from nomothetic data to idiographic applications frequently cannot be determined (Bloom & Fischer, 1982; Nelson, 1983). For example, the interrater reliability for a particular rating scale may be reported in the research literature to be high, yet the raters who use the scale in their own clinic on a daily basis may show inconsistent ratings, especially on some "off" days.

In short, global rating scales have their advantages and disadvantages. Many disadvantages can be offset and the advantages retained if multiple measures are employed; that is, if other more molecular measures (such as self-monitoring or direct molecular observation) are also used in addition to rating scales.

Pros and Cons of Role-Playing and Contrived Measures

Role-playing is used primarily so that interpersonal behaviors (e.g., marital or familial interactions) may be directly observed in the clinical setting. Contrived situations are used to prompt the occurrence of the target behavior. The chief advantages of these measures are twofold. First, they are convenient, since they allow the target behavior to occur at a time and place readily accessible to the therapist. Second, they both permit direct observation of the client's motor behaviors. Measures can be obtained, therefore, that require little inference.

The central question that arises with both role-playing and contrived situations is their concurrent validity with behavior in the natural environment. In other words, the question is whether role-played behavior or behavior occurring under contrived conditions is really representative of naturally occurring behavior. This question with regard to role-playing has been subjected to many empirical tests over the last few years. The general answer to the question is that there are only moderate correlations between role-played and naturally occurring behavior (e.g., Bellack, Hersen, & Lamparski, 1979; Bellack, Hersen, & Turner, 1978, 1979).

To make the question of external validity of role-playing even more difficult to answer, it has repeatedly been shown that role-played performance is highly sensitive to situational variables. Relatively small variations in the role-played scenes or instructions can cause relatively large changes in subjects' performance. For example, Galassi and Galassi (1976) showed that role-played assertive behavior was altered if the stimulus presentation was taped or live, and if single or multiple responses were required of the subject.

Similarly, Higgins, Alonso, and Pendleton (1979) showed that subjects who knew that they were participating in role-playing of assertiveness acted differently from subjects who did not have this knowledge. Likewise, assertive responding in role-played situations was affected by situational parameters: whether a good friend or an acquaintance made the request, whether or not the requesting person expressed a reason, and whether or not other people heard the request (Hopkins, Krawitz, & Bellack, 1981). Since situational variables affect role-played responses, it is really not possible to determine generically the external validity of role-playing (Nelson, 1983).

Another difficulty with using either role-playing or contrived situations to yield measures of change is that the resultant responses must be scored or coded to produce quantified measures. Thus, these measures are subject to the same problems as are other observational measures, problems that are delineated below. More complete discussions of the advantages and disadvantages of role-played and contrived measures have been prepared by Haynes and Wilson (1979), McFall (1977), and Nay (1977).

Enhancing Compliance and Accuracy in Data Collection

Collecting accurate data requires effort. Therefore, some steps should be taken to increase the likelihood that staff members or significant others will comply with data-collection procedures and collect accurate data.

It is quite difficult to assess the actual accuracy of observational data because usually there is no criterion available against which to evaluate accuracy (Foster & Cone, 1980). Therefore, the most common way of evaluating the quality of observational data is by interobserver agreement. In other words, data are collected simultaneously and independently by two observers, and their records are then compared. A high degre of consistency is taken to mean that the observational data are of good quality.

There are three general categories of procedures to calculate interobserver agreement. The first category uses the following formula: agreements divided by agreements plus disagreements multiplied by 100. This category is used mainly for time-sampling and spot-checking methods. An agreement is scored if both observers scored a particular interval or a particular spot check in the same manner. For example, let us say that both a teacher and a teacher aide were simultaneously making spot checks to observe whether or not a student was attending to his work. Of a total of 10 spot checks, the teacher recorded that the boy was attending at five of the spot checks, whereas the teacher aide recorded that he was attending at six of the spot checks. They both agreed that he was not attending at four of the spot checks. The resultant interobserver agreement is nine agreements divided by nine agreements plus one disagreement multiplied by 100, or 90%.

A second category to calculate interobserver agreement is the computation of correlations. The data from one observer form one member of the pair needed to compute correlations, and the data from the second observer form the other member. This correlational procedure can be used with frequency counts, with latencies, and with the various percentage methods noted earlier. In this example, both parents agree to record the latency until their child goes to bed after being told to do so at 8:00 p.m. each evening. The mother records the following minutes over the seven evenings: 35, 16, 100, 18, 25, 70, and 15.

The father records the following minutes over the seven evenings: 30, 12, 90, 15, 25, 80, and 15. These seven pairs can be used to calculate a correlation coefficient that is indicative of interobserver agreement, a correlation of .98.

A third, and least preferred method to calculate interobserver agreement is to divide the smaller observation by the larger observation. Using the seven pairs of numbers listed above results in the following seven quotients: .86, .75, .90, .83, 1.00, .88, and 1.00. The average quotient is .89. This method is highly influenced by the magnitude of the numbers used to form the quotient. Hence, it is used only as a last resort when too few pairs of numbers are available to calculate a correlation coefficient.

Proper ways to calculate interobserver agreement have been hotly debated in the behavioral literature (e.g., Hartmann, 1977). Suffice it to say that observational measures are held in higher regard if high interobserver agreement is obtained than if either low or no agreement is obtained.

It has repeatedly been shown that observers produce higher interobserver agreement if they know that agreement is being assessed and calculated than if they are unaware of this (see review by Kent & Foster, 1977). High agreement can be maintained, however, by random agreement checks (Taplin & Reid, 1973). In collecting observational data, then, the primary observer should be aware that another observer will be collecting agreement data at random, unspecified times. As an example, a mother made a spot check of her 10-year-old son's nocturnal thumbsucking four times per night. Lewis et al. (1981) report that the father or older brother sometimes took agreement data. The ideal here would be if the mother were aware that random checks would occur, but did not know exactly when. To illustrate, if both parents went to check on the son's welfare before retiring for the night themselves, the father could use this opportunity to take occasional reliability checks of the son's thumbsucking.

Although there has been surprisingly little research done on methods to train observers, it makes sense that better data would be collected by trained observers than by untrained observers. Packages to train observers have been described by Wildman, Erickson, and Kent (1975) and by Dancer, Braukmann, Schumaker, Kirigin, Willner, and Wolf (1978).

Procedures to enhance compliance can be applied to data collectors. Such procedures include praise for accomplishments (i.e., regular data collection with high interobserver agreement), verbal and/or written commitments to collect data, and refundable monetary deposits (refundable contingent upon regular, accurate data collection) (Shelton & Levy, 1981).

Reactivity of Observations

Observees, that is, people under observation, sometimes act differently when they are being observed than when they are not being observed. This phenomenon, labeled *observee reactivity,* has been reviewed by Kent and Foster (1977) and by Kazdin (1979). Observee reactivity does not always occur, but the variables that control its occurrence have generally not been empirically determined. When observee reactivity does occur, it limits the external validity of observations. In other words, it is more difficult to generalize from observed to nonobserved occasions, or to assume that observed behavior is similar to nonobserved behavior.

The reactivity of observations was first noted when independent or outside observers were utilized; that is, when observers who were not typically in the observation setting were employed. It was hoped that the use of participant observers or of significant others would reduce or eliminate observee reactivity. In fact, the few studies performed on participant observation have shown that observee reactivity can occur, at least sometimes, even with participant observers who are usually part of the natural setting (e.g., Hay, Nelson, & Hay, 1977, 1980).

One possible solution to the reactivity of observations is to take surreptitious or unobtrusive observations of which the observee is unaware. The use of such unobtrusive measures, however, raises ethical concerns since the observee is not providing informed consent (Kazdin, 1979). Some unobtrusive measures, for example, archival records that are routinely kept, may raise fewer ethical concerns (Kazdin, 1979).

SECTION III
REALISTIC RESEARCH STRATEGIES

Chapter 7
The Essentials of Time-Series Methodology: Case Studies and Single-Case Experimentation

INTRODUCTION

The use of the terminology *time-series methodology* is new to this volume and subsumes several strategies previously described separately. Traditionally, there has been a fairly distinct line drawn between case-study analysis, where no functional analysis or "experiment" actually occurs, and single-case experimental designs. Similarly, the goals of evaluation and research have been seen as dissimilar.

All of these areas are subsumed under time-series methodology, because the essential characteristics of each are shared. Among these are repeated measurement and the necessity of specifying an intervention. Often a baseline of some sort is required. Central to all of these strategies is the need to establish a series of measures on the same individual over a period of time. Thus, the term *time-series methodology*. We recognize the potential confusion that may arise as a result of the well-known statistical procedure termed *time-series analysis*, which is but one way of analyzing such data.

It is our intention in this chapter to lay the groundwork for research and evaluation in applied settings. We view case studies and single-case experiments as lying on a continuum, and the present chapter is a foundation for both.

The goodness of fit between clinically competent decision making and time-series methodology is remarkable. Indeed, we will argue throughout the next several chapters that good clinical and educational practice seems often to involve an implicit type of time-series methodology in that the logic of the two enterprises is so similar. Professionals are often told to assess their clients systematically, to design specific treatments for their clients, and to determine whether or not the intervention has produced a beneficial effect. These common practical guidelines parallel very closely the essential elements of time-series methodology. In some sense it can be argued that good practitioners are already doing evaluations of potential scientific value with most clients they see, if they follow the guidelines required for good professional practice. For example, the practical requirement that the professional systematically assess the client is translated into the research requirement that systematic, repeated measurements be taken of the client's problems. The practical suggestion that specific treatments be designed for the client is modified in time-series methodology only by the requirement that treatments be specified in such a way as to be replicable by other investigators. Finally, the practical recommendation that clinicians determine if their treatments are actually benefiting the client is translated into the requirement that time-series researchers recognize the design strategies that they are using and use design elements appropriately so as to demonstrate and replicate significant effects.

REPEATED MEASUREMENT

The fundamental core of time-series methodology, as is denoted by this name, is repeated measurement of the individual client's behavior over time, whether these behaviors be thoughts, feelings, physiological reactions or motor movements. In contrast to group-comparison research designs, in which only a few measurements (usually pretreatment and posttreatment) are taken, time-series methodology relies on the frequent assessment of clients across time. From these frequent measurements, estimates can be drawn of the degree of variability in the behavior of interest, its level of occurrence, and apparent trends. These estimates are then used to determine the impact of treatment.

It is impossible to know who improved in treatment and by how much unless frequent measures are taken of the individuals involved. This point is often missed in discussions of the relative advantages and disadvantages of time-series versus group-comparison approaches. For example, in the typical group-comparison design in which a premeasure and postmeasure are taken for subjects in both experimental and control groups, measurement error and other extraneous variables are totally inseparable from the treatment effect for any given individual. Thus, if Patient A improves 25% on a particular behavioral measure from pre to post, it is impossible for us to know if this improvement is due to variability in the measurement procedure, to maturational or other extraneous factors, or to treatment itself.

Whether one is doing single-case research or group-comparison research, the full determination of who improved requires repeated measurement. In the clinical arena this is well known. Practical clinical guides often exhort clinicians to "examine regularly and consistently whether therapy is being helpful" (e.g., Zaro, Barach, Nedelmann, & Dreiblatt, 1977, p. 157). No practitioner would be satisfied with only one or two assessments of a client over a period of time that included both the determination of client needs and the design, implementation, and conclusion of treatment. Suppose, for example, your physician happened to take your blood pressure one day and it showed readings that would indicate high blood pressure. If, at that point, your physician failed even to take a second reading and proceeded to lay out a several-month course of treatment, you would certainly have every right to be concerned. If your physician further informed you that no additional assessments of your blood pressure would be taken until the treatment had run a several-month course, it is likely that the physician would have one fewer patient. Incredibly, this is the very tactic which is enshrined in common applied research designs using group-comparison methods. For the practitioner, this type of decision making is out of the question.

As has been discussed in chapters 3-6, the quality of measurement is the cornerstone of all applied work. This point is recognized in rules of good professional practice, but it has been hidden due to the way it has been discussed. For example, practitioners may be advised to try to develop a sensitivity to the client's communication. In fact, this is a call for sensitive measurement of functionally important units of behavior. Good clinicians are often said to be able to discern subtle indicants of client progress and to know how to elicit these cues. This is simply another way of saying that experienced clinicians often are good at informally measuring client behavior and arranging conditions in which these measures can be taken. Thus, an emphasis on securing repeated measures of real quality is nothing more than a more systematic way of doing what applied workers attempt to do anyway.

As was also noted in chapter 3, the measurement system must be standardized. That is, particular measures of applied interest must be taken under consistent conditions. Any condition which might reasonably be expected to influence the measure cannot be allowed to covary with treatment. Usually the best way to protect against this is to keep the measurement procedure as standard as is possible on such dimensions as the time of assessment, the assessor, implicit demands on the client, and the like.

While both of the preceding points regarding the need for quality measures and the need for standardization of measurement are clinically sensible, practitioners often react against this advice. Various reasons can be put forth for this, but probably the biggest is that it is sometimes difficult and time consuming to take systematic measures. At times, it seems far easier for a clinician seeing outpatients, for example, simply to "wing it" than it is to specify treatment goals and to develop measures which will determine whether or not the goals have been reached. In actuality, however, this ease may be illusory. Increasingly, as noted in chapter 2, clinicians and educators are being required by regulations, from both the private and public sector, to specify applied goals and measures of them. Systematic measurement under these conditions often protects the professional's interest at a cost in time and effort that is less than that required by the attempt to defend shortcuts. In addition to pressure from outside sources, the push for quality measurement seems required by the ethics of intervention in applied settings. Anyone who has worked in the applied arena is aware of how easy it is for clients to deceive themselves. Unfortunately, practitioners are also human; the capacity for self-deception is not significantly diminished by possession of an advanced degree. Without systematic measurement, it is quite easy for a practitioner to, in good conscience, claim that a client is improving when in fact this is not true.

Several additional guidelines can be offered for the practitioner conducting repeated measurement in the context of time-series methodology.

Start Your Measurement Early

The first phase of all applied interventions is a period of assessment. Sometimes this phase may be very short (for example, in crisis intervention), and other times the phase may be quite extended. It is important for the use of time-series evaluation in applied settings for the practitioner to begin systematic measurement almost immediately. That is, systematic measurement must begin before the assessment period ends. The reason for this is simple. In applied settings, where clients are paying for services, the practitioner does not have the luxury of obtaining extended measurement when that would delay significantly the onset of treatment. If systematic assessment waits until the end of the assessment period, it becomes impossible to obtain a baseline against which to evaluate the effects of intervention. Several time-series design elements do not require a baseline, but many powerful ones do, and there is no need to throw away the potential for their use due simply to delays in measurement.

Fortunately, the applied needs of the assessment phase can be supported by the use of early repeated measurement. In the beginning of this phase the practitioner is exploring various alternative formulations. Many measures exist which are appropriate for exploratory work and, if they are implemented with an eye towards their future use, they can be turned into systematic measures useful throughout the course of intervention. For example, suppose a client comes in who is extremely anxious. Interviewing during the first session may indicate several possible sources of this anxiety. Rather than wait until it is clear exactly what is producing the anxiety, the practitioner could develop several possible measures at the end of the first session. For example, the clinician might ask the client to record in a diary whenever he or she experiences a significant degree of anxiety (see chapter 4). Similarly, a card-sort procedure might rapidly be developed which contains several possible dimensions contributing to the discomfort (see chapter 5). As time goes on, and the case becomes clearer, some of these measures will probably turn out to be irrelevant, these can then be dropped. If, however, several measures have been taken, it is likely that at least some of them will continue to be valuable. There are other clinical advantages to this as well. Often the collection of systematic measures reveals that apparent problems are really not problems. Further, the nature of the difficulty and possible avenues of remediation can be revealed. Finally, by starting measurement early, it is possible to develop even more adequate measures that coincide more directly with the clinical needs of this situation. These points are often driven home when clinicians fail to develop measures until the last minute. After completing an evaluation based on more informal procedures, a clinician may begin systematic measurement and treatment simultaneously. The measurement process may quickly show that the treatment design was based on an inadequate picture of the situation. These kinds of false starts are destructive clinically and, of course, minimize any potential scientific value that the case may have.

If the practitioner has started measurement early, often the assessment phase will conclude with an adequate baseline already in hand. The possibility of obtaining an adequate baseline is also increased by the range of measures taken early in assessment.

Take as Many Measures as is Reasonable and Practical

If time allows it, good clinicians generally explore a client's problems broadly so as to ensure that the eventual treatment is sensitive to the range of client needs. Of course, the same is true in educational settings. To the extent that measurement systems can be designed that are cheap and unobtrusive, this advice translates into the recommendation that practitioners explore all reasonable avenues of measurement. Assessment can be thought of as a funnel (Nelson & Barlow, 1981). While the initial assessment is quite broad, the information gained from it increasingly tends to narrow the clinical focus. The early use of multiple measures is a critical parallel to this natural process. For example, suppose a client comes into outpatient therapy seeking treatment for an agitated depression. In the first session the clinician may notice that the client is engaging in a number of self-derogatory statements. Rather than wait for a complete picture to emerge, the clinician may begin to keep track of the number of unprompted self-derogatory statements. Later, as the session proceeds, it may become clear that the client is extremely anxious and shows certain social skills deficits. Immediately, some measures to begin to tap into these dimensions can be implemented. For example, the clinician may periodically ask the client how he or she feels on some scale from *no anxiety* to *an extreme amount of anxiety*. Similarly, the clinician may ask the client to fill out a self-report measure of social skills before leaving the session. Through this type of strategy a large number of measures will be generated from which only the most useful and appropriate will ultimately be retained. Obviously, it is possible to burden clients with unnecessary or excessive measurement procedures. In reality it seems to be more of a fear on the part of practitioners than a common, real-life problem. If the clinician is *convinced* that a given measure has potential value, clients will sense this and will experience it as supportive, not excessive.

Use Available Measures

While the quality of measurement is the cornerstone of time-series evaluation, this does not mean that all measures must be of high quality. Often, the clinician or educator does not know what to measure or exactly how to measure it. Similarly, it may be difficult or even impossible to obtain measures of extremely high quality. They may not have been developed yet, or they may not be presently practical for ongoing applied intervention. Rather than abandon the attempt to be systematic because measurement procedures cannot meet some arbitrarily high standard, it is better to take the measures that are possible while simultaneously recognizing their limitations. The power of case-study analyses and single-case experimental designs derive largely from an emphasis on replication. No single case is a "critical experiment." It is the overall picture that is important. Thus, while the contribution of a given case may be limited due to the deficiencies in measurement, it may contribute to an overall sequence of cases which are valuable and scientifically meaningful.

The willingness to accept good measures, if great ones are unavailable, has other benefits. In the process of attempting systematic evaluation, methods may be discovered that will allow more precise evaluation in the future. Similarly, the difficulty in securing adequate measures, while uncomfortable, may motivate a search for better measurement systems. The capacity for applied self-deception should be underlined again here. Abandoning systematic measurement because the most desirable measures are not available makes it possible for the practitioner to deny that treatment is based upon an inadequate assessment, however unintentional this denial might be. If we fail to take systematic measures and rely instead upon intuitive procedures, this does not increase the quality of the assessment. It may, however, increase our ability to forget that fact.

Take Measures Frequently

A final recommendation can be made about the process of repeated measurement. The more frequently measures are taken, the greater the degree of precision. If I take a given measure only very infrequently, it may take a long time for me to determine how much variability exists in the measure due to measurement error and extraneous variables. The number of design options that I can use to evaluate treatment will be limited and the ability for me to discern treatment impact will be correspondingly restricted.

That being said, it should also be noted that it is possible to take measures too frequently. This is particularly the case when the measures are intrusive or are susceptible to factors such as practice or fatigue. Also, many measures are so lengthy or difficult that frequent measurement is impossible. Usually the solution for these problems is to take some measures frequently (those which are easy to implement, fairly unobtrusive, and likely to be agreed to by the client) and supplement these with measures that can only be taken infrequently. Especially if the measures are related, the more frequent measurement will tend to validate and support the less frequent measurement. For example, a rehabilitation therapist working with a stroke victim in a rehabilitation center may not be able to do a comprehensive evaluation of the client's motor skills frequently. These comprehensive assessments often take several hours and it is not practical to take them too often. The clinician could, however, take a simple range of motion measure on a particular limb being worked on, which could then tend to validate at least part of the infrequently taken overall assessment, and vice versa.

As in all of the sections on repeated measurement above, there are additional measurement recommendations to be made. These are covered in chapters 3-6 and should be carefully considered.

SPECIFYING THE INTERVENTION

A critical component of any applied intervention is the degree to which "the techniques making up a particular . . . application are completely identified and described" (Baer, Wolf, & Risley, 1968, p. 95). Any deficiencies in this step will threaten an ability to replicate effects that are achieved. This fact is both a concern and a comfort. It is a concern because replication is the mechanism through which the external validity or general usefulness of time-series methodology is demonstrated. It is a comfort because there is a natural self-correcting effect for errors in specifying the independent variable. Some authors (e.g., Thomas, 1978) have shown an excessive concern for the difficulty posed by this requirement. It is impossible to specify every aspect of an intervention. The practitioner specifying the apparently important variables in treatment may indeed miss many that are critical, such as the personality of the therapist, the arrangement of furniture in the therapy room, the behavior of other students in a classroom, or any of a thousand other possible variables. We do not replicate investigations to see if the exact same conditions will produce the same effects. Obviously, if the conditions are exactly the same, in a determined world the effects will be the same. What we attempt to do when we replicate is to see if the *description* of the conditions is adequate to produce the same effects. Suppose, for example, I claim that self-disclosure on the part of the therapist produces particular reactions in clients under particular conditions. In fact, it may be that only self-disclosure in the context of a particular relationship between a therapist and client will have such an effect. If this is true, then the findings will be inconsistent. Sometimes the effect will replicate and sometimes it will not. What this will show is that the original statement, namely that self-disclosure is the critical variable, needs to be modified. Thus, the specification of the independent variable is not a matter of black and white, nor is it a matter of an endless listing of all conditions present in the intervention. Rather, it is a rule which summarizes the apparently critical components of the intervention which professionals can use as a guide. If the rule is inadequate, this will become clear in future attempts to replicate. Importantly, this is also the way that the adequacy of the rule can be determined. Quite simply, there is no way to know if an intervention has been adequately specified until the long process of replication has occurred.

This discussion points out one reason why case-study analysis or single-case experimental designs need not be limited to "behavioral" interventions. Even abstract or complex intervention principles can be tested if they are sufficiently specified so as to tap into the components of intervention that determine their effectiveness. Conversely, no single-case strategies will save a practitioner's favorite principles if, in fact, these principles are so vague as to be uninterpretable by others or so unimportant that no consistent effects produced by them can be seen. Under these two conditions, however, no one would want to support claims for the importance or efficacy of such principles.

ESTABLISHING THE DEGREE OF VARIABILITY OF BEHAVIOR IN THE CLIENT

An estimate of the degree of variability in the client's behavior (as repeatedly measured) is critical in time-series methodology. It is in the context of this estimate that determinations are made about the level and trend in the behavior and predictions are drawn about the future course of the behavior. This variability (also termed *intrasubject variability*) is the background against which we evaluate all the facts about treatment.

Sources of Variability

It is useful to think of variability as a combination of three sources of control. First, variability can be produced by the measurement procedures.

This source of variability might be thought of as artificial, in that the behavior itself is not varying—it only appears that way. For example, suppose we measure the degree of anxiety felt by a client in response to certain standardized imagined scenes. Suppose further that during one presentation the scenes are read in a very strained voice by the therapist and in another they are read in a very calm tone, and that anxiety ratings track these differences. Unless the practitioner is aware of the variability in measurement, the practitioner may erroneously conclude that the client is sometimes more anxious than other times. In fact, the client is more anxious under some specific and uncontrolled conditions than others.

A second source of variability is that which is due to extraneous variables. Extraneous variables are impactful variables other than the treatment itself. For example, a client may be fatigued one day and energetic the next. Behavior may track these differences. Unlike the previous example, this is a real difference in the behavior, but it is due to a variable (i.e., fatigue) that is not central to the issue at hand. It is impossible to avoid the presence of extraneous variables. Behavior does not occur in a vacuum. Certain kinds of effects, however, are problematic. One type occurs when extraneous variables are not continuously present or not varying systematically. This may lead to an enormous amount of variability in the data as particular variables occur and fail to occur. Essentially you might think of this as a kind of static which will disguise the effects of other variables, much as radio static can make it impossible to hear the actual program. Another kind of problem occurs when some extraneous variable happens to coincide with treatment. This could either be a true coincidence, such as might occur when some strong extraneous variable presented itself simultaneously with the introduction of treatment, or it could be related to treatment in some more systematic way, such as the confounding of social demands from the therapist with the reportedly critical treatment variables. The latter case is really a matter of specifying the nature of intervention into functionally important units as discussed in the previous section. The former case is the driving force for the overall logic of single-case experimental designs. All of these designs are sensitive to the possibility of such coincidental arrangements and attempt to deal with them by making the probability of repeated coincidences unlikely. A third kind of effect of extraneous variables is also possible, but it is less problematic. Sometimes behavior may be changing in a systematic way, due to a continuously present or systematically varying extraneous variable. For example, maturational effects produce a gradual increase in the physical abilities of children. These changes may produce systematic behavioral variation, but if the trends are clear, it is possible to separate these effects from those which are due specifically to treatment.

The third source of variability in the measures taken is the treatment itself. It is this impact that the practitioner wishes to assess. It is important to underline, however, that an ability to see the impact of treatment is dependent upon an ability to separate it from variability due to measurement error and extraneous variables. Essentially, when we have weeded out alternative sources of variability, we are left with the treatment effects.

There is a more philosophical reason for the need to establish the degree of intrasubject variability. The goal of applied intervention is to improve client functioning. Improvement is essentially a matter of intrasubject variation. The only way to estimate intrasubject variability is to take repeated measurements within an individual across time and to assess the variability directly. Differences between people are not the same as differences within people. Reliance on infrequent measurement of many individuals is not a shortcut to a determination of individual improvement. This logical fact is fairly easy to demonstrate. For example, the top of Figure 7.1 shows a situation in which intrasubject variability is extremely low and yet intersubject variability is extremely high. The bottom of Figure 7.1 shows that intrasubject variability can be high when intersubject variability is low.

When variability within subject is assessed with many subjects, both types of variability are known. The reverse is not true. Regardless of how many subjects are assessed infrequently, variability within a client cannot be known. Regardless, then, of the methodology chosen, the estimation of intrasubject variability is an essential component of applied research.

What is Stability?

Estimating the degree of intraindividual variability occurs along two continua. One is based solely on a physical dimension. If we have a series of events measured along some physical dimension, we can speak of the degree of variability in that set of data. For example, data could be said to be highly variable when the average deviation from the mean is high and relatively stable when the average deviations are low. The concept of variability as a purely physical property, however, has its limitations. Estimates of variability only have meaning because of the use to which these estimates will be put. For example, physicists would be appalled at the degree of variability (in purely physical terms) shown in the behavior of animals in operant chambers. These same operant researchers, in turn, would be appalled at the degree of physical variability tolerated in applied research. For the purposes of measuring the speed of light, physicists cannot tolerate even the most infinitesimal degree of physical variability. For measuring the effect of a particular schedule of reinforcement, much more physical variability may be tolerable. Thus, the second continuum used to evaluate variability is its utility. This is not a purely physical quality. Rather, it is an evaluation of that physical quality relative to a methodological task.

What then is an acceptably small degree of variability? The logic of time-

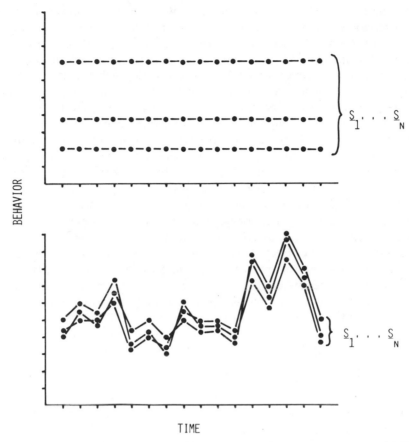

Figure 7.1. An example of the independence of intrasubject and intersubject variability. In the top figure, intersubject variability is high and intrasubject variability is low. In the bottom figure, the reverse is true. Intrasubject variability, therefore, cannot be estimated by knowledge of intersubject variability.

series methodology and of applied work generally suggests that data must be stable in the following sense: The influences of measurement error and extraneous variables are sufficiently limited or sufficiently clear so as to enable a clear statement about the effects of the independent variable at its expected strength. In other words, the degree of variability seen cannot eliminate an ability to see expected effects.

The word *stability* has been used by others to mean that the data have no trend and that the degree of physical variability is small. This definition of stability is problematic for several reasons. For one, as we have just argued, variability criteria based solely on absolute physical dimensions are arbitrary. Another difficulty is that this use of the term confuses the issue of trend with the issue of variability around that trend. Behavior which shows no trend is *stationary*. It can be shown, however, that nonstationary data can still be *stable* in the sense defined above, when a particular set of conditions has led to a systematically changing behavioral pattern. This trend may be due to the consistent effect of some extraneous variable, such as maturation. As long as the extraneous variable does not covary systematically with treatment, it may be quite possible to discern treatment effects from the background effects causing the steady trend. Practitioners very often do not see stationarity in their clients' behavior. Clients may be gradually deteriorating or gradually improving, and intervention may still be required.

There is another, more logically based problem with the overemphasis on stationarity as opposed to stability. There is the misperception that stationary data are necessarily less influenced by extraneous variables and therefore only stationary data are adequate. For example, Johnston and Pennypacker (1981) have claimed that any trend in the data eliminates an ability to separate treatment effects from the effect of extraneous variables. Suppose, however, two extraneous variables were present which canceled each other out? Say that a clinician was interested in the social functioning of a child. Maturational effects might be improving the ability of the child to interact socially while the deterioration produced by social isolation might be working in the opposite direction. It is conceivable that these two variables could cancel each other out so evenly as to produce stationarity in the behavior of interest. Any intervention with this child, however, would be an intervention in the context of the effects of social isolation and maturation. If the effect of isolation were not present, and the resulting trend was a gradual improvement, then treatment would be seen in the context of the effect of maturation as an extraneous variable. Both have equal scientific status. Thus, stationarity does not relieve us from the duty to identify important extraneous variables, nor is it necessary for time-series evaluation to achieve stationarity in measurement.

Throughout the sections that follow, we will use the word *stable* in the sense defined above. This need not be a problem since most of the recommendations made by others, which use a more limited sense of the term, are equally valid when the word has been defined more functionally. With the exception of the definition, the rules remain intact.

Let us return then to the question of how much variability can be tolerated in the data or, stated differently, how we can know when our measures are stable. Since we cannot rely purely on physical components of variability to answer this question, the answer can only be stated conditionally. To put it bluntly, it all depends. It depends on our knowledge of the treatment and its effects; on our knowledge of the particular behavior, disorder, or deficiency, and its known course or its response to treatment; on our knowledge of a particular measure that we have used of the behavior and how sensitive it is to actual changes that occur; and on our knowledge of the effects of a whole constellation of external conditions and extraneous variables that surround our attempt to evaluate the effects of this particular intervention on this particular client in his or her particular situation. Fortunately, practitioners are in the best position to make this judgment. One crucial variable is how large a change we expect to find. For example, consider the data shown in Figure 7.2. If the expected outcome is that shown in the top part of the figure, then the first phase is far too variable for our purposes. If, conversely, we anticipate the effects in the bottom part of Figure 7.2, then these same data are perfectly adequate. If we anticipate a sudden effect of treatment, we can tolerate a greater degree of variability than if the effects would be gradual. If the intervention is likely to influence the degree of variability in the data, in addition to its impact on the level or trend in the data, then a greater degree of variability in the preceding phase could be accepted. Indeed, sometimes variability is itself the target dimension.

When variability is itself the target, again the degree of change must be considered. Examine the data in Figure 7.3. The baseline is inadequate if the effects we hope for are those on the top right. If we hope to see the effects shown on the bottom, the baseline is probably sufficiently stable.

Sometimes none of these questions concerning the likely effects of an intervention can be answered with certainty. In such a situation, the lower the degree of variability in a physical sense the better. The clinician or educator, however, may not have the luxury of tinkering with the situation until extremely stable data are produced. In these situations, the experienced practitioner will simply rely on his or her clinical judgment. The experienced single-subject researcher must rely on his or her best guess. Both applied interventions and thorough evaluation contain many elements within them that are more artistic than they are scientific.

Aids for Determining Stability

A number of different attempts have been made to guide the researcher by the specification of particular stability criteria. We have already discussed problems with using purely arbitrarily set levels of physical variability. Criteria can be specified, however, which function more as judgmental aides than as arbitrary cutoffs. One is to look at the anticipated effects and to see if there is likely to be much overlap between one phase and another. If there is little or no overlap, then the phase is more likely to be said to be stable. Similarly, a practitioner could specify that several days must go by with no deviation above X percent of the mean for those days. This is really a stationarity criteria, but the percentage of deviation could be said to reflect the requirements of the situation. More formal statistical means are also available. One particularly interesting statistic is called a *C-statistic*. It is useful

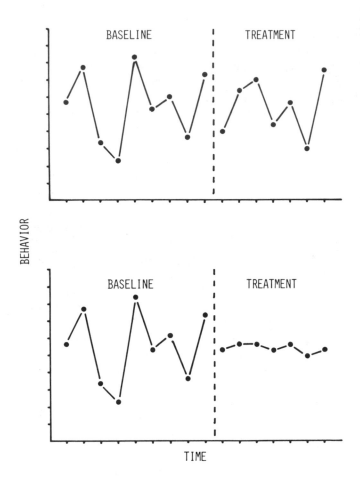

Figure 7.2. An example of how data with the same amount of variability can be nonstable or stable, depending upon the expected results. If the results at the top are expected, the data are nonstable. If the results at the bottom are expected, the data are stable.

primarily where estimates of stationarity are needed. Essentially it is a statistical procedure which compares the overall variability in the data set to the variability which occurs from one data point to the next (Killeen, 1979; Tryon, 1982). This allows statements to be made about the presence or absence of trends in the data (since trends produce greater overall variability but not point-to-point variability). Another method is simply to graph the data which have been collected and to graph the anticipated results in the next phase. If the expected effects can be clearly seen, then the data may

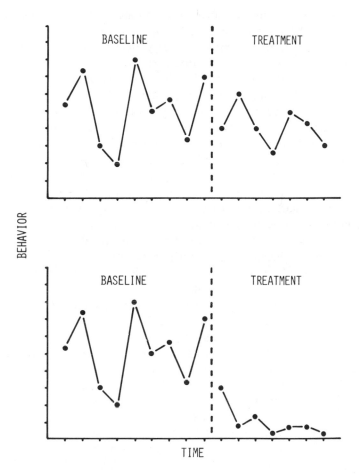

Figure 7.3. Another example of how the adequacy of baseline is a relative concept. In this case, the unusual target for treatment is a reduction in variability. If the results at the top are expected, the stability shown in baseline is inadequate. If the results at the bottom are expected, the baseline probably is adequate.

be sufficiently stable. Of course, our estimates can be wrong and we may have proceeded with a set of data that are not sufficiently stable. This is parallel to the situation in which a clinician moves ahead, thinking that the clinical needs are clear, and then finds that additional factors were operating which were not obvious.

There is a final way to think about predictions of effects. Instead of thinking of anticipated effects as a prediction of what *will* happen, think of them as a statement of what the minimum change is that would be satisfying. In other words, at what point would you feel as though some meaningful changes had occurred? This does not seem to require so much a prediction of future events as a statement of current values. If your data are too variable to see the minimum change you would hope for, then they are not stable.

A related question to the one of stability is that of the number of data points needed to estimate stability. Any estimate of variability which is based on fewer than three data points cannot distinguish trend and variability around that trend. The more data points that are collected beyond three data points the better. There is no maximum. Estimates that are based on a few data points are defensible under several conditions. First, if the degree of variability seen is extremely low (for example, if three data points in a row were on or near the same exact score), then the need for a large sample might be mitigated. Similarly, if the effects expected are very large, then the number of data points in the estimates of stability might be correspondingly reduced. When there is a disorder that we know a great deal about and where there is a known course, then a small sample (or even one measurement) may suffice to indicate the level and trend in the behavior. If the measure is of extremely high quality, then fewer data points would be needed. Thus, there is no absolute answer to the number of data points needed. Indeed, as in clinical practice itself, there are few absolute answers throughout all of time-series methodology. Just as in any applied situation, when you are in the dark you need more information to be sure where you are. To the extent that you are *not* in the dark about the effects that are anticipated, or the quality of the measure, or the course of the behavior, to that extent you can cut corners on the number of measurements required.

Ideally, estimates of stability are similarly based throughout the course of the study. For example, if the length of several phases is similar, then we have more confidence that effects shown in one phase are not fundamentally different than those in another. This is not a hard and fast rule, however. Sometimes we are forced to base our estimates of stability in some phases on far fewer data points than there are in others. As will be discussed in subsequent chapters, this can produce a distortion in our ability to discern actual effects. Often trade-offs need to be made. As elsewhere, the solution is to replicate the effects.

What to do When Data are not Stable

There are basically four things that a practitioner can do when faced with data that are unstable. The first strategy is probably the most important; namely, to analyze sources of variability. One of the main advantages of collecting systematic individual data is the way that this highlights potential sources of control over the phenomena of interest. If, for example, baseline data showed several periods in which the client was functioning at a level that would be acceptable after treatment, then the obvious thing to do is to attempt to discern what it is about those periods that is producing improved functioning. There are three methods to use when attempting to analyze sources of variability. First, possible effects due to measurement error should be explored. Any inconsistency in the measurement process could easily produce excessively variable data. The second strategy is to examine the data and attempt to identify major extraneous variables that might produce the instability. These can be then controlled or eliminated, more or less one at a time, until stability emerges. For example, Figure 7.4 shows the hypothetical record of a child in school. Notice that there are several distinct periods when this child's on-task behavior reaches dramatically low levels. On examination it may be determined that these days are associated with an inadequate breakfast, inadequate sleep, or some other extraneous condition. The practitioner at this point can either eliminate data points associated with particular extraneous conditions and continue to do so throughout the rest of treatment, or an effort could be made to eliminate or stabilize the conditions themselves. For example, the data could be put aside on the days in which the child has an inadequate breakfast or the child could be enrolled in a free breakfast program. A third strategy is to attempt to control all possible extraneous variables. This is essentially the strategy chosen by those who do laboratory research, and it is possible in some circumstances to create a parallel condition in applied settings. By controlling for all conceivable variables, stability may emerge, but the cost is often high for those in applied settings.

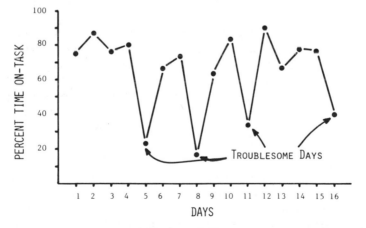

Figure 7.4. An example of how systematic, repeated measurement sets the occasion for analyzing extraneous sources of variability. The child's behavior is only problematic on days 5, 8, 11, and 16. If the source of control over the behavior on these days can be identified, treatment might be greatly aided.

A second major strategy when data are excessively variable, is to wait for a more stable pattern to emerge. Often stability is temporarily disturbed by extraneous factors. This is particularly likely in baseline when, for example, clients may expect sudden change, may be attempting to improve their situations, may be examining their difficulties more systematically than previously, and so on. Essentially, this advice can be summarized this way: if the picture is unclear, wait a while to see if clarity emerges. It may be better to wait than to plunge ahead unnecessarily. As the picture becomes clearer, it may be more obvious that treatment is not necessary or perhaps should be directed at a different target than thought previously.

A third major strategy is to examine the temporal unit of analysis. Measures are often collected in a particular temporal unit due to matters of convenience and not to clinically defensible considerations. For example, clients are often asked to self-record in hourly or daily blocks. The more meaningful unit of analysis may be much larger; say, weekly or monthly. If the actual phenomenon makes more sense in larger temporal units, then the data may be blocked or intraclient averaged. This is accomplished simply by calculating the mean for the data appearing during set blocks of time. The data shown in Figure 7.5 reveal what often occurs when data are blocked or intraclient averaged. The top graph shows the raw records for a daily measurement system while the bottom graph shows those same data ranged into blocks of 2-day periods. As you can see, the data are much more clear in the lower than the upper graph.

It is important that practitioners not deceive themselves by this process of blocking. The variability in the behavior itself is not changed by the way that we choose to examine our data. Put another way, blocking will often reduce the variability in data but it will never reduce the variability in behavior. Nevertheless, variability in behavior need not always be highlighted. This might be better understood by examining a similar measurement situation. Suppose an instructor wished to assess the level of performance of a student. An essay exam might be given in which several specific questions are asked. Each of these questions will be scored, but the total performance on the exam will consist of the sum of scores on the individual questions. This situation is much like that faced by a practitioner considering the use of intraclient blocking. Because we do not really care about the answers to individual questions, blocking is natural and sensible.

Consider a similar case in which a married couple has come in for treatment. The clinician may ask the couple to record the number of pleasing and displeasing things done by the partner. These records will undoubtedly be collected daily, not because daily records are the best picture of marital functioning, but because the clients will better be able to keep track of their records that way. Despite the claims of some purists, it is no more dangerous to collect these data into larger and more meaningful units than it is to score

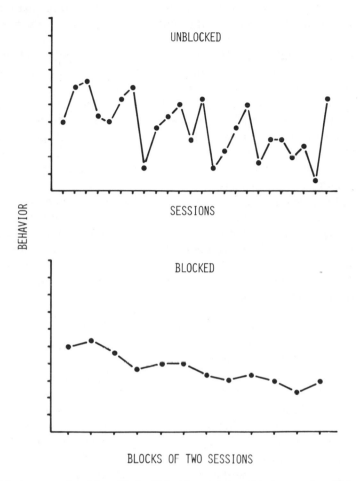

Figure 7.5. An example of the effect of blocking or intrasubject averaging. This should be done only when the temporal unit of analysis is too small relative to the phenomena being examined.

a test based on the overall performance rather than consider each question in isolation. Marital arguments, for example, are probably not best viewed on a daily basis. All couples probably have some bad days, but only disturbed couples may be likely to have many bad days. Thus, the average level of disturbance over several days or even longer may be a more meaningful unit of analysis.

There is a danger when blocking or intraclient averaging is used totally on a post hoc basis without applied justification. The danger is that the particular temporal unit chosen just happened to lead to stable data because of a chance coincidence between this unit and the variability observed. This possibility can be guarded against by replicating findings based on blocked data with additional clients. If these additional clients can be evaluated successfully using the same blocking interval, then the practitioner may be more confident that the interval chosen is appropriate. In questionable circumstances it is always best to maintain the smaller temporal unit at the data-collection phase so that the inherent variability in the behavior can be viewed in a more fine-grained way. The case of the instructor giving an essay examination can illustrate the point. While it may not be useful to consider the student's performance on a question-by-question basis for the purpose of determining the overall course grade, the examination itself must be scored question-by-question. The instructor might notice that the performance on a particular question is quite poor, while the performance on another question is quite good. This may be due to the quality of the lecture covering that material, to the quality of the background reading, or to other events which may give clues about how best to instruct the student. In a similar manner, blocked data may be best for viewing the overall impact of a program, but it is often advisable to retain and perhaps even to present the data collected in smaller temporal units in addition to the larger ones.

A final strategy that a practitioner can take when faced with excessively variable data is simply to proceed anyway. This advice should be followed only when there is some real need to proceed, such as immediate clinical demands. The advice to proceed anyway is not a call for "sloppy" clinical work or for inadequate evaluation. Rather, it is a recognition that sometimes corners must be cut. It is better to attempt an evaluation despite the corners being cut than to abandon all hope of an evaluation due to a failure to meet some arbitrary standard. Often, in the attempt to analyze a case despite the high variability in the data, something may be learned which may assist the clinician in future cases. At times the intervention may have such a powerful effect that an unexpectedly clear picture may emerge despite seemingly excessive variability. In any case, by collecting systematic data the practitioner is being responsible and will be able to account for his efforts to those who may require this information, including the client.

ACCOUNTABILITY: CONTINUITY OF CASE STUDIES AND SINGLE-CASE EXPERIMENTATION

The purposes of time-series methodology range from accountability to the production of new scientific knowledge. Essentially, up to this point the focus has been on measuring client progress and specifying treatment. These elements are central to any attempt to be acountable. The growing emphasis on accountability at all levels was described in chapter 2. If you look up *accountability* in the dictionary you will find that the word comes from a root word meaning *to count*. Giving an account implies reporting the facts: the count.

An *account* has other meanings too, such as *the statement of a relation*. In the same way, pure accountability in the applied environment sets the stage for more complex goals. As you move beyond accountability, not only can you say what you did, you can say something about what it means.

When you do this, you begin to go beyond the case-study level to the single-case experimental level. You move from mere description to an analysis. This is a continuum. For example, in chapter 12 we will explore how pure accountability efforts can be combined to support the development of scientific knowledge. Similarly, in chapters 8-11 we will explore ways that the professional can increase scientific output in the analysis of individual cases. For instance, one of the most natural clinical designs is the A/B (a period of baseline followed by a period of treatment). This design in itself is not usually an experimental design. Yet it can easily form the basis of experimental designs, with very little additional effort. Once we are accountable it is only a small step to the creation of scientific knowledge. It requires two additional steps: replication and the creative use of single-case design elements.

This entire book is built on accountability, yet you will not see a separate chapter on accountability, or even on case studies. This is because we feel that time-series methodology should be viewed as a whole. There is no clear dividing line between the uses to which it is put. The next three elements of time-series methodology, however, primarily apply when the goal goes beyond simple accountability.

REPLICATION

The logic of all time-series analysis requires replication of effects. In the applied setting this requirement is increased because of the methodological compromises often forced there. In addition, the external validity or generalizability of our knowledge depends on many systematic replications of effects across many clients and settings.

There are two areas where replication is important. One is replication within a single evaluation. Often this is replication within a subject, while at other times it involves replication across several subjects. Time-series research depends on the principle of unlikely successive coincidences. A single coincidence is rarely thought of as unlikely. As the number of coincidental effects increases, our confidence in the reality of the effects seen increases. Ways of replicating effects in this way will be discussed in chapters 8-10.

The second type of replication that is critical to the success of time-series methodology is replication across clients. When a particular effect has been seen in a particular individual and a rule or description has been derived to explain the important conditions, we usually have little confidence that this description is, in fact, adequate. As other practitioners use this description to guide their attempts to treat similar cases, the adequacy of the description will be tested. It is only in this process that errors in our ability to describe the actual functionally important variables will appear. This, of course, is the process of clinical replication (see chapters 2 and 12).

AN ATTITUDE OF INVESTIGATIVE PLAY

Undoubtedly the biggest difference between group-comparison research and time-series methodology is the overall approach encouraged. Time-series research should be a dynamic, interactive enterprise in which the design is always tentative, always ready to change as significant questions arise in the process. There should be *an attitude of investigative play*. The practitioner should have decided on a general strategy to follow in evaluating a particular applied question. This strategy, however, is not a detailed statement of such things as a length of phases, sequence of conditions, and the like. To follow such a course means that the practitioner cannot respond to the demands of the situation as they arise. This is simply not good practice. For example, clinical guides often advise clinicians to "be prepared to alter your style if dealing with a client in response to new information" and "be prepared to have many of your hypotheses disproved" (Zaro et al., 1977, p. 28). A practicing clinician cannot afford to go into a treatment session (much less a whole series of sessions) with an absolute commitment to follow a particular course of action. One of the common mistakes made by professionals attempting to do time-series evaluations is to attempt to use time-series tools as they have been taught to use group-comparison procedures. This virtually eliminates the applied environment as an appropriate place to do science. Clients' data often do not conform to the preset mold; they often do not confirm preset hypotheses. When unanticipated effects are seen, the clinician must be ready to abandon previous ideas and to let the client's data be the guide. In group-comparison research, however, the design is planned in detail beforehand and then simply carried out. Indeed, it is often recommended that there be no possibility of evaluating client progress during the course of the intervention itself. Probably the most extreme example of this is double-blind research, most often used to test out new drugs. While this may be appropriate for endeavors that are specifically research oriented, it is inappropriate for those attempting to combine scientific and applied goals.

One way of increasing the attitude of investigative play is to graph data frequently and in several different ways. Just as good clinicians often examine their case notes and assessment materials between client visits, the examination of client data allows discrimination of interesting patterns or leads which need to be followed. By adopting such an intellectual stance, unexpected or even undesirable data patterns can often be clues on how best to treat this client and how to interpret particular behavioral phenomena.

The dictionary defines *play* as *having fun while taking part in a game.* A *game* is defined as *a plan or scheme or a contest with certain rules.* An *investigation* is defined as *a careful search or a detailed examination.* Thus, an attitude of investigative play means approaching the task in such a way that the practitioner finds some intrinsic enjoyment or value in the game of investigation; that is, the careful search for an answer to the client's problems. As in all games, there are certain set rules and expected outcomes. The practitioner "wins" the game by learning how to be of help. The kind of play involved in applied exploration is not something which diminishes the seriousness of the task. To the contrary, it supports the practitioner in following leads that are presented and in maintaining a commitment to excellence.

If, in the process of exploration, a particular phenomenon emerges or a particular anomaly occurs, a good practitioner (and a good scientist) will pursue it and use it. Suppose, for example, a client drops out of therapy for a time. Instead of being seen as something which has interfered with an ongoing evaluation, it might be used as a period during which the maintenance of treatment gains can be assessed. Similarly, if a client shows some real difficulty in the course of treatment, it could be viewed as an opportunity to learn more about the phenomenon rather than as an interference with some preset notion about how the case would proceed.

KNOWLEDGE OF DESIGN ELEMENTS

It is our claim that the logic of applied decision making and that of single-case design is very close, and often identical. If so, the practitioner with a knowledge of design elements will usually be able to fit design tools to practical needs. It is to these tools that we now turn.

Chapter 8
Within-Series Elements

INTRODUCTION

In this chapter we will begin to identify the logical structure of time-series methodology. For the practitioner this is important for two reasons. First, the logical structure of clinical and educational practice can be related to specific ways of designing applied evaluations. Practitioners already use most of the logical elements of this methodology. They often just do not know that they do. Second, at times it is beneficial to use these design elements and logical maneuvers deliberately, to improve clinical decision making. Recall that the purpose of this book is to relate time-series methodology to the on-line applied environment. Thus, we are not interested here in requirements that would improve the output of knowledge if they interfere in any significant way with service goals. Such conflicts are possible, but it is also true that the self-discipline and rigor produced by an effort to be systematic have many clinical benefits.

In this chapter, and those that follow, we will emphasize the logic of single-case design elements, not the form of completed designs. The creative use of time-series methodology in the exploration of applied phenomena may be enhanced by emphasizing design elements or tools rather than numerous completed designs. For example, designs such as an A/B/A or B/C/B have often been described as separate designs even though their logical structures are identical. In fact, all single-case designs are built from a small set of building blocks. There are potentially as many specific single-case designs as there are designs for brick buildings, and the core elements of each are as simple. In these chapters we will attempt to distill all time-series work into a few core elements, organized by the nature of their estimates of stability and the logic of their data comparisons. In this way, we hope that we can underline the similarity between the logical units of time-series methodology and the common strategies reflected in applied decision making. Just as a practitioner may need to switch strategies as work progresses and be ready to draw upon different logical maneuvers in order to determine what is actually going on with the client, in the same way the practitioner conducting time-series evaluations must be aware of the range of logical design alternatives available at any moment.

There are three fundamentally different kinds of single-case experimental strategies. By far the best known are the *within-series elements*. (The other two types will be described in the next two chapters.) In within-series elements, changes seen within a series of data points across time, in a single measure or set of measures, are analyzed. Each data point is seen in the context of those that immediately precede and follow it; that is, the series of interest is built in real time. Groups of data points are collected together according to the consistency of the specifiable conditions under which they were collected. Each consistent condition thus constitutes a *phase* in the series. Like the individual points themselves, phases are evaluated in the context of phases that precede and follow them, that is, in real time.

There are two groups of elements based on this strategy: simple phase changes and complex phase changes. In this chapter we will describe the logic of each of these types and delineate the specific elements which utilize this logic. We will start by describing the simple phase change, and then we will point out how it may actually be used in a clinical case. Following this, we will describe the complex phase-change elements.

THE SIMPLE PHASE-CHANGE ELEMENT

The cornerstone of many of the popular time-series strategies is the *simple phase change*. This element consists of (a) establishment of the stability, level, and trend within the series of data points across time taken under similar conditions, (b) a change in the conditions impinging upon the client while maintaining consistency of measurement procedures, and (c) examination of concomitant changes in the stability, level, or trend in a series of data points taken under the new conditions. This strategy is a within-series strategy in that systematic changes seen within a series of data points across time are examined.

A common example of a simple phase change occurs when data are repeatedly collected during a baseline period and continue to be collected during a subsequent treatment period. By tradition, this is termed an *A/B* design (*A* always refers to baseline, *B* to the first identified treatment or treatment element, *C* to the second identified treatment or element, etc.). If the stability, level, or trend shown in A changes when B is implemented, B may be responsible and our confidence that treatment produces an effect increases. How much it increases is a function of many factors. We will discuss these in more detail later.

What we are doing in a simple phase change is using the first phase (in combination with everything we know from other sources) to determine the nature of the phenomena of interest and to project into the future. Against that background, we then examine the patterns shown in the second phase. If there are major changes in the expected patterns, then we suspect that an effect has occurred.

Even a single simple phase change can accomplish many desirable goals. First, it allows the practitioner to be accountable. This is important on several grounds, from the demands of third-party payers to professional and ethical requirements. The cornerstone of accountability is being able to give an accurate report (an account) of what the clinician did and what progress the client made. A simple phase change will do just that.

Second, even this simple design element will begin to allow statements to be made about the likelihood that improvement is due to treatment. Suppose, for example, that an A/B design seems to show a clear treatment effect. If we know that this treatment has been shown to be effective in controlled experimental work with other clients, our confidence increases that the apparent treatment effect with this client is real. (This issue will be discussed in chapter 12). At times the level of knowledge obtained may approach that of an experimental analysis. Suppose, for example, that we know, based on other information, that a particular behavior is resistant to change and rarely, if ever, gets better spontaneously. Suppose, further, that a long and steady baseline is present. Dramatic effects following treatment implementation may yield knowledge that approaches a level of confidence appropriate to controlled experiments. An example might be the social withdrawal of a chronic schizophrenic. This behavior rarely changes spontaneously. Sudden major and permanent improvement following treatment might be quite convincing indeed.

In most cases, however, a single simple phase change will need to be bolstered by replication, either within the same client or across clients. Time-series methodology is built upon replication as the source of ultimate confidence in the knowledge produced. The effect can be replicated in many different ways, as we will see in this and subsequent chapters. One common way is to repeat the phase change, but now in reverse order. To continue with our example of an A/B design, this strategy would yield an A/B/A design. If the changes seen in the second phase now change yet again with the third phase, then our confidence in the effect increases incrementally. This simple phase-change process could be repeated indefinitely. Each sequence would form a specific design; for example, A/B/A/B or B/A/B. Two different treatments can be compared in exactly the same manner; for example, B/C/B or C/B/C/B. All of these specific forms are identical logically, although the certainty of knowledge which is possible differs, and the specific kinds of questions one is asking vary.

The evaluation of effects in all within-series designs is based on an examination of patterns of changes in the stability, level, and trend shown in the data. These changes can be of different magnitudes, latencies, and consistency. Figure 8.1 presents several examples of changes in these various characteristics representing improvement. The changes which are most dramatic are those which are (a) of very large magnitude, (b) closely related in time to the phase change, and (c) consistent throughout the phase.

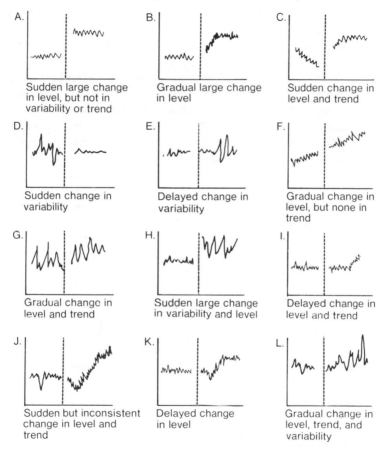

Figure 8.1. Some examples of changes in variability, level, and trend in a simple phase change.

To get a sense of how these factors can combine, consider each of the 12 graphs in Figure 8.1. Graph A shows a change in level only. Because the change is sudden, steady, and large (relative to background variability), this effect seems fairly strong. Graph B shows a similar effect, except that the change is more gradual. Here the effect is less clear because of the gradualness of change. The magnitude is large, however, and the effect is fairly believable. In Graph C the same gradual effect occurs, but this time there is also a change in trend since the baseline was proceeding in an opposite direction. The net effect is to increase the believability of the result. Graph D shows only a sudden change in variability. This effect is not particularly believable because many extraneous factors can cause sudden decrease in variability alone. It would probably need to be replicated before much confidence in the effect would be possible. Graph E shows a delayed change in variability, which is even weaker. Few conclusions can be drawn from these data. Graph F is also quite flawed. Since the trend is exactly the same, few would suggest that this could show an effect without proper controls and replication. Graph G is similar to Graph B except the variability is greater. The increased variability weakens the conclusion. Graph H is similar to Graph A, except variability is greater. This weakens it, but the effect is still so large that the effect seems fairly clear. All the other graphs are relatively weak, primarily because of inconsistent or delayed effects. Through replication, of course, all of these could be shown to be real effects, but the determination that an effect probably did occur usually cannot rest solely on data such as these.

When we have determined that a change has probably occurred, this does not mean that we can conclude that our single phase change was responsible for it. The most critical difficulty is that we never know what would have happened had we not changed phases as we did. Were this not true, we would be able, with a single pre- and a single post-data point, to determine whether or not a particular intervention had worked with a client. What we are relying on is the plausibility of the overall picture that is shown.

There are many factors that could threaten the internal validity of changes that are seen. Internal validity refers to the extent to which the effects seen are due to the stated treatment (Campbell & Stanley, 1966; Cook & Campbell, 1979). Table 8.1 summarizes some of these threats.

In phase-change designs with individual clients, there are three basic issues: Did something in the client's world happen to coincide with the phase change? Is the assessment device consistently applied? Are there effects due to time or repeated assessment that began to occur near the phase change? (There are other threats to internal validity, but most of these apply primarily to group-comparison approaches.)

Single-case experimental designs are organized around efforts to limit the plausibility of these possibilities. The major strategy is to replicate the effects, while allowing other factors (e.g., number of assessments, timing of the phase change) to vary. In the design options that follow, we will periodically point out how this goal is accomplished.

Table 8.1. Major Alternative Explanations for Effects Seen in a Time Series

1. Coincidental events	Events in the client's world happened to coincide with changes in conditions so as to mimic treatment effects.
2. Time alone	Processes such as maturation, learning, or other gradual effects associated with time alone mimic treatment effects.
3. Assessment	Repeated assessment produces changes that mimic treatment effects.
4. Instrumentation shift	Changes in the measuring instrument itself mimic treatment effects.
5. Regression to the mean	The tendency for scores to show a central tendency mimics treatment effects.

USING THE SIMPLE PHASE CHANGE

The simple phase change provides an example of the manner in which time-series methodology fits the logic of good applied practice. In this section we will describe the sequence of events faced by a practitioner in a simple case. We will attempt to show how the simple phase change can be used to develop knowledge in a single case. The reader should be cautioned, however, that this may be a bit artificial. When a practitioner begins to work with a client (whether it is an individual, group, agency, etc.), it is rare that the applied question will be obvious from the start. The practitioner must approach the case as a process of investigation and exploration. Thus, all of the design tools ideally should be available for use as specific questions arise. The practitioner should not have decided, for example, that a simple phase change is the only design tool that will be used with a particular client.

Establishing the First Phase (e.g., Baseline)

Typically, a therapeutic relationship begins with a period of assessment. This assessment serves two functions. It helps reveal the nature of the client's situation, and it allows the practitioner to determine whether or not the problem is deteriorating, improving, or is stationary. If the guidelines described in chapter 7 have been followed, when this period ends a baseline will be in hand. If not, it is usually wise to wait until a baseline is established, since it is only then that we can be confident that intervention is warranted. Sometimes, however, we must proceed immediately to intervention before a thorough assessment is completed. This is particularly likely when the client is in crisis or the problems are particularly severe and obviously in need of intervention. The guidelines offered here apply as well to the situations in which intervention has proceeded before a baseline has been obtained as they do to the more usual case when a thorough assessment period is possible.

Several recommendations have been offered as to the adequacy of obtained baselines (or first phases in general). One consideration is the length of the phase. This issue applies to the length of any phase in a within-series strategy. The purpose of repeated assessment is to enable the establishment of estimates of stability, level, and trend within the individual. In the absence of other information, it is impossible to separate these three aspects of data until a minimum of three measurement points have been collected. Even then, more are highly desirable. If one data point is collected, no estimates of trend will be possible and the data will by definition be stable. When two data points have been collected, an estimate of level is available but variability and trend will be indistinguishable. It is only when three data points have been collected that stability, level, and trend can begin to be separated. The suggestion that phases include at least three data points is not an absolute one, but it is also not an artificial one. In the normal applied situation, it is difficult to know whether or not the picture that the client is presenting at any given point in time is representative or if the problem is rapidly improving or deteriorating. These questions are as important to good practice as they are to time-series methodology. The suggestion that at least three data points be collected can be translated into the more usual clinical advice to know where you are and where you are going with a particular client. Sometimes, however, various considerations modify the recommendation for several data points in a particular phase. There may be other information available on the problem being measured. For example, the disorder may have a known history or course, such as the social withdrawal of a chronic schizophrenic. In this situation it may not be as important to assess the stability of the behavior because, on other grounds, we expect that it will be fairly stable. At other times, we may have an archival baseline available, such as records from previous therapists, or reports from individuals in the client's environment about past adjustment. In these situations, even a single data point may confirm what is already suspected or known, based on other sources of information, and the treatment may then proceed. At first glance this might seem to be lethal to the single-case experimental analysis of such a case. In fact it is not, because the practitioner has many other design tools available to make up for short phases. For example, the simple phase change might be repeated later within the same client, or the effects might be replicated with others. All of this is not to say that phases consisting of many data points are not desirable. They are, and often the applied situation will naturally produce long phases. For example, if the case is particularly complex or difficult but treatment need not begin immediately, an extended assessment period is common. Certainly in the treatment phase it is not unusual for phases to be lengthy. Particularly if assessment data are collected frequently the situation in which very few data points are available can often be avoided.

A second consideration is the stability of baseline. All of the earlier comments (chapter 7) apply here. There is one possible addition to those recommendations. If it is difficult to obtain stability within a phase, it may be possible to use a design which is more robust in this regard. An example might be the alternating-treatments design which will be discussed later in the chapter on between-series strategies (chapter 9).

A final consideration is the level and the trend shown in the first phase. The level must be such that the following phase makes sense. For example, if the client is in baseline, the level of problem behavior must be such that a subsequent phase is warranted. The trend shown in the first phase should also be one which justifies a phase change. When the following phase is expected to produce increases in the data, then either a declining or a flat trend is highly desirable. If decreases are expected, then rising or flat trends are beneficial. These are not rigid rules and they are not arbitrary. In terms of logic, they mimic good clinical and educational practice. If a client were to come in who had a rapidly improving situation before treatment had even begun, then most practitioners would recommend putting off intervention until the need for it becomes clear. If the client is improving, but is improving slowly, and treatment is expected to accelerate that improvement noticeably, then intervention might be justifiable. In the same way, a slowly improving baseline is adequate for the purposes of single-case experimental analysis if the treatment is expected to be relatively powerful. The suggestion that stationary or deteriorating baselines are most desirable before intervention is not an artificial appeal for unfortunate client circumstances just so that effects can be seen. Rather, it is a recognition that the need for, and beneficial effect of, treatment will be most easily demonstrated in such circumstances. These are exactly the same kinds of considerations which lead utilization review boards or third-party payers to look first for evidence of a clear difficulty that is not improving on its own.

Once again, it is important to emphasize that all of these considerations actually apply to any phase in a within-series strategy including the first in a simple phase change. The logic of the simple phase change (and complex phase changes) is the same whether one is going from a condition that one has arbitrarily termed *baseline* to one termed treatment, or whether one is going from one treatment to another. After all, a baseline period is really a type of treatment. It is the treatment that the world happens to be applying to the client at that particular time.

Implementing the Second Phase (e.g., Treatment)

Once the first phase (for example, the baseline phase) has been established, then it is possible to move to a second phase. We are assuming that baseline has now been collected and treatment is ready to begin. Before treatment begins, the practitioner may wish to consider whether there are variables that need to be controlled before intervention. For example, the practitioner may suspect that the client will be highly susceptible to social influences and that almost any kind of well-justified intervention will work due to a placebo or social-demand effect. This may be important in helping us understand the characteristics of the client; for example, in determining whether or not the problem seen is itself due to the client's suggestibility. It may also be important in that it will prevent us from using a more difficult, costly, or risky intervention with the client if that is not necessary. Under these conditions the practitioner may wish to begin not with treatment, but with a variant of it that will eliminate these possible alternative explanations for any effects that might be seen. This parallels good clinical and educational decision making and may even fit in with legal requirements, such as the requirement that the least restrictive alternative treatment available be implemented first. If, when the less restrictive intervention is put in place, a strong effect is seen, then there will be no need to go on to a more difficult treatment. Conversely, if the intervention produces no effect at all, then an alternative explanation for any subsequent effects will have been eliminated, the case may be better understood, and the logic of time-series methodology will allow an intervention phase to begin. This will be discussed in more detail shortly.

Another consideration is that treatment ideally should begin at full force if possible. When one is going from one phase to another, it is desirable for the difference between the two phases to be maximal. Gradual shifts between phases can minimize apparent differences between them. This has been pointed to as a major deficit in single-case experimental designs (Thomas, 1978), but actually this strategy protects well against false positives in this situation. Gradual implementation will tend to make strong and obvious changes in performance less likely. Delayed effects can be validated, however, by replication. Further, if effects are seen immediately, gradual implementation will not invalidate those effects. Gradual implementation can cause false negatives but not false positives.

Acting on Results

When the second phase is implemented, there are logically only three possible outcomes: no apparent improvement, deterioration, or improvement.

No Improvement

If there is no change, there are at least three reasonable courses of action. One is to wait for a period of time to see if treatment will have a delayed effect. The second alternative is to try a totally different type of treatment. A third course is to add or subtract elements from the treatment package. The logic of these last two recommendations should be discussed. If a phase produces no change in the data, then it is reasonable to assume that the behavior of interest has not been altered by the treatment condition. To the extent that this can be assumed, there is no impediment to moving on to another treatment or adding an element to treatment which might be more effective. Essentially this makes the first treatment phase part of baseline. Consider the data shown in Figure 8.2, for example. Since B added nothing, the B phase can be considered (with caution) part of the A phase. There is a tendency to think of baseline as a vacuum, but it is not. Baseline is just a name for all the things in the world of the client that surround the behavior as it is. Some of these things are relevant to the behavior, but most probably are not. An ineffective B phase can be thought of as just yet another variable that is not related, and thus the client is still in baseline. (This is written, "A=B".)

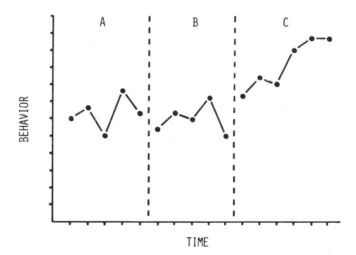

Figure 8.2. A hypothetical example of an A=B/C design. This is normally considered functionally equivalent to a simple phase change, because B is thought to be part of the first phase.

Of course, it is possible that an ineffective treatment produced a changed state of affairs which now interacts in some way with subsequent treatment.

For example, suppose I teach a retarded child to imitate, but I find that it does not improve his social skills. Suppose I then mainstream the child into a normal classroom. I may find an increase in social skills. It may be possible that the ability to imitate was critical to the impact of the normal classroom. Imitation may be necessary but not sufficient. As phases are added, the plausibility of equivalence between baseline and ineffective treatment phases is jeopardized further. An $A=B=C=E=F/G/F/G$ design, where nothing works until G, seems inherently weak.

The solution to these problems is to replicate systematically any effects ultimately found. For example, in the design above the practitioner would want to test treatment G with a similar client (an $A/G/A/G$ design might be a good way to do this). Similarly, the effects of mainstreaming without prior training in imitation might be attempted with other retarded children.

These three possible paths (wait, try a new treatment, change the old treatment) are the same courses of action which seem advisable on applied grounds. Sometimes treatment will work if the practitioner sticks with it, but if still no change is apparent a responsible professional will try something else. In the applied situation, if the first treatment produced no effect, the practitioner would not normally turn to a major reassessment of the client (e.g., baseline) although this is certainly one option. In the same way, the logic of single-case experimental design does not require a return to baseline following an ineffective treatment phase, but it certainly would permit it.

Deterioration

If the treatment produces deterioration, then the course both clinically and methodologically is clear. The treatment should be terminated. At this point, the behavior could once again improve (or at least stop its deterioration) or it could continue to deteriorate. If it does the former, then the clinician will have documented an iatrogenic effect of treatment which is itself often a significant contribution to clinical knowledge. Iatrogenic effects have long been documented in applied literature (such as that of psychotherapy, Bergin & Strupp, 1972). Unfortunately, relatively little is known about our treatment failures. They tend to be hidden in the "error variance" of group-comparison studies. The present approach may allow the experimental documentation of negative findings, since it goes beyond affirming the null hypothesis to documenting actual deterioration. If individual client characteristics can be related to such deterioration, an important (if unpleasant) contribution to the applied literature can be made. Conversely, if the behavior continues to worsen when treatment is withdrawn, then it may be that the intervention was not responsible for the deterioration.

Improvement

The last possible effect during the second phase is that improvement could be seen. If so, there are several possibilities which present themselves. If the improvement is less than maximal, the practitioner may wish to add to the treatment or change the treatment to produce an even more rapid improvement. This parallels the suggestion made in going from the first phase to the second phase; namely, that if improvement exists which is substantially less than that desired, it is possible to move into a subsequent phase. A more likely course of action is to continue with the successful treatment. The clinician could choose to continue this until the successful conclusion of the case. If so, the end result would be an A/B or a "case-study" design. The A/B design may itself often make a contribution to the clinical literature. These cases can be accumulated into series of cases which can be analyzed as a clinical replication series, as discussed in chapter 12. This is an extremely useful option and is part of the core of empirical clinical practice. In addition, if the client has another similar problem or if the problem occurs in several different situations, or if another similar client is available, then it is possible to apply the same treatment to these other problems, situations, or clients, and secure an experimental design in this way. This is termed a *multiple baseline* and is discussed in chapter 10. The final course of action is also experimental: specifically, to withdraw the treatments or to implement a treatment placebo. If improvement then slows or actually reverses, one can conclude that a treatment effect is likely.

Withdrawal Strategies

The use of the withdrawal is a popular tool in single-case experimental designs. Since the use of this strategy was probably overemphasized in the early literature on single-case designs, several difficulties were highlighted which were sometimes mistakenly taken to be characteristic of a time-series approach more generally.

There are many potential problems with the withdrawal of an apparently effective treatment. On the face of it, it appears as though the purpose of withdrawal is to produce a deterioration in the client's performance. Cast in this way, it obviously raises ethical issues since the client is coming to treatment to get better. If the client were to see the withdrawal as arbitrary it would certainly raise issues in terms of client fees, possible morale problems, and possible neutralization of subsequent effects due to these difficulties. When other persons are involved in treatment (such as treatment staff or the client's family), withdrawal may lead to a lack of cooperation on the part of others.

But, there are many counterarguments. First, if the treatment is known to be effective, then withdrawal is not necessary. If it is not known to be effective with this client, then withdrawal may serve an important function. Good clinical practice requires the avoidance of the unnecessary use of ineffective treatment. Physicians recognize this issue in the common practice of drug holidays. *Drug holidays* are nothing more than scheduled periods of withdrawal in which the opportunity presents itself for the assessment of the continued need for treatment. It is not the purpose of a drug holiday to produce client deterioration. The main purpose is to avoid unnecessary treatment.

Second, few interventions are such that the treatment can be continued indefinitely. Eventually there will be a treatment withdrawal; the issue is a matter of timing. Withdrawal allows the assessment of maintenance of treatment effects. There is no requirement that withdrawal be done in order to produce deterioration.

Third, withdrawals are often created by clients naturally in the course of treatment. Clients may go on vacations, become ill, temporarily drop out of treatment, move away for a period of time, be unable to attend treatment sessions due to competing situations, and the like. These can be encompassed in ongoing applied evaluations by examining the data taken during or after these periods, but before reimplementation of active treatment. These "natural withdrawals" are not as methodologically desirable as withdrawals determined by the practitioner. They are more likely to reflect variables which might impact on the behavior of interest. For example, a client may drop out of treatment for reasons that also will produce deterioration in the target behavior. Therefore, practitioners should always specify the reasons for treatment withdrawal. If the withdrawals are occurring naturally, they should investigate the reasons for the withdrawal and stress considerable caution and need for replication when presenting the cases. Nevertheless, natural withdrawals can aid in an analysis of treatment effects.

Fourth, withdrawals need not be long and drawn out. Even a very short withdrawal, if it is accompanied by a clear change in the behavior seen, can increase the practitioner's confidence substantially in the treatment effects. The slight delay in treatment that withdrawal imposes should be weighed against the methodological and applied value.

Fifth, a good rationale will most often be helpful in minimizing problems of withdrawals. An absolutely honest rationale may often times work very well. A client may be told, for example, that treatment had been fairly successful so far, but it is not clear that there continues to be a need for it, so it seems wise to take a short breather and see where things go. At other times, a somewhat deceptive rationale may be used. The client may be told that this is a point in which normally there is a pause and that at times this may lead to further improvement. This inducement of positive expectancies should be handled with considerable care, as would placebo interventions of any sort.

Sixth, withdrawals are often naturally produced by the practitioner in the course of treatment itself by a change of problem focus. The practitioner may, after a period of some progress on a particular issue, turn to other issues of importance. During this time, assessment of these other issues may be occurring that might constitute a kind of natural baseline for the original problem. This is withdrawal in much the same way that the period of assessment when the client comes in for treatment is considered to be baseline, although active initial assessment is ongoing.

Finally, treatment withdrawals can often have a clear clinical benefit for clients. Three outcomes are likely during a withdrawal. The behavior may level off or continue to improve or it may deteriorate. If it levels off or continues to improve, then the client may be convinced that treatment has indeed been successful and that the problem is now more fully under control. Conversely, if the behavior deteriorates, the client may (if the withdrawal has been appropriately handled) see this as confirmation that treatment is necessary and is successful. An example from one of our own cases might underline this point. A woman came in complaining of difficulty in a competitive sport. She was lifting weights competitively and had done quite well until she failed to make a lift in front of a number of men who worked out with her at the gymnasium. Following this failure, she began to lose confidence in her ability to lift the weights and her pounds-lifted declined. Treatment consisted of a cognitive preparation strategy combined with an anxiety management procedure. The total weights began to increase. (See Figure 8.3). After a period of time, the client was told to work out without using the cognitive preparation strategy. A rationale was given that now that progress had been achieved, the cognitive preparation might be mere rote and might actually interfere with her ability to increase her lifts. Subsequent workouts went poorly and she was unable to lift the weights that she had been lifting previously. She came back to treatment now convinced that therapy was required and was important in her improvement. She became more involved with therapy at that point and improved even more. Thus, appropriately handled, withdrawals can be a kind of testing ground both for the clinician and for the client.

The withdrawal phase need not be thought of only as the return to baseline. As is pointed out above, it may include placebo treatment elements. There are several ways in which this is accomplished other than those already mentioned. For example, the treatment may be applied to another behavior that may not actually be of interest to the analysis, but provides a handy comparison to evaluate the impact of intervention on the first problem on which measures are continuing. If the treatment consisted of some kind of contingent delivery of consequences or similar procedures, this phase might include the noncontingent delivery of the same consequences.

This advice might seem strange at first. Logically, if a particular phase change (e.g., A/B) has been effective, then replication would seem to require conducting the phase change in reverse order (B/A) rather than going

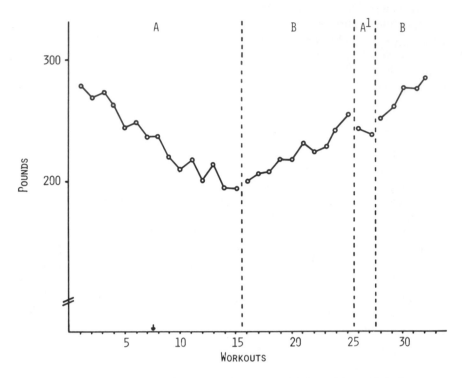

Figure 8.3. An example of the use of a short withdrawal in a clinical case.

to a variant of baseline. In fact, however, it is impossible to "go back to baseline" in a literal sense. The second baseline phase in an A/B/A, for example, is baseline in the context of an immediately preceding A/B sequence. Suppose B consisted of attention from a teacher for a given behavior. The return to baseline is now a type of extinction phase—it is not literally a return to the first phase. (For this reason, there are many possible explanations if the behavior during the second baseline phase differs from the first.) The second baseline must be functionally similar to the first, but not necessarily identical in form. For example, a placebo condition and a baseline condition are thought to be equivalent by definition. Often the data do not bear this out, of course, but if they do, then functional equivalence is confirmed. Thus, it is acceptable to use a placebo condition in the second baseline phase. If the data for the two phases are similar, the placebo can serve the same functions as the purer type of withdrawal. The only risk is that the second baseline phase may be shown to differ from the first, in which case additional analysis would be needed to find out why.

The Third Phase

If the practitioner has returned to the first condition (following an improvement seen during the second), three outcomes are once again logically possible: no change, deterioration, or improvement. If the behavior deteriorates, then the practitioner would probably reimplement treatment until the case was successfully concluded (e.g., an A/B/A/B design). Other options are available, such as determining the effective components of treatment through an interaction design element. These more complex design options will be described below.

If the behavior shows continued improvement, then several options are available. If the improvement continues at a noticeably lower rate than that seen in the earlier phase, then the practitioner may wish to reimplement treatment. This parallels once again the recommendation made about the shift from the baseline phase. If the rate of improvement seen continues to be high, then the practitioner could wait to see if improvement will continue or will slow. Sometimes the behavior will soon stop improving or may even deteriorate, perhaps due to a short-lived carry-over effect from the second phase. If it does not, there seems to be little applied need to intervene further, because the problem is solved. The practitioner can allow the case to continue to a successful conclusion and store these data. This becomes an A/B design with what amounts to a follow-up phase (the second baseline phase). The sequence can be repeated with other clients as was suggested above with an A/B design. This will be discussed in detail in chapter 10. If the effect replicates, then the practitioner would be in the enviable position of having documented a treatment which is so strong that once delivered it continues to produce improvement even when withdrawn. This is not really as implausible as it may sound. Many treatments are thought to produce relatively permanent changes in the client's environment. For example, a client who has received therapy that established more successful relationships with other people will then live in a much different world than before. Another alternative in this situation would be to apply the same treatment to a different behavior in the same individual or the same behavior in different situations. Once again this would produce a multiple baseline (chapter 10).

If no change is seen when the second phase is withdrawn, that is, if the behavior neither deteriorates nor continues to improve, then all of the options just described remain open. Reimplementation, however, is particularly attractive. Much of the early work on single-case designs emphasized the need for a withdrawal phase and for a clear "reversal" of the behavioral patterns seen. This harks back to the time when these designs were used primarily in the context of animal operant work. In the animal laboratory there is an assumption that current behavior is primarily a function of immediately present environmental variables. Demonstrating this control consists of the ability repeatedly to return to the same level when the same external conditions are continuously in force. Thus, behavior is usually expected to be in one predictable and steady state in the presence of a specific variable and in another predictable and steady state in the presence of a second. Under these assumptions, if the behavior failed in the second return to baseline phase to look very much like the data in the first baseline phase (in terms of level, stability, and trend), then experimental control would not have been thought to be demonstrated.

Fortunately, it is only the history of single-case methodology that leads us to look for such reversals. It is not required by the logic of the designs themselves. The clinician or educator does not assume that the current level of behavior is primarily a function of the immediately present environmental variables. Usually the assumption is quite explicit that the current level of behavior is heavily influenced by historical variables or variables not under clinician or client control. Further, the practitioner is not seeking to establish a steady state of responding under a particular specifiable condition. Typically, the target is client improvement rather than achievement of some particular steady state. That is, the practitioner expects improvement in the presence of a particular treatment that would be greater than what might occur in its absence. The actual level of the behavior may be a less important issue. The data shown in Figure 8.4 may help make the point.

The top half of the figure shows an A/B/A/B sequence in which withdrawal produces less improvement but no deterioration in the behavior of interest. The bottom half of the figure shows the same data calculated as a difference score from the trend established in the previous phase (or the same phase in the case of the first phase). When plotted in terms of improvement (i.e., in terms of a change from the predicted pattern) a classical reversal emerges. What is reversing is not the level of the behavior but its trend. This does not mean that the bottom part is a better way to present the information. Both are perfectly adequate. The point is that the top figure, which appears to show a pattern which some might say does not demonstrate a clear effect, actually does show a clear effect when the data are thought of in terms of improvement rather than just absolute level.

COMPLEX PHASE-CHANGE ELEMENTS

The simple phase change is designed to answer relatively simple questions, such as whether or not a treatment works or whether or not one treatment works better than another. The logic of a phase change may be utilized in more complex ways. In these strategies the simple phase change is coordinated into a series of phase changes in which there is an overall integrative logic to the particular sequence of phases.

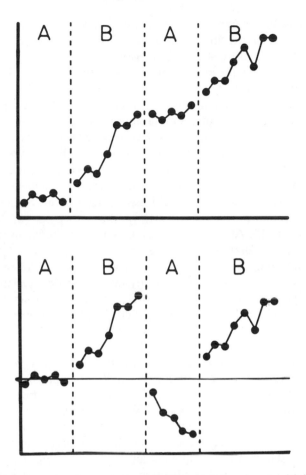

Figure 8.4. An example of two ways of looking at data when a withdrawal is not associated with a change in level. The bottom graph calculates the data seen in the top in terms of a change from the trend set in the previous phase. The line in the bottom graph represents the trends set by the previous phase. Both versions are equally correct, but the bottom one makes obvious the control exerted over improvement, if not level, by the intervention and its withdrawal. (From Hayes, S.C. Single case experimental designs and empirical clinical practice. *Journal of Consulting and Clinical Psychology,* 1981, *49,* 193-211.)

Interaction Element

The interaction element is a sequence of phase changes which is designed to assess the contributions of one or more treatment elements. For example, suppose a treatment approach consisted of two distinguishable elements (B and C). Suppose, further, that this package had been shown to be effective, perhaps utilizing an A/B+C/A design. The relative contributions of the elements could be determined by systematically adding or subtracting one of the elements from the other. A number of specific sequences are possible (e.g., B/B+C/B; C/B+C/C; B+C/C/B+C; B+C/B/B+C). Just as with a simple phase change, the number of times that the element is added or subtracted is indefinite.

The logic of an interaction element is identical to a simple phase change. In fact, it is really a form of a simple phase change, but the question is a bit more complex. It is asking what is the combined effect of treatment components compared to one alone. You can see that the logic is the same if you were to write the designation for an A/B/A design with the equally correct designation A/A+B/A. Typically, the interaction element is combined with elements which allow the practitioner to determine whether or not the treatment element or treatment package works at all (e.g., A/B/A/B/B+C/B). At times, however, this may be known already and the interaction element may occur by itself.

The attempt to discern which are the active components of treatment for a given client is important both clinically and scientifically. Single subject researchers have tended recently to ignore component analyses of treatment packages (Hayes, Rincover, & Solnick, 1980). Clearly, however, a client has a right to expect that treatment will consist of essential elements. If treatment packages are left in their combined form indefinitely, then a great deal of superstitious behavior on the part of practitioners is possible. For example, early medical treatments often consisted of complicated regimens, in which active elements were mixed with unnecessary ones. Persons might be advised to avoid night air, shut all windows, and drink potions, when in fact the critical issue was to keep mosquitoes out of the house (a side effect of closing the windows). Since intervention is not without risk (e.g., the potion might itself be dangerous), component analysis allows safer treatment. This example also points to another advantage in component analyses. At times, particular elements of treatment may have implications for our understanding of the needs of the individual client or of the nature of the disorder itself. By alternating these specific components it is possible to ascertain the nature of the disorder to a greater degree, which might then lead to greater understanding and treatment advances. If we know, for example, that only closing the windows has an effect, it might help us find the true cause of the disease (i.e., mosquitoes).

Interaction design elements usually emerge in two ways in practice. In the first instance a treatment package is working. The question arises whether the effect would continue if an element of the package were removed. Usually this shift should be made before an entirely satisfactory state has been achieved. Otherwise, removal of elements is assessing maintenance of effects, not their production. (There are other design elements which do just this, however. See Rusch & Kazdin, 1981).

For example, suppose an educator develops a new math program. It consists of a new self-paced curriculum, special quizzes to provide regular and detailed feedback, teacher praise and support, and peer tutoring. If math skills are now gained more rapidly, it may be worthwhile to remove an element (say, peer tutoring) and see if this improved rate of gain will continue. If it does not, reimplementation will allow a second assessment of the original package. This is an example of an A/B+C/B/B+C design (where B represents the whole package, except peer tutoring). If no change occurs when the element is withdrawn, others could be withdrawn until some decrement is noticed. The final element could then be reintroduced. The logic of this is the same as that described earlier regarding an A=B/C sequence. In the present example, suppose we view peer tutoring, quizzes, teacher praise, and a new curriculum as separate elements. Suppose we implement the package, show an effect, and then withdraw peer tutoring, and no change occurs. We might then withdraw teacher praise. Suppose no change occurs. Then we withdraw the quizzes, and progress slows, so we reimplement the quizzes. This complicated example of an interaction element could be written this way: A/B+C+D+E=B+C+D=B+C/B/B+C.

The second major way an interaction element naturally arises in practice is when a treatment approach has an effect that is not maximal. We may then decide to add an element which might increase the effect. If it does, a brief withdrawal (and reimplementation so as to end on the best package) will document the effect. To return to our earlier example, suppose our new, self-paced curriculum alone produces an effect, but it is not maximal. We add quizzes and get clear improvement. The quizzes are then withdrawn and reimplemented. The resulting design is an A/B/B+C/B/B+C. Note that the interaction element alone does not show the effect of treatment relative to baseline. For that, other elements need to be added. For example, the refined package could now be tested against baseline with others (e.g., in an A/B+C/A/B+C design). The present example also demonstrates how interaction elements will naturally tend to distill complex packages and build up simpler ones into maximally efficient units.

Combining Simple Phase Changes to Compare Two Different Treatments

A simple phase change which compares two different treatments only makes sense if it is known that at least one of the treatments is effective in the first place. If this is not known, a comparison of the two treatments may show only that one treatment works better than the other. Both may actually be ineffective or even harmful. We cannot know this for certain until comparisons are made to baseline performance. One way to accomplish treatment comparison goals and to document the effectiveness of treatment is to combine an A/B/A with an A/C/A. The resulting A/B/A/C/A sequence allows us to determine both whether or not B and C are effective and, though the comparison is not elegant, to generate some data on whether or not B is more effective than C. This last question is not answered in an elegant manner because noncontiguous data are being compared, namely the data in the B phase with those in the C phase, and order effects are also possible. Typically, this problem is handled by conducting a similar analysis with other subjects, but with a reversal of the sequencing of the two treatments. For example, another client may receive an A/C/A/B/A sequence.

In evaluating the data emerging from time-series evaluations, data which are closer together in time are more easily compared than those which are separated by larger temporal intervals. Many extraneous variables are more likely to occur given a longer temporal interval than a shorter one. For example, maturation or learning-related changes are not likely over short intervals but become more likely as time goes on. For this reason, comparisons of data which are contiguous are stronger than comparisons of those which are further apart in time. This influences strongly the logic of single-case experimental designs. An attempt is usually made to arrange conditions in such a way that the more critical comparisons are being made in contiguous conditions. As with most of the rules guiding single-case experimentation, this is a matter of degree and not an absolute issue. Several designs, including an A/B/A/C/A, violate aspects of this rule. When it is violated, attempts are typically made to control for some of the threats that it raises. Controlling for order effects in the A/B/A/C/A design is an example.

The considerations involved in conducting such a sequence mimic very closely those which were described earlier for the simple phase change. Clearly, however, many patterns of data outcome could undermine an original intention to conduct an A/B/A/C/A analysis. For example, if the data in the second baseline phase failed to show a slowing of improvement established in the first treatment, then it would make no sense to implement a second type of treatment any more than it would to reimplement the first treatment for a second time (e.g., in an A/B/A/B sequence). The point here is that these designs tend to emerge naturally in the course of treatment. It is a mistake to decide beforehand to follow a particular sequence of phases rather than to allow the information being collected from the client to guide the emerging design in a dynamic and interactive way.

Sometimes a simple phase change for a given treatment will then justify a more direct treatment comparison. For example, an A/B/A might be followed by a B/C/B/C sequence, resulting in an A/B/A/B/C/B/C (to control for order effects, an A/C/A/C/B/C/B would also be needed with additional clients). In this case, the first four phases established the effectiveness of one treatment. This can then be used as a kind of benchmark to evaluate a second treatment (the last four phases).

In these types of designs, order effects can be very troublesome. In an A/B/A/C/A, for instance, the second treatment may not work as well as the first, precisely because it *is* the second treatment. The patterns shown must be consistent when controls are added for order.

An example of an A/B/A/C/A design is given by Harmon, Nelson, and Hayes (1980). In this study, conditions were compared which were designed to improve depressed clients' mood (B) or their activity (C). The purpose of the study was to answer the question: Do people get depressed mood because they do less, or do they do less because of their mood? A well-known side effect of self-monitoring is reactivity (see chapter 4) which was used to increase mood or activity specifically. Clients were given timers which buzzed periodically throughout the day. During one condition, they immediately rated their mood. During another condition they rated pleasant activity. During baseline, no frequent ratings were made. Overall ratings of mood and activity were also taken at the end of each day throughout the entire study. Nine depressed clients took part (all were also in a weekly therapy group). Three each completed A/B/A/C/A, A/C/A/B/A, and baseline-only sequences. The data of interest are whether measures of mood improve when pleasant activity is increased and if measures of pleasant activity improve when mood is improved (see Figure 8.5).

Note that mood improves when pleasant activity increases, regardless of the sequence. Note also that activity does not increase as much when mood is increased, again regardless of order. Thus, we can conclude that improvements in mood are more likely to follow changes in activity than vice versa. Because the same effects are shown in different clients experiencing the conditions in reversed order, order effects are ruled out. This study also demonstrates the use of a baseline-only control, which will be discussed in chapter 10.

Changing Criterion Element

This element (Hall, 1971; Hall & Fox, 1977; Hartmann & Hall, 1976) is based on a fundamentally different type of reasoning than the elements that have been described thus far. It emerges when it is possible arbitrarily to specify the pattern that a given behavior should show in a particular period, and to change the specification repeatedly. If the behavior repeatedly and closely tracks the criteria specified, then it is reasonable to believe that the criteria themselves are responsible for the changes. Usually, the criteria would specify a given level that the behavior must reach. For example, a clinician may tell a socially withdrawn client to strike up at least two conversations per week. After a period of time this criterion may be changed (e.g., to four per week) and the degree to which the behavior then tracks the new criterion can be determined. The logic of a changing-criterion design element, however,

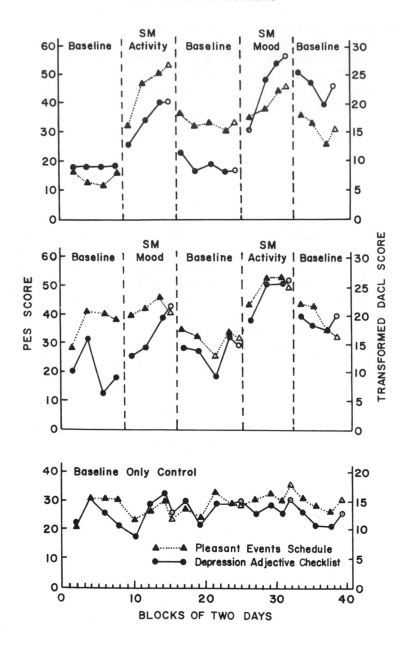

Figure 8.5. An example of an A/B/A/C/A design. (From Harmon,T., Nelson, R.O., & Hayes, S.C. Self-monitoring of mood versus activity by depressed clients. *Journal of Consulting and Clinical Psychology,* 1980, *48,* 30-38.)

could relate as well to criteria related to variability or to trend as it does to level. For example, a clinician could encourage a client to set upper and lower boundaries on calorie intake if the client tended alternately to binge and starve.

Figure 8.6 shows hypothetical data for a socially withdrawn client. As part of the treatment, specific goals for the number of social contacts with others are repeatedly set. If the data shown in Figure 8.6 resulted, a reasonably strong case could be made for a treatment effect.

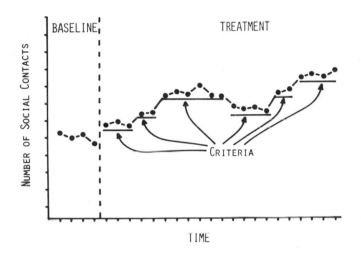

Figure 8.6. A hypothetical example of a changing-criterion design.

Because the source of information about treatment effects in a changing-criterion design element is the relationship between repeated changes in the criteria and similar changes in the behavior itself, it is important that the criteria changes not mimic common behavioral patterns that might occur naturally. There are at least four things to consider. First is the number of criterion shifts. If only one or two criterion shifts are made, then there will naturally be relatively little information about the correspondence between the criterion and behavior. This is basically the same issue as that of the number of replications in a simple phase change. Each criterion shift provides an opportunity for a replication of the effect seen. At the absolute minimum, of course, at least two criteria are required, but most studies using this design have used four or more criterion shifts. A second issue is the length of the subphase in which a single criterion is in force. In some versions of this design, researchers have left the criterion in force for a very short period of time. An example is provided by Friedman and Axelrod (1973), who lowered the number of cigarettes to be smoked each day, for a client, from a high of 38 cigarettes to a low of zero (see Figure 8.7). None of the criteria were enforced for more than two or three days. The problem with this is that it does not enable a clear assessment of the correspondence between the criterion and the behavior. The stability, level, and trend in the behavior are all important determinants of correspondence. If extremely short subphases are utilized, it will be impossible to assess all of these sources of information.

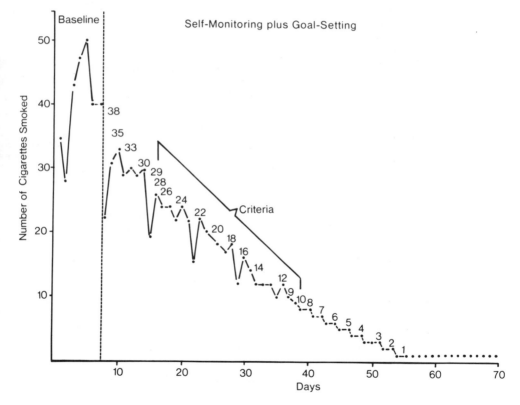

Figure 8.7. An example of a changing-criterion design. (From Friedman, J. & Axelrod, S. *The use of a changing-criterion procedure to reduce the frequency of smoking.* Unpublished manuscript. Temple University, 1973)

In addition to recommending that the criteria be held for a sufficiently long period of time to determine correspondence, it is also important that the criteria be shifted at irregular intervals. Many behavior-change patterns approximate a gradual increase or decrease in behavior. If criterion shifts are regular, and especially if the length of the subphases is short, the resulting expected behavior pattern will be a gradual and steady increase or decrease. It is better to have some subphases somewhat longer than others so that any cyclic or periodic changes in the behavior will not coincide with criterion shifts.

A third method of increasing the likelihood of detecting a relationship between behavior and criteria is to alter the magnitude of the criterion shifts themselves. Often the changing-criterion design element is used when gradual improvement is expected. It may not be possible or even advisable to shift a criterion in a dramatic way. This does not mean, however, that the magnitude of criterion shifts should be consistent. Just as with the length of the subphases, it is desirable to have some criterion shifts greater than others.

A final method of increasing the precision of the design is to change the direction of the criterion shifts (e.g., Hall & Fox, 1977). If it is possible to do so, the relaxation of a stringent criterion allows a kind of reversal, very much like an A/B/A/B design. In this case, however, instead of baseline, the reversal consists of a return to an earlier criterion level. Perhaps one way to think of this would be to think of it as a B'/B"/B'''/B"/B'''. In other words, the treatment is partially withdrawn by returning to a more relaxed level. What is different about all of this compared to the simple phase change and its variations is that we have some prior expectation of the specific patterns that should be seen in a particular phase or subphase. The changing-criterion design has been most popular when used with behaviors that tend to change gradually. It is particularly well suited to situations in which the client is learning new things in a gradual way or is gradually eliminating a problematic behavior. It does not require any withdrawal of treatment and, in fact, is logically useful even when no baseline assessment phases are possible.

One main difficulty with the use of the changing-criterion design is in determining whether or not the behavior seen fits the series of specifiable criteria during intervention. Each of the main characteristics of data, namely variability, level, and trend, enter into a determination of correspondence. Consider the case in which a client comes in for assistance in reducing smoking. Imagine that a series of stepwise reductions in level of smoking permitted is attempted. If the data are quite variable and, in particular, if some of the days exceed the set criterion in a particular phase, then it will be difficult to determine whether or not the behavior is tracking the criteria. Similarly, if the criterion is not changed for a period of time and yet there is a trend in the behavior, then this would undermine the conclusion that the behavior is tracking the criteria. If the criteria are stable, then ideally the behavior seen should also be stable. The level itself may also be a matter of difficulty.

If a criterion was set of 30 cigarettes per day, for example, and the client actually smoked an average of only ten cigarettes a day, it is not persuasive evidence of the power of the criterion itself. (For an example of such a situation, see Dietz & Repp, 1973).

The four recommendations given earlier will diminish the problem of determining the degree of correspondence. Additional analytic aids may be needed, however. One possibility is to present the data (and not the criteria) to persons skilled in time-series methodology and ask them to guess when criteria were changed and by how much. It is then possible to check the correspondence between the hypothesized and actual criteria. For example, the data at the top of Figure 8.8 are the data from Dietz and Repp (1973), presented without any criteria. The reader may wish to identify apparent shift points and guess what the actual criteria were. The bottom of the figure shows the actual criteria. Various statistical means can then be used to assess correspondence. For example, first a *hit* could be defined. This could mean identifying the exact time of a criterion shift or, if more liberal rules are desired, being within some set distance of it. Once a hit is defined, the rates of hits and misses expected due to chance alone can be determined and compared to the obtained values with, say, a chi square. A similar strategy could be used for assessing criterion levels. The point is that the obviousness of correspondence between the criteria and obtained data is itself measurable, although methods remain to be agreed upon.

Figure 8.9 shows an example of a series of planned criterion shifts when the level of the behavior is being used to identify the criteria. Notice that this planned series alters the length, magnitude, and direction of criteria changes. Just as with phase changes more generally, it is important that the changes fit into the clinical routine, but it is also important to be mindful of the reasons why the criteria were shifted. The clinician should not go into the case with an expected series of criterion shifts, such as that shown in Figure 8.9. Rather, the appropriate criterion shifts should merge in the context of therapy with an eye towards issues of magnitude, length, and direction. If the criterion shifts are heavily influenced by particular client behaviors, it is important to identify that source of control in the description of the procedure. For example, if the criteria are shifted only when the client requests that they be made more stringent, then a shift seen in the behavior might be due to the same factors that led the client to request the shift and not to the criterion itself. As with other phase-change designs, the solution to this seems to be to allow the natural tendency to shift criteria at particular times but to rely on replication and articulation of the reasons for the shift to control for possible confounding factors.

The changing-criterion design has another weakness—it cannot be applied if there are no clear criteria for the client. Many therapies seek fairly general

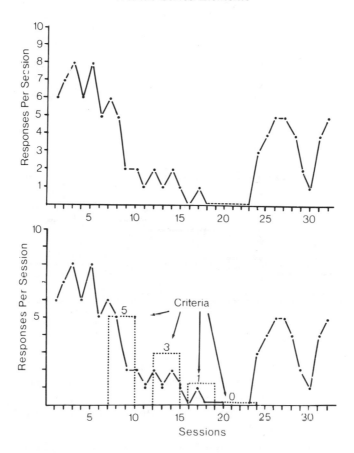

Figure 8.8. An example of a changing-criterion design. The weakness of this example is the brevity of criteria, their regular changes, and the poor fit in the early subphases. (From Dietz, S.M., & Repp, A.C. Decreasing classroom misbehavior through the use of DRL schedules of reinforcement. *Journal of Applied Behavior Analysis*, 1973, *6,* 457-463.)

improvement, and it is not possible or even desirable to set specific criteria for change. In these situations other designs are more appropriate.

Parametric Design Elements

At times the practitioner is interested in the relative effectiveness of several variations of a particular treatment arranged along some kind of continuum. For example, the clinician may be interested in the effectiveness of a particular amount of therapist self-disclosure. Each of these values of a particular treatment could be considered to be a distinct treatment, and the design

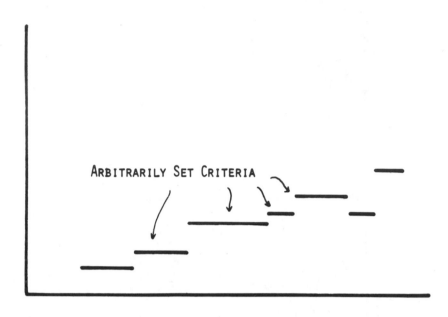

Figure 8.9. An example of ways to vary criteria so as to avoid excessive regularity.

options already described could be used to test the parameters of a given intervention. The parametric nature of the comparisons, however, opens up additional options. One common strategy which is quite popular in the basic experimental literature, although rarely seen in the applied literature, is to increase the parameter of interest and then to decrease it. This ascending-descending sequence amounts to a replication of each value of the intervention so that the nature of the relationship between treatment parameters and outcome can be obtained. For example, suppose four different levels of a particular treatment were being compared (let's call them B, B', B", B"'). One sequence which would test the relative impact of these treatment variations would be an A/B/B'/B"/B"'/B"/B'/B/A sequence. If at any point the clinician wished to investigate particular parameters more closely, it would be possible to add alternations of that value to other values of interest (e.g., B'/B"/B'/B"). The difference in this design is that we have some a priori reason to believe that the conditions are closely related, differing only on a specifiable parameter. To the extent that this is true, it strengthens the logical structure of the design and allows somewhat weaker controls in phase sequencing to be used. In some ways this is similar to the logic of a changing-criterion design in which expectations about the impact of treatment drawn from our knowledge of the criterion allow us more flexibility in phase sequencing. It differs from the changing criterion in that no expected reaction pattern is required, and thus the data are evaluated in the normal manner and not in terms of correspondence to a criterion.

An example of the uses of such a design is in an attempt to relate drug levels to response. If various levels of the drug were tried, an orderly dose-response relationship should emerge. The results ideally should show some orderly relationship to treatment values. The relationship need not be linear. Figure 8.10 shows some idealized data from such a design. The top of the graph shows a linear relationship between treatment value (e.g., dosage level) and outcome. The bottom shows a curvilinear relationship. Both are fairly convincing. Note, however, that the patterns are replicated—that is, each value shows a specific and replicable pattern. When this is not true, the design cannot distinguish order effects from treatment effects.

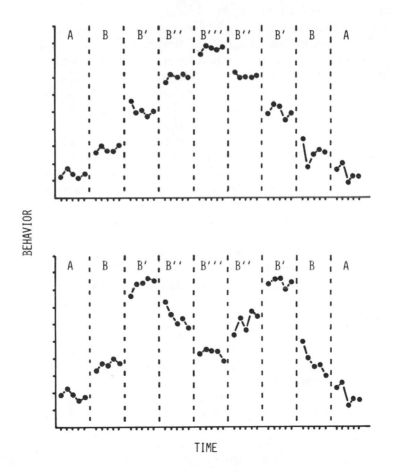

Figure 8.10. Two examples of a parametric design.

Periodic Treatments Element

The phase-change strategies often seem to imply that treatment is either present or absent. The idea that treatment is a more continuous variable is foreign to these designs. In the applied environment, however, a continuous notion is quite common. For example, suppose a clinician sees a client for a weekly outpatient therapy session. When is treatment present? Clearly, treatment is present in the therapy situation itself, but what about measures taken after treatment? Is treatment present in the week after a therapy session? Or is this baseline? Most applied workers would, if pressed, probably point to a continuous, rather than digital, perspective. It is a matter of degree.

Little work has been done to date attempting to fit treatment as a continuum to the continuum of client responses. The analytic methods needed to do this are not well developed.

One major reason for this may be that much of the logical structure of single-case experimental designs was drawn from the animal operant literature. In this environment it is quite easy to say precisely when a particular treatment is in force and precisely when it is not. The interventions are intrusive and can be continuously present in the animal's environment. In the applied situation this is often not the case. Intervention may be confined to treatment sessions which may occur only irregularly. For example, in the typical outpatient therapy situation, the client is likely to see the clinician no more than 1 hour per week for treatment. It becomes somewhat arbitrary in this situation as to what is considered to be data collected during treatment and what is considered to be follow-up data, unless the intervention is obviously continuously present, such as a token economy with a noncompliant child. Thus, behavior shown by the client outside of the therapy environment itself may be thought of as more or less treatment related, rather than dichotomously related to treatment or no treatment.

The periodic treatments design (PTD) draws upon this observation (Hayes, 1981). The notion is that a consistent relationship between the periodicity of treatment sessions and periodicity of behavior change can demonstrate therapeutic effects. It can be used when the frequency of measurement far exceeds the frequency of treatment sessions. The PTD is particularly useful when treatment sessions are irregularly scheduled, so that normal periodicity cannot mimic true effects. If improvement is more rapid in a given period following treatment than at other times, then a treatment effect can be identified. For example, there may be sudden improvements or jumps in the data following treatment. If this is consistent, despite irregular spacing of treatment sessions, the sessions are probably responsible.

Figure 8.11 shows some hypothetical data which are designed to exemplify the principle. The top half of the figure shows the hypothetical record of positive social interactions, self-recorded daily by a client. Arrows on the abscissa show days when the client saw a psychotherapist for therapy sessions. The treatment sessions occur at varying intervals, and periods of improvement only follow them. This relationship is made particularly salient in the bottom half of the figure, which presents the same data in difference-score form. (Each pair of data points is calculated as a difference from the preceding pair. The line in the bottom represents each preceding pair value.) Naturally, these data do not show what it is about the therapy sessions that would produce the effect. It could be simply the placebo value of going for any kind of treatment, or it could relate to more specific therapeutic aspects. This same criticism applies to other phase change designs where a treatment is simply compared to no treatment.

The PTD is not limited to situations in which immediate and dramatic effects occur after treatment. The essential move in this design is to view time from treatment as a continuous treatment-related variable. It is an analogic, nondigital perspective on what is treatment related and what is not (cf. Lindsley, 1968). This continuous variable is then compared to outcome (also a continuous variable). Delayed effects, if consistently shown, could also be related to treatment.

To fit the PTD into more usual perspectives, it is possible to create a type of simple phase-change design out of it. Suppose you were willing to assume that the data closest to treatment sessions are more likely to reveal treatment-related effects. It is then possible to create "phases" by identifying some cutoff point between "treatment" and "baseline." Consider the data shown at the top of Figure 8.12. If we somewhat arbitrarily take the midpoint between treatment sessions as a cutoff, we can create phases that appear exactly like a simple phase change. To highlight these data further, we could calculate them in difference-score format (the difference from the trend set in the previous phase), showing the dramatic pattern at the bottom of Figure 8.12.

As this example reveals, a PTD draws on the logic of within-series designs, but it adds in the notion of a treatment continuum. This can be forced back into a digital form (as above) but the design does not demand it. As we get used to analogic perspectives on the presence or absence of treatment, data such as those shown in Figure 8.1 may appear more normal. How we will analyze these data is still unclear, however, because the PTD is still so new.

In real life, data analysis may not always be a problem. The data shown in Figure 8.13 are actual data from a clinical case (Hayes, 1978). This client was extremely fearful of snakes. Two extended sessions of exposure were used to treat the client. Daily measures of the degree of approach on a visual avoidance measure (Hayes, Nelson, Willis, & Akamatsu, 1982) are shown in the figure. Note that the client improves dramatically after each session and shows no subsequent deterioration. It seems highly likely that treatment was responsible. This case also shows how naturally a PTD can fit into professional practice.

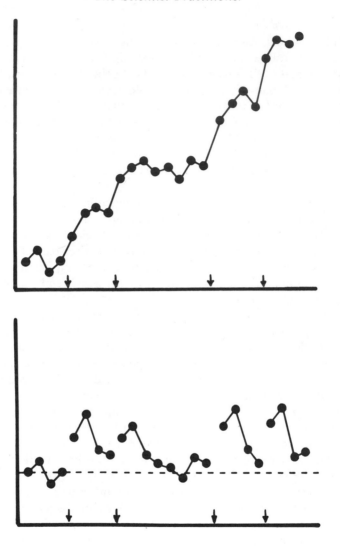

Figure 8.11. An example of a periodic treatments design. (From Hayes, S.C. Single-case experimental design and empirical clinical practice. *Journal of Consulting and Clinical Psychology,* 1981, *49,* 193-211.)

FOLLOW-UP

Regardless of the particular kind of strategy used to evaluate the single case, the practitioner can and probably should include a follow-up phase. The follow-up phase amounts to an extension of the final treatment phase. Even though treatment is no longer in force, the assumption is that if treat-

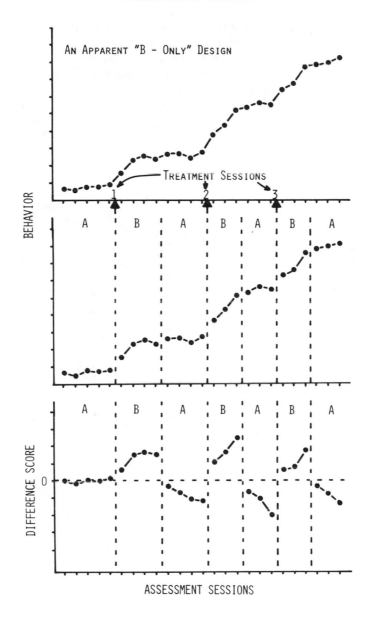

Figure 8.12. An example of a periodic treatments design. The top figure would normally be considered a B-only design. If we consider *treatment* and *baseline* to be time close to, or removed from, treatment sessions, the pattern shown in the middle results. When these data are recalculated in terms of the change from the trend established by the preceding "phase," the bottom version is formed (the horizontal line represents the trend set in the previous phase). The three forms are equally correct, but the degree of control is more obvious when steps are taken to highlight the changes.

ment has been effective, it will be maintained during follow-up. In a sense
this is very similar to placebo interventions which follow baseline. You might
recall that earlier in the chapter we described how phases that are equivalent
to baseline can be considered to be part of baseline. In the same way,
behavioral patterns which continue after the termination of treatment are
generally considered to be part of the treatment phase; that is, a long-term
result of treatment.

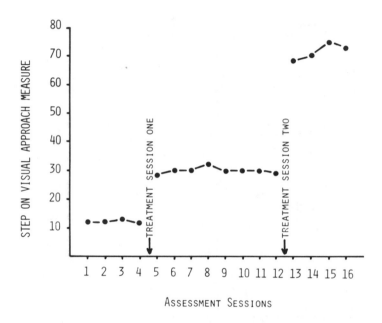

Figure 8.13. A case example of the periodic treatments effect.

There are logical difficulties with some of these assumptions for particular
single-case designs. For example, if several different phases preceded follow-
up, it may be that any maintenance which is shown is due to the entire sequence of phases and not to the final treatment. This is the problem of
multiple-treatment interference (Hersen & Barlow, 1976; Kratochwill, 1978).
The difficulties here are no different than the difficulties presented for the
interpretation of any phase in a single subject design. The answer is also
similar: replication. If maintenance is only shown when a particular sequence
is present, then sequence is important.

EVALUATING THE RESULTS OF WITHIN SERIES STRATEGIES

When the conditions have been properly arranged, several evaluative outcomes are possible. It is possible that the magnitude of the effect is such that anyone examining the data and understanding the fundamentals of single-case designs would determine that an effect has occurred. Depending on our background knowledge about the problem, even a few replications may be extremely convincing. At other times, the effects which are seen may not be of such a size that the effects are certain. Quite a bit has been said about this problem. For example, it is known, based on several studies (e.g., Furlong & Wampold, 1982), that even experienced single case researchers will disagree about the meaning of some data patterns. This puts the applied worker in an apparently uncomfortable position. It is possible to collect information on a client and still not be certain what to say about the data when they have been collected.

Various rules have been suggested to circumvent these issues. Many researchers have recommended, for example, that statistical evaluations be applied in such situations (e.g., Kazdin, 1976; Kratochwill, 1978). Indeed, a number of techniques are available which might be of assistance here. Unfortunately, even if the statistical analyses are done, we are not necessarily left with any increase in our knowledge of the effect, although we may feel more certain.

The usual argument for the necessity of statistical inference goes this way:

1. Science demands valid judgments.

2. If judgments are to be valid, they must be reliable.

3. Different judges disagree; therefore, their judgments are unreliable.

4. If they are unreliable, the judgments are also invalid.

5. Judgments made solely on the basis of statistical inferential tools are reliable.

6. Therefore, judgments made on the basis of statistical inference are valid.

Several logical errors occur here. Even if validity requires reliability (which is not necessarily so), reliability does not imply validity. If we determined the validity of effects by the shoe size of the authors, we would have perfect reliability, but presumably no validity. It must be shown, therefore, that statistically aided judgments actually are better; that they improve our ability to predict or to control phenomena. With single-case designs, no such data yet exist. When they do, we will then know how helpful statistical inference is to the practitioner using time-series designs.

The other area of concern in the syllogism is the use of interjudge variability as a measure of reliability. In fact, if some judges are very good at picking up real effects and others are not, interjudge "unreliability" may result. Intra-judge reliability may be quite high. Yet only a portion of the judges may make consistently valid judgments.

This issue has a clear relationship to a phenomenon often seen in practi-tioners. In the applied environment, some individuals seem to be very effec-tive at picking up on subtle client characteristics and knowing what kinds of interventions are likely to be effective. Many practitioners seem especial-ly adept at drawing from the techniques developed by others, making them part of their armamentarium, and mastering their use. Others seem to have a difficult time understanding what the client's needs are or learning from the clinical experience of others. Unfortunately, the same seems to be true of single case experimental data.

No data yet exist on what good applied scientists attend to when making effective judgments about single-case data. The rules offered throughout this book are largely based on logic, and could yet prove to be incorrect. Table 8.2 summarizes a few of these rules. The task of the scientist-practitioner is to learn how to read results in an effective way, in precisely the same way that the task of a practitioner is to learn to be sensitive to a client's true needs.

Table 8.2 Some Common Rules in Evaluating Time-Series Data

1. Evaluate effects relative to background variability.

2. Replicated effects are more believable.

3. The more applications the more believable are the data.

4. The more consistent the effects, the more believable.

5. The larger the magnitude of change (given background variability and previous knowledge about the behavior), the more believable.

6. Immediate effects are more believable.

7. Large changes in level, or level and trend, are more believable.

8. Effects which rule out alternative explanations are more believable.

Chapter 9
Between-Series Elements

INTRODUCTION

In within-series strategies, assessment of variability, level, and trend is made within a series of measurements taken across time. To do this, it is essential that several measurements be taken successively under a given condition (e.g., baseline, or a given treatment). In other words, a phase is required. Another way to group data points is needed, however, when conditions change too rapidly for there to be several measures in a given condition. Suppose, for example, you notice that an acquaintance responds quite differently to different greetings. Sometimes when you see him you use an informal greeting. Invariably, he smiles and returns the greeting. Other times you use a more formal greeting, and then he only nods grimly. Common sense will quickly tell you that your greeting style is responsible for the differences, but note that no stable sequence of three or more measurements in the same condition (i.e., a phase of formal or informal greeting) is required. Are you mistaken in the logic of your conclusion? No, what you have done intuitively is to combine his reactions first by greeting condition and then across time within condition, rather than to do it by successive measurements alone. This produces two series across time (e.g., formal and informal greeting). Differences between these two series provide the evidence of an series effect.

This is the logic of *between-series* design elements. They do not need to contain phases (although phase-change elements can be added as the overall design is constructed), because the estimates of stability and trend are organized by condition across time and not by time alone. There are two basic types of between-series design elements: the alternating-treatments design and the simultaneous-treatments design.

THE ALTERNATING-TREATMENTS DESIGN ELEMENT

The logic of the alternating-treatments design element (ATD) is based simply on the rapid and random (or semirandom) alternation of two or more conditions (Barlow & Hayes, 1979). By *rapid,* what is meant is that the frequency of possible alternation is about as great as the frequency of the meaningful unit of measurement. If, for example, the clinical phenomenon is best measured in weekly units, there should be a possibility of a change in condition about once a week. In the ATD, a single data point associated with one condition may be preceded and followed by measurements associated with other conditions. Because of this, there is no opportunity to assess stability, level, and trend within consistent phases. Rather, these assessments are obtained within conditions, by arranging data points sequentially associated with a condition or treatment each into a separate series. If there is a clear separation between such series, differences among conditions are inferred.

The idea of a rapid alternation of conditions is not a new one, but the essential logic of it has occasionally been clouded. Operant researchers have long used rapid alternation of conditions to assess effects of schedules of reinforcement. At least two types have been used. In a multiple schedule, two or more schedules of reinforcement, each associated with a clear external stimulus to signal the schedule in force, is rapidly alternated (Barlow & Hersen, 1973; Hersen & Barlow, 1976; Leitenberg, 1973; Reynolds, 1968; Sidman, 1960; Ulman & Sulzer-Azaroff, 1975). A mixed schedule (Reynolds, 1968) is similar except no clear external event signals which condition is in place (more on this difference later). The logic of the comparisons made in these designs, however, does not restrict its use to the study of schedule of reinforcement effects, nor is the presence or absence of external cues critical. Properly understood, the ATD is one of the most powerful and applicable design elements in all of time-series methodology. It has been greatly underused only because its essential nature and practical uses have been hidden by historical artifact.

Consider the following example that emerged naturally in the treatment of a clinical case. The design has some problems which will be instructive later, but it also demonstrates the logical structure of an ATD. One of us (S.C.H.) once noticed while supervising a student therapist that an alternation of conditions was naturally occurring. When the student was uncomfortable, he would move back from the client and would tend to be more formal, cold, and predictable. At other times he would lean toward the client and would be more spontaneous, warm, and self-disclosing. What emerged in his clients was a predictable pattern—clients quieted down and became more defensive when the therapist was leaning back, but more open and self-disclosing when he was leaning forward. This somewhat whimsical example illustrates the essential logic of the design element. Suppose the therapist took the small additional step of deliberately scheduling the "lean back" and "lean forward" periods and the client behaved as shown in Figure 9.1. Because of the consistently higher level of self-disclosure shown in the "lean forward" condition, we would conclude that the therapist's behavior was controlling the client's reactions. With additional controls (mentioned later) we might be able to show what it was specifically about the therapist's actions that was critical.

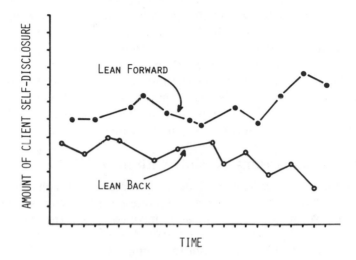

Figure 9.1. A hypothetical example of the effects of therapist behavior on client self-disclosure.

Note that the comparison is made between series. Any changes shown within each series are unanalyzed and may be due to extraneous factors, such as history, maturation, and the like. In the ATD itself, there are no phases, although by random assignment sometimes there may be three or more data points in a row in the same condition. One could think of this as an extremely rapid A/B/A/B design (cf. Campbell & Stanley's 1963 discussion of an *equivalent time samples* design), but they differ significantly. First, as we have already noted, the nature of the assessment of variability, level, and trend differs. Second, the nature of treatment comparisons differ. Third, order effects are less likely (due to rapid, random alternation), but multiple-treatment interference is perhaps more likely. Multiple-treatment interference occurs when the effect of one treatment is different in the presence of another treatment than in its absence. Such interference is not always undesirable, as we will discuss later. Finally, an ATD can incorporate three or even more conditions. A within-series comparison is difficult with three or more conditions and considerable thought must be given to the specific sequence of phases (e.g., an A/B/A/C/A).

Although we have termed this design element the *alternating treatments design,* it should be clear that *treatments* is used here to refer to the condition in force, not necessarily therapy. Baseline conditions can be alternated with specific therapies as easily as two or more distinct therapies can be alternated. Whether or not this is needed depends upon the specific question being asked. If the question is "does therapy B work?" then baseline either must be alternated with B, or other design elements must also be used, such as a baseline phase both before and after the ATD element. For example, Figure 9.1 does not show that therapist behavior (i.e., leaning forward and being warm) increased client self-disclosure over doing nothing in particular—it increased it only relative to what was shown when the therapist leaned back and acted more formally. Similarly, the apparent trend in the "lean forward" condition does not show that the client is improving relatively to doing nothing special. If this information is important, baseline conditions would be needed either as part of the ATD or as part of a phase-change strategy.

Types of Comparisons Possible with an ATD

The ATD can either be used alone or in combination with other design elements. It can be used to answer many questions that emerge in the applied environment. Several investigators have compared treatment and no treatment in an ATD. For example, O'Brien, Azrin, and Henson (1969) compared the effect of following and not following suggestions made by chronic mental patients in a group setting on the number of suggestions made by these patients. Doke and Risley (1972) alternated daily the presence of three teachers versus the usual one teacher and noted the effect on planned activities in a classroom (contingencies on individual versus groups were also compared in an ATD later in the experiment). Redd and Birnbrauer (1969) alternated reinforcement and no reinforcement using two adult therapists. Zimmerman, Overpeck, Eisenberg, and Garlick (1969) and Ulman and Sulzer-Azaroff (1975) are other early examples.

A representative study comparing two treatments is provided by Agras, Leitenberg, Barlow, and Thomson (1969). This study examined the effects of therapist praise on a severely claustrophobic client. The subject was a 50-year-old female whose symptoms intensified following the death of her husband some 7 years before being admitted as a research patient in a psychiatric unit. When admitted the patient was unable to remain in a closed room for longer than 1 minute without experiencing considerable anxiety. As a consequence of this disorder, the patient's activities were seriously restricted.

During the study, the patient was asked, four times daily, to remain inside a small room until she felt she had to come out. Time in the room was the dependent measure. During the first four data points representing treatment (see Figure 9.2), the patient kept her hand on the doorknob. Before the fifth treatment data point (sixth block of sessions), the patient took her hand off the doorknob, resulting in a considerable drop in times.

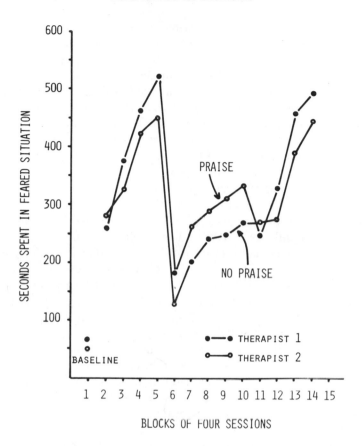

Figure 9.2. Data obtained during the experimental modification of claustrophobic behavior. Two therapists alternated in praising or not praising performance. (Redrawn from: Agras, W.S., Leitenberg, H., Barlow, D.H., & Thomson, L.E. Instructions and reinforcement in the modification of neurotic behavior. *American Journal of Psychiatry*, 1969, *125*, 1435-1439.)

During treatment, two therapists alternated sessions with one another. One therapist administered social praise contingent on her remaining in the room for an increasing period of time. The second therapist maintained a pleasant relationship but did not praise her in any way for time spent in the room. In the second experimental phase the therapists switched roles, but returned to their original roles in the third phase. The data indicate that praise consistently increased performance relative to no praise. Note, however, that no firm statements can be made about the effect of these two exposure treatments relative to no treatment (no exposure).

Another example of a two-treatment comparison is provided by a case from our own files. The client was a 32-year-old, single male who was socially anxious. Often in such situations it is difficult to determine if the person is socially unskilled or simply anxious. In this case, we hedged our bets and alternated an anxiety-management and a social-skills training approach. As can be seen in Figure 9.3, the anxiety-management approach was consistently more effective in improving this client's social skills. Note again, however, that we cannot say for sure that treatment was effective relative to doing nothing at all, only that the two treatments differed. In this case the two treatments are fairly well developed, however, and the need for a thorough evaluation of the impact of treatment is lessened. Because of our long history of experience with these treatments, the rising slope seen in Figure 9.3 can be credibly thought of as a treatment effect, but it is weakly demonstrated (by what is essentially an A/B with a one-point baseline).

Thus, two or more treatments are usually compared in an ATD alone when they are of known effectiveness, and it is the relative effectiveness that is primarily at issue. In clinical case management it is often a good idea to collect a baseline even in these conditions to make it more credible that a treatment effect occurred. In Figures 9.2 and 9.3, for example, at least a single point of baseline was collected.

Another clinical example is provided in a case from Hayes, Hussian, Turner, Anderson, and Grubb (in press). The client was a 38-year-old female with a driving phobia. The phobia had progressed to the point where even driving a few blocks would create intense anxiety attacks. After a short baseline, sessions of systematic desensitization were begun, either with or without cognitive coping training being added. As can be seen in Figure 9.4, the coping plus desensitization package worked better than desensitization alone.

This case also makes another point in that it shows that the ATD can be used to study the additive effects of treatment components as well as two entirely different treatment regimens. Even more analytic studies would be possible. For example, the role of a variety of "nonspecific" factors could be assessed using an ATD. A treatment protocol could be followed exactly in the same way each session, except that therapist warmth or some other such variable could be alternated.

In addition to analyzing treatments and treatment elements, an ATD can be used to analyze the effects of different therapists, times of treatment administration, and the like, as Ulman and Sulzer-Azaroff (1975), McCullough et al. (1974), and Browning (1967) point out. This could be accomplished by collapsing data points across interventions and examining the therapeutic effects of two quickly alternating therapists. This comparison could be made more elegantly by having two or more therapists alternate quickly in the administration of a single treatment.

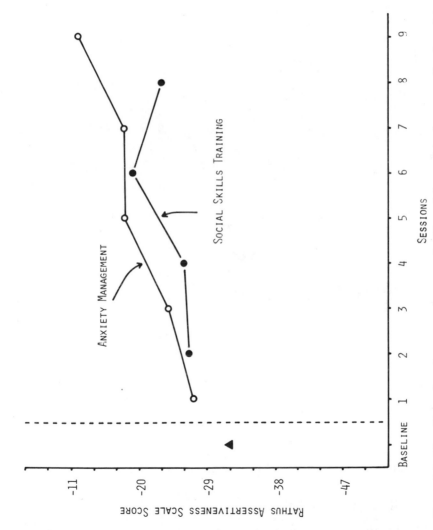

Figure 9.3. The effect of anxiety-management and skills-training approaches on a client's social anxiety.

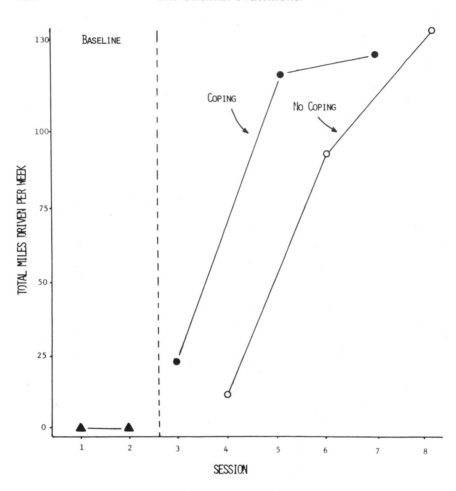

Figure 9.4. The effects of desensitization with or without cognitive coping on miles driven by a driving phobic.

The ATD is also quite useful in assessment, as discussed below.

Advantages of an ATD

The ATD element has a number of distinct advantages (Barlow & Hayes, 1979; Ulman & Sulzer-Azaroff, 1975). First, it does not require withdrawal of treatment, or if one is used in the ATD itself, it need not be lengthy. If two or more therapies are being compared, the question, which one works best? can be answered without a withdrawal phase at all.

Occasionally, a primitive type of an ATD often emerges naturally. Just as there are natural withdrawals as in a phase-change design, there are natural alternations with baseline as in an ATD. More will be said about this later, but one example might be the following. Suppose treatment occurs every other week, but measures are taken every week. You could think of this as an ATD, in which the therapy weeks and baseline weeks are being alternated. Notice the similarity between this logic and that of the PTD.

The lack of a necessary withdrawal is a distinct advantage for an ATD. It limits the practical and ethical problems posed by the absence of treatment that would otherwise occur (see chapter 8).

A second advantage is that the comparison can be made more quickly than in a withdrawal design. McCullough et al., (1974) for example, effectively compared two treatments in four days. Withdrawal designs, on the other hand, require relatively stable baselines followed by at least three, and usually more, data points in each of at least three phases (A/B/A). As Ulman and Sulzer-Azaroff note (1975), this efficiency also allows sudden termination of the experiment, with the likelihood of having obtained usable data. A withdrawal design, on the other hand, must be carried through to completion.

This rapidity allows an ATD to be used in circumstances that are not well suited to phase-change designs. One such situation occurs when measurement is cumbersome, lengthy, costly, aversive, or necessarily infrequent. For example, suppose a stroke victim is being treated in a physical rehabilitation center. A complete workup of the patient's muscular functioning may require several hours of careful testing by two staff professionals. Obviously, such measures cannot be taken frequently. Suppose they could only be taken once a month. If an A/B/A/B design were being used, and if at least three data points were taken in each phase, this would mean 12 months to ask the simplest kind of question (Does treatment work?). With an ATD, the minimum time period would be reduced considerably. Suppose a measure is taken at the very beginning, then after 1 month of treatment, then after 1 month of maintenance, and then after 1 more month of treatment. Suppose the data shown in Figure 9.5 are the result. In only about 3 months, we could begin to conclude that treatment was effective.

One reason why comparisons can be made more rapidly is that only two data points are absolutely required in each series. With two data points we can assess, but not distinguish, variability from trend. In an ATD, however, assessment of variability is drawn in part from all of the data, not just those with a single series. Thus, a pattern like that shown in Figure 9.5 could be caused by variability only if it were very large and happened to coincide perfectly with treatment alternation. With such a small number of data points,

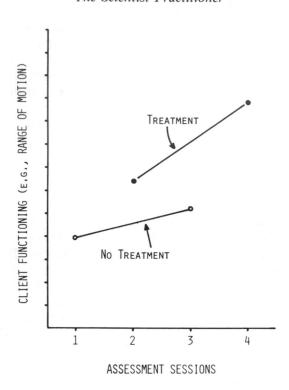

Figure 9.5. A hypothetical example of an assessment of effects of treatment using an ATD when measures are infrequent.

this is not an unreasonable possibility, but the lengthy measures that would force such infrequent alternation are also often known to be quite stable.

There is another advantage of the rapid conclusions possible with an ATD: it can be used in a single therapy session. Few other designs allow this. For example, one of our students told a client in desensitization to occasionally prepare for some of the scenes by repeating a comforting statement to herself. When it was pointed out that this accidental alternation allowed a test of the role of cognitive coping on rapidity of progress, the anxiety data for each scene were reexamined. During the first treatment session, anxiety was much lower following the coping statement, an effect which was then deliberately replicated in several subsequent sessions (Hayes et al., in press). The point of this is that conclusions were possible in a single therapy session. There are some situations, such as in crisis intervention, where this may be a distinct advantage. This example also illustrates how ATDs emerge naturally in clinical practice.

Another advantage of the ATD is the possibility of proceeding without a formal baseline phase. Ulman and Sulzer-Azaroff (1975), in considering this point, suggest that behaviors yielding chronically unstable baselines can be studied with this design. In applied research, a common observation is behavioral improvement during baseline, which does not allow for introduction of any but the strongest treatments in the usual withdrawal design (Hersen & Barlow, 1976). But this does not present a problem for the ATD. No baseline is required.

A final major advantage of the ATD is its insensitivity to background trends more generally. Suppose, for example, that we are examining a behavior that is continuously changing, perhaps due to maturation. In such a situation, all conditions are likely to be associated with improvement. In a phase-change design this presents special problems. Treatments must be quite effective to show additional improvement, especially because of the added difficulty of distinguishing within phase variability from trend. In an ATD, consistent increases in improvement will be easily noticeable. Figure 9.6 presents an example. Note that every data point represents an improvement over the previous one. Despite this, the advantages of B over A are obvious. Many behaviors (e.g., academic skills, physical abilities) do tend to show continuous transition, and the ATD is particularly useful for their analysis.

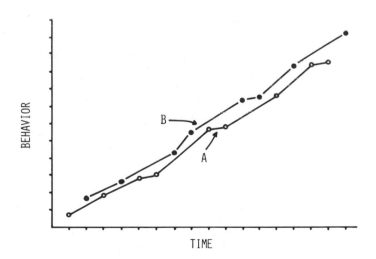

Figure 9.6. An example of ATD data in which each data point improves on the preceding one, and yet an effect is still seen.

Considerations in the Use of an ATD

Several issues must be considered before using an ATD. Some of the more important dimensions are the following:

Should there be an Attempt to use Discriminative Stimuli?

We originally suggested that exteroceptive stimuli were required in an ATD (Barlow & Hayes, 1979). That is, we said each condition must have a readily identifiable signal so that the client can discriminate which treatment condition is in effect. Actually, the logic of the ATD does not *require* such stimuli, although with humans they are nearly unavoidable (Hayes, Levy, & Barlow, 1982). It is this latter fact and the field's history of including such stimuli in most animal uses of these designs (mixed schedules are the rare exception, see Reynolds, 1968), that cause the confusion. There are times when a discriminative stimulus can be avoided, and an ATD will still be useful. For example, a patient might be given an active drug and a placebo in an ATD. The logic of the design will still allow the comparison to be made.

While discriminative stimuli are not reqired in an ATD, they are often quite useful. In certain conditions they will tend to produce clearer tests of two or more conditions. They help the conditions become more distinct. After experience with the cues and the conditions they signal, clients may begin to react in part to the cues themselves (this is why they are so popular in animal work, where the consistent reactions that result are desired). Suppose, for example, that Teacher A praises a child for asking questions, while Teacher B does not. After a period of time, when the child sees Teacher A the questions will be more likely, *before* the praise is delivered. Thus, discriminative stimuli (in this case the teachers themselves) will tend to magnify and clarify existing differences.

If proper discriminations are made, treatments that are topographically very similar (e.g., 5 min. versus 10 min. time-outs) can be compared. This can be established by using instructions as discriminative stimuli in applied research. If one is comparing 5 versus 10 min. time-out periods for disruptive behavior in children, there are few reasons why one would not describe the treatments as each became appropriate, particularly since someone would most likely describe these conditions in the normal use of this procedure in the natural environment.

If the alternation of conditions is also associated with the alternation of stimuli, then additional considerations emerge. Take, for example, our earlier illustration of the lean-forward-be-warm, lean-back-be-cool case study. It could be that the client's responses are controlled not by the therapist responses (warm versus cool) but by the therapist posture itself, independent of its association with therapist reactions. This is entirely plausible. It may be harder to self-disclose to a person leaning back from you.

In such situations, the potential effect of the stimuli must be controlled. One way to do this is to reverse the association between the stimuli and treatment, either with another client or with the original client in a subsequent phase. The stimuli should be counterbalanced. For example, the clinician could lean back and be warm. If the client then gradually starts to self-disclose more when the therapist leans back, the suspected impact of the therapist affect will be confirmed. The use of this control was shown earlier in the example of the claustrophobic praised for approach (Agras et al., 1969). Because the differences could have been due to therapist effects, and not to praise per se, the conditions were reversed twice during the course of therapy (see Figure 9.2).

This control is only necessary when the signaling or discriminative stimuli could reasonably have an impact, and are arbitrarily related to what is thought to be the active elements of treatment. If they are not arbitrary, such a control is not needed or possible. For example, suppose two semantic therapies are compared. The nature of the verbal interchange may be a stimulus, but it is impossible to reverse it because the stimulus is part of the intervention. If the stimuli are unlikely to affect outcome, it is not essential to counterbalance them. For example, if colored lights or a tone were used, such control may often be unnecessary.

It is probably likely that the clinician will at least consider counterbalancing when it is most needed. This is true because the use of signals usually requires some deliberate planning. If it seems that counterbalancing is needed, it should occur after a clear difference between treatments has emerged.

At times it may be desirable deliberately to *avoid* any connection between arbitrary stimuli and treatment. The advantage of this is that it would immediately eliminate the possibility that the stimuli are responsible (cf. Kazdin, 1982). For example, if multiple therapists are used, they could be randomized across interventions from the very beginning, rather than associated with a given treatment and then counterbalanced. If treatment itself is strong, this alternative may be a very useful one, because it shortens the analysis Thus, the use of discriminative stimuli help effects to be seen, but they may entail some ultimate cost in time and effort.

How Many Alternations are Needed?

The minimum number of alternations is two, but a larger number is highly desirable. The more frequent the alternations, the more opportunities there are for the series to diverge or overlap. Since the fundamental comparison in an ATD is the degree of divergence and overlap between the series, increasing these opportunities increases the precision of the analysis.

The frequency of alternation is limited by several factors. First, alternation can occur no more often than the meaningful unit of measurement. The word *meaningful* is meant to convey the importance of temporal measurement units that are appropriate to the task. (You may recall the discussion of this issue as it related to intrasubject averaging in chapter 7.) For example, if the nature of the behavior is such that it is most meaningful when viewed as a weekly average, then weekly alternations are the most rapid that could be done. It would be foolish to present the data in, say, daily units, just so that more rapid alternation is possible. The measurement frequency should be dictated by the nature of the behavior, not the design.

A second limitation on alternation frequency is that alternation can occur no more often than the time during which treatment effects are strong. Some treatments are known to have effects which linger for considerable periods of time (e.g., drugs with long half-lives). If they are analyzed with an ATD, the frequency of measurement and alternation must be adjusted to fit these time frames. If this rule is broken, it will simply decrease the likelihood of detecting an effect, so it is not a reason to disbelieve clear differences actually found in an ATD.

It should be clear that the "rapidity" of alternation in an ATD is relative to the behavior and its proper unit of measurement, not real time. Some investigators have defined ATDs in other terms. For example, Kazdin (1982) states that an ATD is inappropriate with behaviors which change slowly. "Because two (or more) interventions are usually implemented on the same day, it is important that the intervention not take too long with a given session to begin to show its effects" (Kazdin, 1982, p. 189). This need not be a limitation, since the rapidity of alternation is relative only to measurement. The amount of time to show an initial effect is probably a good operational definition of the meaningful temporal unit of measurement for that behavior. If change will take at least a month to see at all, why express the data in finer units? If data are taken (or collapsed) monthly, then monthly alternation would be, by definition, rapid.

How Should Treatments be Alternated?

The answer to this question requires an understanding of threats to the validity of an ATD or the ability of the ATD to answer the question being asked. Foremost among them is the as yet unknown magnitude of multiple-treatment interference existing in the ATD. Since this issue is important, we will now spend some time discussing the problem of multiple-treatment interference.

Multiple-treatment interference. Multiple-treatment interference (Campbell & Stanley, 1963) or condition change interactions (Ulman & Sulzer-Azaroff, 1975) poses the question: Will the results of Treatment B in an ATD where it is alternated with Treatment C be the same as when Treatment B is applied in isolation?

Applied research and clinical practice more generally are fraught with treatment interference. Our clients are experiencing a variety of events before and between treatments. One client may have recently lost a family member, another flunked an exam, a third had sexual intercourse, and a fourth been mugged on the way to a session. It is possible that these clients may repond differently to treatment than otherwise would have been the case, and these historical factors account for some of the enormous intersubject variability seen in comparing two treatments. ATDs, on the other hand, attempt to control for this experience by dividing each subject in two and administering two or more treatments within approximately the same period of time. As with all applied research, the results may be affected by interaction with events occurring in the environment. But, within a single case, ATDs handle outside interference very effectively.

The special problem posed by the ATD is the degree to which one experimental treatment impacts on another. There are three concerns: sequential confounding, carry-over effects, and an alternation effect (Barlow & Hayes, 1979; Ulman & Sulzer-Azaroff, 1975).

Sequential confounding refers to the fact that Treatment C may be different following Treatment B. In an A/B/A/C/A design, for example, we do not trust the comparison of B and C because any differences may be due to order. It may not be B versus C, it may be first versus second. This is why an A/B/A/C/A must be coupled with an A/C/A/B/A, to control for order.

The solution proposed for this in an ATD is random or semirandom sequencing. If many alternations are possible, and the results are consistent, it becomes extremely unlikely that a particular sequence could be responsible for the differences. Consider the following sequence: BCCBCBBCBCBBBCCBCCBCCCB. If the beginning and later sections of the two series continue to show consistent differences, despite random sequencing, order effects are unlikely to be responsible. If they are, the data will not replicate, and we will know soon enough.

Carry-over or contextual effects refer to the influence of one treatment on an adjacent treatment, irrespective of overall sequencing. These effects may be divided into *contrast* and *induction* (Ulman & Sulzer-Azaroff, 1975; Reynolds, 1968). Both terms refer to a change in the pattern of behavior in one condition caused by the presence of another condition. In contrast, the behaviors in the two conditions change in a direction opposite to each other. In induction (or generalization), the two behaviors change in the same direction.

For example, a mild punisher may be effective when applied alone. When even stronger punishers are also used, however, the greater suppression in the strong punishment condition may be associated with a loss of suppression in the mild condition.

Contrast is a common finding, even in humans (e.g., Waite & Osborne, 1972). In animals the effects tend to be fairly small (Dunham, 1968; Freeman, 1971) and transient. In humans, however, our ability to influence our own environment may lead to more permanent contrast and generalization effects.

There are several ways to reduce carry-over effects. Random sequencing of conditions is helpful, particularly in avoiding generalization. Suppose we were to claim that Treatment B will always act to increase the behavior shown in the following period. Since both B and C will be next about as often, this will tend to distribute the carry-over effects and still allow a reliable comparison of the two treatments.

The use of short treatment periods has also been shown to be helpful in reducing carry-over effects (O'Brien, 1968). Separation between treatment sessions is also valuable. For example, Powell and Hake (1971) minimized carry-over effects in a study comparing two reinforcement conditions by presenting only one condition per session, a situation that usually obtains in applied research (e.g., Agras et al., 1969; McCullough et al., 1974). It is interesting to note that similar procedures have been suggested to minimize carry-over effects in the traditional within-subjects group approach (Greenwald, 1976).

Finally, a third issue in studying carry-over effects are those due to the speed of alternation of treatment, which can be termed an *alternation effect*. For example, in multiple-schedule work in basic research where carry-over effects have been studied, schedules are alternated by the minute rather than once or twice a day, or even less often, as is now typical in applied research. Rapid alternation seems to heighten carry-over effects, particularly contrast, as noted above (Powell & Hake, 1971; Waite & Osborne, 1972). But alternation must be frequent enough to allow data to be compared and, in some cases, for discriminations to be formed. The appropriate speed of alternation that allows meaningful comparisons but minimizes carry-over effects will probably depend on the particular question asked.

With these steps and in view of the nature of applied research, including the ability of humans to discriminate quickly and efficiently, it would seem that carry-over effects should not be a stumbling block to the internal validity of an ATD. But, as Ulman and Sulzer-Azaroff (1975) note, "In the absence of a systematic investigation, however, such interaction remains unspecified, and any generalization based on this design should be qualified accordingly" (p. 389).

There are two reasons why carry-over may not present a major problem: it is often beneficial, and it can be identified. Contrast can be a particularly desirable carry-over effect in an ATD. Contrast will not reverse the relative positions of two treatments. For example, suppose Treatment B leads to better performance than Treatment C. In an ATD, B may be even better and C even worse than usual, but carry-over cannot make C better than B. In other words, an ATD can be a kind of methodological magnifying glass. A magnifying glass distorts the world, but it does so in order to help us to see the world. The differences seen are real differences, though they may appear larger than they "really are."

As an example, suppose we are comparing a self-instructional approach to a rote-drill approach in the teaching of math skills. Suppose we knew that the self-instructional approach was, in reality, only slightly better than the rote-drill approach. Contrast effects will tend to make the differences appear larger in an ATD. For instance, the student noticing the difference may expect more progress in the self-instructional condition and may begin to dread the less useful drill sessions. Such effects may enhance the differences even more.

External validity is a matter of the utility and generality of our descriptions of results. Clear differences seen in a properly controlled ATD are real differences. As long as we remember that a between-series design asks about differences between series and not about the nature of the individual series itself, our conclusions will not be jeopardized.

Fortunately, it is possible to assess directly the extent to which such effects are present. Sidman (1960) suggests two methods. One is termed *independent verification,* which essentially entails conducting a control experiment in which one or the other of the component treatments in the ATD are administered independently. For example, two treatments might be compared through an ATD in a direct replication across three subjects. Three more subjects might then receive baseline, followed by Treatment B, in an A/B fashion. The second treatment could be administered to a third trio of subjects in the same manner. Any differences that occur between the treatment administered in an ATD or independently could be due to carry-over effects. Alternatively, these subjects could receive Treatment B alone, followed by an ATD alternating Treatments B and C, returning to Treatment B alone. An additional three subjects could receive Treatment C in the same manner. Trends and levels of behavior during either treatment alone versus the same treatment in the ATD could be compared.

A more elegant method is termed *functional manipulation* by Sidman (1960). In this procedure, the strength or intensity of one of the components is changed. For example, if comparing flooding and a gradual, structured approach to the feared object in the treatment of fear, the amount of time in flooding could be doubled at one point. Changes in fear behavior occurring during the second unchanged treatment (structured approach) could be attributed to carry-over effects.

The study of treatment interaction can be interesting in its own right. Some treatments juxtaposed in fast alternation could prove more effective than either component alone. That is, alternation effects, mentioned above, could prove therapeutic. For example, in some unpublished work carried out several

years ago, a sadistic rapist was treated by daily alternation of orgasmic reconditioning using first a sadistic fantasy and second an appropriate heterosexual fantasy. Sexual arousal to the appropriate fantasy seemed to increase
more quickly during the fast alternation than during orgasmic reconstruction-
ing to the appropriate fantasy alone (Abel, Blanchard, Barlow, & Flanagan,
1975). This may represent a contrast effect or possibly an intensification of
the therapeutic effect due to a sharpening of stimulus control. The appropriate
method for studying these alternation effects would be to juxtapose a period
of fast alternation with a period of slower alternation. This has recently been
done (Leonard & Hayes, in press) and has demonstrated that fantasy alternation does indeed produce strong changes in sexual arousal patterns and
that these are clearer with fast than with slow alternation.

Alternation Recommendations

The bottom line of this discussion is that it is desirable to alternate randomly or semirandomly and to keep a careful eye on possible carry-over effects. If they are likely to be present and are thought to be a problem, alternation might be slowed somewhat and treatments separated into distinct
sessions.

At times, even random alternation will by chance lead to short phases of
three more sessions of the same type in a sequence. If the number of possible alternations is very high, this may not be a problem. In many applied
situations, however, the practitioner does not have unlimited possibilities to
alternate conditions. Since the comparisons are made between series, phases
of the same treatment are to be avoided. The solution is to put an upper
limit on the number of possible sequential treatment sessions of the same
type. For example, the treatments could be alternated randomly (say, by the
flip of a coin) but no more than three of the same type in a row.

Natural Alternation

There are times when treatment alternation occurs naturally. Two examples
were given earlier: The alternation in coping instructions in a desensitization
paradigm, and the lean-forward-lean-back case. The problem with natural
alternation is that it is particularly likely to be influenced by events which
will also influence the behavior of interest. For example, the therapist may
be leaning back and reacting coolly because of the content of the *client's*
speech, not vice versa.

The same issue was raised earlier with regard to within-series designs.
Natural alternation is useful, but practitioners should state the reasons for
the alternation, if known, and should interpret the results very cautiously.
Even better, a period of deliberate alternation should be included. If both

the natural and deliberate alternation lead to the same outcome, the results are considerably strengthened.

One form of natural alternation is practically ubiquitous in situations in which treatment is confined to short periods (e.g., therapy sessions), and measurement occurs more often. For example, suppose a client is receiving regular, 1-hour-per-week, outpatient therapy. Suppose further that measures are taken immediately before and after the treatment session. The pre- and postsession data could be separated into two series, and treated as an ATD. In some situations, this pre-post version of an ATD may provide meaningful data. For example, exposure-based treatments with phobic clients often produce fairly large gains immediately after a treatment session. If a client had repeatedly improved from presession to postsession, and if the gains were stable, a pattern like that shown in Figure 9.6 earlier would be seen, where A is the pre- and B the postmeasure (see Thyer & Curtis, 1982).

Similarly, suppose that in the same situation the week is divided into the half-week period immediately after and immediately before therapy. Measures collected during these two periods could be gathered into two series and compared.

The weakness of these approaches is that alternation is not random and correlation with extraneous variables is possible. For instance, it is possible that deficits in performance immediately before treatment are due to the impending session; improvement afterward may be due to elation over the fact that therapy is concluded for another week. This weakness can be mitigated somewhat if the timing of therapy is randomized. The reader might recognize the logic of this as essentially the same as a periodic treatments design (see chapter 8).

Despite the difficulties, if it is known that the behavior is fairly resistant to change, and if effects are clear, a pre-post ATD can provide meaningful data. The client may be improved right after treatment and simply maintain the gains until the next session. If so, the two series (pre and post) will clearly diverge (see Figure 9.6). This strategy, of course, would be particularly useful for accountability in applied settings.

Is a Baseline Needed?

A baseline is not required by an ATD, but it can be quite useful. All baselines allow both a description of client functioning and a prediction about future course. If an ATD is done comparing two treatments (after a baseline), this will allow some assessment of the impact of treatment per se (essentially an A/B design), as well as of the differential treatment effects (from the ATD phase). If baseline can also be continued in the ATD phase, an elegant comparison is possible. Any sources of influence that might have coincided with the ATD phase can be ruled out as the cause of improvement during treatment.

An alternative is to withdraw treatment after the ATD phase, or to multiple-baseline the ATD phase (see chapter 10). These combinations build upon the logical structure of these other design units and do not need a special analysis.

How Many Series Can be Compared?

An ATD weakens as the number of series increases, because the time between the same intervention increases, the number of trials of a given intervention decreases, and sources of multiple-treatment interference increase. This makes it less likely that a result will be found, but it does not jeopardize any clear results that are seen.

One way to arrive at an upper limit is to consider the number of data points that are likely to be collected before termination and then decide (based on knowledge about the stability of the behavior and the likely magnitude of effect) how many data points would be needed at a minimum in each series. Two is the absolute lowest value, but four or more are more common. Then divide the second number into the first. That will give the upper bounds on the possible number of different series.

An example of an ATD using three series is presented in Figure 9.7. These data are from the series of cases mentioned earlier (Hayes et al., in press) analyzing the effects of cognitive coping on progress through a desensitization hierarchy. This particular client had a severe case of astraphobia, and stayed in her basement much of the time in fear of potential storms. The data shown are latency-to-anxiety measures taken during the conduct of desensitization.

These data show less anxiety for the coping than the no-coping scene (an effect described earlier with the driving phobic). In this case, however, the client was also required to spell distractor words during some scene presentations. Apparently, the coping statement effect was not due to mere distraction. Note that although these results seem clear, the frequency of measurement is quite high and still the precision of the analysis is beginning to suffer. In very few cases would it be wise to analyze more than four conditions in an ATD, and in probably most situations, three is a reasonable upper limit.

How Much Overlap is Acceptable?

In evaluating the ATD (or STD for that matter, see below), the degree of divergence and overlap between the series are the data of interest. No clear standards have emerged in evaluating between-series results. If there is no overlap between the series, and several data points are in each series, then few would doubt the effect. If there is overlap, other issues arise. First, is the percentage of overlap small relative to the number of data points? If it

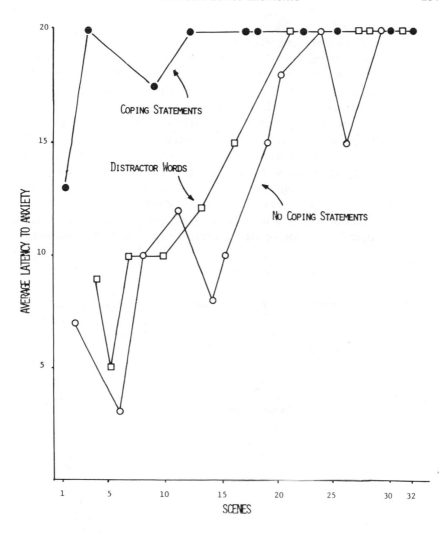

Figure 9.7. An example of ATD data in which three series are compared in a client with astraphobia. (A longer latency means less anxiety.)

is small (say 10-20%), then the differences are more likely to be real. This is particularly so if the number of data points is large, if the magnitude of the divergence is large, and if the magnitude (as well as percentage) of overlap is small. Second, is the behavior known to be fairly stable? If so, the results will probably be more reliable. If the behavior is extremely variable, chance alone can produce divergent series, especially if the number of alternations is small. Third, is there a trend in divergence and convergence? An example is shown in Figure 9.8. These are the data from an airplane phobic client in the study mentioned earlier on the effect of cognitive coping on progress in desensitization (Hayes et al., in press). Notice that there is a clear convergence as the two series progress. The orderliness of the data suggest that the results are generalizing to the untreated scenes, not that there is no difference between the two. This was then tested by alternating a reminder *not* to use the coping statements with the statements. The data once again diverge. Then the original conditions were then reinstated and the data converged once more. (This is also a good example of the combination of design elements to answer specific questions. This particular design does not even have a name, but it is a logical extension of design tools we have already discussed.)

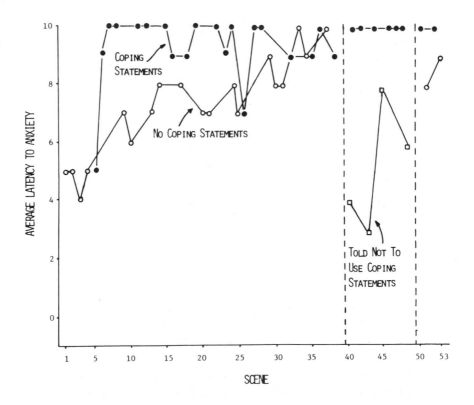

Figure 9.8. An example of series convergence in an ATD and its analysis.

Providing a Rationale

The use of an ATD in actual clinical practice may at first seem cumbersome. In fact, it is not. Clinicians may wonder, for example, what people will think if treatment is alternated rapidly. Usually, the truth works as a beautifully effective rationale. For example, a client might be told:

> Well, it appears as though there are two aspects to your problem. On the one hand, you are having quite a hard time with managing your level of stress and anxiety. On the other hand, you also seem to need help with learning how to take better control of your life. Rather than work only on one aspect of your problem, I think we should work on two fronts. I've found it to be quite helpful with others in the past. Two basic approaches strike me as possibly useful, biofeedback and assertiveness training. What I'd like to propose is that sometimes we concentrate on anxiety management and sometimes on learning new skills. I'm not sure which will be most helpful, and in this way we'll cover all the bases. If, later on, it appears that one approach is better than another, we could then concentrate on that.

Naturally, a real rationale would be more subtle, but this gives the basic idea. Clients are usually very receptive to such an approach if the clinician is convinced of the value of it.

Often no need for a special rationale exists because clients will not notice the ATD. Clients do not necessarily expect consistent therapy sessions. For example, if the clinician wants to compare two treatments, usually it is because both seem relevant. If it seems that way to the clinicians, it may also seem that way to the client.

Unusual Types of ATDs

ATDs Across Behaviors or Settings

An unusual form of the ATD can be used to document the effect of a single treatment if it can be applied to several problem behaviors or to behaviors in several problem situations, or combinations of both. For example, suppose a client has spasticity in both an arm and a leg and each seems amenable to treatment by EMG biofeedback. The biofeedback treatment could be applied randomly to each area in turn. Separate measures could be taken on each bodily measure. This creates, in effect, a separate ATD for each measure as the treatment is alternated between treatment of the arm and leg.

Figure 9.9 shows an example of what might result. The top graph is a kind of ATD in which treatment of the arm is alternated with a placebo (treatment of the leg), while the reverse is true of the lower graph.

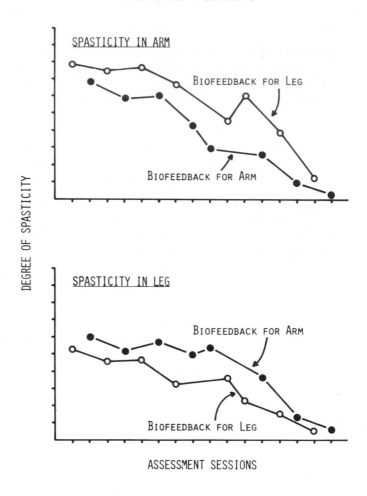

Figure 9.9. A hypothetical example of an ATD across behaviors.

There are several possible advantages in this use of the ATD. It evaluates the effect of treatment without any withdrawal, and yet allows fairly strong statements about the effects of treatment. This is permitted because the specific effects allow intervention with one behavior to be a kind of baseline (or placebo) for another. Another advantage of this design is that it does not require that the behaviors be completely independent. To the extent that they are not independent, the series will draw closer together, but as long as there is consistent differential effectiveness, the series will diverge. This is the same point made earlier about the relatively robust nature of an ATD when background trends exist. The one requirement of this use of the ATD is that it must not be likely that treatment of one behavior makes the other worse. In that case, iatrogenic effects could mimic treatment effects.

The Use of an ATD as an Idiographic Assessment Procedure

The rapidity of conclusions possible with an ATD offer another interesting use of the design: as an assessment procedure. In many areas, practitioners are told to distinguish between two closely related types of problems, or clients, and to apply different treatments to each. For example, a person with a social skills problem might be thought to be suffering from excess anxiety (requiring anxiety-relief procedures), or deficit skills (requiring direct skill training). Similarly, physical therapists may be told that some types of muscle problems respond best to dry heat, while others require whirlpool treatments. These kinds of distinctions are notoriously difficult to make and often they are merely logically (not empirically) based (Nelson & Hayes, 1979). The empirical clinician can use an ATD to make these decisions in a way that is not only empirical, but is individually tailored to the client.

For example, in a recent study, McKnight, Nelson, and Hayes (1982) rapidly alternated cognitive therapy and social skills therapy for a group of depressed clients. Importantly, those who improved best following a specific treatment in the early part of therapy, continued to do so throughout (see also Figure 9.3). This means that a clinician could conduct an ATD for a short time, determine the best treatment, and then throw all treatment resources into this condition. This basic strategy has been described (although in different terms) by earlier researchers (e.g., Kazdin, 1977, 1982; Kazdin & Hartmann, 1978). They recommend including a baseline as well, although none is really required (or it could be in the ATD itself).

McCullough et al. (1974) is a good case example. Following a 5-day baseline of the amount of cooperative behavior shown by a disruptive 6-year-old boy, two treatments were introduced for 4 days: (1) social praise for cooperative behavior and ignoring uncooperative behavior and (2) social reinforcement for cooperative behavior plus removal from the classroom for 2 minutes for uncooperative behavior. Treatment was administered during both a morning session and an afternoon session, and the two treatments were alternated during the day such that one treatment was offered in the morning and the other in the afternoon. Across all four days, the time of administration of a particular treatment (a.m. or p.m.) was counterbalanced. The effect of the two treatments are presented in Figure 9.10. The praise plus time-out treatment seemed to increase cooperative behavior more than the other treatment in the ATD phase and therefore was continued in the next phase.

In this design, the baseline allows a statement of the problem, the ATD allows an individual assessment of which treatment is most likely to work,

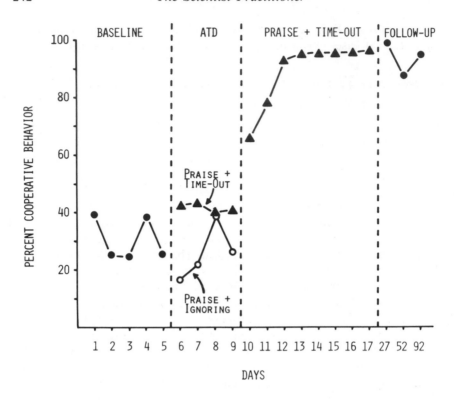

Figure 9.10. The percentage of observation periods in which the client emitted cooperative behavior during baseline, ATD, praise plus time-out, and follow-up phases. (Redrawn from McCullough, J.P., Cornell, J.E., McDaniel, H.H., & Mueller, R.K. Utilization of the simultaneous treatment design to improve student behavior in the first-grade classroom. *Journal of Consulting and Clinical Psychology,* 1974, *42,* 292. The labeling has been changed to reflect our view of the design. Although the authors call this an STD, it fits our definition of an ATD.)

and the final phases allow a check on whether the treatment is, in fact, associated with further improvement.

The use of an ATD for idiographic assessment will also permit the verification of common assessment distinctions. For example, suppose an MMPI profile suggested that a client was depressed *and* anxious, but that the depression was probably secondary to excessive anxiety. In such a situation, treatment of anxiety might be expected to be most effective. To evaluate this, treatments aimed at anxiety and depression could both be used in an ATD fashion. If the MMPI prediction proved correct in the ATD results, the *treatment validity* (Nelson & Hayes, 1979) of the assessment would be confirmed.

Surprisingly few assessment distinctions have been subjected to this kind of analysis. When they have, positive results are not always obtained. In some of our own cases, dramatically counterintuitive results have even been found, such as clients who improve more in objective social skills following anxiety-based treatment rather than social skills treatment (see Figure 9.3), but who also show more improvement in anxiety following skill treatment than following anxiety treatment. Teasing out the dimensions we need to decide on the most effective treatment requires the intensive analysis of many individuals. For example, in the McKnight et al. (1982) study, we were able to predict which treatment would work best in 9 out of 9 individual clients by a series of self-report measures of irrational cognitions and social skills. This then confirms the utility or treatment validity of this measurement.

THE SIMULTANEOUS-TREATMENT DESIGN ELEMENT

The only other true between-series design element is the simultaneous-treatment design (Browning, 1967). The STD is a more generic term for a *concurrent schedule* (Hersen & Barlow, 1976; Reynolds, 1968). The implication that a distinct schedule of reinforcement is attached to each "treatment" produces the same unnecessary narrowness as the mixed or multiple schedule does for an ATD. Browning's (1967) term, *simultaneous-treatment design,* seems more descriptive and suitable. Both terms adequately describe the fundamental characteristic of this design, the concurrent or simultaneous application of two or more treatments in a single case. This contrasts with the fast alternation of two or more treatments in the ATD. The best example of the use of a STD in applied research is the original Browning (1967) experiment, also described in Browning and Stover (1971).

Browning (1967) first obtained a baseline on the number of incidences of grandiose bragging in a 9-year-old emotionally disturbed boy. Six staff members who worked in the boy's residential cottage participated in the simultaneous application of three treatments: (a) positive interest and praise contingent on bragging, (b) contingent verbal admonishment, and (c) ignoring. At any one time, two of the staff were assigned to each condition. The boy was free to approach any of the staff members. What is of interest here is how much time the boy spent with staff members who were responding in a given way. To control for possible differential effects with individual staff, each team administered each treatment for one week in a counterbalanced order. For example, the second group of two therapists admonished the first week, ignored the second week, and praised the third week. The idea is that the boy "would seek out and brag to the most reinforcing staff and shift to different staff on successive weeks as they switched to S's preferred reinforcement contingency" (Browning, 1967, p. 241).

The data from Browning's subject (see Figure 9.11) indicate a preference for verbal admonishment, as indicated by frequency and duration of bragging and a lack of preference for ignoring. Thus, ignoring became the treatment of choice and was continued by all staff. There may be instances, however, when preference for a treatment may have little relation to its effectiveness. This point will be discussed below.

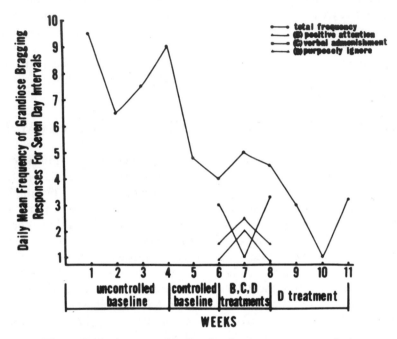

Figure 9.11. An example of a simultaneous treatment design.

In an STD, then, the treatments are available simultaneously. The subject chooses which one is applied. As in a concurrent schedule in animal operant work, the purpose of the design is to measure preference, not effectiveness. It is unlikely that the client will be equally exposed to each treatment. In fact, the very structure of an STD ensures that the client will not be equally exposed to all treatments (except in the unlikely event that both treatments are equally preferred.)

Many current issues in clinical science are issues of preference, and an STD may be useful in addressing them. It seems frequently the case that individuals will avoid treatment if it is not preferred. Attendance is essentially a component of treatment, and one which will, in part, determine its effectiveness. For example, in fear-reduction research it has been suggested that implosive therapy is more aversive than systematic desensitization and, therefore, maybe ultimately less effective, due simply to dropouts. The hypothesis about preference could be tested with an STD.

At times (as in the Browning, 1967, example), a knowledge about preference has more direct implications for treatment. For example, a clinician working with a retarded child may use an STD to determine which consequences are most preferred. This consequence could then be used as part of a treatment program. In most situations, however, preference and effectiveness should not be expected to coincide. For example, a fearful person may choose the least aversive treatment, not necessarily the most effective.

The STD is particularly useful for some types of assessment questions. For example, in an investigation of the connection between paranoia and homosexuality, Zamansky (1958) showed paired pictures of males and females to male paranoid schizophrenics and measured the amount of time spent watching each picture in the pair. King and Lockhart (1977) employed a similar procedure in an effort to assess erotic preferences for pictures of different parts of the body. In this study, subjects could respond on either of two telegraph keys. On a variable interval, responses on a given key would produce a slide of a breast, leg, and so on. In this way, preference could be measured behaviorally by the frequency of presses, say, on the "breast" key versus the "leg" key. Consistent subject preferences were shown.

Because of its limited focus, an STD is not well suited for the general evaluation of treatment outcome. Rather, it is useful in the assessment of preference, be it for identification of meaningful consequences, assessing clinical behavior, or identifying treatment preferences.

Chapter 10
Combined-Series Elements

INTRODUCTION

There are several design strategies which combine both between-series and within-series elements into a logically distinct and coordinated whole. These are what we term *combined-series* elements. Combined-series elements are not just the logically consistent sequencing of design elements in which each element stands as an independent unit. Combinations of this sort are very important, but they require no special categorization. We will describe some ways of sequencing and combining design elements in chapter 11. An example might be the inclusion of an ATD in between an A and a B phase (e.g., Kazdin & Hartmann, 1977). This sequence has special advantages (such as identifying a treatment most likely to be effective in the ATD phase and then confirming its worth in the B phase), but they are a direct extension of the component units. Conversely, true combined-series design elements result in unique characteristics that are not simply the characteristics of the components.

THE MULTIPLE BASELINE

The most common combined-series design element is the multiple baseline. The multiple baseline consists of a coordinated series of simple phase changes in several different series in which the phase changes occur at different points in real time and after different first phase lengths. By arranging for the phase change to occur in this way, several simple phase changes are elevated into a much stronger whole.

The term *multiple baseline* is something of a misnomer (Actually, the term *multiple phase change* might be clearer and more descriptive. The term *multiple-baseline* is probably too firmly entrenched to make a change worth the confusion, however). Any series of phase changes can be arranged in this way, whether or not one of the phases is a baseline. For example, several B/C phase changes could easily be collected into a multiple baseline. To make sense of the term, it may help to recall that, in a sense, the first phase in a simple phase change is always a kind of "baseline" for the second phase, whether or not the first phase is a baseline in the sense of "no treatment."

The purpose of a multiple baseline is to control for the principle weaknesses of the simple phase change. In a simple phase change, it is very rare that the change in behavior will be sudden enough or large enough, and the knowledge about the stability of the behavior strong enough to conclude firmly that any differences seen are due to the phase change. The first phase provides some protection against assessment-related effects (e.g., instrument drift or reactivity) and time-related processes (e.g., maturation), but the protection is by no means complete (see chapter 8). The multiple baseline strengthens the protections against effects of this kind. The most lethal difficulty with a single, simple phase change is the possibility that some impactful extraneous event has coincided with the timing of the change in conditions. There is usually no way to rule this out. That is the main reason why a simple phase change is generally thought to be preexperimental until it is replicated (e.g., in an A/B/A/B). (As noted throughout the book, however, the A/B, or case study, is on a continuum with single-case experimental designs and makes a crucial contribution to science.) The multiple baseline is particularly useful in ruling out this threat to the internal validity of an effect shown in a simple phase change. It does this, as will be discussed below, by attempting to replicate the phase change in more than one series, and by using each subsequent series as a control condition for the earlier series.

The different series can be any which are likely to be functionally independent and which are likely also to respond to the same treatment. The different series can be created in different clients, with different behaviors, in different settings, or any combination of these. The specific phase change must, however, be functionally identical in each series. Typically, the same first condition must yield to the same second condition, because it is alternative explanations for a specific phase change effect that are being eliminated.

The Logic of the Multiple Baseline

An example of a multiple baseline might be as follows: Suppose you were examining the effects of computer-based instruction versus normal classroom instruction on math performance. Rather than implement the program across all three classes of 4th graders in a given school, you might choose to stagger the implementation in such a way that each of the classes serves as a control for the others. Often this is the most practical for other reasons (e.g., personnel requirements of the program implementation), but it also produces special experimental characteristics.

Suppose that the data shown in Figure 10.1 resulted. As noted earlier, the change seen in the first phase would not normally be particularly convincing (unless we had strong reason on other grounds to believe that the trend set in the first phase will always normally continue—i.e., unless the behavior has a very well known course). By replicating the results in other series, regardless of sequencing, the strength of our conviction would increase (see chapter 12). But the multiple baseline arranges the phase changes in a unique way so that specific between-series comparisons are possible.

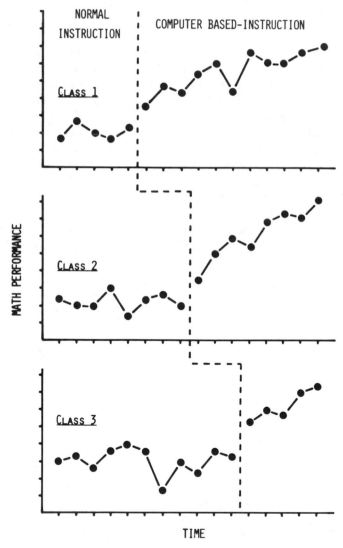

Figure 10.1. A hypothetical example of a multiple baseline.

Figure 10.2 shows the sequence of comparisons in a typical three-series multiple baseline. The first comparison is the within-series comparison at the first phase change. The considerations in determining if an effect may have taken place are identical to those discussed in chapter 8. The second set of comparisons is between the first and second, and first and third series. Since the second and third series are uninterrupted, they provide a between-series, "baseline-only" control for the effect seen in the first series. If the effect seen in the first series was due to assessment or time-related changes, it should have also been seen in the other series since they were exposed to just as much assessment over just as long a period of time. Thus, the different lengths of the first phase in each series allows a control for some of the threats to the validity of a single, simple phase change.

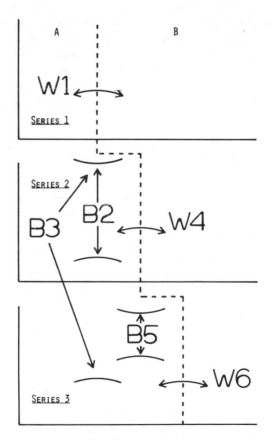

Figure 10.2. The within- (W) and between- (B) series comparisons in a multiple baseline. The numbers refer to the normal sequence of comparisons. (Note that the B does not refer to treatment, as it has elsewhere in the book.) By staggering the phase changes across series, several between-series comparisons are possible, which control for the weaknesses of a simple phase change.

The next comparison is within the second series, at the phase change. If an effect occurs here, but not previously, it controls for extraneous events in real time (i.e., grandma moved out, the boss resigned, the client got sick), which might have produced the effect in the first series. Because of the nature of this control, it is important that the phase change in the second series occur at a different point in real time than the change in the first.

If the series are being collected simultaneously, then having different first phase lengths will naturally lead to this. It could be possible to start one series earlier than the other, and then end up changing both series at the same time (but with different lengths of baselines). This is undesirable since it reduces considerably the control provided by the second phase change.

When the second phase change occurs, once again the uninterrupted series is examined for concomitant effects. This between-series comparison replicates the controls provided by the earlier between-series comparisons (B2 and B3 in the figure). Finally, the phase change on the third series (W6) replicates the control provided by the earlier phase change (W4). Thus, a total of six primary comparisons are made in a typical three-series, multiple baseline. If all the results are supportive (e.g., see Figure 10.1), this provides strong evidence of an effect, and controls well for the weaknesses in each of the simple phase changes considered separately.

When to Implement a Multiple Baseline

A multiple baseline can be used at any point in a design containing multiple series. It is most common at the beginning of a design, but it could easily be used later. The bottom of Figure 10.3 provides an example. Treatment was implemented all at once in each series but withdrawn in a multiple-baseline fashion. The advantage of this, compared to the more usual arrangement (see top of Figure 10.3), is that it strengthens the analysis considerably by (a) providing three additional between-series comparisons (B1, B2, and B3 in the figure) and (b) strengthening the effect of the three withdrawals by "unconfounding" them with events in real time.

Sometimes a multiple-baseline element is repeated in a single design, either to replicate the entire comparison or to conduct another comparison. This strategy is particularly useful when the first comparison raises a question which could be asked using the second phase as a baseline for a third phase. For example, suppose an employee exercise program has included feedback about the amount of exercise performed by each shift. This program has been evaluated by implementing the program in a staggered fashion across shifts, and has shown reliable changes in employee fitness. The program manager, however, notes that the employees seem to be claiming that they do more exercise than they really do, apparently in order to make their shift look good. The manager decides to continue the program, but now to give

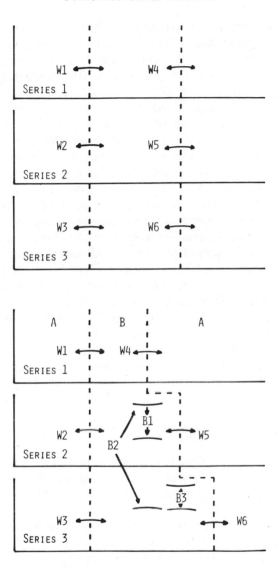

Figure 10.3. Demonstration of how a multiple baseline can add to the strength of an analysis regardless of where it occurs. The top of the figure is strong, but the bottom is even stronger because it adds three between-series comparisons (B1-3) to the six within-series comparisons (W1-6).

feedback to employees about the actual fitness of their shift (e.g., the average strength of each shift's employees). In this way, the manager reasons, employee faking or "just going through the motions," will not have any payoff.

This sequence would be described as an A/B+C/B+D, where B is the exercise program, and C and D are the types of feedback given to the shifts. An A/B+C/B+D design is essentially two different, unreplicated phase changes. It is like two A/B designs put together. By arranging them in a multiple baseline, however, these weaknesses would be largely resolved.

Figure 10.4 shows the options the manager could use in implementing the third phase. The top of the figure shows one type of sequential multiple baseline. It is useful, but it has a problem. Note that phase B+D always occurs after a set amount of phase B+C. Suppose treatment B+C has a delayed effect, such that effects improve after a set amount of time. This is not totally implausible. Many interventions take a period of time really to take hold (or to fall apart). Such effects could mimic a strong effect for fitness feedback (B+D). This would probably be discovered when the order was reversed in another set of subjects (see below), but there is another alternative, shown at the bottom of the figure. This arrangement (or variations on it) is stronger because it controls for phase length (and events that might correlate with it) as well as controlling for coincidental events in real time. The overall repeated multiple baseline allows us to conclude that fitness feedback is probably better than exercise feedback in motivating employee changes. To strengthen this conclusion, the entire program could be replicated, with the fitness feedback now occurring first, or additional simple phase changes within each shift could confirm the effects. This is needed because the third phase could have an effect due to the fact that it is novel, or the second treatment, and not due to fitness feedback per se.

Staggering Phase Changes

If one series has an initial phase that is only slightly shorter than the next, it limits the precision of the between-series comparisons in a multiple baseline. For that reason, fairly large overlaps are often desirable and often emerge naturally.

The timing of phase shifts is quite important. Consider the data shown in Figure 10.5, for example. Note that the effects for the first phase change have not yet been shown before the phase change on the second series is implemented. This is a fairly serious flaw in most instances, because we are not then sure if the change in the first series was a side effect of whatever caused the change in the second. It is even possible that an extraneous variable produced both changes.

Recall that the purpose of a multiple baseline is to control for alternative explanations for an effect seen in a simple phase change. If there is no effect, there is no reason to control for these alternative explanations. Only when a reasonably clear and stable effect has apparently been shown in the first series should the second be interrupted.

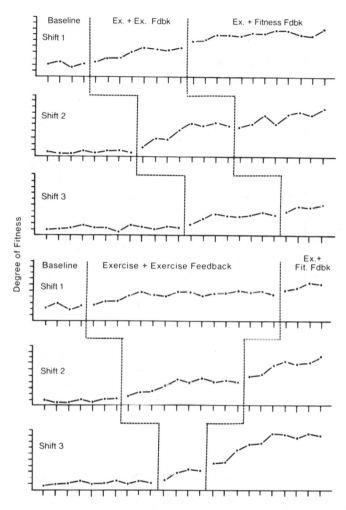

Figure 10.4. A hypothetical example of the sequencing of two multiple-baseline elements. The top of the figure has a problem because the third phase is always implemented after second phases of the same length. The bottom arrangement is stronger and more convincing.

This means that the precise sequencing of phase shifts must not be rigidly planned beforehand. The idealized patterns shown earlier might lead the reader to suppose that a clinician or educator could carefully lay out the timing of phase shifts before even beginning an evaluation. In fact, the client lays these out by the results shown. In a sense, the client is in charge of the design options — the practitioner is responsible for recognizing them and choosing the best one.

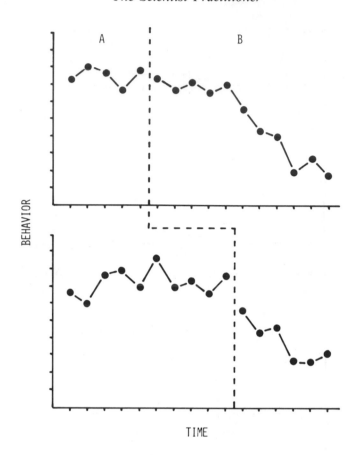

Figure 10.5. An example of improper timing of a phase change in a multiple baseline. The phase change in the second series occurs before an effect has been shown in the first series. This weakens the analysis considerably because the whole purpose of the between-series comparisons in a multiple baseline is to control for alternative explanations for observed within-series effects (see Figure 10.2).

The Number of Series Needed

No absolute rule can be given about the number of phase-shift replications required between series in a multiple-baseline element. The logic of the maneuver applies as well to a single replication as to several—it is simply that each additional series strengthens our confidence that much more. Thus, the clinician should not feel as though the element is useless when only two series are compared, though more are desirable.

If strong results are produced in two series, the phase change has been replicated once and a single, between-series comparison has provided some control for assessment of time-related effects. Other things being equal, an A/B/A might be as powerful, since it too replicates a phase change once. In some ways, however, the multiple baseline may be more powerful, because the phase change is replicated exactly. In an A/B/A, the replication of the A/B phase change is produced by an opposite phase change — B/A. This is often quite reasonable, but at times it is not. For example, if A is baseline and B is a strong program of reinforcement for performance, the second A phase may be thought of as extinction, not just as baseline. A decrease in performance in the second A phase may thus be due to the sequence (B to A), not to the functional equivalence of the two phase changes (i.e., A/B and B/A). The problem with this is that the pattern of responses may mimic a true replication. In a multiple baseline, the sequence in each series is the same, and thus the replication it provides carries fewer assumptions about the equivalence of the two phase changes. Partly for these reasons, a multiple baseline across three or more series is powerful indeed when properly conducted and when clear patterns are evident.

If several series are compared in the usual way, the design can become too long. This is because the need to wait for clear effects after a phase change extends the first phase in the remaining series that much more. The extension is especially troublesome if the first phase is truly baseline. It raises ethical problems (the need to begin treatment) and other problems caused by excessively long phases such as rigidity in the client's behavior, morale problems, and the like.

One solution is to shift two or more series at the same time. Suppose nine series were compared, for example. Three phase shifts across groups of three series each would accomplish the multiple baseline more rapidly than nine separate staggered phase changes. This is shown in Figure 10.6. Notice that the top arrangement allows relatively small amounts of overlap, and, even so, treatment is in force for only a short time in the last few series. If effects were slow in a given series, the onset of each phase would be pushed back accordingly.

It is not as critical that the second phase be of varying lengths. The primary between-series comparisons are between the interrupted and uninterrupted series, not between interrupted and formerly interrupted series (see Figure 10.2). It is more elegant to continue the second phase until all the phase changes have occurred, primarily because the long second phase tests a kind of maintenance effect. Nevertheless, it is not required.

Interdependence of Series

Much has been made of the need to avoid the multiple baseline when the specific series are interdependent (e.g., Kazdin & Kopel, 1975). If a phase

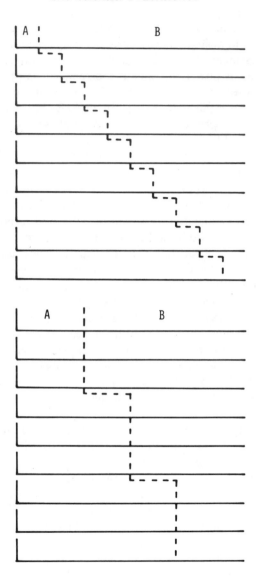

Figure 10.6. An example of alternatives for staggering phase changes when many series exist. Normally the bottom alternative will be more practical.

shift in a multiple baseline is accompanied by behavior change not only within series, but also between series, it is difficult to distinguish uncontrolled effects from true treatment effects. For example, in a multiple baseline across series produced by several different behaviors, changes in one behavior may produce changes in another because of actual processes of response generalization caused by treatment, or it could be that changes in both series are due to extraneous variables. Leitenberg (1973) has argued that, "If general effects on multiple behaviors were observed after treatment had been applied to only one [in a multiple baseline across behaviors], there would be no way to clearly interpret the results"(p. 95). While this argument seems sound, it should not be thought of as a weakness of a multiple baseline.

Independence need not be *assumed,* rather it is, in part, being *tested.* Often, no clear statement can be made a priori about the independence of series. Indeed, it is often clinically desirable that series not be independent. Processes of response generalization and setting generality, for example, are critically important and often desirable.

Suppose a clinician is treating a person with multiple phobias. Measures are taken on each, and after a time treatment is begun on one. As it improves, suppose the other phobias also improve. The clinician should immediately abandon the earlier design decision and explore this unexpected, but exciting finding. One way to do this might be to withdraw treatment for a short period. If all the phobias then slow their rate of improvement, experimental evidence of a general therapeutic effect would be provided. Put another way, lack of independence is not a problem so much as it is an opportunity to study generalization effects.

The reader should recognize that this opportunity can be used only if time-series methodology is viewed in a creative, dynamic way. As we have emphasized repeatedly, the practitioner should never be committed to a design. Rather, tentative decisions are made pending the data themselves. In applied interventions this is good advice in any case.

Some degree of interdependence between series can actually be tolerated in a multiple phase change, particularly if it is not strong or if several series are available (Kazdin, 1980). Suppose, for example, that a strong increase in the treated series is associated with a slight increase in the untreated series. If this untreated series stabilizes and then improves rapidly when specifically treated, few would argue that no effect has been shown. Similarly, if three or four series show the effect and one or two others show interdependent patterns, the most likely conclusion is that the effect is real but that not all the series are independent. If this seems softheaded, consider how unlikely it would be to get strong phase-change effects in several series by chance alone. This is so unlikely, that not every series need show clean effects.

An example is shown in Figure 10.7. These are the data for an elderly female client who was being treated for depression following being raped by her nephew (Hayes & Barlow, 1977). The client had a severe cleft palate, which had been repaired only as an adult, and was extremely socially anxious, particularly about public transportation. As part of her overall treatment, a social anxiety intervention was begun, focusing on six examples of three separate classes of feared transportation-related events: comments about her looks, questions about her voice, and strange looks. As is shown in the figure, the client improved immediately following treatment aimed at four of six separate situations (two "comments" situations, and two "questions" situations). The remaining situations improved without specifically being treated, but the rapidity and consistency of the earlier effects make the entire evaluation fairly believable.

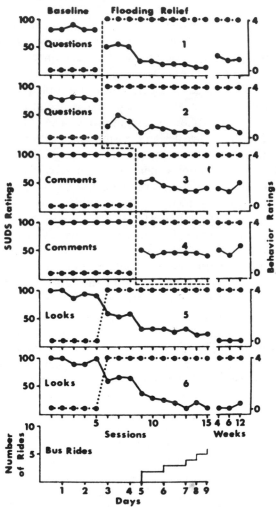

Figure 10.7. An example of a multiple baseline across situations. (From Hayes, S.C. & Barlow, D.H. The use of flooding relief in a case of public transportation phobia. *Behavior Therapy,* 1977, *8,* 742-746. Reprinted with permission from the Association for Advancement of Behavior Therapy.)

Ineffective Phase Changes

Sometimes an intervention is attempted which shows no effect in the first leg of a multiple baseline. In this situation, two basic alternative strategies are possible. Sometimes it is important to see if an effect will be shown in the remaining series. For instance, a treatment might be thought to be effective for three different types of behaviors. When no effect is shown on one behavior, the practitioner may still believe that the intervention would work with the remaining behaviors. Rather than continue to work on the first behavior, the multiple baseline across behaviors might be extended to the second series. If an effect is shown there, an opportunity is provided to investigate the differential responsiveness of the behaviors.

A more common alternative, discussed in chapter 8, would be to go on to another condition (e.g., in an A=B/C sequence). This third condition could then be implemented in the other series (e.g., those still in the A phase). If this seems to violate the rule that a multiple baseline must compare the same phase change in each series, recall that an A=B/C is considered functionally equivalent to an A/C. That is, as long as no effect is shown (A=B), we are still thought to be in baseline. This is not necessarily true, but in a sense, this type of multiple baseline tests that assumption since A/C phase changes are implemented on the remaining series. If an A=B/C is not equivalent to an A/C, then the effects should differ. If they do, the option is opened for studying the role of B in the eventual outcome of C.

For example, suppose a rehabilitation therapist attempted to treat a client with several muscular problems, using a new kind of ultrasound therapy. Finding no effects, suppose heat treatments were used, now with good effects (so far, an A=B/C). If the heat treatments did not then work in other muscles, the specific muscular problems might differ, or the ultrasound treatment may have aided in the impact of the heat treatments, despite its apparent ineffectiveness. This could be studied by trying the ultrasound with the problematic muscles, and if there is no effect, to intervene again with the heat treatment as had been done in the first series.

At times, ineffective phases are expected in a multiple baseline. When it is important to control for possible alternative explanations for a simple phase change, it is sometimes useful to try this condition first in ome of the series. The multiple baseline can also incorporate this approach. For example, Hayes, Johnson, and Cone (1975), designed a noncoercive litter-control procedure for use in a youth prison. The prison officials suggested simply giving the prisoners "areas of responsibility" and demanding that they keep these areas clean. A voluntary program was implemented in which some items of indigenous litter had been secretly marked. Prisoners collecting and turning in litter which contained marked items (thus proving it had been picked up from the grounds) received extra pay or privileges. The program was implemented in a multiple-baseline fashion across three areas of the compound, with a fourth serving as a baseline-only control. It seemed unlikely that assigning areas of responsibility would contribute, but the prison officials could have interpreted any beneficial results as due to this. Accordingly, when the intervention was implemented in Area 1, the prisoners were simultaneously told that Area 2 was their responsibility. As is shown in Figure 10.8, change occurred only in the treated area. A similar strategy was followed in Areas 3 and 4. In this design, Areas 1 and 3 are A/Bs, while Area 2 is an A-C/B, and Area 4 is an A-C. This shows how ineffective phases can deliberately be worked into multiple baselines to control for various possibilities.

Heterogeneity Versus Homogeneity of Series

Originally, Baer et al. (1968) suggested that multiple baselines should be done across series of the same type. Thus, a multiple baseline could be done with a similar behavior in two or more clients (across people); two or more behaviors in one client (across behaviors); or with the same behavior, done by the same person, in two or more settings (across settings). The logic of the design element, however, does not require this. Any combination of series can be used, as long as the phase change is identical. For instance, a multiple baseline could be implemented across Behavior A in Setting Z, Behavior B in Setting Y, and Behavior C in Setting X. Equally logical, but more unusual, a multiple baseline could be conducted across Behavior C in Person X, Behavior B in Person Y, and Behavior A in Person Z.

The specific series that are selected allow some statements to be made about likely areas of generalization for the effects seen. If several clients with the same disorder were used, and if strong and consistent data were used, it makes it more likely that effects will generalize across people. If results are replicated across settings, then results in one setting are more likely to generalize to another for similar clients. Note, however, that we will not have demonstrated generality across clients. Mixing types of series (person, behavior, setting) provides a more ambitious program of generalization. In other words, some depth is being traded for breadth. Whether or not this is a wise move depends upon the generality of the results. If they are highly general, replication across types of series will advance our knowledge most rapidly. If the results are real, but very specific, tests across the same kinds of series may be more cautious and may reduce the likelihood that we will falsely reject effective interventions.

The Natural Multiple Baseline

The multiple baseline across people is probably one of the clearest examples of a natural design element that arises in practice. Nothing could be more

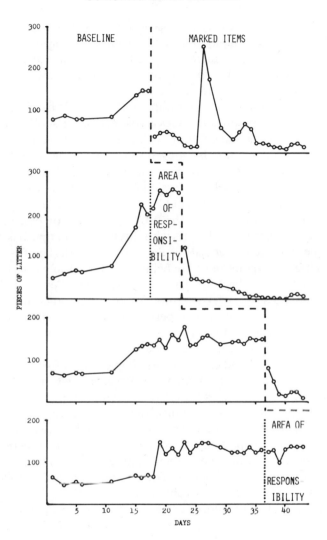

Figure 10.8. An example of the use of ineffective phases in a multiple baseline to control for alternative explanations. (Redrawn from Hayes, S.C., Johnson, V.S., & Cone, J.D. The marked-item technique: A practical procedure for litter control. *Journal of Applied Behavior Analysis,* 1975, *8,* 381-386. Used with permission from The Society for the Experimental Analysis of Behavior.)

natural to clinical work than an A/B and it is the simple phase change that is the basis of a multiple baseline. There are several ways a natural multiple baseline can emerge. One way is to save several identical A/Bs done with several clients, usually (but not necessarily) with similar problems. Individual clients will inevitably have differing lengths of baseline (often widely so), due to case complexities or to matters of convenience. Thus, sequential cases usually lead to a multiple baseline across people.

Some of the earliest applied literature on the multiple baseline (e.g., Baer et al. 1968) said that multiple baselines across persons should always be done at the same time in the same setting with the same behavior. Saving cases, with perhaps periods of months or even years separating each, violates this rule, but fortunately the logic of the strategy does not really require it. If the time of the phase shift differs in real time from client to client, it is unlikely that important external events could repeatedly coincide with the phase changes. The control exerted by the different lengths of baseline remain.

There are two primary difficulties with this type of multiple baseline, compared to the type recommended by Baer et al. (1968). The first difficulty is fairly subtle. If several clients are being seen at the same time in the same place, then a multiple baseline across persons may allow a slightly more elegant control because any extraneous variables (i.e., other than treatment) that produced an effect for the first person are probably simultaneously present for the other clients. In a sense, extraneous variables are not just randomized, they are also held constant across cases. If a terrible snowstorm occurred just as the second condition was implemented for Person 1, it also occurred at the corresponding moment for Persons 2 or 3. In a natural multiple baseline across cases this added form of control is not present. Instead, the improbability of successive coincidences controls for the effect of extraneous variables. In fact, however, the difference between the two is very small. What is literally present for two people may not be functionally present for both (e.g., one may not even take note of the snowstorm, the other may be greatly concerned about it). There is an advantage to following the advice of Baer et al., but it is probably fairly small.

The second problem is more severe. It was touched upon in the earlier discussion of natural withdrawals. If the clinician is allowing the case itself to determine the exact length of baseline, there is the danger that the same factor which indicated that it is time to change phases is correlated with processes that produce behavior change. The main practical protections against this difficulty are replication (e.g., including several cases in natural multiple baselines), information (e.g., reporting in detail why each phase change occurred when it did for each client), and considerable caution. If the reasons for changing phases vary widely from client to client, it is unlikely that a third variable consistently produced changes in the second phases. Hopefully, some of the clients will have had treatment implemented at a particular moment for reasons that are fairly arbitrary. For example, the assessment phase may be quite routine and yet differ in length between clients simply because of scheduling issues.

It is also essential that clinicians report all cases attempted, not just those showing the desired effect. If the effect is not seen in some of the cases, the clinician should attempt to find out why (indeed this seems required by good clinical practice). A careful examination of possible differences between individuals which might account for variable results may lead to treatment solutions for nonresponsive clients. Data showing subsequent response would increase our knowledge about mechanisms producing change and about boundary conditions of a given treatment (see chapter 12).

The opportunities to use the multiple baseline element in practice are many. Multiple baselines often form naturally across behaviors due to the tendency for practitioners to tackle subsets of problems sequentially rather than all at once. Figure 10.9 shows one such example (from Hayes, Brownell, & Barlow, 1978). This client was an inpatient who came in complaining of sexual arousal to sadistic rape and exhibitionism. He was also a very active heterosexual. He had raped at least one female and had been arrested for exposing himself. Physiological and self-report measures were taken of all three arousal patterns.

It was natural to begin treatment (self-administered covert sensitization) with one problem area. In this case, exhibitionism was selected because the client was in danger of being arrested for this more recent but currently stronger pattern. As therapy eliminated the client's arousal pattern to exhibitionism, no effect was noted on sadistic arousal. This was then successfully targeted for treatment. A similar effect occurred.

This is a fairly dramatic case, resulting in interpretable data, despite the fact that only two series were compared. What is important to note is that this emerged out of routine clinical work. It was a natural design. The course and sequence of treatment probably would have been the same without the systematic measures, but these measures allowed firm conclusions to be drawn and shared with the profession.

Natural multiple baselines across settings or time are less common but occur when practitioners treat problem behavior shown in one specific condition or time of day first, rather than treating the problem all at once. The case mentioned earlier, concerning the depressed and anxious woman with a cleft palate, provides an example. Rather than attempt to deal with all situations at once, we targeted them two at a time—a natural multiple baseline across situations. The litter program shown in Figure 10.8 is another example.

The multiple baseline is probably one of the best designs available for practitioners. It does not require withdrawal, it is fairly simple, and applied opportunities for its use abound once systematic measures are being taken.

THE CROSSOVER DESIGN

In our discussion of multiple baselines, we pointed out that Baer et al. (1968) recommended that only one dimension (e.g., people, behavior, situa-

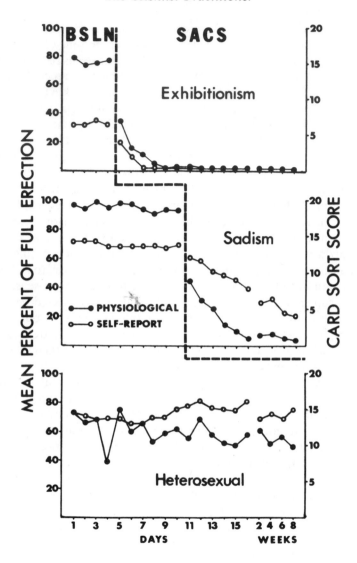

Figure 10.9. An example of a multiple baseline across situations that emerged naturally in the treatment of a patient with multiple sexual deviations. Note the use of a baseline-only control. *SACS* stands for *self-administered covert sensitization*. (From Hayes, S.C., Brownell, K.D., & Barlow, D.H., The use of self-administered covert sensitization in the treatment of exhibitionism and sadism. *Behavior Therapy,* 1978, *9,* 283-289.)

tion) be allowed to vary, and that this does indeed provide some additional control by factoring out external sources of influence. That is, any external event that might influence the outcome occurs simultaneously for all series.

The crossover is drawn from this logic and that of similar group-comparison approaches (see Kazdin, 1980). In it, two concurrent phase changes occur, one in the reverse order of the other, each on a separate series. For example, a B/C sequence might be conducted on one behavior and a C/B sequence on another. By changing phases at the same time, in the same place, after phases of the same length in each series, external sources of influence are kept equivalent in each series. If consistent within-series effects are shown in each series (e.g., if B is greater than C in each case), the likelihood of the effect is increased beyond that of the component simple phase changes were they not synchronized.

Suppose an educator wishes to test the value of two different comprehensive curricula. In one the publisher uses programmed texts, while the other is more traditional. Two different subjects are identified (say, math and English). Several students are assessed repeatedly and carefully. In math, the programmed text is used first, then after a month or so, the traditional text is used. The reverse is true in English. If the programmed text is clearly better in both cases, we are much more likely to believe it than if the same sequence had occurred in both subject matters. Such things as time of year, events in the classroom, and so on are held constant. If a third variable was responsible for the improvement in English when the programmed text was used, why did math acquisition slow at the same point? Thus, extraneous variables are controlled by keeping them equivalent throughout for both series.

Crossovers will occasionally emerge naturally in clinical or educational settings. Suppose a client comes in with two problems. One problem is in need of immediate treatment, and treatment begins while baseline is collected on the second problem. After a time, treatment is stopped on Problem 1 and simultaneously begun on Problem 2. This is a natural crossover, created by a shift in problem focus.

The crossover elements can be used to strengthen a design such as an A/B/A/B when more than one series is available (e.g., there are two problems). Rather than conduct the same sequence on each behavior, the sequences can be timed in a crossover fashion. Figure 10.10 provides an example. Note that the patterns, while relatively weak in each series, are made more believable by the crossover, because an extraneous variable would have to have exactly opposite effects on each series to produce the result.

When a crossover consists entirely of two simple phase changes, it is important that it be replicated. This is because complex order effects are still possible. For example, novelty might have an opposite effect on two series. With replication this becomes less plausible.

The main advantage of a crossover is that it does not require an absence of treatment, and it is a very simple design. It can be added easily to within-series designs of all kinds, whenever two or more series are available.

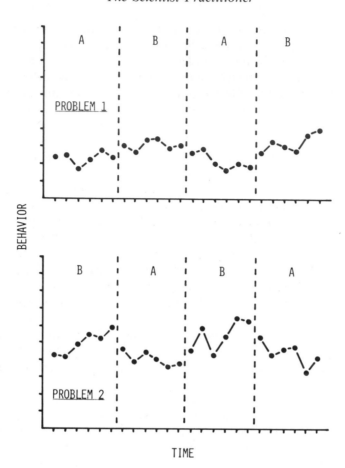

Figure 10.10. An example of the use of a crossover. Each series shows a fairly weak treatment effect, but the crossover arrangement makes the effect much more convincing because of the simultaneous acceleration and deceleration across series.

THE CONSTANT-SERIES CONTROL

Many times there are problems that are repeatedly assessed and left in a single condition throughout (usually baseline). These data can be examined as a type of between-series comparison (e.g., Brownell et al., 1977; Hayes & Cone, 1977) and can be combined with other within-series comparisons. The logic of this comparison is identical to the between-series comparisons made in a multiple-baseline design (see Figure 10.2). Changes occurring elsewhere and not in the control series are more likely to have been produced by treatment (cf. Campbell & Stanley's (1963) equivalent-time-samples design).

The purpose of the constant-series control is to reduce the likelihood that extraneous events, cyclical effects, and the like, could have been responsible for the changes seen. If they were, the reasoning goes, why didn't the constant series also change in the same way? For this to be a sensible point, it is important that the constant series could reasonably be expected to be susceptible to extraneous source of influence. For example, if the constant-series control was the gender identity of a transsexual and the treated series was the client's depressed mood, the lack of changes in the constant series would add little to the analysis because gender identity is notoriously stable.

The most common type of constant-series control is the use of baseline-only when several series are available. If the practitioner has been comparing, say, baseline to treatment in one series, the remaining series might produce a natural baseline-only control. It may be targeted for treatment, for example, but is left untreated because the client must move. Figure 10.11 presents an example.

In the top series, an A/B/A/B has been conducted on one problem, while the bottom series represents an untreated problem. Because changes occur only with treatment, the data are strengthened. Essentially, three between-series are available to supplement the within-series changes.

Baseline is not the only type of constant-series control. Sometimes only treatment has been implemented: a "B-only" (cf. Browning & Stover, 1971). A treatment-only control can be helpful in much the same way as a baseline-only control. Consider the hypothetical data in Figure 10.12. Note that while improvement is constant in the treatment-only control, it subsides when treatment is withdrawn in the first series. This heightens the believability of the withdrawal effects. The downturn is much less likely to have been due to extraneous events, maturation, delayed effects of treatment, and so on. All of these explanations, if true, presumably should have impacted on the treatment-only series. It also controls for any unlikely order effect (that treatment will work only after a formal baseline).

The constant-series control, like all elements that use more than one series, can be applied to any type of series: that organized by person, problem, situation, time of day, or any combination of these. Different series are relevant to different questions, and they emerge in different ways. For example, consider the use of constant-series controls across people. This element provides a home for those cases in which only treatment is given and those in which treatment is never given. As anchors in a series of cases they provide additional control and precision to the analysis. Figure 10.13 shows two examples. At the top, a multiple baseline across cases has been created. While the multiple baseline itself is strong without the constant-series controls, the treatment-only control eliminates the likelihood of an order effect and strengthens the between-series comparisons at each of the phase changes. The baseline-only control strengthens the between-series comparisons further. At the bottom,

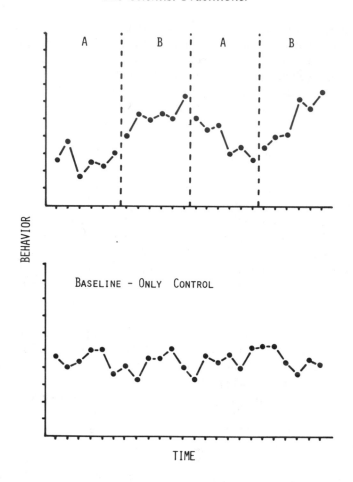

Figure 10.11. An example of the baseline-only version of a constant-series control.

the constant-series controls perform the same function for an A/B/A/B design. Note that any design elements would be strengthened in the same way by using these controls.

Constant-series controls emerge very naturally in the course of applied practice. For example, a client may have multiple problems. A practitioner may immediately launch into treatment of some problems. These may be particularly severe, or they may be particularly obvious so that the practitioner might move into treatment, perhaps even in the first session, without feeling the need for additional assessment before beginning. These would form a treatment-only control. Other problems may remain on the back burner. They are clearly problems and they are being repeatedly measured, but needs in other areas are being pursued while their treatment is being

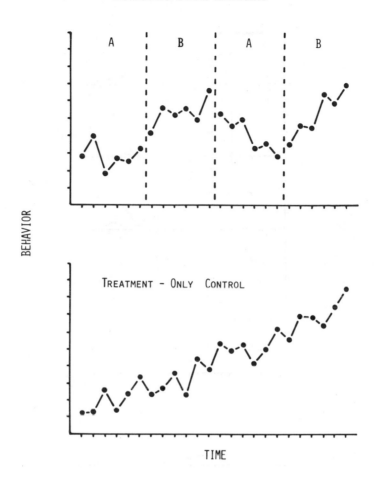

Figure 10.12. An example of the treatment-only variant of a constant-series control.

postponed. These would form a baseline-only control. These two constant series elements would make a contribution to whatever is done on the other problems. Suppose that the only actual analysis done is an A/B on a third problem. The combination of a treatment-only control, a baseline-only control, and an A/B could elevate a collection of weak (but nonintrusive) design elements into a meaningful design if the resultant data were clear.

THE TRUE REVERSAL

Treatment withdrawal is often termed a *reversal* and it is common to hear a design which includes a withdrawal (e.g., an A/B/A/B) called a *reversal design*. Actually, the data themselves are sometimes expected to reverse dur-

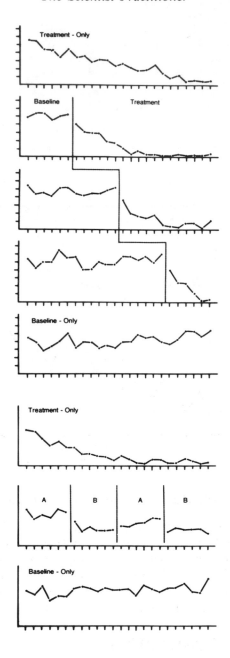

Figure 10.13. Two examples of how constant series controls add to the precision of any analysis.

ing a withdrawal (though we have argued that this is not required). The design itself is not a reversal.

Leitenberg (1973) originally made the distinction between reversal and withdrawal designs. A reversal design is one in which instead of being withdrawn, treatment is deliberately reversed. For example, if a child is being encouraged to play with peers, she may then be encouraged to play with adults and not with peers (e.g., Allen, Hart, Buell, Harris, & Wolf, 1964).

While the reversal is not necessarily a combined-series design, it usually is one because separate measures will be kept on the two targets. Figure 10.14 provides an example from Allen et al. (1964).

As one behavior increases, the other is expected to decrease. In addition, the sequence within a series is evaluated much as in an A/B/A except that the second baseline is a deliberate reversal of treatment. The true reversal is seldom seen for at least two reasons. First, it seems hard to justify ethically in most applied situations. A withdrawal has some similar problems, but many redeeming features. The use of a true reversal would be quite rare in normal practice (except perhaps a paradoxical intervention, but there the expected result is not deterioration). The second problem with a true reversal is that it does not fit many interventions well. Many interventions are not "reversible." Consider an educational intervention, for example. How could it sensibly be reversed? Would you attempt to teach the opposite of what you just taught?

Combined-series design elements, as has been seen, put together between- and within-series elements in a new way, with an identifiable and distinct logic. They are new design units, built from other design units. Design elements can also be combined in a manner that does not involve new logical units. This occurs in practice when the tools we have already described are sequenced in a particular way to attempt to analyze applied phenomena. It is to this that we now turn.

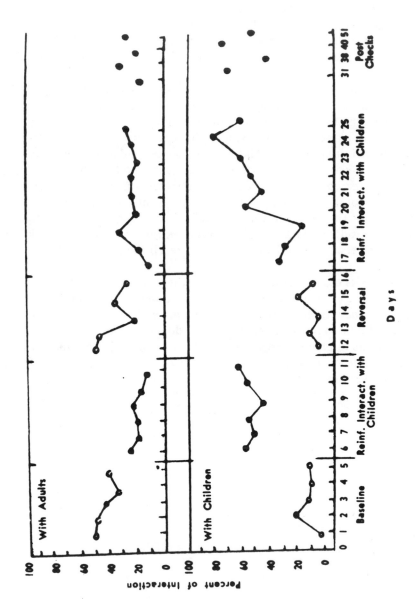

Figure 10.14. An example of a true reversal design (From Allen, K.E., Hart, B., Buell, J.S., Harris, F.R., & Wolf, M.W. Effects of social reinforcement on isolate behavior of a nursery school child. *Child Development*, 1964, *35*, 511-518.)

Chapter 11
Issues, Ethics, and Examples in the Use of Time-Series Methodology in Practice

COMBINING DESIGN ELEMENTS

In a way, the topic of this chapter is the topic of the book. Yet there are a variety of issues that have not yet been addressed that have to do with the actual use of the various tools we have been describing.

Throughout this book we have repeatedly emphasized that time-series elements are not completed structures that are simply laid on top of professional activities. Properly used, designs are the results of creative strategies used to solve applied problems. Time-series elements are combined as the need for them emerges. It is quite possible to create designs that literally have no name, as would be the case with a particular combination of elements never before used. The practitioner should not feel as though there is some vulnerability in using a "new design" in such a situation. If the design elements are well worked out, and are used appropriately, the completed design need not be familiar.

To combine design elements, it is important to keep track of two basic issues: what question needs to be answered, and what design tools that can answer that question best fit the specifics of the situation.

Which Design Element to Use

Table 11.1 presents some clinically important questions and examples of the various design elements useful in each situation. Within any row of this table various elements can be combined to address a given clinical question. As different questions arise, different elements can be used (draw from different rows).

Consider the first question, Does a treatment work? Several additional questions then need to be answered in a particular situation in order to arrive at reasonable design options which fit the situation. Panel 11.1 presents

Table 11.1. Examples of the Use of Design Elements to Answer Specific Types of Clinical Questions

CLINICAL QUESTION	DESIGN TYPE		
	WITHIN SERIES	BETWEEN SERIES	COMBINED SERIES
Does a treatment work?	A/B/A/B . . . , B/A/B/A . . . , A/B (see combined designs) Periodic treatments design Changing criterion design	Alternating treatments (comparing A and B) Alternating treatments across behaviors or situations	Multiple baseline across settings, behaviors, or persons comparing A and B Replicated crossovers (comparing A and B)
Does one treatment work better than another, given that we already know they work?	B/C/B/C/ . . . , C/B/C/B	Alternating treatments comparing B and C)	Replicated crossovers (comparing B and C) Multiple baselines (comparing B and C and controlling for order
Does one treatment work, does another work, and which works better?	A/B A/C/A combined with A/C/A/B/A	Alternating treatments (comparing A and B and C)	Multiple baseline comparing A and B and C and controlling for order)
	Or combine any element from Row 1 with any element from Row 2		
Are there elements with a successful treatment that make it work?	B/B+C/B B+C/B/B+C C/B+C/C B+C/C/B+C	Alternating treatments (comparing, for example, B and B+C)	Multiple baseline (comparing B and B+C, and C and B+C) Replicated crossovers (comparing B and B+C, and C and B+C)
Does the client prefer one treatment over another?		Simultaneous treatments (comparing B and C)	
Does a treatment work, and if it does, what part of it makes it work?	Combine any elements from Rows 1 or 3 with any element from Row 4		
What level of treatment is optimal?	Ascending/descending design (B'/B'/B')	Alternating tyreatments (comparing B and B')	Multiple baseline (comparing B B' and controlling for order) Replicated crossovers (comparing B and B')

(From Hayes, S.C. Single case experimental design and empirical clinical practice. *Journal of Consulting and Clinical Psychology*, 1981, *49*, 193-211.)

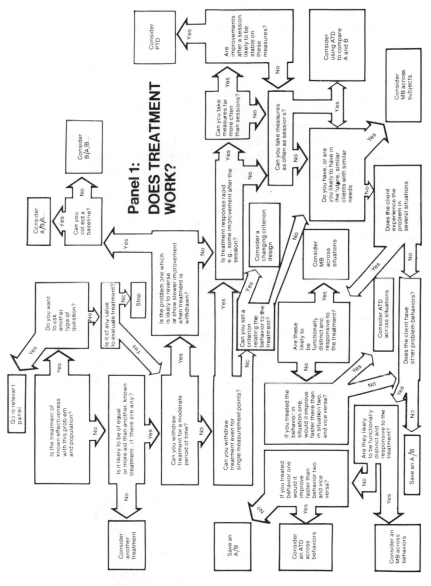

Panel 1: DOES TREATMENT WORK?

Go to relevant panel

Is the treatment of known effectiveness with this problem and population? — No → Is it likely to be of equal or more aid than another known treatment, if there are any? — Yes → Do you want to ask another type of question? — No → Is it of any value to evaluate treatment? — No → **Stop**

Is it of any value to evaluate treatment? — Yes → Is the problem one which is likely to reverse or show slower improvement when treatment is withdrawn? — Yes → Can you collect a baseline? — Yes → **Consider A/B/A...** / No → **Consider B/A/B...**

Is the treatment of known effectiveness... — No → Consider another treatment

Is it likely to be of equal or more aid... — Yes → Can you withdraw treatment for a moderate period of time? — No → Is the problem one which is likely to reverse or show slower improvement when treatment is withdrawn? — No → Is treatment response rapid e.g., some improvement after the session? — Yes → Can you take measures far more often than sessions? — Yes → Are improvements after a session likely to be stable on these measures? — Yes → **Consider PTD**

Are improvements after a session likely to be stable on these measures? — No → Can you take measures as often as session is? — No → **Consider using ATD to compare A and B**

Can you take measures far more often than sessions? — No → Can you take measures as often as session is? — Yes → Do you have, or are you likely to have in the future, similar clients with similar needs? — Yes → **Consider MB across subjects**

Can you withdraw treatment for single measurement points? — Yes → Can you set a criterion relating the behavior to the treatment? — Yes → **Consider a changing criterion design**

Can you set a criterion relating the behavior to the treatment? — No → Are these likely to be functionally, distinct and responsive to the treatment? — Yes → **Consider MB across situations**

Are these likely to be functionally, distinct and responsive to the treatment? — No → Does the client experience the problem in several situations? — Yes → **Consider ATD across situations**

Does the client experience the problem in several situations? — No → Does the client have other problem behaviors? — Yes → Are they likely to be functionally distinct and responsive to the treatment? — Yes → **Consider MB across behaviors**

Are they likely to be functionally distinct and responsive to the treatment? — No → **Save an A/B**

If you treated the behavior in situation one, would it improve faster there than in situation two, and vice versa? — No → **Save an A/B**

If you treated behavior one would it improve faster than behavior two and vice versa? — No → **Consider an ATD across behaviors**

Do you have, or are you likely to have in the future, similar clients with similar needs? — No → Does the client experience the problem in several situations?

Panel 11.1. Does a treatment work?

275

a flowchart which summarizes some of the major options for Row 1 of Table 11.1. Notice that there is almost *always* an option that could work. Sometimes, there are several options.

When there are several options, it may be beneficial to employ redundant design elements. For example, in Row 1 of Table 11.1, there are several within-, between-, and combined-series options. Consider a simple case. Suppose a rehabilitation therapist is treating three spastic clients with biofeedback. Suppose the original plan is to do an A/B/A/B with each (see the top of Figure 11.1) This is reasonable, but what if the treatment is so effective it causes improvement that does not slow with treatment withdrawal? It would cost very little to stagger phases across clients (see the middle of Figure 11.1). That way, a simple multiple baseline would be formed which would allow an analysis of irreversible rates of improvement. Suppose, however, that the treatment only works with some people, *and* it causes irreversible improvement. A multiple baseline will not solve this problem. One possibility is to conduct an ATD in the treatment phases (bottom of Figure 11.1). That way the effects can be documented at the level of the individual. If the treatment only works with some people, this can be ascertained.

Thus, the use of multiple tools increases the flexibility and precision of the analysis. We are not suggesting that such an elaborate design is needed or even desirable in most situations. The point is that the practitioner should consider the use of redundant design tools when it is practical and when the individual advantages of each may be needed. The practitioner needs constantly to be aware of emerging design options and to set things up so that the design can react and change as the data come in. Table 11.1 may provide a structure for this. The practitioner should monitor the nature of questions that emerge (i.e., What row are we now in? What row are we likely to be in later?) and consider the options in each row. Which fit best? If more than one fits, can they be combined? What are the costs and benefits?

Panel 11.2 shows another flowchart, this one aimed at Rows 2 and 3 of Table 11.1. There are many other questions that could bear on the options selected, but this chart summarizes the major ones. The chart (and the one in Panel 11.1) mimics the decision-making process an experienced empirical practitioner would follow. The reader should develop his or her skills to a point where most of these questions are intuitively available. A good way to do this is to work through Panels 11.1 and 11.2 several times with hypothetical or actual situations.

"STRETCHING" THE GUIDELINES FOR TIME SERIES METHODOLOGY

Time-series elements are not "all-or-none" devices. This book has taken a very liberal stance about the essential continuity between elegant, absolutely

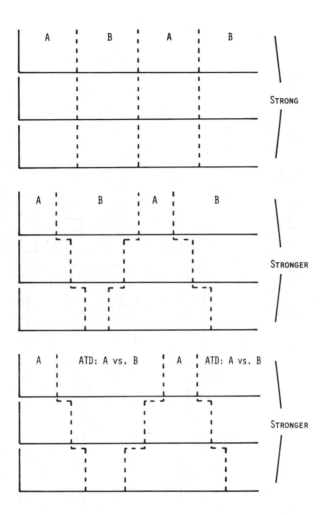

Figure 11.1. An example of ways design elements can be combined to increase the strength of an analysis.

defensible design options and imperfect but possibly valuable ones. How far can the basics be liberalized?

Repeated Measurement

Different elements can be stretched to different degrees. Consider repeated measurement. Without repeated measurement, there cannot be a series of data points with which to evaluate variability and trend. Few situations will allow simple pre-post measurement to be of any use in time-series methodology. There are a few exceptions, however, even to one of the most

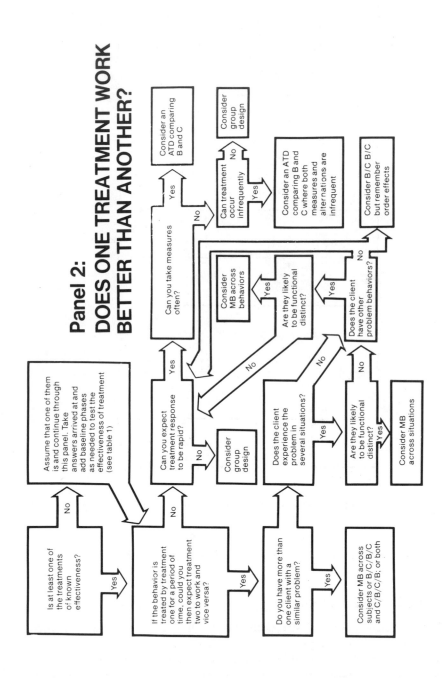

Panel 2:
DOES ONE TREATMENT WORK BETTER THAN ANOTHER?

Is at least one of the treatments of known effectiveness?

Assume that one of them is and continue through this panel. Take answers arrived at and add baseline phases as needed to test the effectiveness of treatment (see table 1)

If the behavior is treated by treatment one for a period of time, could you then expect treatment two to work and vice versa?

Can you expect treatment response to be rapid?

Consider group design

Can you take measures often?

Consider an ATD comparing B and C

Can treatment occur infrequently

Consider group design

Consider an ATD comparing B and C where both measures and alternations are infrequent

Consider MB across behaviors

Are they likely to be functional distinct?

Does the client have other problem behaviors?

Consider B/C B/C but remember order effects

Do you have more than one client with a similar problem?

Does the client experience the problem in several situations?

Are they likely to be functional distinct?

Consider MB across situations

Consider MB across subjects or B/C/B/C and C/B/C/B; or both

Panel 11.2. Does one treatment work better than another?

basic of rules. Sometimes we know so much about the stability and course of a particular phenomenon that even single data points are useful. Examples are hard to find in the behavioral sciences, but they occur regularly in medicine. Suppose we were treating a client with a form of cancer that was virtually always fatal and which almost never went into remission. Even a single observation of a dramatic reversal would be potentially worthwhile because we know so much about the expected nature and course of the disorder.

Systematic Measurement

Even more basically, suppose measurement is unsystematic, perhaps anecdotal. In some few situations, anecdotal information is scientifically useful. It may be, for example, that a particular constellation of factors should not be possible, given a particular point of view. Unsystematic data, collected even once, might call this into question if that constellation is apparent. Suppose, for example, it was claimed that true transsexuals never change their sex role identity. Suppose further, that it is clear from anecdotal evidence that a client once fit the definition of a transsexual, but has since changed his identity. This anecdote might provide important and worthwhile evidence. Similarly, someone might claim that all depressed married women are angry at their husbands. If I can find even one that does not show this, an anecdotal report of it may be meaningful.

The methodological rules we have described should not be thought of in legalistic ways. The overall strategy is more important than individual guidelines. The long-term research program is more important than any individual rule violation. This point deserves some additional discussion.

The Purpose of the Methodology

The products of science are statements of relations that are based on verifiable experience. Unlike purely experiential disciplines (e.g., mysticism) which eschew the development of rules or laws as an important output, or purely social enterprises (e.g., law) which develop rules without the requirement that they be verifiable in experience, science attempts to walk a middle line between the two.

Scientific methodology is nothing more than a set of guidelines which permit others to have access to the experiences which support particular statements. In a sense, methodology is a way we isolate ourselves from the capacity we have to deceive ourselves. It is all too easy to see things in a particular way because of our hopes, expectations, wishes, desires, fears, and so on. Practitioners are well aware of this, of course. Concerns about "countertransference," about the "Rosenthal effect," and the like are due to this sense of the ease with which we deceive ourselves. Scientific methodology is a way of protecting ourselves from our own folly.

Methodology is valuable to the extent that it does this. It is not a matter of following rules for rules' sake. There is no hidden vault containing "rules of scientific methodology." Nor is it a matter simply of logic or carefully crafted argument. Methodological rules can be logical and still be poor rules. We have attempted to show, for example, that the supremely logical structure of group-comparison research simply has not worked well in applied disciplines, not because it is not logical, but because it does not work very well in this situation.

The point here is that the rules contained in this book should be taken with a grain of salt. Some of our sensible-sounding recommendations may ultimately turn out not to be very helpful. Logic will not decide this — the progress of the field will — and the only way to decide is to test it.

It is quite possible to assess this empirically. For example, no one has yet done a study to see if the use of time-series elements make clinical success more or less likely with a given case. It seems likely that it will, yet this is ultimately an empirical question. Individual clinicians can test the usefulness of time-series methodology themselves, by examining the impact it has on their work. Do people get better when a systematic evaluation is done? Are baseline data helpful in formulating successful treatments? Are things learned which can then be applied to other cases? It is these kinds of outcomes which determine the value of methodology.

The answer to the question, How far can we stretch the methodology? is then clear: Until the methodology no longer makes a contribution. It is not clear how far that will be. For certain violations, nature may extract a high price. For others, the cost may be low. Applied disciplines need more experience with this approach before we will know how liberal we can be. It seems better simply to do as rigorous a job as we can than to set excessively narrow standards and give up in disgust because they can't be met.

THE CONTRIBUTION OF "CASE STUDIES"

At some point, enough niceties are missed so that an analysis is no longer viewed as a single-case experimental design. It is often then called a *case study,* although we have subsumed both of these under the rubric *time-series methodology.* Case studies range from purely anecdotal reports to well-crafted, simple phase-change designs. The issues they present differ, depending on their exact nature.

As mentioned above, in this text nonexperimental designs (e.g., A/B designs) have not been clearly distinguished from their more elaborate brethren. This is because time-series methodology includes designs which lie on a continuum in terms of the *degree* to which they are "experimental." The distinctions between them are dependent on a host of factors, and weaker forms can become stronger through various means. For example, we have pointed to a number of ways A/B designs can be integrated into more sophisticated analyses (such as a multiple baseline). In the chapter that follows, we will describe another use for A/B analyses — in clinical replication series. Earlier (in chapter 8) we mentioned the use of the A/B in providing for accountability.

In time-series methodology, the case study is of use because it is part and parcel of a general methodological approach — it blends smoothly into more and more sophisticated analyses. Without an interest in case analysis, the entire methodological structure we are advocating is seriously weakened.

Traditional research methodologists have tended to put case studies into a separate (and lower) class. Their functions are seen as quite limited. Case studies are said to be of use primarily because they suggest hypotheses, for example. While this is surely so, it can amount to damnation by faint praise because virtually anything can suggest hypotheses. Such a view discourages practitioners from analyzing their cases. Without this beginning, where will more elaborate analyses come from?

If case studies are thought of as anecdotal case reports, then it is true that they have a limited scientific function. Once repeated and systematic measurement is in place and interventions specified, however, the role expands. In particular, the practitioner attempting this type of case analysis will not be certain (before the case is concluded) what the level of scientific product will be. The opportunities abound, as we have argued, to raise the level of knowledge, while simultaneously meeting client needs. Even those analyses that end up at a lower level (e.g., a B-only, an A/B) will form a foundation for additional work.

By encouraging case studies, we increase the likelihood of even more meaningful output. If practitioners are discouraged from doing case studies, why should they use time-series methodology at all? In this sense, an openness to case analysis and to the case studies that may often result is a cornerstone of applied time-series methodology.

ETHICAL ISSUES

Several important ethical issues arise in the use of time-series methodology for practical evaluation. Unless these issues are properly viewed, they can present significant barriers to empirical practitioners. The biggest source of ethical difficulties comes from the mixture of scientific and practical goals in the approach we have advocated here.

Is Time-Series Methodology Ethically Defensible in Practice?

Society has always been ambivalent about science. The pursuit of knowledge is frightening because it implies a willingness to enter unknown and perhaps undesirable places. The motivation and sense of balance of the scientist is thought to be critical. Knowledge is a genie that, once let out, is difficult indeed to return to the bottle.

These very human worries are reflected in such disparate arenas as the biblical story of Creation (in which humankind's fall from grace is caused by eating from the tree of knowledge); movies about "mad scientists" who pursue knowledge at the expense of human values; or current concerns about computers, genetic engineering, test-tube babies, and so on. The point is not that these worries are unjustified. The point is that our ambivalence about science must be recognized, and placed in proper perspective. Restraints on the pursuit of knowledge must be applied only to situations that warrant it.

Society has generated a large number of rules to protect human subjects. These include procedural protections, such as the submission of research proposals to human-subjects committees, as well as specific mandated activities on the part of a researcher, such as the acquisition from the subjects of informed and written consent to the research procedures involved. Quite apart from the formal legal requirements which surround the term *research,* there are a number of informal requirements as well. These can range from the ethical practices in a particular applied profession (such as the standards set forth by the American Psychological Association) to the individual, idiosyncratic application of ethical and moral guidelines to these activities. Should these protections be applied to clients who are treated by empirical practitioners? Does the kind of time-series methodology advocated here turn clients into human subjects, and practice into formal research?

If it does, the whole purpose of this book is unattainable. Practitioners could not function if their routine professional work was seen as formal research, with all of the additional protections that implies. There seems to be, however, an important difference between research and time-series evaluation.

The Distinction Between Research and Evaluation

A good deal has been written about this distinction, but advances in evaluation procedures and recent changes in the protection provided to human subjects have produced an environment in which this issue is particularly critical. First, we should examine the verbal distinctions we make between research and treatment, and second, examine the functional importance of these variables and the societal mechanisms that have sprung up around them.

The dictionary defines *research* as *the careful hunting for facts or the truth*. This sense of research is clearly quite compatible with treatment. After all, successful treatment involves a kind of investigation of the world of the particular client. This sense of the word *research* is not what people are talking about when they talk of protection for human subjects.

Over the years, research has come to mean a search for objective facts in which regard for the welfare of the "subjects" is very much secondary to the development of scientific knowledge. Perhaps because of dramatic instances of abuse (particularly in medicine), a number of guidelines have been developed to protect research subjects.

This second sense of the word *research* is often not compatible with professional practice. Clients are not necessarily subjects, and research which puts knowledge first and the client second is, by definition, distinct from the normal activities of a practitioner. Thus, in our usual use of the term, research is basically incompatible with practice.

In common language, when do people usually call something research? Generally, people seem to do it based on appearance. The left side of Table 11.2 presents several characteristics which appear particularly salient in making this distinction.

Table 11.2. Some Defining Characteristics of Research and Evaluation

TREATMENT RESEARCH	TREATMENT EVALUATION
1. Systematic data collected	1. Systematic data collected
2. Intervention specified	2. Intervention specified
3. Subject selected on basis of scientific needs	2. Clients selected on usual clinical criteria
4. Questions selected on scientific grounds	4. Questions selected on the basis of client needs
5. Publication or presentation may result	5. Publication or presentation may result
6. Design tools used to answer scientific questions	6. Design tools used to answer clinical qustions

Note that most of these characteristics have to do with the apparent, formal or structural characteristics of the activity. For example, if systematic data are collected, the activity is likely to be thought to be research, regardless of the goal of the activity.

The problem with this, as it applies to the clinical or educational environment is apparent by considering the right side of Table 11.2. Empirical practice has many of the structural aspects of formal research. The presence of any of these characteristics is likely to cause the kind of evaluation we have talked about in this book to be termed formal research. Yet the two are very different.

On functional grounds, treatment research and treatment evaluation seem quite distinct. Their goals and purposes are different. The goal of science is to develop better organized statements of relations between events. In other words, the goal is a better rule or law. The goal of treatment is to improve client functioning. The two are easily distinguished at the extreme. When the two goals are mixed, confusion can result, unless careful distinctions are made.

Table 11.3 shows a division of activities based on the mix of scientific and treatment goals.

Table 11.3. The Distinction Between Treatment, Treatment Evaluation, Treatment Research, and Research

TREATMENT	PURE EVALUATION	TREATMENT ~~RESEARCH~~ *Evaluation*	TREATMENT RESEARCH	PURE *Research*
Pursuit of better organized scientific statements	None	Secondary	Primary	Primary
Pursuit of better client outcome	Primary	Primary	Secondary	None

At least four activities seem distinguishable. In pure treatment, the only goal is improved client outcome. In treatment evaluation, the primary goal is client outcome, but the practitioner would also like to be able to *say* something about it (e.g., Did the client improve due to treatment? What was the real problem? What about treatment was helpful? How many other clients could benefit by this approach?). In treatment research, the goal is primarily the generation of better organized scientific statements. Client improvement is always hoped for, but is secondary. A specific client's needs are to be accommodated to the research project, if possible, but the individual client's needs did not start the sequence of events and are not the central issue. In pure research on applied problems, client improvement is not even a secondary goal in any immediate sense. Survey research or research in experimental psychopathology would be an example.

The problem is that it is harder to see the goals of an activity than it is to see the form of the activity. Look again at Table 11.2. Note that it is in the areas that are easy to see (e.g., Are data collected?) that research and evaluation are similar. They differ in areas that are more difficult to discern (e.g., Why are you collecting data?). Thus, on the surface, research and evaluation look quite similar. An empirical practitioner could easily be mistakenly thought of as "doing research on clients;" it could falsely be said that "clients are being used as guinea pigs;" and so on.

There are a number of short- and long-term consequences, both for the client and the practitioner, which accrue when treatment is elevated to treatment evaluation or to treatment research. Since, in treatment research, increased client functioning is only a side effect of the main goal of generating better organized scientific statements, treatment research would seem to decrease the probability that an individual client would be helped by participating. In treatment evaluation, however, scientific goals are subsumed under the goal of increasing client functioning. Thus, treatment evalution seems to increase the likely benefits of treatment with little increased risk. As we have argued throughout this book, treatment evaluation is a matter of adopting an empirical approach to treatment. It seems likely to make interventions more systematic, with better information supporting clinical decisions. It is hard to see how this could fail to help therapy (although this assumption has not yet itself been tested empirically). Indeed, our current societal posture at times seems to assume that if the intervention is poorly specified; if goals are unclear; and if measures are weak, infrequent, or nonexistent, then there is *less* of an ethical worry. Our own cultural ambivalence about science has turned vice into virtue, sloppiness into safety.

Every client can be viewed as an opportunity to conduct a new experiment, to ask new questions, and to increase our knowledge about behavior and its treatment, all in the context of actual professional work. In light of the above, this work should not be considered treatment research. It is treatment evaluation. This is the case despite the fact that it might yield publications, or presentations; despite the fact that it involves the refinement of scientifically important statements. If this activity is allowed to be termed *research* and if this label then leads to the application of the legitimate protections given to research subjects, then the strangulation of empirical clinical and educational work is not far behind. We could very easily find ourselves in a position where the conduct of empirical intervention is discouraged, by virtue of the immediate negative consequences occurring to a practitioner attempting to conduct it; and treatment which failed to specify its target, its procedures, or its outcome could become the officially encouraged mode of intervention.

The Necessity of Evaluation

There is a flip side to this coin. Do we have an ethical obligation to promote treatment evaluation? If so, how?

There are strong ethical arguments to be made for evaluation. Without repeated, systematic measurement how can a professional *really* know if the client is progressing? Isn't there an ethical need to be sure of this? Similarly, without careful specification of treatment, how can a practitioner *really* inform the client or others of its nature? Is not this ethically required?

If good practice requires the essentials of time-series methodology, it seems strange that the approach described in this book has had relatively limited application. There are several reasons and possible solutions.

First, most practitioners only take research methodology courses which emphasize group-comparison approaches. Part of our argument throughout has been that practitioners have been given the wrong tools for on-line evaluations. The solution may be to expand practitioners' training to include specific courses on time-series methodology.

Second, even with the tools in hand, professionals face multiple barriers to their use. The clinical and educational environment can be a hectic place. It is easier, in the short run, to be loose in planning and implementing intervention. The solution may be for agencies to encourage (or even require) evaluation and to provide the resources it needs. Indeed, third-party payers are beginning to require systematic data on clients (see chapter 2). Agencies should provide training for support staff (e.g., in measurement skills) and use salary and promotion to encourage empirical work. Agency policies should encourage proper presentation of evaluation data.

Finally, this entire approach is still quite new. The kinds of measures and designs needed in the on-line clinical and educational environment are just now being developed. Often we do not know what a client needs. It is hard to be systematic in such a situation. Even with dedication, only a certain proportion of a typical professional's clients will present problems clear enough or known enough to be defined and measured specifically. Even when that is handled, the client may drop out of treatment, or suddenly present an entirely new problem. The hard truth is that empirical practice requires dedication and persistence. A practitioner with real dedication would probably end up with an evaluation worth sharing in a minority of the cases first presenting themselves. Yet think of what could be accomplished if we had systematic evaluations on only a small number of the clients practitioners treat. Our entire field would, in a matter of months, have a larger data base than has emerged in decades.

The Ethics of Experimental Therapy

It frequently happens that clients present problems for which there are no known, demonstrably effective interventions. Normally, the practitioner will make an educated guess about what might work. The treatment might be known to be effective in similar areas, or it might seem to be logically related to the problem at hand, or it may simply be common. In this situation, the client is receiving an experimental therapy — one of unknown effectiveness.

In normal applied practice, this is often not obvious. Practitioners tend to have considerable faith in their approach and it is only with careful questioning that it might be clear that there are little or no data to support the intervention. In time-series evaluations, the experimental nature of such treatment is often more obvious, because it is well defined. In a way, this can be disconcerting, because careful evaluation may help us to see what we do not know as well as what we do. Thus, on-line evaluations may be discouraged on the grounds that clients should not be subjected to experimental interventions. But the evaluation is not what makes it experimental. It just keeps us from fooling ourselves when it is.

If an experimental treatment is being used because of the evaluation (and not client needs), then that is a different matter. At that point the enterprise is formal research, not evaluation, and the full protections given research subjects are required.

Sometimes you will hear it said that evaluation is *only* needed when treatment is experimental. If it is well developed, so the view goes, why evaluate it?

Actually, evaluation of interventions of known effectiveness is worthwhile for several reasons. First, there are instances when treatment will not be maximally effective with a specific client. In such a case, treatment modifications or alternatives can be implemented when there are reasons to believe that these modifications may be more effective. In this way, the techniques we use can gradually be refined and questions on client-treatment interactions, or which forms of treatment are most effective with which clients, can be addressed. Second, other questions about the intervention, such as the degree of generalization across responses or situations, will emerge naturally. Third, accountability alone is a good reason for evaluation. Finally, repeated replication across many clients is the way we determine the generality of results of the treatment across treatment settings and therapists as well as clients. Accumulation of evaluations of many cases is the primary topic in the next chapter.

Ethical Issues Raised by Evaluation

Evaluation does not relieve the practitioner of the need for general ethical conduct. Issues of informed consent in applied practice, competence, proper professional relationships, and so on, are not reduced one iota by evaluation. These topics, however, are beyond the scope of this book.

Evaluation does raise three major classes of additional ethical concerns, however. First, the practitioner must never do research in the name of evaluation without providing the client with the full protection given research subjects. Evaluation must be in the service of immediate clinical and educational goals. For example, if a practitioner selects a treatment target because of its scientific interest and not clinical need, this is research, not evaluation.

If a practitioner seeks out a client to ask a predetermined question of interest, this is research, not evaluation. If effortful, costly, or time-consuming measures are taken that have little or no practical purpose, but are used because they will strengthen the data base, then this is research, not evaluation.

Table 11.4 describes several issues that should be examined. The practitioner must be honest in answering these questions. If the evaluation process is not fostering good practice, then it is not really evaluation.

The second major issue raised is confidentiality. Careful evaluation increases our knowledge of the client. If we then present our results, it is critical that the client's confidentiality be protected. This is a general problem in applied fields. An anecdotal case report presents the same difficulties. The solution is to ensure absolute confidentiality or, if that is not possible, to secure client consent for any possible breaches of confidentiality. One way to do this is to have the client sign a "consent for services" which describes what information will be collected and how it will be used. Alternatively, if data are presented that might allow the client to be identified, nonpertinent information can be removed or changed. If needed information might allow client identification (a rare situation), the client should be asked to consent in writing to its use.

A third and final area of concern is that an empirical approach to intervention may take more time, effort, or money, particularly in the early stages of intervention. Usually, a person raising this issue will view these costs as needless, and therefore unethical. If they are in the service of a client, however, they may actually be required for effective intervention. If quality intervention requires more work, then saving a client this effort may be penny-wise and pound-foolish.

Additional protective devices may need to be generated which are unique to treatment evaluation. For example, the decreased privacy which is entailed by the publication or presentation of treatment evaluations may require some examination by persons other than the practitioner. Agencies interested in encouraging treatment evaluations could set up committees which would review presentations or publications of treatment evaluations with the specific goal of diminishing reasonable threats to invasion of privacy. They might also encourage practitioners to obtain consent for the kind of evaluations that are being performed. The same committees might review the work of practitioners doing no evaluations and design methods to encourage more evaluation. It would be important to arrange conditions so that it is harder to be sloppy than to be systematic.

Table 11.4. Questions to Ask Oneself to Prevent Doing Research in the Name of Evaluation

PRACTICAL ISSUES	TREATMENT RESEARCH	TREATMENT EVALUATION
How did the client come to be in treatment?	Sought for project	Routine channels
Why is the client being kept in therapy?	To be evaluated	Client need
Why was the target behavior selected?	Scientific interest	Client need
Why are these measures being taken?	To make a better case to the scientific community	To assess client progress
Why is intervention being timed this way?	Research purposes	Client need
Why is this intervention being used?	Scientific interest	It seems most likely to be of aid
Why is this intervention being changed?	Scientific interest	To help the client, or to clarify client need
Why are control conditions used?	To establish a scientifically valid affect	To help better understand the client's needs

Chapter 12
Clinical Replication

INTRODUCTION

In previous chapters, the various measurement and procedural strategies of time-series methodology were outlined. The outstanding feature of this approach, of course, is the intensive analysis of the individual case. In chapter 2, clinical replication was described as a process wherein practitioners, using a well-specified treatment or intervention accumulate a series of cases presenting with the same problem, such as depression or headache, and so on. In the course of intervening with this series of clients, the practitioner using time-series methodology observes and records successes and failures, analyzing, where possible, the reasons for this individual variation. The purpose of this chapter is to suggest a set of guidelines for accumulating a clinical replication series.

In a previous book (Hersen & Barlow, 1976), clinical replication was distinguished from direct and systematic replication strategies by its emphasis on the replication of a well-defined intervention or treatment for well-defined clinical (or educational) problems with a large number of clients. In addition, this intervention would be administered as it would normally be delivered in the applied setting in order to determine the generalizability of effectiveness from research to treatment settings. Direct and systematic replication, on the other hand, are strategies more often concerned with establishing generalizability of a specific experimentally established functional relation between an experimental procedure and a behavior. Often this relation includes only one component of a treatment program as applied to one isolated facet of behavior. Interested readers are referred to Hersen and Barlow (1976) or Barlow and Hersen (in press) for descriptions of direct and systematic replication strategies.

QUESTIONS ADDRESSED BY CLINICAL REPLICATION

Chapter 2 describes data from a clinical replication series as making a very important contribution to the research process. This contribution consists primarily of a determination of the extent of effectiveness of a procedure and the generality of that effectiveness with a series of individuals through field testing the procedure. Data from these series are capable of providing answers to the unanswered questions of applied research on therapeutic interventions. A properly conducted clinical replication series, even without single-case experimental analysis, can rule out most or all threats to internal validity and contribute to causal statements on the effectiveness of an intervention. The strength of this statement may approach or equal conclusions one can draw from true experimentation (e.g., Kazdin, 1981). But the contribution from a clinical replication series highlighted in this chapter concerns generality of findings.

Specifically, there are several unanswered questions that can be addressed by clinical replication. First, using a well-defined, clinically significant criterion of improvement and applying an intervention in its most powerful form, how many of a series of clients improve? It would be important, of course, to answer this and subsequent questions in as many different settings as possible around the world to establish maximum generality of findings. Second, how many clients show limited improvement that would not be judged clinically significant by practitioners, who would then be forced to consider additional or alternative interventions? Third, how many people fail to improve or perhaps even deteriorate during administration of the intervention? Fourth, what are the reasons for limited improvement or deterioration?

Paying close attention to nonclinical improvement and failures, as well as successes, the practitioner in the process of clinical replication will "try to describe and account for what happened" (Cronbach, 1975, p. 124) by looking at similarities and differences among failures and successes along a number of dimensions. Such dimensions would include, but not be limited to, procedural differences in the application of the intervention (e.g., successful clients may have been seen more frequently than nonsuccessful clients). It is also possible that different therapists applying apparently similar procedures will produce different rates of success. While a search for therapist variables that may influence outcome has not been fruitful in the context of more traditional psychotherapy research (Parloff, Waskow, & Wolfe, 1978), it is entirely plausible that some therapist variables might show up in the context of a large clinical replication series. For example, less experienced therapists applying specific procedures in the same setting under supervision might not achieve the extent of success of more experienced therapists. (It should be noted that recent evidence does not support experience of therapists as an important variable, at least in the context of fear-reduction procedures (Marks, 1981).

But, most practitioners and researchers will look for differences among the clients themselves, assuming that the parameters of the intervention and the practitioner are relatively constant across a series, to find important clues to account for differential response. For example, Rachman (1978) and Barlow and Mavissakalian (1981) have pointed out that phobics with high autonomic responding in phobic situations might respond differently to a standard treatment than those without this type of response, as measured, for example, by heart rate. Most recently, Ost, Jerremalm, and Johansson (1981) confirmed this hypothesis with social phobics. Any number of other client variables, of course, might be associated with differential response to treatment (e.g., Norton, DiNardo, & Barlow, 1983).

Answers to the questions listed above, followed by intensive local observation of factors associated with differential response to treatment applied in its most powerful form, should then point the way to more systematic research on client-therapist interactions in both applied and research settings. This research, in turn, would lead to more careful and thorough assessment of all clients on variables found to be important predictors of response to treatment as well as a determination of what variations or additions to specific interventions would be needed for clients who are not likely to benefit from an otherwise successful intervention.

THE SEQUENCE OF CLINICAL REPLICATION IN THE RESEARCH PROCESS

Clinical replication has been a frequent activity for practitioners and researchers over the decades, and although the results of many clinical replication series, both large and small, have appeared in the literature and had substantial impact on practice. Nevertheless, there has been little in the way of conceptualizing the precise role that this activity plays in advancing our knowledge or its proper sequence in the research process. When first defining clinical replication and providing examples of its use, Hersen and Barlow (1976) noted that clinical replication ideally should come after a technique-building approach. For example, in developing a new comprehensive treatment for depression, someone might actually construct a series of components, each targeted at various aspects of depression (i.e., cognitive, motor activity, somatic symptoms, etc.). Each component would first be tested individually on the specific aspect of depression for which it was targeted (e.g., Azrin & Besalel, 1981). Following a determination of which individual components worked and which did not for specific targets within the diagnostic category of depression, a package treatment would be constructed. This treatment could then be tested in a clinical replication series to establish generality of findings across clients (at least). In fact, this was how Lovaas and his colleagues proceeded in their very important clinical replication series on autistic children (Lovaas, Koegel, Simmons, & Long, 1973). After testing individual treatment components on various aspects of autism, Lovaas et al. constructed a comprehensive intervention and examined the effects of this intervention on a series of children. While all children improved, these investigators observed that some children did not improve to a clinically important extent and, through intensive local observation, speculated on the reasons why. This series, in fact, probably comes closest to following the progression of research outlined in the Agras and Berkowitz (1980) model described in chapter 2.

This seems an ideal use of clinical replication. After experimental verification of effectiveness of a treatment and component analysis of the necessary and sufficient conditions for a treatment to be effective, generality of findings would be established through clinical replication. Within the series, of course, further analysis of reasons for failure and additions to treatment that remediate that failure are possible and desirable through the use of single-case experimental designs.

Nevertheless, it is recognized that the world, including the scientific world, does not always proceed in such an orderly fashion, and that many major clinical replication series have appeared prior to the research necessary to demonstrate, first, the effectiveness of the intervention when compared against no treatment or some good attention placebo, and, second, the component analysis. In other words, in the most usual case a treatment is developed by an innovative practitioner, based on some familiarity with prior research and theory and/or intuitive judgments concerning the necessary components of an effective intervention. This is followed by a systematic "research-dismantling" strategy wherein the components of treatment are further refined, improved, and often reassembled. Frequently this results in a treatment which bears little resemblance to the original treatment. For example, Wolpe's (1958) series, as described in chapter 2, sparked the substantial thrust of research on fear reduction that eventually resulted in an intervention based on *in vivo* exposure bearing little resemblance to systematic desensitization in imagination.

We would suggest that a clinical replication series to establish generality of findings following a technique-building effort is preferable, and in many ways the ideal progression of research. Nevertheless, innovative practitioners who feel that they have developed an effective intervention for a difficult problem will undoubtedly proceed with a clinical replication series and, in some cases, this will be of considerable value to the scientific community if it is ultimately published. It should be stated at this point that there are also grave dangers associated with the publication of "innovative" clinical replication series, particularly if the guidelines described below are not followed. The history of the human services, and all health-related fields, is replete with dramatic but untested "miracle cures" that seem to have worked in one setting with one practitioner, but were later proved useless. Some of these procedures were actually dangerous. Thus, the guidelines described below should be followed since this will rule out some threats to internal validity or the degree of confidence that one has in the actual efficacy of the treatment as opposed to alternative explanations (e.g, Kazdin, 1981). The value of these innovative series would be greatly increased, of course, by the presence within the series of single-case experimentation demonstrating the effectiveness of treatment and elucidating the important components of treatment through a component analysis. Thus, the guidelines to be described below apply equally to an initial innovative clinical series, particularly with experimental analyses embedded within it, or to one that is attempting to establish generality of findings after a technique-building progression of research.

GUIDELINES FOR CLINICAL REPLICATION

The Lemere and Voegtlin Series

In chapter 2, the substantial influence of clinical replication series on practitioners was described, regardless of whether the series appears before or after firm research support for the effectiveness of the intervention is available. While some examples were described briefly, many more examples could have been cited. One particularly interesting example is the well-known and highly influential series conducted in the 1940s on chemical aversion approaches applied to the treatment of alcoholism (e.g., Lemere & Voegtlin, 1950). This series was remarkable in many ways, and from a technical point of view is probably the best example of a clinical replication in the literature.

The outcome of this impressive series, conducted with over 4,000 alcoholics, demonstrated that 60% were fully abstinent at a 1-year follow-up. The usual effect of the appearance in print of this series occurred. That is, despite the difficulty in arranging the administration of this intervention, it was widely adopted, and hospitals were set up specifically to administer this program. It is interesting to note that this procedure has never been subjected to the kinds of experimental inquiry that would determine in a clear, functionally analytic way its effectiveness; and yet, because of the publication of this clinical replication effort, it is still used in many hospitals. For example, Wiens, Montague, Manaugh, and English (1976) have recently reported similar results, in that 63% of a large group were abstinent at 1-year follow-up. These figures are even more impressive if one examines the results of Lemere and Voegtlin's analysis of successes and failures (intensive local observation), demonstrating as it does a variety of factors associated with success or failure. For example, both procedural and client variables predicted success. If clients were available for, and received, two or more booster sessions during the year following treatment, the probability of remaining abstinent was 95%. Strong middle-class social support systems were also highly related to success (e.g., Voegtlin, Lemere, Broz, & O'Hallaren, 1942). While chemical aversion therapy, intrusive and medically risky as it is, and requiring as it does close inpatient supervision, is not administered as widely as it once was, noted experts in the area of addictive behaviors still recommend that chemical aversion therapy should at least be considered for every alcoholic (Nathan & Lansky, 1978). This recommendation is made despite a fuller understanding of the social context of alcoholism that now exists and the availability of a large number of alternative treatment approaches (e.g., Paolino & McCrady, 1977). Based largely on this pioneering work, other investigators (e.g., Elkins, 1980) have adopted alternative procedures designed to accomplish very similar goals that are less physically intrusive and can be applied entirely in imagination. After 40 years, these procedures (e.g., covert sensitization) are likely to take the place of chemical aversion therapy where it is still employed. But, the wide influence of this technique, which continues to this day, was due at least in part to the careful observations made by these investigators. For our purposes, it is helpful to look briefly at the major features of this series that account for its impact, and in so doing outline the guidelines essential for a successful clinical replication series.

The first guideline concerns the selection and definition of clients. Clearly, little will be communicated from a clinical replication series if a practitioner defines clients very vaguely; for example, "neurotics" or "learning disabled." Classification of clients based on objective, detailed descriptions is essential before one can begin to talk about the effects of treatment, including successes and failures. Within the area of mental health, the advent of DSM-III is seen by most as a significant advance in the empirical, nontheoretical description and initial classification of emotional and behavioral problems (Barlow, 1981) and this shorthand notation may often suffice. But, nothing will be lost, and much will be gained by as clear and detailed a description of the presenting problem and background variables as is possible. For instance, many practitioners who see a large number of clients in one particular category may automatically exclude certain clients from their treatment, based on preconceived notions of who will benefit and who will fail. These clinical intuitions are often based on extremely valuable clinical experience derived from informal clinical replication series that are continually going on in every practitioner's setting. For example, a practitioner treating agoraphobics may have observed in the past that two or three clients addicted to narcotics (to take an extreme example) did not benefit from treatment. Therefore, he or she will treat no further clients with narcotic addictions. The difficulty with the selection criteria is that the systematic observations of failures will then be lost to the community of practitioners at large once the results of a clinical replication series are reported. It would certainly be preferable to deal with all clients who meet a widely agreed-upon criterion of problem definition, such as DSM-III, so that systematic observation of failures or partial successes could be reported. Failing this, a practitioner should certainly note very carefully those clients who were excluded for practical or other a priori considerations and the reasons why. Returning to our example, the alcoholics in the Lemere and Voegtlin series were well enough described that social class and degree of social support were later identified through intensive local observation as variables critically implicated with success.

The second requirement is the existence of a clearly defined, replicable, intervention procedure. That is, a procedure described in enough detail that other experienced and qualified practitioners could apply it after some initial acquaintance with the procedural details of intervention. Very seldom is this guideline fulfilled in clinical research or reports of clinical replication series. Even more direct behavioral treatments are often described in a very cursory fashion with important procedural details omitted. However, while workshops, clinical demonstrations, and certainly advanced clinical training will always be necessary to communicate the essentials of intervention, clearly described procedures rather than vague references to "psychotherapy" or "physical therapy" will entice practitioners to take those few steps necessary to become further acquainted with a successful procedure. Although physically intrusive, such that medical supervision was necessary, the emetic aversive technique was well described, such that it could be applied in relatively pure form at other centers across the country.

A third guideline requires that measures of change must be reliable and valid and should be as nonreactive as possible. Guidelines for this type of measurement were described in chapter 3 and examples provided in chapters 4-6. In the Lemere and Voegtlin series, the estimates of change consisted of abstinence or well-defined periods of relapse, corroborated by reports from relatives. Of course, since drinking and intoxication are at least clearly observable problems, rather good, socially valid estimates of this problem were readily available even in the 1940s.

These measures of change must also yield reliable estimates of extent of success. This is necessary in order to differentiate improvement that is clinically significant and important from change that might be in the positive direction but is not sufficient from the point of view of either the client or the practitioner and would most usually result in additional efforts to achieve clinically important change. This is evident in the Lemere and Voegtlin (1950) series where the particular issue at hand, problem drinking, could be categorized into total abstinence, occasional problem drinking, or baseline problem drinking.

Finally, in any clinical replication series, the investigators must attend to failures as well as to limited success in their clients and engage in intensive local observation in an attempt to determine factors associated with this differential response. Lemere and Voegtlin (1950) and their associates performed this in an admirable way and determined that various procedural and client variables, particularly in combination, were associated with relapse, as noted above.

Contrast this approach and its 30- to 40-year impact with other series published contemporaneously that examined outcome as percentage of success with one form of psychotherapy or another. Many of these were reviewed at the time by Eysenck (1952) and few, if any, described replicable treatments or measures that allowed determination of individual response to treatment. At least partly for this reason, many of these interventions have long since disappeared from the mental health scene.

These four factors, described above, comprise the guidelines for a successful, scientifically important, clinical replication series. In the next section we will examine the presence or absence of these factors in several well-known and important clinical replication series, some of which have already been mentioned, as well as some lesser known, somewhat smaller or more recent series, in order to illustrate these guidelines in a variety of contexts.

The Wolpe Series

The one series mentioned throughout this book, which can be said to have sparked the new wave of research on anxiety disorders in general and phobia in particular, was the series reported in 1958 by Wolpe. It is useful to examine this series in the context of the four criteria described above in a step-by-step fashion. In this book, Wolpe reviews data on 210 clients seen over a period of many years. However, in the book itself, only data on the last 88 cases are reported in detail, since information on the initial 122 cases had been reported previously. Thus, this analysis will concern only the 88 cases reported in Wolpe's book (1958).

Selection

Wolpe is very clear on this and notes that he accepted every case with a diagnosis of neurosis, no matter how long-lasting or how severe the case, and irrespective of whether or not there was previous treatment. Clearly excluded, according to Wolpe, were psychotics and psychopaths. This, of course, would not be an adequate definition today, but was quite precise given the climate of classification in the mid-1950s. Particularly helpful, even now, are the capsule descriptions of the major presenting problems for every one of the 88 cases, in a table covering approximately six printed pages in the text. A further breakdown by conventional diagnostic classifications is not particularly helpful at this point in time, since the classifications have changed considerably. Nevertheless, the specification of such target problems as agoraphobia, claustrophobia, exhibitionism, impotence, insomnia, interpersonal anxieties, and the like, many times in combination with a given case, greatly assist the practitioner in determining what kind of client was in treatment, even without the assistance of current, up-to-date classification schemas.

A further inclusion criteria imposed by Wolpe required that the client receive "adequate" amounts of therapy. Wolpe regarded this, usually, as a positive response by the client or 40 sessions, whichever came first. This is a rather rigorous inclusion criteria. Much to Wolpe's credit, he does note that in cases whose status was doubtful, the decision to include or exclude was discussed with another prominent psychiatrist. If exclusion was decided upon, descriptive notes on these cases were provided. In light of our present knowledge, a far preferable strategy, of course, would be to include data on *all* clients who qualified for the series and presented to the office of the practitioner, including those who dropped out of treatment before "adequate" therapy was administered, the time at which they dropped out (for example, early versus late), followed by intensive local observation to determine any pattern of events associated with refusing further treatment.

Intervention

Most practitioners, if asked about Wolpe's original series, would probably respond that it described the application of systematic desensitization in imagination to phobias. In fact, the intervention procedures employed were just as diverse as the distribution of client problems. Of the 88 clients, more (58) were treated with assertiveness training than were treated with desensitization (57). Of these, 30 clients received both desensitization and assertiveness training. Other treatments used for specific cases included relaxation, abreaction under hypnosis, carbon dioxide treatment (used by Wolpe to induce relaxation), avoidance conditioning, and "retraining of breathing" (in the case of a severe stammer due to respiratory spasm). Once again, to Wolpe's credit, these diverse treatments were specified, at least by name, and given the clear description of these treatments provided at other points in the book, one can be reasonably sure what Wolpe was doing. Nevertheless, one could hardly call this a test of desensitization, or even fear-reduction procedures as we know them today. Rather, in keeping with Wolpe's purpose at that time, the series describes the application of a number of treatments falling under the rubric of behavior therapy to diverse, nonpsychotic, adult problems, most of which (63 out of 88) presented with some anxiety, according to Wolpe. It must be pointed out, of course, that Wolpe's purpose at this time was to demonstrate an alternative method of treating neurotic disorders to the prevailing psychoanalytic approach.

Measures

Categorization of change was based on Knight's (1941) criteria which sub-divided outcome into five categories ranging from *apparently cured* to *unim-proved*. But Wolpe really only used three: the first category, *apparently cured;* the second category, *much improved;* while the last three categories, *moderately improved, slightly improved,* and *unimproved,* were lumped together and regarded by Wolpe as failures. These outcomes, of course, based as they were on Wolpe's private practice in South Africa, relied solely on the judgment of the therapist. Wolpe clearly recognized the problems with this approach, even then, and attempted to correct for bias by introducing the Willoughby Scale, a currently little-used questionnaire measuring anxi-ety or neuroticism in a variety of situations. Unfortunately, this question-naire was not always given, for various reasons, and when it was given, the administration was in a pre-post fashion. Nevertheless, in a large percentage of the cases, data from this subjective questionnaire, filled out by the pa-tient, supplemented the very precise (for that time) categorization of therapist judgment of success. The marked increase in reliable and valid methods of measuring outcome for use in the practitioner's office (see chapters 3-6) make it much easier today for practitioners to collect these kinds of data.

Analysis of failures

The final guideline comprises the most important scientific function of the practitioner, identification and analysis of those clients only partially suc ceeding or failing. In Wolpe's table, 10 out of the 88 clients fell into the last three categories of Knight's (1941) criteria, signifying less improvement or failure. These clients are described and a rather detailed note is provided for nine of them. Failure in several of these cases was precipitated by "resen sitization" after a particularly traumatic, unforeseen incident, while in many of the others a variety of interpersonal problems seemed to interfere with the progress. Other data are included for one wishing to analyze this clinical replication series in more detail, such as the therapeutic time span in months, the number of sessions, as well as the sex and age of the subjects. And, as promised, Wolpe provided notes on three cases who were not included in the analyses.

Summary

The strengths of this series are remarkable when one considers the qual-ity of evidence available to practitioners at that time. In this context, the cases were clearly described, although heterogeneous by today's standards, the intervention procedures were objective and replicable, although once again heterogeneous, and the outcome criteria were communicable to practitioners and represented the state of the art of objectivity at that time. It is clear to see, from our perspective 25 years later, why this series generated the interest and subsequent clinical research that it did. The progression of this research was traced in chapter 2, leading us to our more powerful and more fully understood treatments for anxiety reduction.

The Maletzky Series

A particularly elegant example of a major clinical replication series that would serve in many ways as a model for practitioners dealing with large numbers of clients, homogeneous on a particular presenting problem, has been described by Maletzky (1980). Over a period of 9 years in his private practice, Maletzky treated 186 exhibitionists, primarily with a procedure called *"assisted" covert sensitization.* As indicated elsewhere (Barlow, 1981), the results of this well-conducted and convincing series demonstrate that 85% of an unselected group of exhibitionists presenting for treatment evidenced marked clinical improvement after follow-ups of from 1 to 9 years, a remarkable result and one of the more powerful effects from a psychosocial treatment yet observed. Measuring up against the guidelines, several elegant features of this replication series became evident along with the usual shortcomings.

Selection

Exhibitionism is a clearly defined target problem and it is unusual to come across controversy regarding the presence or absence of this behavior. Furthermore, given the social unacceptability of exhibitionism, immediate treatment is often required, even though other problems may be present in clients seeking help for this behavior. Of clients presenting with this problem, Maletzky reports no exclusionary criteria. Of course, it would have been preferable for Maletzky to actually say that no one presenting for exhibitionism was excluded from treatment, or perhaps that one or two people turned out to be psychotic in addition and were excluded. But, in any case, we must presume that no one was excluded, once it was clear that exhibitionism was the presenting problem, including those who were under legal contingencies at the time of referral. Individual descriptions of the 186 subjects in tabular form is not presented, although a rather detailed summary of client characteristics provides a good substitute. In this summary, Maletzky describes referral source, age (the clients were surprisingly young, with an average age of 28.2 years), average length of existence of the problem behavior, and other averaged characteristics of this behavior, such as number of apprehensions per exposure, and so on. Twenty-one of these cases presented with several maladaptive sexual approach behaviors, including three clients for whom exposure was associated with subsequent rape. The fact that this is a rare occurrence is substantiated by additional literature in Maletzky's report. While this description is helpful, the average response of a large group of subjects does not really communicate much. Generally, the more information about individual clients the better, and tabular data describing number of clients falling in specific age ranges, and so on, would probably be more useful than the average age for the whole series. Nevertheless, this only becomes really important when one begins intensive local observation to differentiate those who succeed and those who only partially succeed or fail.

An additional, extremely positive feature of this series is the use of a variety of therapists in addition to Maletzky and an analysis of the differential impact of these therapists. For example, 50% of the first 155 clients were treated by "psychiatric personnel" without professional degrees but with extensive training in behavioral methods under the direction of Maletzky. Thirty-nine percent were treated by Maletzky himself, while the remaining 11% were treated by other professionals. An analysis revealed no differences in treatment effectiveness as a function of therapist or therapist training. Naturally, these data will be more meaningful when replication series in different settings, using Maletzky's general therapeutic package, appear for comparison.

Intervention

A strength of this series is the specificity of the intervention procedures. Although not exactly the same package of procedures was applied to each and every client (this would be extremely unusual in any clinical series), one core procedure, "assisted" covert sensitization, was applied to virtually all clients. Assisted covert sensitization is a procedure where intense descriptions of the chain of events leading up to the undesirable behavior, in this case exhibitionism, are integrated with aversive consequences of the client's choosing, such as nausea and vomiting. This imaginal process is "assisted" by providing the client with a vial of a foul-smelling substance. Maletzky used valeric acid. Using various methods of analysis, the therapeutic effectiveness of the adjunctive procedures, sometimes combined with assisted covert sensitization, were evaluated both alone as well as in combination with the core procedure as compared to the core procedure alone. The adjunctive procedures included such techniques as thought-stopping; masturbatory conditioning to more acceptable heterosexual practices; environmental control, where subjects were asked to avoid locations where exhibitionism occurred frequently in the past; and occasional aversive behavior rehearsal, in which exhibitionists would exhibit themselves under contrived circumstances to women collaborating with the therapist. Data described in this series indicate that adjunctive procedures alone had only small effects in some clients and that the combination of adjunctive procedures and "assisted" covert sensitization over a large number of clients did not seem to result in any distinct clinical advantage over the core procedures alone. Of the 186 clients, 104 received assisted covert sensitization, with just an occasional assist from one other adjunctive procedure, while 63 received the core procedure with a variety of adjunctive procedures. Some 19 clients received only some other procedure, such as covert sensitization, without the presence of the aversive odor. Nevertheless, Maletzky plays it safe, as would most clinicians. He currently employs many of these adjunctive procedures, all of which are explicitly described, with his clients, because they take very little extra time and some clients report subjective benefit from one or another of them. Since the clinical (and existing experimental) evidence does not necessarily support the use of these procedures, every practitioner will make his or her own decision on whether to use them, but the impressive data from this series overwhelmingly supports the use of assisted covert sensitization in the treatment of exhibitionism.

Measures

The measures in this series are particularly clear, and once again represent the current state of the art of the use of practical and realistic dependent measures within the practitioner's office. Not only is self-monitoring of relevant urges, fantasies, dreams, exhibitionistic acts, and masturbation present for almost all subjects, but these data were often corroborated by police records and reports from significant others. In addition, a very clever *in vivo* behavioral test was used, wherein exhibitionists were presented with an idiosyncratic situation in their own environment that had previously been associated with a high frequency of exhibitionism. Finally, there are penile plethysmograph records using equipment that is now available for practicing clinicians, who may treat large numbers of sexual problems. Thus, one would have nearly as much confidence in these specific and clinically relevant measures of change as one would have in the most complete and thorough clinical research report coming out of our more advanced laboratories for studying sexual behavior.

Analysis of Failures

Maletzky carefully examined the records of 20 subjects out of the 186 who were categorized as failures, in that they engaged in subsequent exhibitionistic behavior. Brief mention is also made of seven clients who left treatment early and therefore could not be said to have received treatment. Maletzky looked at these data from a number of different perspectives and found that most variables or factors did not differentiate successes from failures. For example, duration of exposing, number of incidents, prior legal record, time of entry into treatment program, or presence of adjunctive techniques was not correlated with treatment response. However, several factors did stand out. For one thing, the failures were considerably younger than the succeeders, and secondly, these clients were usually "disgruntled" about the lack of immediate success. Thus, Maletzky computed a measure which he termed *velocity of change*. This measure was computed by summing weekly changes and frequency data for the first 4 treatment weeks and averaging the changes. The velocity of change was 4.1 for overt behaviors, but for the 20 failing subjects the corresponding figure was 1.4. Maletzky hypothesizes that these 20 young failures were more easily frustrated and highly impatient, resulting in early pessimism and a bad response. Maletzky subsequently altered his therapeutic procedure for young clients. He provided more frequent early contact, more demonstrable positive feedback, and more initial environmental support to these clients. For example, he now sees these people two to three times a week, but for briefer durations, and sees family members to enlist their support of the client through the early phases of treatment.

Summary

This series tells us more about the treatment of exhibitionism than any data from our clinical research laboratories yet produced. Although relatively recent, it is clear that it is having an enormous impact. In many ways, Maletzky anticipated each and every guideline that we proposed for the conduct of useful and meaningful clinical replication series. With his inherent curiosity, he also demonstrated not only the possibilities, but also the importance of carrying on applied research within the context of practice. Of course, an extremely important step will be replication of these results in other centers. Unlike the Masters and Johnson, series where other practitioners seeing similar numbers of patients were reluctant to publish their series, it is hoped those practitioners in the position of dealing with large numbers of exhibitionists will be as careful in recording their interventions and results as was Maletzky, so that we may increase our knowledge of the generality of findings of these evidently powerful techniques.

The Masters and Johnson Series

This series has been, in all likelihood, the single most influential piece of work ever published for practitioners who deal with sexual problems. One book, describing direct behavioral interventions for the varieties of sexual dysfunction in a large population of males and females, literally revolutionized the treatment of these problems, such that presumably very few practitioners today treat sexual dysfunction without some use of these procedures. While these direct behavioral procedures have been integrated into other theoretical systems (e.g., Kaplan, 1974), and a variety of explanations have been made for success, they still comprise the primary set of intervention procedures for these problems. Thus, no chapter on clinical replication could avoid an examination of this important work. But, a review based on the guidelines reveals that while there are considerable strengths to this series, there are also several distinct weaknesses that limit the amount of information available to practitioners.

Selection

First, because of the way the program was set up, and because of some a priori decisions made by the investigators, the clients were highly selected. Some of the criteria included having the time and financial resources to travel to St. Louis and spend two weeks away from home, family, and employment. Referral from some authority, such as health professionals, clergy, and so on, was also necessary, as well as some ascertainment that the married couple otherwise had a stable marriage, communicated well, and were both strongly interested in participating in the program. Questions were also asked of the referring authority about the adaptation of the couple to their community. Finally, the couple, before coming to St. Louis, had to agree to cooperate with the program for 5 years following its termination. Obviously, this produced a very highly restricted group of people, which limits the ability to generalize the results to the more usual flow of clients presenting with this problem in a more typical setting.

Nevertheless, the cases that were treated are most often richly and thoroughly described, such that practitioners can readily identify similar cases presented in their clinic. Furthermore, from the point of view of contributing to the research process and making etiological contributions of various factors, numerous data gleaned from the individual histories and experiences during treatment are provided and broken down into various categories. These factors are then related to treatment outcome. For example, the seeming contribution of religious orthodoxy to impotence in males and the fact that clients falling in this category failed most often during treatment for their impotence represents the first time that the seriousness of this issue was recognized.

Intervention

This area has caused considerable difficulty in the years following Masters and Johnson's 1970 report. There seem to be several reasons for this. First, the authors do describe their treatment procedures extremely well. In fact, the clarity of their intervention programs for the various dysfunctions, as described, is undoubtedly one of the reasons that their program has been so widely adopted. Nevertheless, there is accumulating evidence that these therapists may have actually introduced a considerable number of additional clinical procedures and tactics as they tried to do the best they could for their clients. Hints of this have occurred in the various books describing their intervention (cf. Barlow, 1980; Zilbergeld & Evans, 1980). There is, of course, nothing at all wrong with this tactic; in fact, any clinician who does not employ additional procedures if they seem appropriate could be questioned. But, for our purposes, it seems that many of these procedures were not described. Zilbergeld and Evans (1980) attribute the failure of many sex therapists to approach the rate of success reported by Masters and Johnson to this deficit in communication.

Measures

In this area, Masters and Johnson also deserve considerable credit. But, on the other hand, problems have emerged in the way they reported their data which limit its usefulness to practitioners. Attempting to be as conservative as they could in their reports, certainly an admirable goal, they decided upon the now well-known failure rates rather than success rates. This means that after choosing an arbitrary criterion (for example, providing orgasmic opportunity for the female partner in at least 50% of attempts at sexual intercourse, in the case of premature ejaculation), Masters and Johnson reported their results in terms of clients who initially failed to reach this criterion. They reasoned that since relapses might occur, one could not talk of success until the 5-year follow-up. Although they did conduct the 5-year follow-up on people they could reach, and reported the results, the primary statistics communicated around the world were initial failure rates. Fortunately, sexual dysfunction is a rather straightforward, observable problem by both the client and the partner, and the direct interviews of both partners to ascertain sexual functioning would seem to be an adequate basis for determining success or failure in these cases. Furthermore, except for secondary impotence in males, relapse rates over the 5 years, in those clients who could be reached, seemed minimal. Nevertheless, this dichotomous manner of reporting results obscures degrees of improvement that are to be found in any clinical series and precludes detailed analysis of those clients who did well from those who improved minimally. For example, there were probably some clients with premature ejaculation who were able to provide orgasmic experiences for their partner (assuming one agrees that this is a reasonable criterion) 80% of the time or more. Perhaps another group ranged from 40 to 60% of the time, and yet a third group ranged from 20 to 40%. Even the third group can be said to have improved somewhat if the baseline was zero. More important, one client reaching the level of 45% would be classified as a failure while the next, reaching 55%, would be a success. A far more preferable system would be to report the range of responses and proceed with an analysis to provide more information to practitioners on the type of response likely from clients walking into their office. Of course, the provision of base rates of sexual functioning using these criteria would also be of considerable assistance so one could judge how far each client, or the group as a whole, moved in relation to this criteria. These base rates were not provided.

Analysis of failures

Here Masters and Johnson make perhaps their greatest contribution. They recognize the importance of documenting failures to the development of comprehensive and effective treatments, and repeatedly report on factors that seem to influence failure. In some excellent examples, as in the case of secondary impotence described above, failures are described in tabular form as a function of clinically important factors. The results for religious orthodoxy have already been mentioned. Furthermore, Masters and Johnson devote a full chapter at the end of their book to a description of treatment failures. Nevertheless, in retrospect, the information could have been more systematic. For example, presumed causes of failure are not provided in any kind of an organized way for other categories of sexual dysfunction. Again, the chapter on treatment failures is really just a summary of selected cases of failure where the authors discuss or describe the occasional idiosyncratic marital problem or procedural errors on the part of the therapist that seem to be associated with a therapeutic failure. It is not clear how representative these cases are in the context of all failures in their series. And, as in most series discussed thus far, Masters and Johnson did not systematically analyze the reasons for failure using appropriate time-series methodology. However, the documentation of factors associated with failure is certainly a first step.

Summary

One can question the figures of percentage failure, or after-5-years percentage of success, in relation to the total number of people seen. Using one of many possible strategies in determining their results, Masters and Johnson chose to report only known failures at follow-up. That is, those who upon interview, either immediately after treatment or after 5 years, were determined to have failed or to have relapsed. But they excluded from follow-up approximately 30% of the clients who could not be reached. Many reports of outcome of a given intervention routinely include these data in the category of failures; and this, of course, might change quite dramatically some of the failure rates, depending on the distribution of these unreachable clients in the various categories. Masters and Johnson cannot really be faulted for this, it is simply a matter of choosing one strategy over the other and they do make it clear just how they compiled these results. But the results, even with their highly selected sample, might look considerably worse. If this had been communicated rather than the more restricted and more positive failure rates that were reported, the impact of the series on practitioners might have been somewhat different, and some of the frustrations being voiced by many who cannot seem to replicate Masters and Johnson's success might not have occurred.

FEASIBILITY OF CLINICAL REPLICATION

The major series described above to illustrate the guidelines of clinical replication were all chosen for their historical significance, their size and clinical impact, and the fact that they were carried out by working practitioners in strictly applied settings going about their business of treating clients. Obviously, the concept of clinical replication or the contribution of this type of effort to the research process was not considered in any formal way when these series were undertaken. Nor is it realistic to expect the average practitioner to accumulate routinely series of 100 to 200 or more cases of a relatively homogeneous disorder. Nevertheless, in this era of increasing specialization, a larger number of clinical and educational practitioners are concentrating on certain specific problems (e.g., phobia, attention deficit disorder). Within these specialty clinics, which may have either a clinical or a research focus or both, there is an increasing concern with documenting and analyzing treatment failures. An example of this type of effort carried out by Foa will be described below (Foa, 1979; Foa, Grayson, Steketee, Doppelt, Turner, & Latimer, 1983). Thus, one major source of clinical replication data will be the large number of specialty clinics around the country.

Additionally, despite the fact that the majority of practitioners continue to see a variety of clients limited only in a very broad way to areas such as adult clinical, child clinical, learning disabilities, and the like, a wealth of information is available from these sources concerning the replication of various treatments with a variety of populations. While it would be unrealistic to expect series of 100 or more from these sources, it is not unrealistic to look for series of 20 to 30 clients homogeneous with regard to a given problem. When multiplied by the literally thousands of practitioners, most of whom will become increasingly accountable in the years ahead, using procedures such as those described in this book, the potential yield of useful information is limitless.

To cite an example, one of the more popular treatments introduced in the last several years is cognitive therapy for depression (Beck, Rush, Shaw, and Emery, 1979). Because of wide publicity, the initial report of successful results, and the numerous workshops and training opportunities available to clinicians wishing to use this procedure, there is little question that at present it is a widely used technique in the treatment of depression. However, aside from a few preliminary studies (e.g., Kovacs, Rush, Beck, & Hollon, 1981), we know little about the overall effectiveness of this technique and even less about the generality of this effectiveness across clients and situations. In view of the fact that this therapy is at present widely used by a variety of well-trained therapists, clinical replication, in the space of several years, would yield data on the generality of effectiveness of this procedure across thousands of cases if only a small percentage of therapists now practicing this procedure compiled data on 20 or 30 of their cases and made these data available. As our systems for accountability advance, third-party payers, government agencies, and ultimately all practitioners may routinely have access to this type of information. As noted in chapter 2, the NIMH collaborative study (1980b) examining the effectiveness of this treatment might also contribute to this goal if therapists are allowed the flexibility to employ the procedure of clinical replication. But the major purpose of this trial is not to produce the type of information that would be forthcoming from a clinical replication series.

EXAMINING FAILURES

One of the best examples in recent years of an analysis of failures coming out of a specialty clinic or clinical research center is Foa's (1979) description of 10 severe, obsessive-compulsives who did not respond to her otherwise successful program consisting of exposure and response prevention for compulsive rituals.

Severe obsession-compulsives, of course, always report an overwhelming fear of contamination or catastrophe. Rituals of various kinds, usually washing or checking, are then carried out to prevent this catastrophe or contamination from occurring or spreading (e.g., excessive washing, checking locks, requesting reassurance, etc.).

In the best tradition of intensive local observation, Foa observed two factors that seemed to differentiate very clearly the 10 failures from the majority of successes. The first she termed *overvalued ideation.* Most obsessive compulsives state that their fears are irrational or senseless when asked directly, and report that it would be unlikely that the consequences would occur despite the fact that they feel compelled to behave as if a real danger exists. In contrast, four of Foa's ten failures reported strong beliefs that their underlying fears were, in fact, realistic and that their rituals actually did prevent the occurrence of disastrous consequences. For example, one client was afraid of inflicting mental retardation on her son through her own contact with retarded people. Another feared contracting tetanus from contact with sharp objects, while still another feared contact with leukemia germs that would cause the death of her husband and children. Elaborating on the cognitive processes in this last case, Foa describes a woman with above-average intelligence who reported sitting in a beauty parlor one day and hearing the woman sitting next to her tell the beautician that she had just come back from the children's hospital, where she had visited her grandson who had leukemia. The client immediately left, registered in a hotel, and washed for three days. Her reasons for this were that she would transmit leukemia germs to her husband and children if she was in contact with them and they would then die. She reported that although she could transmit them to her children, she was immune to these germs herself. She was asked if she had talked to specialists about the rationality of these thoughts and she mentioned that she had talked to several specialists, "They all tried to assure me that there are no leukemia germs, but medicine is not that advanced; I am convinced that I know something that the doctors have not yet discovered. There are definitely germs that carry leukemia" (Foa, 1979, p. 170). All four of these clients described by Foa were unable to admit some irrationality in these fears. Once again, the more usual obsessive-compulsive might say something like, "Yes, I know there are no leukemia germs, and that I can't really transmit it, but the fear still overwhelms me and I'm compelled to wash so that I'll feel more comfortable around my family."

In another four clients, Foa observed a second characteristic that seemed to differentiate these failures from more successful clients: the presence of severe depression. Specifically, on a rating scale of 0-8, the mean depression rating for all clients was 4.8 before treatment and 2.8 after treatment. But these four clients who failed manifested severe depression, with a mean of 7.8 on this scale. One client had severe psychomotor retardation which prevented her from carrying out routine household chores. The other three were agitated depressives with frequent crying spells. Of the 10 failures, two additional clients displayed combinations of both overvalued ideation and depression.

Since Foa collected multiple self-report measures during treatment, she was able to identify possible reasons why these clients did not do as well. Specifically, the former two groups failed to show habituation while being exposed repeatedly to their fear-producing situations. That is, these clients reported little or no decrement in anxiety during exposure trials when compared to the typical client. Although the clients with depression, as compared to the clients with overvalued ideation, demonstrated slightly different patterns, neither showed the habituation that seems necessary for successful response to treatment. In an important step, Foa reported that at least some of the depressives later responded to treatment after first being treated for their depression. This type of analysis greatly strengthens conclusions one can draw about the association of depression with failure. Replication in other clinics, where failures were also identified as being depressed, all but confirms it (e.g., Marks, 1973; Rachman & Hodgson, 1980).

With regard to overvalued ideation, Foa speculates that much more detailed, in-depth attention to cognitive change would be necessary to deal with these clients. This observation and identification of a factor associated with failure would have been considerably strengthened by subsequent analysis, using time series methodology, which would demonstrate that changing these cognitions would lead to improvement in the obsessive-compulsive disorder. Nevertheless, this attention to failures may prove to be the most important contribution to the developing treatment of obsessive-compulsive disorders since the origination of exposure and response prevention as a major treatment modality in the last decade. Of course, more detailed, in-depth, prospective tests combined with replication in other centers, particularly with cognitive factors, will be necessary to confirm these factors as important predictors. In a subsequent report, Foa and her colleagues (Foa et al., 1983), using sophisticated statistical analyses, extended their observations on depression and habituation and correlated these factors with other variables that may be important in predicting outcome in a detailed look at the process of failure with this treatment.

In summary, we can learn from this interesting series that analysis of failures is comprised of three loosely related steps. First, factors associated with failure or minimal success are identified in the context of a clinical replication series. Naturally, not all factors identified will turn out to be important. Subsequent analyses will prove that some are unimportant. Second, attention is drawn to these factors, and prospective replication occurs in the same clinic as well as other clinics. Third, and most important, an experimental analysis, preferably using time-series methodology, can be undertaken, both by the practitioner as well as in more sophisticated research centers, to determine and verify the precise course of failure. Foa identified two factors associated with failure. One factor, depression, has also been identified in other clinics around the world. Successfully treating depression can result in a positive response to the original treatment. Finally, further analysis reveals that lack of habituation may be a major reason why depressed obsessive-compulsives don't respond. Thus, thanks to the original clinical observations of Foa (1979), we are quite far along in identifying a very important client-treatment interaction. The investigation of overvalued ideation, however, has not really passed much beyond the stage of initial identification.

Statistical Approaches for Predicting Success and Failure

Recognizing the necessity of determining client-treatment interaction, sophisticated clinical researchers have occasionally employed a somewhat different strategy to address the issue of predicting individual responses to treatment. While only a few such reports have appeared to date, the strategies and procedures necessary to produce this type of report have been around for decades and have been used occasionally as a supplemental analysis in traditional between-group outcome studies. This strategy involves treating a large number of clients in a clinical replication format, examining overall outcome, and then attempting to predict factors associated with outcome based on predetermined criteria, usually scores on psychological tests. These predictions are made statistically, using such procedures as regression analyses, discriminate function analyses, and procedures to determine percentage of variance accounted for (e.g., omega squared). Some investigators, in an effort to determine even more complex factors or chronologically arranged combinations of factors associated with success or failure, have resorted to complex correlational analyses, such as path analysis (e.g., Foa et al., 1983). The basic purpose in most of these procedures is to make probabilistic statements about factors associated with success or failure in subsequent clients undergoing a specific treatment.

One very good example of this type of effort has recently been completed, in the area of psychological treatment of headaches, by Blanchard, Andrasik, and associates (Blanchard, Andrasik, Neff, Arena, Ahles, Jurish, Pallmeyer, Saunders, Teders, Barron, & Rodichok, 1982). This example will be used to illustrate these procedures and to provide a context for comments on the relationship of these procedures to intensive local observation and time-series methodology.

Specifically, 91 clients with chronic headaches were treated with a combination of relaxation and biofeedback in a typical clinical replication format. There were no control groups, comparison groups, nor was there any component analysis of treatment strategies usually associated with traditional outcome research. In setting the stage for this analysis, Blanchard et al. note that the two principal nonpharmacological treatments for headaches are varieties of biofeedback training and relaxation training. Furthermore, numerous controlled, direct comparisons of these two procedures have shown them generally to be equally efficacious. Finally, they observed that direct, controlled conparisons of biofeedback and/or relaxation, in comparison to some control condition in the treatment of headache, have been adequately or even overstudied, with almost all studies showing that either one of these two treatments is superior to no treatment. Thus, this series represents the ideal implementation of a clinical replication strategy following experimental verification of the effectiveness of a treatment.

Different types of headaches were represented among the 91 clients. Thirty-three had tension headaches, 30 had migraine headaches, and 28 combined tension and migraine. Since relaxation is much cheaper, more efficient, and easier to administer than biofeedback, the strategy of the study was to apply relaxation first to all clients, regardless of type of headache, for 10 sessions. Biofeedback was then introduced only for those clients who did not show substantial reduction in headache activity from relaxation therapy. These clients received 12 sessions of either thermal biofeedback for vascular headaches or frontal EMG biofeedback for tension headaches. The notion here is that biofeedback would be administered only to relaxation "nonresponders" to determine if it indeed would be worth the greatly increased cost to put one of these nonresponders through a biofeedback regimen. Naturally, this strategy also allows the investigators to speculate on the mechanisms of action underlying each of these treatments because, if biofeedback works for a relaxation nonresponder, perhaps a different mechanism of action underlies the effectiveness of these procedures.

Since the primary goal of this project was research, a more rigorous and systematic approach to measurement and treatment was observed than is likely to occur in a practitioner's setting. First, all clients were required to complete a 4-week baseline period during which daily ratings of headache were made and numerous psychological tests were administered. Second, the clients, interventions, and measures were exceptionally well described and defined, fulfilling the first three guidelines for clinical replication. Clients presenting with headaches were subjected to extensive diagnostic procedures, including neurological examination, and the categorization of headache type was made by up-to-date, state-of-the-art procedures. Treatment, consisting of relaxation, followed in some cases by one or another type of biofeedback, was standardized to the extent that every step was recorded in a manual; thus, these treatments could be carried out by relatively inexperienced students. Finally, the most up-to-date and sophisticated subjective and physiological assessment of headaches and the various factors thought to be associated with headaches (e.g., background tension and anxiety) were measured, once again, far more extensively than would be likely or even desirable in practice.

The manner in which these measures were quantified allowed Blanchard et al. to set very specific criteria for improvement, a necessary first step for analyzing failures. These criteria were based on data from a validated headache diary and specified a ratio of reduction in headache activity relative to baseline headache activity, referred to as a *headache index*. Clients had to achieve a 50% reduction in headache activity before being considered much improved. Clients not reaching this criterion during the initial relaxation phase were assigned to one of the biofeedback conditions. This "headache index," of course, could be used by any practitioner, making it a very valuable assessment of success or failure.

Although the usual statistical analyses were performed assessing pre-post changes for each treatment, a more stringent and clinically meaningful test of the efficacy of relaxation was calculated to examine the frequency with which individual clients experience useful reductions in headache activity. This analysis demonstrated that 52% of tension headache clients demonstrated at least a 50% reduction in headache activity, while only 25.8% of clients with vascular headache showed this type of improvement. Numbers of clients falling in the categories of unimproved or worse (defined as less than 20% improvement) or slightly improved (defined as 20% to 49% improvement) were also provided. Similar calculations were made for the biofeedback procedures. Overall, relaxation therapy alone produced significant improvement for all three headache groups, with tension headaches responding most favorably, as described above. Biofeedback led to further significant reduction in headache activity for all who received it, with combined migraine and tension headache clients responding most favorably. In the end, after both treatments had been administered to all who qualified, 73% of tension headache clients and 52% of vascular headache clients were much improved (defined as at least a 50% reduction in headache activity).

Before treatment, a number of psychological tests or inventories were administered. These included the MMPI, the Beck Depression Inventory, the State Trait Anxiety Inventory, and a variety of others. Stepwise multiple regression equations were calculated using the psychological test scores alone and also combining these test scores with headache diagnosis to predict average posttreatment headache index score. In addition, in order to conduct a discriminate function analysis, the groups were divided into those who were much improved (50% or greater reduction in headache response) and those who did not meet this criterion, again using the psychological test scores alone as predictors, and then combining the scores with headache diagnosis. This analysis allowed a determination of which two or three test scores would best predict significant improvement.

Considering the multiple regression analysis first, overall results revealed that approximately 32% of the variance in end-of-treatment headache index scores could be predicted after relaxation and 44% of the variance after biofeedback, using the standard psychological test scores. Specifically, several scales of the MMPI and the life-events scale from the Holmes and Rahe Social Readjustment Rating Scale contributed to the prediction of postrelaxation headache index for all clients. However, different psychological tests turn out to be predictive when one attempts to predict the response of distinct types of headaches. Specifically, 40.8, 32.8, and 26.1% of the variance can be predicted in the final headache index for tension, migraine, and combined headache respectively. While this is considered high by current standards of research, it is unlikely to communicate much to the practitioner concerning predictions of response to treatment in individual clients.

Predictions from multiple regression equations, as Blanchard et al. (1982) point out, are much less useful than discriminate function analyses, described below, for determining generality of findings, including predictors of success. Multiple regression, involving as it does a series of correlations between predetermined predictor variables and response to treatment followed by an analysis of the percentage of variance accounted for, leaves no room for assessment of a clinically significant response to a given treatment and the predictors that might be associated with that clinical response.

To take the "best" example above, the psychological tests would account for 40.8% of the variance in predicting response to treatment of those subjects in the study with tension headache (and this is quite high for a psychological study). Assuming for a moment that one could infer to the population of tension headache sufferers (and to the individual client in the practitioner's office) from this sample, then one could say that if this one headache sufferer presented a certain pattern of test results, there is a 40% chance he or she would "respond" to relaxation. Whether this response would be clinically meaningful could not be specified. Furthermore, the figure of 40.8% represents the "average" response of 31 subjects in this group. Problems in generalizing from this hypothetical average to an individual client have been described before (Hersen & Barlow, 1976). For this reason, as well as others, Yeaton and Sechrest (1981) have referred to procedures involving the determination of percentage of variance accounted for as very weak methods for determining strength or generality of effectiveness of a treatment. Much the same can be said for other correlational procedures, such as path analysis, that do not consider individual successes or failures.

Blanchard et al. suggest, quite reasonably, that canonical discriminate function may have considerably more clinical utility, since predetermined clinical criteria of success or failure can be entered into this calculation and predictions can then be made on whether a client will succeed or fail based on these criteria. In this particular study, the criterion, as mentioned above, was at least a 50% reduction on the headache index. Once again, in deference to the practitioner who may wish to use these data, the authors leave the actual classification calculations in manageable form so that practitioners can apply them to their own individual clients. Basically, this calculation reveals that of all patients finishing relaxation, 61.8% could be classified correctly as either successes or failures based on some combination of three of the psychological tests or their subscales. The investigators limited the analyses to three tests rather than the whole battery in the interest of the potential applicability of these procedures to clinical situations. That is, it is easier for a clinician to give three tests rather than a whole battery.

While individual practitioners may not consider this to be a particularly good rate of success (almost 40% would be incorrectly classified even by this simple success-or-failure criterion), the results are somewhat better with individual groups of clients suffering from one particular category of headache. In the best example, the response of the mixed group to the relaxation treatment alone, 85.7% of the clients would be successfully classified. This breaks down to 83.3% of the successes correctly classified, and 86.4% of the failures correctly classified. Thus, since this percentage figure is based on 28 clients, and assuming the representativeness of this sample of all headache sufferers experiencing "mixed" headaches, the individual practitioner would have only a one-out-of-six chance of making an incorrect prediction on his particular client based on two subscales of the MMPI and scores on the Rathus Assertiveness Scale (the tests that turned out to be predictive in this case). That's not bad, and represents a level of prediction seldom, if ever, seen in applied psychological research. Of course, the overall prediction of 61.8% for all headache types is far less satisfactory for predicting the effects of relaxation training, but then it would be in the best interest of the practitioner to properly classify his client into one of the subcategories of headaches to begin with. If this is done, then the range of correct classification ranges from the 85.7% already mentioned for the mixed group, to 73.3% for the migraine group. The lowest percentage of correct classification on this criterion is found for biofeedback treatment of the migraine group, where 71.9% were correctly classified as either successes or failures with only 60% of the failures in this particular group correctly classified (and 82.4% of the successes).

One difficulty with this approach, of course, is the psychological test or subscales that turn out to be the important predictors. In many cases these differ widely from group to group. For example, for the vascular headache group treated by biofeedback, three MMPI subscales were the best predictors of outcome. On the other hand, for all patients finishing relaxation, two calculations from the Life Events Scale and the State Anxiety subscale of the State Trait Anxiety Inventory cluster together as most effective predictors. As the investigators themselves point out, these combinations of test scores defy easy characterization. They conclude that it would probably be naive to expect the same test to predict results for different client groups and for different treatments. Thus, the generality of these predictors is far from a given fact, despite the large sample, and considerably more replication is needed.

Conclusions

Several similarities and differences should be apparent between this effort and the more usual analyses of successes and failures carried out in an applied setting. In the applied setting, the practitioner will examine a number of dimensions in the search for predictors of success and failure, including client variables, therapist variables, other idiosyncrasies of the treatment situation, and perhaps procedural variables relative to the administration of treatment. He or she will not limit him/herself to a couple of tests or other factors with little logical relation to the problem at hand. The practitioner will then attempt to identify those factors that seem associated with success or failure. This, of course, should lead presumably to more prospective observation and tests of factors thought to be associated with failure in subsequent clients and replication in other clinics. The statistical approach, on the other hand, typically concludes in advance which variables will be examined as predictors without the first step of intensive local observation. Usually these predictors are very narrowly construed. The Blanchard et al. series is a good example, with its use of psychological tests or inventories. While Blanchard et al. used these in a sensible fashion, often, in other studies, these are multiplied ad infinitum. These tests, representing as they do answers to questions on a paper-and-pencil inventory administered once before treatment begins, have not proven reliable predictors in the past (Garfield & Bergin, 1978), and even Blanchard et al. admit that the results do not make much sense. Foa's clinical observation of overvalued ideation, repeatedly assessed over the course of treatment, would seem a more intuitively reasonable predictor than a score on a subscale of the MMPI. Other more direct observations of client behaviors during treatment might also prove to be stronger predictors than one-shot psychological tests. Of course, specifying predictors right from the start does have the advantage of being prospective and certainly the investigators cannot be accused of introducing some systematic clinician bias into the identification of important predictive factors.

A second major difference is the reliance on a probabilistic statement, as evidenced in the Blanchard et al. series, with the provision of figures on the "likelihood" of a client's responding in a specific way, given certain test configurations, versus the more individualized type of prediction made thus far in more usual clinical replication series. For example, Foa (1979) identified four individuals who were severely depressed, four with overvalued ideation, and two with both, who were complete failures in her series. Pending further replication and analysis, as outlined in the last section, the practitioner can then determine the extent to which a client he or she is seeing is similar to one of the Foa clients (see chapter 2).

The Blanchard et al. series, advanced and sophisticated as it is, still reports discrimination of successes from failures *on the average;* although, as noted above, this discrimination was done with far greater accuracy than almost any other effort of its kind. A practitioner looking at the series with its 15 to 40% rate of incorrect classifications, would have to gamble that his or her client would respond like one of the correctly classified subjects. Since these subjects are not described much beyond headache type and response on the subscale of various tests, the practitioner would not have much to go on. More detailed individual analysis might examine the 15 to 40% of the clients incorrectly classified on the basis of the various predictors. Were there any apparent differences from those correctly classified? Of course, there is no reason one could not do both types of analyses. But we would suggest that it would be extremely important not to lose sight of the individual as one strives to make clinically relevant predictors available to the practitioner who is seeing individuals.

Both the Blanchard et al. (1982) effort and other clinical replication series described above were initial efforts in the analysis of failures. That is, these series both attempted to identify only those factors associated with failure. The Blanchard et al. report had the advantage of attempting a prospective analysis, but the disadvantage of choosing variables as predictors that were not discovered in a clinically relevant fashion through intensive local observation. Nevertheless, this effort would not be complete by any means without further attempts to determine reasons for failure, so that treatments can be adapted and tailored to all clients experiencing distress.

GUIDELINES FOR CONSUMING CLINICAL REPLICATION DATA

To this point we have discussed guidelines for producing clinical replication series. In this section we present guidelines for consuming these findings.

Table 12.1 presents a checklist of important dimensions for practitioners to consider in consuming research. It lists many questions to consider. By going through the list while examining a given study or clinical replication series you may get a sense of its strengths and weaknesses.

Client Description

First ask yourself if the clients are described in detail. If they are described in detail, examine your own clients and see if they seem similar in respects that you think are probably important (or which you may know to be important) to treatment outcome. Studies which give relatively little detail about the individual subjects may still be valid. Studies that use very different subjects may also be valid. However, they will be so only to the extent that the phenomena that are identified are of such power and generality that issues of client characteristics are relatively unimportant. This may often be true, so you should not reject research out of hand because it used college students, or clinical clients who are poorly described. The point is simply to think this issue through as you examine the research findings. Some problems seem to be quite similar across clients (or even species). Others show a great deal of individual variability. If your problem is of the latter type, client description and similarity is much more important.

Table 12.1. A Checklist of Important Dimensions for Practitioners to Consider

In all cases, a *Yes* indicates greater likelihood of generalization to your situation:

1. Are the clients described in detail? Does your client seem similar to those in the series in most or all important respects?

2. Are the procedures used described in detail sufficient for you to do what was done in all important respects?

3. Does the series specify the conditions (therapist, therapy environment) under which intervention was applied? Are they similar to your own? Are there therapist effects?

4. Are measures taken repeatedly across time so that an adequate individual sample is obtained?

5. Are several different measures taken if there is not one universally accepted measure?

6. Are individual characteristics identified that are related to treatment outcome? Do your clients share the favorable characteristics?

7. If the results are reported in group form, is the percentage of individuals showing the effect reported? Is it high? Are individual data shown?

8. Have the results been replicated? Several times? By others?

9. Are the effects (and differences between effects) strong and clinically meaningful?

10. Does the study experimentally test factors that account for success or failure? If so, are the favorable conditions present in your situation?

11. Have you tried the procedures with your clients? Did you achieve similar results?

Procedural Description

You should then ask yourself if the procedures which are used are described in detail sufficient for you to administer all components of the treatment that you have reason to believe are important to treatment outcome. On this basis, large sections of the applied literature must be questioned. Whatever the value may be, for example, in philosophical discourse about clinical phenomena and interventions, it is extremely unlikely that it will generalize consistently to individual practitioners if it is stated (as it usually is) in such a way as to allow ambiguous conclusions or different conclusions to be drawn about what was actually done. The role of such discussions may be important in generating more specific techniques, principles, and procedures which then may have a degree of external validity. Nevertheless, it is only when procedures are described in detail that they can possibly have a hope of generality, since it is the rules themselves (not the literal findings) which are being generalized to a new situation. This area is probably one in which the differences between reliability and generality are most obvious. Many studies on clinical techniques show obvious effects but do such a poor job of treatment description that any hope of generality is lost.

Intervention Conditions

Then examine the conditions under which the treatment was applied. What kinds of therapists were used? What was the therapy environment like? Do you have any reason to believe that these factors might have a strong impact on the outcome of treatment? If you do, are these factors similar to the ones that exist in your own situation? Only when you have thought through these kinds of issues can you assume that even demonstrably effective techniques used on clients similar to your own will be likely to be effective when you use them. Studies which include several therapists allow an examination of therapist effects. If none are shown, and the therapists spanned a range of characteristics, then this alleviates the concern a bit. If any therapist effects are shown, the goodness of fit between you and the most effective therapists are more critical. If all of the therapists are similar (e.g., all are students or therapists in training), the lack of therapist effects is less meaningful. You should recognize that several single-case designs done by different investigators constitute a kind of assessment of therapist effects.

Repeated Measurement

Were measures taken repeatedly across time so that an adequate individual sample is obtained? You as an individual practitioner could not think of intervening with an individual client until you are fairly sure of the need for intervention. A single assessment may not be enough. Paradoxically, you may be quite willing to take seriously the claims that a particular intervention is effective when a single preassessment has been compared to a single postassessment in several clients. We've already analyzed the logical difficulty with this. If repeated measures are taken, it is usually important that they be presented individually and not just as an aggregate across clients. Among other things, this allows you to assess in considerable detail the goodness of fit between your client's problems and the individuals in the reported research.

Number of Measures

Are several different measures taken if there is not one universally accepted measure? In many clinical areas the identification of client problems is not at all a clear-cut matter. Even in fairly well-defined syndromes such as depression, no single universally accepted measure has emerged to define the disorder. It is risky to assume, for example, that someone who has defined a depressive disorder based on low rates of activity is talking about the same kind of situation as your client, who may show an elevated D scale on the MMPI. If several measures have been taken and the results are parallel with these several measures, there is a greater likelihood that the findings will apply to clients of yours who are similar on some of those measures. Thus, studies with multiple measures are more likely to generalize to other situations.

Identification of Successes and Failures

Did the individual study examine which client characteristics were related to treatment outcome? If it did, what was found? Is your client one who shares the characteristics of those who were treated most successfully? The need for this kind of analysis has already been discussed. Essentially, studies of this sort have generated data-based guesses about rules of generality. Note, however, that the concerns noted earlier apply here. The relationship should be replicable and strong enough to be meaningful. The characteristics identified should be specific and meaningful.

Individual Data

If the results are reported in group form, is the percentage of individuals showing the effect reported? Is it high? Are individual data shown? If you look for data on the effect of interventions on individuals, as recommended here, you will usually be disappointed. The methodological posture we have adopted is currently quite atypical in clinical science. Although the support for this point of view is growing, the huge preponderance of clinical research still clings to some of the worst aspects of group-comparison approaches. Recently, however, some researchers have begun to indicate a box score about how many individuals in a given group showed the effect. For example, a study in which 90% of the patients seemed to improve is probably more likely to generalize to your individual client than one that revealed an impact of similar magnitude but only with, say, 60% of the clients tested.

Replication

Have the results been replicated? How many times? By whom? Every time a finding is replicated, generalizability increases. If the replications are done by several different persons in several different settings and if the findings are relatively consistent, then this is one of the more powerful indications that these findings may apply to your situation. Unfortunately, the picture is often not clear. A finding may have been replicated in a few settings, but not in others. If it has replicated at all, it is quite likely that something is effective about it. The difference in results between studies is due to structural differences between them. The failure to replicate in some settings helps us identify the boundary conditions — the limits of generality. The practitioner must assess whether the conditions he or she is facing are more like the studies that replicated the finding or those that did not.

Strength of Effects

Are the effects strong? In the usual study, we often examine the level of statistical significance and forget the magnitude of the effect shown. It is logical, however, that strong effects will be more generalizable than weak ones. In part, this may be due to issues discussed earlier. Strong effects, for example, will tend to be shown in many (if not all) clients. Thus, the individual consistency is likely to be much higher. This consistency itself implies a kind of generality of findings.

Experimental Analysis of Reasons for Success or Failure

Does the study experimentally test client or situational differences that might relate to the impact of treatment? If so, do your clients or situations show the favorable conditions indicated? This advice has been analyzed in some detail above as the third step in analyzing failures. If a study identifies the boundary conditions of an effect, or conditions which maximize impact, it is providing a richer, more detailed set of rules to guide others. This amounts to a type of experimental test of generality. The decision rules that result seem particularly likely to generalize because of their level of specificity about variables of proven importance.

Testing it Yourself

Have you tried out the procedures with your clients? Did you achieve similar results in the past? There is no better way to know that research findings apply to your situation than to attempt to apply them. The advice offered throughout the rest of this book is that practitioners view themselves as scientists as well. Without these skills, practitioners cannot fully determine the effectiveness of treatment and, therefore, the applicability of treatment. The feedback to the system is reduced and treatments might be accepted which are weak (or rejected though worthwhile). If a treatment is applied to one's own practice in the context of systematic evaluation, over time the truth about applicability will emerge.

Application of the Principles to Clinical Practice

This section has been written primarily from the standpoint of the consumer of research. Throughout, it was presented in terms of the consumption of *others'* research. Yet, when practitioners begin to be more empirical, they are themselves producing evaluations. They are then capable of "consuming" their own evaluations. And all the same rules apply. (Just because we ourselves did it does not mean that the standards change.) If it sounds strange to "consume your own evaluations," translate this statement into normal clinical language. What it means is simply *learning from your own practice*. Look again at Table 12.1, but this time with the set, "These are the things I should do in order to maximize the likelihood that what I learn with one client will transfer to others." Suddenly the guidelines jump out not as dry prescriptions, but as *rules of good practice*.

Consider each point again: *Describing the clients in detail*. What is this but good assessment, careful taking of histories, sensitivity to subtle but critical client characteristics, and the like? *Describing the procedures and conditions in detail*. What is this but a careful and detailed treatment plan? *Repeated measurement*. Are you carefully assessing the client's problems and progress in treatment? *Multiple measures*. Are you doing a fairly broad assessment? Are you keeping your eye on the overall functioning and well being of your client? *Identification of successes* . Are you careful to ensure that the treatment fits the specific needs and strengths of the individual client? *Individual data*. Are you assessing and working for the progress of each and every one of your clients or are you content to say only that overall you do well? *Replication*. Are you using procedures that are likely to work? *Strong effects*. Have you met your treatment goals? *Limitations*. If therapy is not working, do you stop, reassess, and try to determine why it isn't? *Testing it yourself*. Has this intervention worked for you? *Internal validity*. Are you really responsible for change? Was the treatment really needed? Are you utilizing resources appropriately?

The rules to be followed in assessing generalizability closely parallel rules to be followed in good practice. The language differs slightly — the message is the same. Another way you could say this is that the kind of knowledge that is based on the highest standards of practice is the kind of knowledge that is likely to generalize. Unfortunately, it is all too easy to take shortcuts. Much of our knowledge is not based on the highest standards of practice. The recommendations made here, and described in this book, can be seen as guidelines to ensure that practitioners produce and consume knowledge that is consistent with these standards.

References

Abel, G. G., Blanchard, D. B., & Barlow, D. H. (1981). Measurement of sexual arousal in several paraphilias: The effects of stimulus modality, instructional set, and stimulus content on the objective. *Behaviour Research and Therapy, 19,* 25-33.

Abel, G. G., Blanchard, E. B., Barlow, D. H., & Flanagan, B. (1975, December). *A controlled behavioral treatment of a sadistic rapist.* Paper presented at the annual meeting of the Association for Advancement of Behavior Therapy, San Francisco.

Adler, P. T. (1972). Will the Ph.D. be the death of professional psychology? *Professional Psychology, 3,* 69-72.

Agras, W. S. (Ed.) (1978). *Behavior modification: Principles and clinical applications.* (2nd ed.). Boston: Little, Brown.

Agras, W. S., & Berkowitz, R. (1980). Clinical research in behavior therapy: Halfway there? *Behavior Therapy, 11,* 472-488.

Agras, W. S., Kazdin, A. E., & Wilson, G. T. (1979). *Behavior therapy: Toward an applied clinical science.* San Francisco: W. H. Freeman.

Agras, W. S., Leitenberg, H., & Barlow, D. H. (1968). Social reinforcement in the modification of agoraphobia. *Archives of General Psychiatry, 19,* 423-427.

Agras, W. S., Leitenberg, H., Barlow, D. H., Curtis, N., Edwards, J., & Wright, D. (1971). The role of relaxation in systematic desensitization. *Archives of General Psychiatry, 25,* 511-514.

Agras, W. S., Leitenberg, H., Barlow, D. H., & Thomson, L. E. (1969). Instructions and reinforcement in the modification of neurotic behavior. *American Journal of Psychiatry, 125,* 1435-1439.

Albee, G. W. (1970). The uncertain future of clinical psychology. *American Psychologist, 225,* 1071-1080.

Alford, G. S., Webster, J. S., & Sanders, S. H. (1980). Covert aversion of two interrelated deviant sexual practices: Obscene phone calls and exhibitionism. A single case analysis. *Behavior Therapy, 11,* 15-25.

Allen, K. E., Hart, B., Buell, J. S., Harris, F. R., & Wolf, M. M. (1964). Effects of social reinforcement on isolate behavior of a nursery school child. *Child Development, 35,* 511-518.

American Psychiatric Association (1980). *Diagnostic and statistical manual of mental disorders* (3rd ed.). Washington, DC: Author.

Azrin, N. H. (1977). A strategy for applied research: Learning based but outcome oriented. *American Psychologist, 32,* 140-149.

Azrin, N. H., & Besalel, V. A. (1981). An operant reinforcement method of treating depression. *Journal of Behavior Therapy and Experimental Psychiatry, 12,* 145-151.

Azrin, N. H., Hontos, P. T., & Besalel-Azrin, V. (1979). Elimination of enuresis without a conditioning apparatus: An extension of office instruction of the child and parents. *Behavior Therapy, 10,* 14-19.

Azrin, N. H., Naster, B. J., & Jones, R. (1973). Reciprocity counseling: A rapid learning-based procedure for marital counseling. *Behaviour Research and Therapy, 11,* 365-382.

Baer, D. M., Wolf, M., & Risley, T. R. (1968). Some current dimensions of applied behavior analysis. *Journal of Applied Behavior Analysis, 1,* 91-97.

Bakan, D. (1966). The test of significance in psychological research. *Psychological Bulletin, 66,* 423-437.

Bandura, A. (1969). *The principles of behavior modification.* New York: Holt, Rinehart & Winston.

Bandura, A. (1979). On ecumenism in research perspectives. *Cognitive Therapy and Research, 3,* 245-248.

Bandura, A., & Adams, N. E. (1977). Analysis of self-efficacy theory of behavioral change. *Cognitive Therapy and Research, 1,* 287-310.

Barlow, D. H. (1977). Behavioral assessment in clinical settings: Developing issues. In J. D. Cone & R. P. Hawkins (Eds.), *Behavioral assessment: New directions in clinical psychology.* New York: Brunner/Mazel.

Barlow, D. H. (1980). Behavior therapy: The next decade. *Behavior Therapy, 11,* 315-328.

Barlow, D. H. (1981). On the relation of clinical research to clinical practice: Current issues, new directions. *Journal of Consulting and Clinical Psychology, 49,* 147-156.

Barlow, D. H. (1983). Editorial policies of *Behavior Therapy.* The Behavior Therapist, *6,* 32.

Barlow, D. H., Becker, R., Leitenberg, H., & Agras, W. S. (1970). A mechanical strain gauge for recording penile circumference change. *Journal of Applied Behavior Analysis, 3,* 73-76.

Barlow, D. H., & Hayes, S. C. (1979). Alternating treatments design: One strategy for comparing the effects of two treatments in a single subject. *Journal of Applied Behavior Analysis, 12,* 199-210.

Barlow, D. H., Hayes, S. C., Nelson, R. O., Steele, D. L., Meeler, M. E., & Mills, J. R. (1979). Sex role behavior: A behavioral checklist. *Behavioral Assessment, 1,* 119-138.

Barlow, D. H., & Hersen, M. (1973). Single case experimental designs: Uses in applied clinical research. *Archives of General Psychiatry, 29,* 319-325.

Barlow, D. H., & Hersen, M. (in press). *Single case experimental designs: Strategies for studying behavior change.* (2nd ed.). New York: Pergamon.

Barlow, D. H., Leitenberg, H., Agras, W. S., & Wincze, J. P. (1969). The transfer gap in systematic desensitization: An analogue study. *Behaviour Research and Therapy, 7,* 191-197.

Barlow, D. H., & Mavissakalian, M. R. (1981). Directions in the assessment and treatment of phobia: The next decade. In M. R. Mavissakalian & D. H. Barlow (Eds.), *Phobia: Psychological and pharmacological treatment.* New York: Guilford.

Barlow, D. H., Mavissakalian, M., & Schofield, L. (1980). Patterns of desynchrony in agoraphobia. *Behaviour Research and Therapy, 18,* 441-448.

Barlow, D. H., & Seidner, A. L. (in press). Treatment of adolescent agoraphobics: Effects on parent-adolescent relations. *Behaviour Research and Therapy.*

Barlow, D. H., & Wolfe, B. E. (1981). Behavioral approaches to anxiety disorders: A report on the NIMH-SUNY, Albany Research Conference. *Journal of Consulting and Clinical Psychology, 49,* 448-454.

Beck, A. T. (1967). *Depression: Clinical, experimental, and theoretical aspects.* New York: Harper & Row.

Beck, A. T., Rush, A. J. Shaw, B. J., & Emery, G. (1979). *Cognitive therapy of depression.* New York: Guilford.

Beck, A. T., Ward, C. H., Mendelson, M., Mock, J., & Erbaugh, J. (1961). An inventory for measuring depression. *Archives of General Psychiatry, 4,* 561-571.

Beiman, I., Graham, L. E., & Ciminero, A. R. (1978). Self-control progressive relaxation training as an alternative nonpharmacological treatment for essential hypertension: Therapeutic effects in the natural environment. *Behaviour Research and Therapy, 16,* 371-375.

Bellack, A. S., & Hersen, M. (1977). Self-report inventories in behavioral assessment. In J. D. Cone & R. P. Hawkins (Eds.), *Behavioral assessment: New directions in clinical psychology.* New York: Brunner/Mazel.

Bellack, A. S., Hersen, M., & Lamparski, D. (1979). Role-playing tests for assessing social skills: Are they valid? Are they useful? *Journal of Consulting and Clinical Psychology, 47,* 335-342.

Bellack, A. S., Hersen, M., & Turner, S. M. (1978). Role-play tests for assessing social skills: Are they valid? *Behavior Therapy, 9,* 448-461.

Bergin, A. E. (1966). Some implications of psychotherapy research for therapeutic practice. *Journal of Abnormal Psychology, 71,* 235-246.

Bergin, A. E., Garfield, S. L., & Thompson, A. S. (1967). The Chicago Conference on clinical training and clinical psychology at Teachers College. *American Psychologist, 22,* 307-316.

Bergin, A., & Strupp, H. (1972). *Changing frontiers in the science of psychotherapy.* Chicago: Aldine.

Bernstein, D. A., & Nietzel, M. T. (1973). Procedural variation in behavioral avoidance tests. *Journal of Consulting and Clinical Psychology, 41,* 165-174.

Blanchard, E. B., Andrasik, F., Neff, D. F., Arena, J. G., Ahles, T. A., Jurish, S. E., Pallmeyer, T. P., Saunders, N. L., Teders, S. J., Barron, K. D., & Rodichok, L. D. (1982). Biofeedback and relaxation training with three kinds of headache: Treatment effects and their prediction. *Journal of Consulting and Clinical Psychology, 50,* 562-575.

Blanchard, E. B., Andrasik,F., Neff, D. F., Jurish, S. E., & O'Keefe, D. M. (1981). Social validation of the headache diary. *Behavior Therapy, 12,* 711-715.

Bloom, L.J., & Cantrell, D. (1978). Anxiety management training for essential hypertension in pregnancy. *Behavior Therapy, 9,* 377-382.

Bloom, M., & Block, S. R. (1977). Evaluating one's own effectiveness and efficiency. *Social Work, 22,* 130-136.

Bloom, M., & Fischer, J. (1982). *Evaluating practice: Guidelines for the accountable professional.* Englewood Cliffs, NJ: Prentice-Hall.

Boice, R. (1983). Observational skills. *Psychological Bulletin, 93,* 3-29.

Boren, J. J., & Jagodzinski, M. G. (1975). The impermanence of data recording behavior. *Journal of Behavior Therapy and Experimental Psychiatry, 6,* 359.

Borkovec, T. D., Kaloupek, D.G., & Slama, K. M. (1975). The facilitative effect of muscle tension-release in the relaxation treatment of sleep disturbance. *Behavior Therapy, 6,* 301-309.

Bornstein, P. H., Bach, P. J., Heider, J. F., & Ernst, J. (1981). Clinical treatment of marital dysfunction: A multiple-baseline analysis. *Behavioral Assessment, 3,* 335-343.

Bornstein, P. H., Mungas, D. M., Quevillon, R. P., Kniivila, C. M., Miller, R. K., & Holombo, L. K. (1978). Self-monitoring training: Effects on reactivity and accuracy of self-observation. *Behavior Therapy, 9,* 545-552.

Bornstein, P. H., & Rychtarik, R. G. (1978). Multi-component behavioral treatment of trichotillomania: A case study. *Behaviour Research and Therapy, 16,* 217-220.

Boulougouris, J. C., Rabavilas, A. D., & Stefanis, C. (1977). Psychophysiological responses in obsessive-compulsive patients. *Behaviour Research and Therapy, 15,* 221-230.

Bright, P. D., & Robin, A. L. (1981). Ameliorating parent-adolescent conflict with problem-solving communication training. *Journal of Behavior Therapy and Experimental Psychiatry, 12,* 275-280.

Brooks, G. R., & Richardson, F. C. (1980). Emotional skills training: A treatment program for duodenal ulcer. *Behavior Therapy, 11,* 198-207.

Brownell, K., & Barlow, D. H. (1976, September). *Experimental analysis in the treatment of multiple sexual deviations.* Paper presented at the meeting of the American Psychological Association. Washington, DC.

Brownell, K. D., Hayes, S. C., & Barlow, D. H. (1977). Patterns of appropriate and deviant sexual arousal: The behavioral treatment of multiple sexual deviations. *Journal of Consulting and Clinical Psychology, 45,* 1144-1155.

Browning, R. M. (1967). A same-subject design for simultaneous comparison of three reinforcement contingencies. *Behaviour Research and Therapy, 5,* 237-243.

Browning, R. M., & Stover, D. O. (1971). *Behavior modification in child treatment: An experimental and clinical approach.* Chicago: Aldine.

Budzynski, T., Stoyva, J. M., & Adler, C. S. (1970). Feedback:induced muscle relaxation: Application to tension headaches. *Journal of Behavior Therapy and Experimental Psychiatry, 1,* 205-211.

Buros, O. K. (Ed.) (1978). *The eighth mental measurements yearbook* (2 vols.). Highland Park, NJ: Gryphon.

Callahan, E. J., & Leitenberg, H. (1973). Aversion therapy for sexual deviation: Contingent shock and covert sensitization. *Journal of Abnormal Psychology, 81,* 60-73.

Campbell, D. T. (1959). Factors relevant to the validity of experiments in social settings. *Psychological Bulletin, 54,* 297-312.

Campbell, D. T. (1973). The social scientist as methodological servant of the experimenting society. *Policy Studies Journal, 2,* 72-75.

Campbell, D. T., & Fiske, D. W. (1959). Convergent and discriminant validation by the multitrait-multimethod matrix. *Psychological Bulletin, 56,* 81-105.

Campbell, D. T., & Stanley, J. C. (1963). *Experimental and quasi-experimental designs for research.* Chicago: Rand McNally.

Carr, E. G., & McDowell, J. J. (1980). Social control of self-injurious behavior of organic etiology. *Behavior Therapy, 11,* 402-409.

Carver, R. P. (1978). The case against statistical significance testing. *Harvard Educational Review, 48,* 378-399.

Carver, R.P. (1974). Two dimensions of tests: Psychometric and edumetric. *American Psychologist, 29,* 512-518.

Cautela, J. R. (1981). *Behavior analysis forms for clinical intervention* (2 vols.). Champaign, IL: Research Press.

Cautela, J. R., & Upper, D. (1976). The behavioral inventory battery: The use of self-report measures in behavioral analysis and therapy. In M. Hersen & A. S. Bellack (Eds.), *Behavioral assessment: A practical handbook.* New York: Pergamon.

Cavior, N., & Marbotto, C. M. (1976). Monitoring verbal behaviors in a dyadic interaction: Valence of target behaviors, type, timing, and reactivity of monitoring. *Journal of Consulting and Clinical Psychology, 44,* 68-76.

Chassan, J. B. (1960). Statistical inference and the single case in clinical design. *Psychiatry, 23,* 173.

Chesney, M. A., & Shelton, J. L. (1976). A comparison of muscle relaxation and electromyogram biofeedback treatments for muscle contraction headache. *Journal of Behavior Therapy and Experimental Psychiatry, 7,* 221-225.

Christensen, A. (1979). Naturalistic observation of families: A system for random audio recordings in the home. *Behavior Therapy, 10,* 418-422.

Christensen, A., Johnson, S. M., Phillips, S., & Glasgow, R. E. (1980). Cost effectiveness in behavioral family therapy. *Behavior Therapy, 11,* 208-226.

Clifford, D. (1981). Instruments for measuring outcomes in mental health program evaluation: Results of a survey. *Evaluation News, 2,* 54-58.

Claiborne, W. L., & Zaro, J. S. (1979). A development of a peer review system: The APA-CHAMPUS contract. In C.A. Kiesler, N.A. Cummings & G.R. Vanden Bos (Eds.), *Psychology amd national health insurance.* Washington DC: American Psychological Association.

Cohen, E. A., Gelfand, D. M., Dodd, D. K., Jensen, J., & Turner, C. (1980). Self-control practices associated with weight loss maintenance in children and adolescents. *Behavior Therapy, 11,* 26-37.

Cohen, L. H. (1976). Clinicians' utilization of research findings. *JSAS Catalog of Selected Documents in Psychology, 6,* 116.

Cohen, L. H. (1979). The research readership and information source reliance of clinical psychologists. *Professional Psychology, 10,* 780-786.

Cohen, L. H. (1981, August). *Research utilizaton by clinical psychologists.* Paper presented at the annual convention of the American Psychological Association, Los Angeles, CA.

Collins, F. L., & Martin, J. E. (1980). Assessing self-report of pain: A comparison of two recording procedures. *Journal of Behavioral Assessment, 2,* 55-63.

Comrey, A. L., Backer, T. E., & Glaser, E. M. (1973). *A sourcebook for mental health measures.* Los Angeles, CA: Human Interaction Research Institute.

Cone, J. D. (1977). The relevance of reliability and validity for behavioral assessment. *Behavior Therapy, 8,* 411-426.

Cone, J. D. (1978). The Behavioral Assessment Grid (BAG): A conceptual framework and a taxonomy. *Behavior Therapy, 9,* 882-888.

Cone, J. D. (1979). Confounded comparisons in triple response mode assessment research. *Behavioral Assessment, 1,* 85-95.

Conners, C. K. (1969). A teacher rating scale for use in drug studies with children. *American Journal of Psychiatry, 6,* 884-888.

Conte, J. R., & Levy, R. L. (1979, March). *Problems and issues in implementing the clinical research model of practice in educational and clinical settings.* Paper presented at the meeting of the Council on Social Work Education, Boston, MA.

Cook, T. D., & Campbell, D. T. (Eds.) (1979). *Quasi-experimentation: Design and analysis issues for field settings.* Chicago: Rand McNally.

Craighead, W. E. (1978). Report of task force for treatment evaluation and third party payment. *The Behavior Therapist, 1,* 9-10.

Craighead, W. E. (1980). Away from a unitary model of depression. *Behavior Therapy, 11,* 122-128.

Cronbach, L. J. (1975). Beyond the two disciplines of scientific psychology. *American Psychologist, 30,* 116-127.

Cronbach, L. J., & Snow, R. E. (1977). *Aptitudes and instructional methods: A handbook for research on interactions.* New York: Irvington.

Crowe, M. J., Gillan, P., & Golombok, S. (1981). Form and content in the conjoint treatment of sexual dysfunction: A controlled study. *Behaviour Research and Therapy, 19,* 47-54.

Cunningham, C. E., & Linscheid, T. R. (1976). Elimination of chronic infant ruminating by electric shock. *Behavior Therapy, 7,* 231-234.

Cunningham, T. R., & Tharp, R. G. (1981). The influence of settings on accuracy and reliability of behavioral observations. *Behavioral Assessment, 3,* 67-78.

Curran, J. P., Corriveau, D. P., Monti, P. M., & Hagerman, S. B. (1980). Social skill and social anxiety: Self-report measurement in a psychiatric population. *Behavior Modification, 4,* 493-512.

Dancer, D. D., Braukmann, C. J., Schumaker, J. B., Kirigin, K. A., Willner, A. G., & Wolf, M. M. (1978). The training and validation of behavior observation and description skills. *Behavior Modification, 2,* 113-134.

Dapcich-Miura, E., & Hovell, M. F. (1979). Contingency management of adherence to a complex medical regimen in an elderly heart patient. *Behavior Therapy, 10,* 193-201.

Dentch, G. E., O'Farrell, T. J., & Cutter, H. S. G. (1980) Readability of marital assessment measures used by behavioral marriage therapists. *Journal of Consulting and Clinical Psychology, 48,* 790-792.

Dietz, S. M., & Repp, A. C. (1973). Decreasing classroom misbehavior through the use of DRL schedules of reinforcement. *Journal of Applied Behavior Analysis, 6,* 457-463.

Doke, L. A., & Risley, T. R. (1972). The organization of day-care environments: Required vs. optional activities. *Journal of Applied Behavior Analysis, 5,* 405-420

Dörken, H., & Webb, J. T. (1978, March). *Health service practice of licensed/certified psychologists: Training, mobility, clientele, fee-for-service practice and hospital practice.* Paper presented at the meeting of the Southeastern Psychological Association, Atlanta, GA.

Dunham, P. J. (1968). Contrasted conditions of reinforcement: A selective critique. *Psychological Bulletin, 69,* 295-315.

Dunn, L. M., & Markwardt, F. C. (1970). *Peabody Individual Achievement Test.* Circle Pines, MN: American Guidance Service.

Edgington, E. S. (1966). Statistical inference and nonrandom samples. *Psychological Bulletin, 66,* 485-487.

Edgington, E. S. (1967). Statistical inference from N=1 experiments. *Journal of Psychology, 65,* 195-199.

Ehrenfeld, D. (1978). *The arrogance of humanism.* New York: Oxford University.

Elkins, R. L. (1980). Covert sensitization treatment of alcoholism: Contributions of successful conditioning to subsequent abstinence maintenance. *Addictive Behaviors, 5,* 67-89.

Ellis, A. (1962). *Reason and emotion in psychotherapy.* New York: Lyle Stuart.

Emmelkamp, P. M. G. (1974). Self-observation versus flooding in the treatment of agoraphobia. *Behaviour Research and Therapy, 12,* 229-237.

Emmelkamp, P. M. G., & Kuipers, A. C. M. (1979). Agoraphobia: A follow-up study four years after treatment. *British Journal of Psychiatry, 134,* 342-355.

Emmelkamp, P. M. G., & Kwee, K. G. (1977). Obsessional ruminations: A comparison between thought-stopping and prolonged exposure in imagination. *Behaviour Research and Therapy, 15,* 441-444.

Epstein, L. H. (1976). Psychophysiological measurement in assessment. In M. Hersen, & A. S. Bellack (Eds.), *Behavioral assessment: A practical handbook.* New York: Pergamon.

Epstein, L. H., & Abel, G. G. (1977). An analysis of biofeedback training effects for tension headache patients. *Behavior Therapy, 8,* 37-47.

Epstein, L. H., Miller, P. M., & Webster, J. S. (1976). The effects of reinforcing concurrent behavior on self-monitoring. *Behavior Therapy, 7,* 89-95.

Epstein, L. H., Webster, J. S., & Miller, P. M. (1975). Accuracy and controlling effects of self-monitoring as a function of concurrent responding and reinforcement. *Behavior Therapy, 6,* 654-666.

Ericksen, S. C. (1966). Responsibilities of psychological science to professional psychology. *American Psychologist, 21,* 950-953.

Ersner-Hershfield, S. M., Connors, G. J., & Maisto, S. A. (1981). Clinical and experimental utility of refundable deposits. *Behaviour Research and Therapy, 19,* 455-457.

Eyberg, S. M., & Johnson, S. M. (1974). Multiple assessment of behavior modification with families: Effects of contingency contracting and order of treated problems. *Journal of Consulting and Clinical Psychology, 42,* 594-606.

Eysenck, H. J. (1952). The effects of psychotherapy: An evaluation. *Journal of Consulting Psychology, 16,* 319-324.

Eysenck, H. J. (1965). The effects of psychotherapy. *International Journal of Psychiatry, 1,* 97-178.

Fairbank, J. A., DeGood, D. E., & Jenkins, C. W. (1981). Behavioral treatment of a persistent post-traumatic startle response. *Journal of Behavior Therapy and Experimental Psychiatry, 12,* 321-324.

Fairweather, G., Sanders, D., Tornatsky, L., & Harris, R. (1974). *Creating changes in mental health organizations.* New York: Pergamon.

Farkas, G. M., & Beck, S. (1981). Exposure and response prevention of morbid ruminations and compulsive avoidance. *Behaviour Research and Therapy, 19,* 257-261.

Fisher, R. A. (1925). On the mathematical foundations of the theory of statistics. In *Theory of statistical estimation* (Proceeding of the Cambridge Philosophical Society).

Fixsen, D. L., Phillips, E. L., & Wolf, M. M. (1972). Achievement place: The reliability of self-reporting and peer-reporting and their effects on behavior. *Journal of Applied Behavior Analysis, 5,* 19-30.

Flexner, A. (1910). *Medical education in the United States and Canada.* Boston: Merrymount Press.

Foa, E. B. (1979). Failure in treating obsessive-compulsives. *Behaviour Research and Therapy, 17,* 169-176.

Foa, E. B., & Goldstein, A. (1978). Continuous exposure and complete response prevention in the treatment of obsessive-compulsive neurosis. *Behavior Therapy, 9,* 821-829.

Foa, E. B., Grayson, J. B., Steketee, G. S., Doppelt, H. G., Turner, R. M., & Latimer, P. R. (1983). Success and failure in the behavioral treatment of obsessive compulsives. *Journal of Consulting and Clinical Psychology, 51,* 287-297.

Foa, E. B., Steketee, G., & Milby, J. B. (1980). Differential effects of exposure and response prevention in obsessive-compulsive washers. *Journal of Consulting and Clinical Psychology, 48,* 71-79.

Fogel, L. S., & Nelson, R. O. (in press). The effects of special education labels on teachers' behavioral observations, checklist scores, and grading of academic work. *Journal of School Psychology.*

Ford, J. D., & Kendall, P. C. (1979). Behavior therapists' professional behaviors: Converging evidence of a gap between theory and practice. *The Behavior Therapist, 2,* 37-38.

Foster, S. L., & Cone, J. D. (1980). Current issues in direct observation. *Behavioral Assessment, 2,* 313-338

Foxx, R. M., & Martin, P. L. (1971). A useful portable timer. *Journal of Applied Behavior Analysis, 4,* 60.

Frame, C., Matson, J. L., Sonis, W. A., Fialkov, M. J., & Kazdin, A. E. (1982). Behavioral treatment of depression in a pre-pubertal child. *Journal of Behavior Therapy and Experimental Psychiatry, 13,* 239-243.

Frederiksen, L. W., Epstein, L. H., & Kosevsky, B. P. (1975). Reliability and controlling effects of three procedures for self-monitoring smoking. *The Psychological Record, 25,* 255-264.

Freeman, B. J. (1971). Behavioral constrast: Reinforcement frequency or response suppression. *Psychological Bulletin, 75,* 347-356.

Freud, S. (1959). Turnings in the ways of psychoanalytic therapy. In *Collected papers* (Vol. 2). New York: Basic Books. (Original work published 1919.)

Freund, K., Sedlacek, J., & Knob, K. (1965). A simple transducer for mechanical plethysmography of the male genital. *Journal of Experimental Analysis of Behavior, 8,* 169-170.

Friedman, J., & Axelrod, S. (1973). *The use of a changing-criterion procedure to reduce the frequency of smoking.* Unpublished manuscript, Temple University.

Furlong, N. J. & Wampold, B. E. (1982). Intervention effects and relative variation as dimensions in experts' use of visual inference. *Journal of Applied Behavior Analysis, 15,* 415-422.

Gadlin, H., & Ingle, G. (1975). Through the one-way mirror: The limits of experimental self-reflection. *American Psychologist, 30,* 1003-1009.

Galassi, M. D., & Galassi, J. P. (1976). The effects of role-playing variations on the assessment of assertive behavior. *Behavior Therapy, 7,* 343-347.

Garfield, S. L. (1966). Clinical psychology and the search for identity. *American Psychologist, 21,* 353-362.

Garfield, S. L. (1980). *Psychotherapy: An eclectic approach.* New York: Wiley.

Garfield, S. L. (1981). Evaluating the psychotherapies. *Behavior Therapy, 12,* 295-308.

Garfield, S. L., & Bergin, A. E. (Eds.) (1978). *Handbook of psychotherapy and behavior change* (2nd edition). New York: Wiley.

Garfield, S. L., & Kurtz, R. M. (1976). Clinical psychologists in the 1970s. *American Psychologist, 31,* 1-9.

Gauthier, J., & Pellerin, D. (1982). Management of compulsive shoplifting through covert sensitization. *Journal of Behavior Therapy and Experimental Psychiatry, 13,* 73-75.

Geer, J. H. (1965). The development of a scale to measure fear. *Behaviour Research and Therapy, 3,* 45-53.

Geer, J. H. (1977). Sexual functioning: Some data and speculations on psychophysiological assessment. In J. D. Cone & R. P. Hawkins (Eds.), *Behavioral assessment: New directions in clinical psychology.* New York: Brunner/Mazel.

Glaser, R. (1963). Instructional technology and the measurement of learning outcomes. *American Psychologist, 18,* 519-521.

Goldfried, M. R. (1980). Toward the delineation of therapeutic change principles. *American Psychologist, 35,* 991-999.

Goldfried, M. R., & Padawer, W. (in press). Current status and future directions in psychotherapy. In M. R. Goldfried (Ed.), *Converging themes in the practice of psychotherapy.* New York: Springer.

Gottman, J. M., & Markman, H. J. (1978). Experimental designs in psychotherapy research. In S. L. Garfield & A. E. Bergin (Eds.), *Handbook of psychotherapy and behavior change,* (2nd ed.). New York: Wiley.

Greenwald, A. G. (1976). Within-subject designs: To use or not to use. *Psychological Bulletin, 33,* 314-326.

Haley, J. (1978). *Problem-solving therapy: New strategies for effective family therapy.* San Francisco: Jossey-Bass.

Hall, R. V. (1971). *Management series: Part II.* Lawrence, KS: H&H Enterprises.

Hall, R. V., & Fox, R. G. (1977). Changing-criterion designs: An alternate applied behavior analysis procedure. In B. C. Etzel, J. M. LeBlanc, & D. M. Baer (Eds.), *New developments in behavioral research: Theory, method, and application. In honor of Sidney W. Bijou.* Hillsdale, NJ: Erlbaum.

Hamberger, L. K. (1982). Reduction of generalized aversive responding in a post-treatment cancer patient: Relaxation as an active coping skill. *Journal of Behavior Therapy and Experimental Psychiatry, 13,* 229-233.

Hargreaves, W. A., Atkinson, C. C., & Sorensen, J. E. (Eds.) (1977). *Resource materials for community mental health program evaluation.* Rockville, MD: National Institute of Mental Health.

Harmon, T. M., Nelson, R. O., & Hayes, S. C. (1980). Self-monitoring mood versus activity in depressed clients. *Journal of Consulting and Clinical Psychology, 48,* 30-38.

Hart, A. D., & McCrady, R. E.(1977). A unique electronic cueing device providing a tactile signal for behavior monitoring of self or other. *Behavior Therapy, 8,* 89-93.

Hartmann, D. P. (1977). Considerations in the choice of interobserver reliability estimates. *Journal of Applied Behavior Analysis, 10,* 103-116.

Hartmann, W. E., & Fithian, M. A. (1972). *Treatment of sexual dysfunction: A bio-psycho-social approach.* Long Beach, CA: Center for Marital and Sexual Studies.

Hartmann, D. P., & Hall, R. V. (1976). The changing criterion design. *Journal of Applied Behavior Analysis, 9,* 527-532.

Hartshorne, H., & May, M. A. (1928). *Studies in the nature of character. Vol. 1: Studies in deceit.* New York: Macmillan.

Hathaway, S. R., & McKinley, J. C. (1951). *MMPI manual.* New York: Psychological Corporation.

Hay, L. R., Nelson, R. O., & Hay, W. M. (1977). The use of teachers as behavioral observers. *Journal of Applied Behavior Analysis, 10,* 345-348.

Hay, L. R., Nelson, R. O., & Hay, W. M. (1980). Methodological problems in the use of participant observers. *Journal of Applied Behavior Analysis, 13,* 501-504.

Hayes, S. C. (1978, November). *Flooding relief in the treatment of obsessive-compulsive disorders.* Paper presented at the meeting of the Association for Advancement of Behavior Therapy, Chicago, IL.

Hayes, S. C. (1981). Single case experimental design and empirical clinical practice. *Journal of Consulting and Clinical Psychology, 49,* 193-211.

Hayes, S. C., & Barlow, D. H. (1977). Flooding relief in a case of public transportation phobia. *Behavior Therapy, 8,* 742-746.

Hayes, S. C., Brownell, K. D., & Barlow, D. H. (1978). The use of self-administered covert sensitization in the treatment of exhibitionism and sadism. *Behavior Therapy, 9,* 283-289.

Hayes, S. C., & Cavior, N. (1980). Multiple tracking and the reactivity of self-monitoring II: Positive behaviors. *Behavioral Assessment, 2,* 283-296.

Hayes, S. C., Hussian, R. A., Turner, A. E., Anderson, N., & Grubb, T. D. (in press). The effect of coping statements on progress through a desensitization hierrchy. *Journal of Behavior Therapy and Experimental Psychiatry.*

Hayes, S. C., Johnson, V. S., & Cone, J. D. (1975). The marked item technique, A practical procedure for litter control. *Journal of Applied Behavioral Analysis, 8,* 381-386.

Hayes, S. C., Levy, R. L., & Barlow, D. H. (1982). *Clinical realities and the animal laboratory: Competing sources of control over single subject designs.* Unpublished manuscript.

Hayes, S. C., Nelson, R. O., Willis, S., & Akamatsu, T. J. (1982). Visual avoidance: The use of slides in a convenient measure of phobic behavior. *Behavioral Assessment, 4,* 211-217.

Hayes, S. C., Rincover, A., & Solnick, J. V. (1980). The technical drift of applied behavior analysis. *Journal of Applied Behavior Analysis, 13,* 275-285.

Haynes, S. N. (1978). *Principles of behavioral assessment.* New York: Gardner.

Haynes, S. N., Griffin, P., Mooney, D., & Parise, M. (1975). Electromyographic biofeedback and relaxation instructions in the treatment of muscle contraction headaches. *Behavior Therapy, 6,* 672-678.

Haynes, S. N., & Horn, W. F. (1982). Reactivity in behavioral observation: A review. *Behavioral Assessment, 4,* 369-385.

Haynes, S. N., & Wilson, C. C. (1979). *Behavioral assessment.* San Francisco: Jossey-Bass.

Hays, W. L. (1963). *Statistics for psychologists.* New York: Holt, Rinehart & Winston.

Heimberg, R. G., Harrison, D. F., Montgomery, D., Madsen, C. H., & Sherfey, J. A. (1980). Psychometric and behavioral analysis of a Social Anxiety Questionnaire: The Situation Questionnaire. *Behavioral Assessment, 2,* 403-415.

Henson, D.E., Rubin, H.B., & Henson, C. (1979). Analysis of the consistency of objective measures of sexual arousal. *Journal of Applied Behavioral Analysis, 12,* 701-711.

Herink, R. (Ed.) (1980). *The psychotherapy handbook: The A to Z guide to more than 250 different therapies in use today.* New York: New American Library.

Hersen, M., & Barlow, D. H. (1976). *Single case experimental designs: Strategies for studying behavior change.* New York: Pergamon.

Higgins, R. L., Alonso, R. R., & Pendleton, M. G. (1979). The validity of role-play assessments of assertiveness. *Behavior Therapy, 10,* 655-662.

Himadi, W. G., Arkowitz, H., Hinton, R., & Perl, J. (1980). Minimal dating and its relationship to other social problems and general adjustment. *Behavior Therapy, 11,* 345-352.

Hoch, E. L., Ross, A. O., & Winder, C. L. (Eds.) (1966). *Professional preparation of clinical psychologists: Proceedings of the Conference on the Professional Preparation of Clinical Psychologists meeting at the Center for Continuing Education, Chicago, Illinois, August 17-September 1, 1965.* Washington, DC: American Psychological Association.

Hodgson, R., & Rachman, S. (1974). Desynchrony in measures of fear. *Behaviour Research and Therapy, 12,* 319-326.

Hoon, P., Wincze, J., & Hoon, E. (1976). Physiological assessment of sexual arousal in women. *Psychophysiology, 13,* 196-204.

Hopkins, J., Krawitz, G., & Bellack, A. S. (1981). The effects of situational variations in role-play scenes on assertive behavior. *Journal of Behavioral Assessment, 3,* 271-280.

Hops, H., Wills, T. A., Patterson, G. R., & Weiss, R. L. (1971). *Marital interaction coding system.* Eugene, OR: University of Oregon and Oregon Research Institute.

Horan, J. J. (1974). An efficient system for improving observer reliability. *Behavior Engineering, 1,* 1-3.

Hugdahl, K. (1981). The three-systems-model of fear and emotion — a critical examination. *Behaviour Research and Therapy, 19,* 75-85.

Hughes, J. R., Frederiksen, L. W., & Frazier, M. (1978). A carbon monoxide analyzer for measurement of smoking behavior. *Behavior Therapy, 9,* 293-296.

Humphreys, L., & Beiman, I. (1975). The application of multiple behavioral techniques to multiple problems of a complex case. *Journal of Behavior Therapy and Experimental Psychiatry, 6,* 311-315.

Hundert, J., & Batstone, D. (1978). A practical procedure to maintain pupils' accurate self-rating in a classroom token program. *Behavior Modification, 2,* 93-112.

Hundert, J., & Bucher, B. (1978). Pupils' self-scored arithmetic performance: A practical procedure for maintaining accuracy. *Journal of Applied Behavior Analysis, 11,* 304.

Jacobson, E. (1938). *Progressive relaxation*. Chicago: University of Chicago Press.

Jacobson, N. S. (1979). Increasing positive behavior in severely distressed marital relationships: The effects of problem-solving training. *Behavior Therapy, 10,* 311-326.

Jansson, L., & Ost, L. (1982). Behavioral treatments for agoraphobia: An evaluative review. *Clinical Psychology Review, 2,* 311-337.

Jastak, J. F., Bijou, S. W., & Jastak, S. R. (1965). *Wide Range Achievement Test.* Wilmington, DE: Guidance Associates of Delaware.

Jayaratne, S., & Levy, R. L. (1979). *Empirical clinical practice.* New York: Columbia University Press.

Johnston, J., & Pennypacker, H. (1981). *Strategies and tactics of human behavioral research.* Hillsdale, NJ: Erlbaum.

Joint Commission on Mental Illness and Health (1961). *Action for mental health.* New York: Science Editions.

Jones, M. C. (1924). A laboratory study of fear. The case of Peter. *Journal of Genetic Psychology, 31,* 308-315.

Jones, R. R. (1977). Conceptual vs. analytic uses of generalizability theory in behavioral assessment. In J. D. Cone & R. P. Hawkins (Eds.), *Behavioral assessment: New directions in clinical psychology.* New York: Brunner/Mazel.

Jones, R. R., Reid, J. B., & Patterson, G. R. (1975). Naturalistic observation in clinical assessment. In W. T. McReynolds (Ed.), *Advances in psychological assessment, Vol. 3.* San Francisco: Jossey Bass.

Kallman, W. M., & Feuerstein, M. (1977). Psychophysiological procedures. In A. R. Ciminero, K. S. Calhoun, & H. E. Adams (Eds.), *Handbook of behavioral assessment.* New York: Wiley.

Kanfer, F. H., Cox, L. E., Greiner, J. M., & Karoly, P. (1974). Contracts, demand characteristics and self-control. *Journal of Personality and Social Psychology, 30,* 605-619.

Kanter, N. J., & Goldfried, M. R. (1979). Relative effectiveness of rational restructuring and self-control desensitization in the reduction of interpersonal anxiety. *Behavior Therapy, 10,* 472-490.

Kaplan, H. S. (1974). *The new sex therapy.* New York: Brunner/Mazel.

Katell, A., Callahan, E.J., Fremouw, W.J., & Zitter, R.E. (1979). The effects of behavioral treatment and fasting on eating behaviors and weight loss: A case study. *Behavior Therapy, 10,* 579-587.

Katkin, E. S., Fitzgerald, C., & Shapiro, D. (1978). Clinical applications of biofeedback: Current status and future prospects. In H. L. Pick, H. W., Leibowitz, J. E. Singer, A. Steinschneider, & H. W. Stevenson (Eds.), *Psychology: From research to practice.* New York: Plenum.

Katz, R. C. (1973). A procedure for concurrently measuring elapsed time and response frequency. *Journal of Applied Behavior Analysis, 6,* 719-720.

Katz, R. C., & Wooley, F. R. (1975). Improving patients' records through problem orientation. *Behavior Therapy, 6,* 119-124.

Kazdin, A. E. (1974a). The effect of model identity and fear-relevant similarity on covert modeling. *Behavior Therapy, 5,* 624-635.

Kazdin, A. E. (1974b). Reactive self-monitoring: The effects of response desirability, goal setting, and feedback. *Journal of Consulting and Clinical Psychology, 42,* 704-716.

Kazdin, A. E. (1976). Statistical analyses for single-case experimental designs. In M. Hersen & D. H. Barlow (Eds.), *Single-case experimental designs.* New York: Pergamon.

Kazdin, A. E. (1977a). Assessing the clinical or applied importance of behavior change through social validation. *Behavior Modification, 1,* 427-452.

Kazdin, A. E. (1977b). The influence of behavior preceding a reinforced response on behavior change in the classroom. *Journal of Applied Behavior Analysis, 10,* 299-311.

Kazdin, A. E. (1979). Unobtrusive measures in behavioral assessment. *Journal of Applied Behavior Analysis, 12,* 713-724.

Kazdin, A. E. (1980). *Research design in clinical psychology.* New York: Harper and Row.

Kazdin, A. E. (1981). Drawing valid inferences from case studies. *Journal of Consulting and Clinical Psychology, 49,* 183-192.

Kazdin, A. E. (1982). *Single-case research designs: Methods for clinical and applied settings.* New York: Oxford University Press.

Kazdin, A. E., & Hartmann, D. P. (1978). The simultaneous-treatment design. *Behavior Therapy, 9,* 912-922.

Kazdin, A. E., & Kopel, S. A. (1975). On resolving ambiguities of the multiple-baseline design: Problems and recommendations. *Behavior Therapy, 6,* 601-608.

Keefe, F. J., Surwit, R. S., & Pilon, R. N. (1981). Collagen vascular disease: Can behavior therapy help? *Journal of Behavior Therapy and Experimental Psychiatry, 12,* 171-175.

Kelley, J. E., & Lichstein, K. L. (1980). A sleep assessment device. *Behavioral Assessment, 2,* 135-146.

Kelly, J. A., Laughlin, C., Claiborne, M., & Patterson, J. (1979). A group procedure for teaching job interviewing skills to formerly hospitalized psychiatric patients. *Behavior Therapy, 10,* 299-310.

Kelly, J. A., Urey, J. R., & Patterson, J. T. (1980). Improving heterosocial conversational skills of male psychiatric patients through a small group training procedure. *Behavior Therapy, 11,* 179-188.

Kendall, P. C., & Butcher, J. N. (Eds.) (1982). *Handbook of research methods in clinical psychology.* New York: Wiley.

Kendall, P. C., & Norton-Ford, J. D. (1982). Therapy outcome research methods. In P. C. Kendall & J. N. Butcher (Eds.), *Handbook of research methods in clinical psychology* (pp 429-460). New York: Wiley.

Kent, R. N., & Foster, S. L. (1977). Direct observation procedures: Methodological issues in naturalistic settings. In A. R. Ciminero, K. S. Calhoun & H. E. Adams (Eds.), *Handbook of behavioral assessment.* New York: Wiley.

Kent, R. N., O'Leary, K. D., Diament, C., & Dietz, A. (1974). Expectation biases in observational evaluation of therapeutic change. *Journal of Consulting and Clinical Psychology, 42,* 774-780.

Kiecolt-Glaser, J., & Murray, J. A. (1980). Social desirability bias in self-monitoring data. *Journal of Behavioral Assessment, 2,* 239-248.

Kiesler, D. J. (1966). Some myths of psychotherapy research and the search for a paradigm. *Psychological Bulletin, 65,* 110-136.

Kiesler, D. J. (1971). Experimental designs in psychotherapy research. In A. E. Bergin & S. L. Garfield (Eds.), *Handbook of psychotherapy and behavior change: An empirical analysis* (pp 36-74). New York: Wiley.

Killeen, P. R. (1978). Stability criteria. *Journal of Experimental Analysis of Behavior, 29,* 17-25.

King, R. P., & Lockhart, K. A. (1977, May). *A behavioral assessment of preference for erotic visual stimuli.* Paper presented at the meeting of the Midwestern Association for Behavior Analysis, Chicago, IL.

Kirchner, E. P., Kennedy, R. E., & Draguns, J. G. (1979). Assertion and aggression in adult offenders. *Behavior Therapy, 10,* 452-471.

Kiresuk, T. J., & Sherman, R. E. (1968). Goal attainment scaling: A general method for evaluating comprehensive mental health programs. *Community Mental Health Journal, 4,* 443-453.

Knight, R. P. (1941). Evaluation of the results of psychoanalytic therapy. *American Journal of Psychiatry, 98,* 434-446.

Kolko, D. J., & Milan, M. A. (1980). Misconception correction through reading in the treatment of a self-injection phobia. *Journal of Behavior Therapy and Experimental Psychiatry, 11,* 273-276.

Korman, M. (1974). National conference on levels and patterns of professional training in psychology: The major themes. *American Psychologist, 29,* 441-449.

Kovacs, M., Rush, A. J., Beck, A. T., & Hollon, S. D. (1981). Depressed outpatients treated with cognitive therapy or pharmacotherapy: A one-year follow-up. *Archives of General Psychiatry, 38,* 33-42.

Kraemer, H. C. (1982, November). *Some statistical issues in meta-analysis.* Paper presented at the meeting of the Association for the Advancement of Behavior Therapy, Los Angeles, CA.

Kratochwill, T. R. (1977).N=1. An alternative research strategy for school psychologists. *Journal of School Psychology, 15,* 239-249.

Kratochwill, T. R. (1978). *Single-subject research: Strategies for evaluating change.* New York: Academic Press.

Kratochwill, T. R., & Piersel, W. C. (in press). Time-series research: Contributions to empirical clinical practice. *Behavioral Assessment.*

Kubany, E. S., & Sloggett, B. B. (1973). A coding procedure for teachers. *Journal of Applied Behavior Analysis, 6,* 339-344.

Kubany, E. S., Weiss, L. E., & Sloggett, B. B. (1971). The good behavior clock: A reinforcement/time out procedure for reducing disruptive classroom behavior. *Journal of Behavior Therapy and Experimental Psychiatry, 2,* 173-179.

Lacey, J. I., Bateman, D. E., & Van Lehn, R. (1953). Autonomic response specificity: An experimental study. *Psychosomatic Medicine, 15,* 18-21.

Lamontagne, Y. (1978). Treatment of a tic by prolonged exposure. *Behavior Therapy, 9,* 647-651.

Lande, S. D. (1980). A combination of orgasmic reconditioning and covert sensitization in the treatment of a fire fetish. *Journal of Behavior Therapy and Experimental Psychiatry, 11,* 291-296.

Lang, P. J. (1968). Fear reduction and fear behavior: Problems in treating a construct. In J. M. Shlien (Ed.), *Research in psychotherapy, Vol. 3.* Washington, DC: American Psychological Association.

Lang, P. J. (1971). The application of psychophysiological methods to the study of psychotherapy and behavior modification. In A. E. Bergin & S. L. Garfield (Eds.), *Handbook of psychotherapy and behavior change.* New York: Wiley.

Lang, P. J. (1977) Physiological assessment of anxiety and fear. In J. D. Cone & R. P. Hawkins (Eds.), *Behavioral assessment: New directions in clinical psychology.* New York: Brunner/Mazel.

Lang, P. J., & Lazovik, A. D. (1963). Experimental desensitization of a phobia. *Journal of Abnormal and Social Psychology, 66,* 519-525.

Larsen, J., & Nichols, D. (1972). If nobody knows you've done it, have you? *Evaluation, 1,* 39-44.

Layne, C. C., Rickard, H. C., Jones, M. P., & Lyman, R. D. (1976). Accuracy of self-recording on a variable ratio schedule of observer verification. *Behavior Therapy, 7,* 481-488.

Lazarus, A. A. (1961). Group therapy of phobic disorders by systematic desensitization. *Journal of Abnormal and Social Psychology, 63,* 504-510.

Lazarus, A. A. (1967). In support of technical eclecticism. *Psychological Reports, 21,* 415-416.

Leger, L. A. (1979). An outcome measure for thought-stopping examined in three case studies. *Journal of Behavior Therapy and Experimental Psychiatry, 10,* 115-120.

Lehrer, A. (1981). Not a science. *APA Monitor, 12,* 42.

Leitenberg, H. (1973). The use of single-case methodology in psychotherapy research. *Journal of Abnormal Psychology, 82,* 87-101.

Leitenberg, H. (1974). Training clinical researchers in psychology. *Professional Psychology, 5,* 59-69.

Leitenberg, H., Agras, W.S., Butz, R., & Wincze, J. (1971). Relationship between heart rate and behavioral change during the treatment of phobias. *Journal of Abnormal Psychology, 78,* 59-68.

Lemere, F., & Voegtlin, W. L. (1950). An evaluation of the aversion treatment of alcoholism. *Quarterly Journal of Studies on Alcohol, 11,* 199-204.

Leonard, S. R. (1981). Sex related motor behavior change: A demonstration of empirical clinical practice. *Behavioral Assessment, 3,* 403-410.

Leonard, S. R., & Hayes, S. C. (in press). Sexual fantasy alternation. *Journal of Behavior Therapy and Experimental Psychiatry.*

Levi, L., & Anderson, L. (1975). *Psychosocial stress: Population, environment, and the quality of life.* Holliswood, NY: Spectrum.

Levin, S. M., Barry, S. M., Gambaro, S., Wolfinsohn, L., & Smith, A. (1977). Variations of covert sensitization in the treatment of pedophilic behavior. *Journal of Consulting and Clinical Psychology, 45,* 896-907.

Levy, R. L. (1977). Relationship of an overt commitment to task compliance in behavior therapy. *Journal of Behavior Therapy and Experimental Psychiatry, 8,* 25-29.

Lewinsohn, P. M., & Arconad, M. (1981). Behavioral treatment of depression: A social learning approach. In J. F. Clarkin & H. I. Glazer (Eds.), *Depression: Behavioral and directive intervention strategies.* New York: Garland.

Lewis, M., Shilton, P., & Fuqua, R. W. (1981). Parental control of nocturnal thumbsucking. *Journal of Behavior Therapy and Experimental Psychiatry, 12,* 87-90.

Liberman, R.P., & Wong, S. (1980, November). *Personal communication.*

Liberman, R. P., & Smith, V. (1972). A multiple baseline study of systematic desensitization in a patient with multiple phobias. *Behavior Therapy, 3,* 597-603.

Linden, W. (1980). Multi-component behavior therapy in the case of compulsive binge-eating followed by vomiting. *Journal of Behavior Therapy and Experimental Psychiatry, 11,* 297-300.

Lindsley, O. R. (1962). A behavioral measure of television viewing. *Journal of Advertising Research, 2,* 2-12.

Lindsley, O. R. (1968). A reliable wrist counter for recording behavior rates. *Journal of Applied Behavior Analysis, 1,* 77-78.

Lipinski, D. P., Black, J. L., Nelson, R. O., & Ciminero, A. R. (1975). The influence of motivational variables on the reactivity and reliability of self-recording. *Journal of Consulting and Clinical Psychology, 43,* 637-646.

Lipinski, D. P., & Nelson, R. O. (1974). The reactivity and unreliability of self-recording. *Journal of Consulting and Clinical Psychology, 42,* 118-123.

Lobitz, W. C., & LoPiccolo, J. (1972). New methods in the behavioral treatment of sexual dysfunction. *Journal of Behavior Therapy and Experimental Psychiatry, 3,* 265-271.

Locke, H. J., & Wallace, M. (1959). Short marital adjustment and prediction test: Reliability and validity. *Marriage and Family Living, 21,* 251-255.

Lorr, M., & Klett, C. J. (1966). *The inpatient multidimensional psychiatric scale manual.* Palo Alto, CA: Consulting Psychologists Press.

Lovaas, O. I., Koegel, R., Simmons, J. Q., & Long, J. D. (1973). Some generalization and follow-up measures on autistic children in behavior therapy. *Journal of Applied Behavior Analysis, 5,* 131-166.

MacPhillamy, D., & Lewinsohn, P. M. (1975). *Manual for the pleasant events schedule.* Unpublished manuscript.

Madle, R. A., Neisworth, J. T., & Kurtz, P. D. (1980). Biasing of hyperkinetic behavior ratings by diagnostic reports: Effects of observer training and assessment method. *Journal of Learning Disabilities, 13,* 35-38.

Mahoney, K. (1974). Count on it: A simple self-monitoring device. *Behavior Therapy, 5,* 701-703.

Mahoney, M. J. (1974). *Cognition and behavior modification.* Cambridge, MA: Ballinger.

Mahoney, M. J. (1977). Some applied issues in self-monitoring. In J. D. Cone & R. P. Hawkins (Eds.), *Behavioral assessment: New directions in clinical psychology.* New York: Brunner/Mazel.

Mahoney, M.J., Moura, N.M., & Wade, T.C. (1973). The relative efficacy of self-reward, self-punishment, and self-monitoring techniques for weight loss. *Journal of Consulting and Clinical Psychology, 40,* 404-407.

Mahoney, M. J., Moore, B. S., Wade, T. C., & Moura, N. G. M. (1973). The effects of continuous and intermittent self-monitoring on academic behavior. *Journal of Consulting and Clinical Psychology, 41,* 65-69.

Mahoney, M. J., & Thoresen, C. E. (1974). *Self-control: Power to the person.* Monterey, CA: Brooks-Cole.

Maletzky, B. M. (1974). "Assisted" covert sensitization in the treatment of exhibitionism. *Journal of Consulting and Clinical Psychology, 42,* 34-40.

Maletzky, B. M. (1980a). "Assisted" covert sensitization in the treatment of exhibitionism. In D. J. Cox & R. J. Daitzman (Eds.), *Exhibitionism: description, assessment and treatment.* New York: Garland.

Maletzky, B. M. (1980b). Self-referred versus court-referred sexually deviant patients: Success with assisted covert sensitization. *Behavior Therapy, 11,* 306-314.

Marks, I. M. (1973). New approaches to the treatment of obsessive-compulsive disorders. *Journal of Nervous and Mental Disease, 156,* 420-426.

Marks, I. M. (1978). Flooding (implosion) and allied treatments. In W. S. Agras (Ed.), *Behavior modification: Principles and clinical applications* (2nd ed). Boston: Little, Brown.

Marks, I. M. (1981). New developments in psychological treatments of phobias. In M. R. Mavissakalian & D. H. Barlow (Eds.), *Phobia: Psychological and pharmacological treatment.* New York: Guilford.

Mash, E. J., & Terdal, L. G. (Eds.) (1976). *Behavior therapy assessment.* New York: Springer.

Masters, W. H., & Johnson, V. E. (1970). *Human sexual inadequacy.* Boston: Little, Brown.

Mathews, A. M. (1978). Fear-reduction research and clinical phobias. *Psychological Bulletin, 85,* 390-404.

Mathews, A. M., Gelder, M. G., & Johnston, D. W. (1981). *Agoraphobia: Nature and treatment.* New York: Guilford.

Mathews, A. M., Teasdale, J., Munby, M., Johnston, D., & Shaw, P. (1977). A home-based treatment program for agoraphobics. *Behavior Therapy, 8,* 915-924.

Mattos, R. L. (1968). A manual counter for recording multiple behaviors. *Journal of Applied Behavior Analysis, 1,* 130.

Mavissakalian, M. R., & Barlow, D. H. (Eds.) (1981). *Phobia: Psychological and pharmacological treatment.* New York: Guilford.

Mavissakalian, M., & Michelson, L. (1982). Patterns of psychophysiological change in the treatment of agoraphobia. *Behaviour Research and Therapy, 20,* 347-356.

McCullough, J. P., Cornell, J. E., McDaniel, M. H., & Mueller, R. K. (1974). Utilization of the simultaneous treatment design to improve student behavior in a first-grade classroom. *Journal of Consulting and Clinical Psychology, 42,* 288-292.

McFall, R. M. (1977). Analogue methods in behavioral assessment: Issues and prospects. In J. E. Cone & R. P. Hawkins (Eds.), *Behavioral assessment: New directions in clinical psychology.* New York: Brunner/Mazel.

McGlynn, F. D. (1980). Successful treatment of anorexia nervosa with self-monitoring and long distance praise. *Journal of Behavior Therapy and Experimental Psychiatry, 11,* 283-286.

McGuire, W. J. (1973). The Yin and Yang of progress in social psychology: Seven koan. *Journal of Personality and Social Psychology, 28,* 446-456.

McKnight, D., Nelson, R. O., & Hayes, S. C. (1982). *Cognitive and social deficits in clinical depression: A treatment validity analysis.* Unpublished manuscript.

McLaughlin, J. G., & Nay, W. R. (1975). Treatment of trichotillomania using positive coverants and response cost: A case report. *Behavior Therapy, 6,* 87-91.

McNamara, J. R., & Bechtel, J. E. (1975). A fixed or variable interval pocket programmer. *Journal of Behavior Therapy and Experimental Psychiatry, 6,* 229.

McPherson, F. M., Brougham, L., & McLaren, S. (1980). Maintenance of improvement in agoraphobic patients treated by behavioural methods — a four-year follow-up. *Behaviour Research and Therapy, 18,* 150-152.

McReynolds, W. T., & Stegman, R. (1976). Sayer versus sign. *Behavior Therapy, 7,* 704-705.

Meehl, P. E. (1978). Theoretical risks and tabular asterisks: Sir Karl, Sir Ronald, and the slow progress of soft psychology. *Journal of Consulting and Clinical Psychology, 46,* 806-835.

Meichenbaum, D. (1977). *Cognitive-behavior modification: An integrative approach.* New York: Plenum.

Melamed, B. G., & Siegel, L. J. (1975). Self-directed in vivo treatment of an obsessive-compulsive checking ritual. *Journal of Behavior Therapy and Experimental Psychiatry, 6,* 31-35.

Meyers, A., Mercatoris, M., & Artz, L. (1976). On the development of a cognitive self-monitoring skill. *Behavior Therapy, 7,* 128-129.

Milby, J. B., Meredith, R. L., & Rice, J. (1981). Videotaped exposure: A new treatment for obsessive-compulsive disorders. *Journal of Behavior Therapy and Experimental Psychiatry, 12,* 249-255.

Miller, A. J., & Kratochwill, T. R. (1979). Reduction of frequent stomachache complaints by time out. *Behavior Therapy, 10,* 211-218.

Miller, B. V., & Bernstein, D. A. (1972). Instructional demand in a behavioral avoidance test for claustrophobic fears. *Journal of Abnormal Psychology, 80,* 206-210.

Mischel, W. (1968). *Personality and assessment.* New York: Wiley.

Mischel, W. (1973). Toward a cognitive social learning reconceptualization of personality. *Psychological Review, 80,* 252-283.

Monti, P. M., McCrady, B. S., & Barlow, D. H. (1977). Effect of positive reinforcement, informational feedback, and contingency contracting on a bulemic anorexic female. *Behavior Therapy, 8,* 258-263.

Nathan, P. E., & Harris, S. L. (1980). *Psychopathology and society* (2nd ed.). New York: McGraw-Hill.

Nathan, P. E., & Lansky, D. (1978). Management of the chronic alcoholic: A behavioral viewpoint. In J. P. Brady & H. K. H. Brodie (Eds.), *Controversies in psychiatry*. Philadelphia: Saunders.

National Institute of Mental Health (1971). *A distillation of principles on research utilization* (Vol. 1). Washington, DC: U. S. Government Printing Office.

National Institute of Mental Health (1980a). *Final report of NIMH conference No.RFP NIMH ER-79-0003, Behavior therapies in the treatment of anxiety disorders: Recommendations for strategies in treatment assessment research*. Unpublished report.

National Institute of Mental Health (1980b). *NIMH treatment of depression, collaborative research program (pilot phase), revised research plan, January 1980, Psychosocial Treatments Research Branch*. Bethesda, MD: Author.

Nay, W. R. (1977) Analogue measures. In A. R. Ciminero, K. S. Calhoun & H. E. Adams (Eds.), *Handbook of behavioral assessment*. New York: Wiley.

Nelsen, J. C. (1981). Issues in single-subject research for non-behaviorists. *Social Work Research and Abstracts, 31-37.*

Nelson, C. M., & McReynolds, W. T. (1971). Self-recording and control of behavior: A reply to Simkins. *Behavior Therapy, 2, 594-597.*

Nelson, R. O. (1977). Methodological issues in assessment via self-monitoring. In J. D. Cone & R. P. Hawkins (Eds.), *Behavioral assessment: New directions in clinical psychology*. New York: Brunner/Mazel.

Nelson, R. O. (1983). Behavioral assessment: Past, present, and future. *Behavioral Assessment, 5, 195-206.*

Nelson, R. O., & Barlow, D. H. (1981). Behavioral assessment: Basic strategies and initial procedures. In D. H. Barlow (Ed.), *Behavioral assessment of adult disorders*. New York: Guilford.

Nelson, R. O., & Bowles, P. E. (1975). The best of two worlds—observations with norms. *Journal of School Psychology, 13, 3-9.*

Nelson, R. O., Boykin, R. A., & Hayes, S. C. (1982). Long-term effects of self-monitoring on reactivity and on accuracy. *Behaviour Research and Therapy, 20, 357-363.*

Nelson, R. O., Hay, L. R., Devany, J., & Koslow-Green, L. (1980). The reactivity and accuracy of children's self-monitoring: Three experiments. *Child Behavior Therapy, 2, 1-24.*

Nelson, R. O., Hay, L. R., & Hay, W. M. (1977). Comments on Cone's "The relevance of reliability and validity for behavioral assessment." *Behavior Therapy, 8, 427-430.*

Nelson, R. O., & Hayes, S. C. (1979). Some current dimensions of behavioral assessment. *Behavioral Assessment, 1, 1-16.*

Nelson, R. O., Lipinski, D. P., & Black, J. (1975). The effects of expectancy on the reactivity of self-recording. *Behavior Therapy, 6, 337-349.*

Nelson, R. O., Lipinski, D. P., & Boykin, R. A. (1978). The effects of self-recorders' training and the obtrusiveness of the self-recording device on the accuracy and reactivity of self-monitoring. *Behavior Therapy, 9, 200-208.*

Newman, F. L. (1979, November). *Global scales: Strengths, uses, and problems of global scales as an evaluation instrument*. Paper presented at the meeting of the Pennsylvania Evaluation Network, Philadelphia, PA.

Norton, G. R., DiNardo, P.A., & Barlow, D. H. (1983). Predicting phobics' response to therapy: A consideration of subjective, physiological, and behavioural measures. *Canadian Psychologist, 24, 50-59.*

Obler, M. (1973). Systematic desensitization in sexual disorders. *Journal of Behavioral Therapy & Experimental Psychiatry, 4, 93-101.*

O'Brien, F. (1968). Sequential contrast effects with human subjects. *Journal of the Experimental Analysis of Behavior, 11,* 537-542.

O'Brien, F., Azrin, N. H., & Hensen, K. (1969) Increased communications of chronic mental health patients by reinforcement and by response priming. *Journal of Applied Behavior Analysis, 2,* 23-29.

Odom, J. V., & Nelson, R. O. (1977). The effect of demand characteristics on heart rate during the behavioral avoidance test. *Perceptual and Motor Skills, 44,* 175-183.

O'Leary, K. D., & Johnson, S. B. (1979). Psychological assessment. In H. C. Quay & J. S. Werry (Eds.), *Psychopathological disorders of childhood* (2nd ed.). New York: Wiley.

O'Leary, K. D., & O'Leary, S. G. (1977). *Classroom management: The successful use of behavior modification* (2nd ed.). New York: Pergamon.

Ollendick, T. H. (1981) Self-monitoring and self-administered overcorrection: The modification of nervous tics in children. *Behavior Modification, 5,* 75-84.

Ost, L. (1978). Behavioral treatment of thunder and lightning phobias. *Behaviour Research and Therapy, 16,* 197-207.

Ost, L., Jerremalm, A., & Johansson, J. (1981). Individual response patterns and the effects of different behavioral methods in the treatment of social phobia. *Behaviour Research and Therapy, 19,* 1-16.

Ostow, M. (1981). Letter to the editor. *Science, 212,* 984.

Paolino, T. J. & McCrady, B. S. (1977). *The alcoholic manager: Alternative perspectives.* New York: Grune & Stratton.

Parloff, M. B., Waskow, I. E., & Wolfe, B. E. (1978). Research on therapist variables in relation to process and outcome. In S.L. Garfield & A.E. Bergen (Eds.), *Handbook of psychotherapy and behavior change: An empirical analysis* (2nd ed.). New York: Wiley.

Parsonson, B. S. & Baer, D. M. (1978). The analysis and presentation of graphed data. In T.R. Kratochwill (Ed.), *Single subject research: Strategies for evaluating change.* New York: Academic.

Patterson, G. R., Cobb, J. A., & Ray, R. S. (1973). A social engineering technology for retraining the families of aggressive boys. In H. E. Adams & I. P. Unikel (Eds.), *Issues and trends in behavior therapy.* Springfield, IL: Charles C. Thomas.

Patterson, G. R., Ray, R. S., Shaw, D. A., & Cobb, J. (1969). *Manual for coding family interaction.* Available from ASIS/NAPS, c/o Microfiche Publications, 440 Park Ave So, New York, NY 10016 (Document No.01234).

Patterson, G. R., & Reid, J. B. (1970). Reciprocity and coercion: Two facets of social systems. In C. Neuringer & J. L. Michael (Eds.), *Behavior modification in clinical psychology.* New York: Appleton-Century-Crofts.

Paul, G. L. (1969). Behavior modification research: Design and tactics. In C. M. Franks (Ed.), *Behavior therapy: Appraisal and status.* New York: McGraw Hill.

Perry, N. W. (1979). Why clinical psychology does not need alternative training models. *American Psychologist, 34,* 602-611.

Peterson, D. R. (1968). *The clinical study of social behavior.* New York: Appleton-Century-Crofts.

Peterson, D. R. (1976a). Is psychology a profession? *American Psychologist, 31,* 572-581.

Peterson, D. R. (1976b). Need for the Doctor of Psychology degree in professional psychology. *American Psychologist, 31,* 792-798.

Powell, J., & Hake, D. F. (1971). Positive versus negative reinforcement: A direct comparison of effects on a complex human response. *Psychological Record, 21,* 191-205.

Prigatano, G. P., & Johnson, H. J. (1974). Autonomic nervous system changes associated with a spider phobic reaction. *Journal of Abnormal Psychology, 83,* 169-177.

Prinz, R. J., Foster, S., Kent, R. N., & O'Leary, K. D. (1979). Multivariate assessment of conflict in distressed and non-distressed mother-adolescent dyads. *Journal of Applied Behavior Analysis, 12,* 691-700.

Proshansky, H. M. (1972). For what are we training our graduate students? *American Psychologist, 27,* 205-212.

Quay, H. C. (1977). Measuring dimensions of deviant behavior: The Behavior Problem Checklist. *Journal of Abnormal Child Psychology, 5,* 277-289.

Quilitch, H. R. (1972). A portable, programmed audible timer. *Journal of Applied Behavior Analysis, 5,* 18.

Rachman, S. J. (1974). Primary obsessional slowness. *Behaviour Research and Therapy, 12,* 9-18.

Rachman, S. J. (1978). *Fear and courage.* San Francisco: W. H. Freeman.

Rachman, S. J., & Hodgson, R. I. (1974). Synchrony and desynchrony in fear and avoidance. *Behaviour Research and Therapy, 12,* 311-318.

Rachman, S. I., & Hodgson, R. I. (1980). *Obsessions and compulsions.* Englewood Cliffs, NJ: Prentice-Hall.

Rachman, S. J., & Wilson, G. T. (1980). *The effects of psychological therapy* (2nd ed.). New York: Pergamon.

Raimy, V. C. (Ed.) (1950). *Training in clinical psychology (Boulder Conference).* New York: Prentice-Hall.

Rankin, G. (1982). Control rather than abstinence as a goal in the treatment of excessive gambling. *Behaviour Research and Therapy, 20,* 185-187.

Raush, H. L. (1974). Research, practice, and accountability. *American Psychologist, 29,* 678-681.

Ray, R. L., & Kimmel, H. D. (1979). Utilization of psychophysiological indices in behavioral assessment: Some methodological issues. *Journal of Behavioral Assessment, 1,* 107-122.

Ray, W. J., & Raczynski, J. M. (1981). Psychophysiological assessment. In M. Hersen, & A. S. Bellack (Eds.), *Behavioral assessment* (2nd ed.). New York: Pergamon.

Redd, W. H., & Birnbrauer, J. S. (1969). Adults as discriminative stimuli for different reinforcement contingencies with retarded children. *Journal of Experimental Child Psychology, 7,* 440-447.

Rehm, L. P., Fuchs, C. A., Roth, D. M., Kornblith, S. J., & Romano, J. M. (1979). A comparison of self-control and assertion skills treatments of depression. *Behavior Therapy, 10,* 429-442.

Reid, W. J. (1979). Evaluation research in social work. *Evaluation and Program Planning, 2,* 209-217.

Resick, P. A., Forehand, R., & McWhorter, Q. (1976). The effect of parental treatment with one child on an untreated sibling. *Behavior Therapy, 7,* 544-548.

Reynolds, G. S. (1968). *A primer of operant conditioning.* Glenview, IL: Scott, Foresman.

Risley, T. R., & Hart, B. (1968). Developing correspondence between the non-verbal and verbal behavior of preschool children. *Journal of Applied Behavior Analysis, 1,* 267-281.

Roberts, M. W., McMahon, R. J., Forehand, R., & Humphreys, L. (1978). The effect of parental instruction-giving on child compliance. *Behavior Therapy, 9,* 793-798.

Robin, A. L., Kent, R. N., O'Leary, K. D., Foster, S., & Prinz, R. (1977). An approach to teaching parent and adolescent problem-solving communication skills: A preliminary report. *Behavior Therapy, 8,* 639-643.

Robin, A. L., & Weiss, J. (1980). Criterion-related validity of observational and self-report measures of problem-solving communication skills with distressed and non-distressed parent-adolescent dyads. *Behavioral Assessment, 2,* 339-352.

Robinson, J. C., & Lewinsohn, P. M. (1973). Behavior modification of speech characteristics in a chronically depressed man. *Behavior Therapy, 4,* 150-152.

Roe, A., Gustad, J. W., Moore, B. V., Ross, S., & Skodak, M. (1959). *Graduate education in psychology. Report of the conference sponsored by the E&T Board.* Washington, DC: American Psychological Association.

Rogers, T., Mahoney, M. J., Mahoney, B. K., Straw, M. D., & Kenigsberg, M. I. (1980). Clinical assessment of obesity: An empirical evaluation of diverse techniques. *Behavioral Assessment, 2,* 161-181.

Romanczyk, R. G., Kent, R. N., Diament, C., & O'Leary, K. D. (1973). Measuring the reliability of observational data: A reactive process. *Journal of Applied Behavior Analysis, 6,* 175-184.

Rosen, J. C. (1981). Self-monitoring in the treatment of diurnal bruxism. *Journal of Behavior Therapy and Experimental Psychiatry, 12,* 347-350.

Ross, A. O. (1963). Deviant case analysis: Neglected approach to behavior research. *Perceptual and Motor Skills, 16,* 337-340.

Ross, A. O. (1981). Of rigor and relevance. *Professional Psychology, 12,* 319-327.

Royce, W. S., & Arkowitz, H. (1978). Multimodal evaluation of practice interactions as treatment for social isolation. *Journal of Consulting and Clinical Psychology, 46,* 239-245.

Royer, F. L., Flynn, W. F., & Osadca, B. S. (1971). Case history: Aversion therapy for fire setting by a deteriorated schizophrenic. *Behavior Therapy, 2,* 229-232.

Rusch, F. R., & Kazdin, A. E. (1981). Toward a methodology of withdrawal designs for the assessment of response maintenance. *Journal of Applied Behavior Analysis, 14,* 131-140.

Rush, A. J., Beck, A. T., Kovacs, M., & Hollon, S. (1977). Comparative efficacy of cognitive therapy and pharmacotherapy in the treatment of depressed outpatients. *Cognitive Therapy and Research, 1,* 17-37.

Rush, A. J., Khatami, M., & Beck, A. T. (1975). Cognitive and behavior therapy in chronic depression. *Behavior Therapy, 6,* 398-404.

Sakheim, D. K., Barlow, D. H., & Beck, J. G. (1983) *Diurnal penile tumescence: A pilot study of functional and dysfunctional males during waking assessment.* Unpublished Manuscript.

Sanavio, E. (1982). An operant approach to the treatment of writer's cramp. *Journal of Behavior Therapy and Experimental Psychiatry, 13,* 69-72.

Sanders, R. M. (1971). A timeout procedure for the modification of speech content: A case study. *Journal of Behavior Therapy and Experimental Psychiatry, 2,* 199-202.

Sargent, J. D., Green, E. E., & Walters, E. D. (1972). The use of autogenic feedback training in a pilot study of migraine and tension headaches. *Headache, 12,* 120-125.

Schindele, R. (1981). Methodological problems in rehabilitation research. *International Journal of Rehabilitation Research, 4,* 233-248.

Schover, L. R. (1980). Clinical practice and scientific psychology: Can this marriage be saved? *Professional Psychology, 11,* 268-275.

Scriven, M. (1967). The methodology of evaluation. In R. W. Tyler, R. M. Gagne, & M. Scriven, *AERA monograph series on curriculum evaluation No. 1.* Chicago: Rand-McNally.

Sechrest, L. (1975). Research contributions of practicing clinical psychologists. *Professional Psychology, 8,* 413-419.

Seymour, F. W., & Stokes, T. F. (1976). Self-recording in training girls to increase work and evoke staff praise in an institution for offenders. *Journal of Applied Behavior Analysis, 9,* 41-54.

Shadish, W. R. (1980). Nonverbal interactions in clinical groups. *Journal of Consulting and Clinical Psychology, 48,* 164-168.

Shahar, A., & Marks, I. (1980). Habituation during exposure treatment of compulsive rituals. *Behavior Therapy, 11,* 397-401.

Shakow, D. (1976). What *is* clinical psychology? *American Psychologist, 31,* 553-560.

Shakow, D., Hilgard, E. R., Kelly, E. L., Luckey, B., Sanford, R. N., & Shaffer, L. F. (1947). Recommended graduate training program in clinical psychology. *American Psychologist, 2,* 539-558.

Shapiro, D. A., & Shapiro, D. (1982). Meta-analysis of comparative therapy outcome research: A critical appraisal. *Behavioral Psychotherapy, 10,* 4-25.

Shapiro, D. A., & Shapiro, D. (1983). Comparative therapy outcome research: Methodological implications of meta-analysis. *Journal of Consulting and Clinical Psychology, 51,* 42-53.

Sheehan, D. J., & Casey, B. (1974). Communication. *Journal of Applied Behavior Analysis, 7,* 446.

Shelton, J. L., & Ackerman, J. N. (1974). *Homework in counseling and psychotherapy.* Springfield, IL: Thomas.

Shelton, J. L., & Levy, R. L. (1981). *Behavioral assignments and treatment compliance.* Champaign, IL: Research Press.

Shuller, D. Y., & McNamara, J. R. (1970). Expectancy factors in behavioral observation. *Behavior Therapy, 7,* 519-527.

Sidman, M. (1960). *Tactics of scientific research.* New York: Basic Books.

Sieck, W. A., & McFall, R. M. (1976). Some determinants of self-monitoring effects. *Journal of Consulting and Clinical Psychology, 44,* 958-965.

Siegel, L. J., Dragovich, S. L., & Marholin, D. (1976). The effects of biasing information on behavioral observations and rating scales. *Journal of Abnormal Child Psychology, 4,* 221-233.

Silver, B. V., & Blanchard, E. B. (1978). Biofeedback and relaxation training in the treatment of psychophysiologic disorders: Or, are the machines really necessary? *Journal of Behavioral Medicine, 1,* 217-239.

Sintchak, G., & Geer, J. (1975). A vaginal plethysmograph system. *Psychophysiology, 12,* 113-115.

Sirota, A. D., & Mahoney, M. J. (1974). Relaxing on cue: The self regulation of asthma. *Journal of Behavior Therapy and Experimental Psychiatry, 5,* 65-66.

Smith, M. L., & Glass, G. V. (1977). Meta-analysis of psychotherapy outcome studies. *American Psychologist, 32,* 752-760.

Snow, R. E. (1974). Representative and quasi-representative designs for research in teaching. *Review of Educational Research, 44,* 265-291.

Sobell, L. C., & Sobell, M. B. (1978). Validity of self-reports in three populations of alcoholics. *Journal of Consulting and Clinical Psychology, 46,* 901-907.

Spanier, G. B. (1976). Measuring dyadic adjustment: New scales for assessing the quality of marriage and similar dyads. *Journal of Marriage and the Family, 38,* 15-38.

Spivack, J. & Swift, M. (1967). In M. Swift, *Devereux elementary school rating scale manual.* Devon Pa: Devereux Foundation.

Spivack, G., & Swift, M. (1973). The classroom behavior of children: A critical review of teacher-administered rating scales. *Journal of Special Education, 7,* 55-89.

Spurr, J., & Stevens, V. J. (1980). Increasing study time and controlling student guilt: A case study in self-management. *The Behavior Therapist, 3,* 17-18.

Stampfl, T. G. (1967). Implosive therapy: The theory, the sub-human analogue, the strategy and the technique: Part I. The theory. In S. G. Armitage (Ed.), *Behavior modification techniques in the treatment of emotional disorders* (pp. 22-37). Battle Creek, MI: V. A. Publication.

Stevens, S. S. (1958). Measurement, statistics, and the schemapiric view. *Science, 161,* 849-856.

Stricker, G. (1973). The doctoral dissertation in clinical psychology. *Professional Psychology, 4,* 72-78.

Stricker, G. (1975). On professional schools and professional degrees. *American Psychologist, 30,* 1062-1066.

Stricker, G. (1979). Criteria for insurance review of psychological services. *Professional Psychology, 10,* 118-122.

Strupp, H. H. (1968). Psychotherapists and (or versus?) researchers. *Voices, 4,* 28-32.

Strupp, H. H. (1981). Clinical research, practice, and the crisis of confidence. *Journal of Consulting and Clinical Psychology, 49,* 216-220.

Stuart, R. B., & Stuart, F. (1972). *Marital pre-counseling inventory.* Champaign, IL: Research Press.

Taplin, P. S., & Reid, J. B. (1973). Effects of instructional set and experimenter influence on observer reliability. *Child Development, 44,* 547-554.

Tasto, D. L. (1977). Self-report schedules and inventories. In A. R. Ciminero, K. S. Calhoun, & H. E. Adams (Eds.), *Handbook of behavioral assessment.* New York: Wiley.

Teasdale, J. D., & Fennell, M. J. V. (1982). Immediate effects on depression of cognitive therapy interventions. *Cognitive Therapy and Research, 6,* 343-352.

Tharp, R. G., & Gallimore, R. (1975). The ecology of program research and evaluation: A model of successive evaluation. In L. Sechrest, S. G. West, M. A. Phillips, R. Redner & W. Yeaton (Eds.), *Evaluation studies review annual, Vol. 4.* Beverly Hills, CA: Sage.

Thelen, M. H., & Ewing, D. R. (1970). Roles, functions, and training in clinical psychology: A survey of academic clinicians. *American Psychologist, 25,* 550-554.

Thomas, E. J. (1978). Research and service in single-case experimentation: Conflicts and choices. *Social Work Research and Abstracts, 14,* 20-31.

Thorne, F. C. (1947). The clinical method in science. *American Psychologist, 2,* 161-166.

Thyer, B. A., & Curtis, G. C. (1982, May). *The repeated pretest-posttest single-subject experiment: A new design for applied behavior analysis.* Paper presented at the Association for Behavior Analysis, Milwaukee, WI.

Tryon, W. W. (1982). A simplified time series analysis for evaluating treatment interventions. *Journal of Applied Behavior Analysis, 15,* 423-429.

Turner, R. M., & Ascher, L. M. (1979). A within-subject analysis of stimulus control therapy with severe sleep-onset insomnia. *Behaviour Research and Therapy, 17,* 107-112.

Tyler, F. B., & Speisman, J. C. (1967). An emerging scientist-professional role in psychology. *American Psychologist, 22,* 839-847.

Tyler, R. W., (1931). What is statistical significance? *Educational Research Bulletin, 10,* 115-118; 142.

Ulman, J. D., & Sulzer-Azaroff, B. (1975). Multielement baseline design in educational research. In E. Ramp & G. Semb (Eds.), *Behavior analysis: Areas of research and application.* Englewood Cliffs, NJ: Prentice-Hall.

Van Heuven, P. F., & Smeets, P. M. (1981). Behavioral control of chronic hiccupping associated with gastrointestinal bleeding in a retarded epileptic male. *Journal of Behavior Therapy and Experimental Psychiatry, 12,* 341-345.

Voegtlin, W. L., Lemere, F., Broz, W. R., & O'Hallaren, P. (1942). Conditioned reflex therapy of alcoholic addiction: Follow-up report of 1042 cases. *American Journal of Medical Science, 203,* 525-528.

Wade, T. C., Baker, T. B., & Hartmann, D. P. (1979). Behavior therapists' self-reported views and practices. *The Behavior Therapist, 2,* 3-6.

Waite, W. W., & Osborne, J. G. (1972). Sustained behavioral contrast in children. *Journal of the Experimental Analysis of Behavior, 18,* 113-117.

Walk, R. D. (1956). Self-ratings of fear in a fear-invoking situation. *Journal of Abnormal and Social Psychology, 52,* 171-178.

Walker, H. M., Hops, H., & Greenwood, C. R. (in press). The CORBEH research and development model: Programmatic issues and strategies. In S. Paine, T. Bellamy & B. Wilcox (Eds.), *Human services that work.* Baltimore: Brookes.

Walls, R. T., Werner, T. J., Bacon, A., & Zane, T. (1977). Behavior checklists. In J. D. Cone & R. P. Hawkins (Eds.), *Behavioral assessment: New directions in clinical psychology.* New York: Brunner/Mazel.

Waranch, H. R., Iwata, B. A., Wohl, M. K., & Nidiffer, F. D. (1981). Treatment of a retarded adult's mannequin phobia through in vivo desensitization and shaping approach responses. *Journal of Behavior Therapy and Experimental Psychiatry, 12,* 359-362.

Waskow, I. E., & Parloff, M. B. (Eds.) (1975). *Psychotherapy change measures.* Washington, DC: National Institute of Mental Health.

Watson, D. & Tharp, R. (1972). *Self directed behavior: Self modification for personal adjustment.* Monterey, CA: Brooks Cole.

Watson, J. P., & Marks, I. M. (1971). Relevant and irrelevant fear in flooding — A crossover study of phobic patients. *Behavior Therapy, 2,* 275-293.

Weed, L. (1968). Medical records that guide and teach. *New England Journal of Medicine, 278,* 593-600.

Weekes, C. (1972). *Peace from nervous suffering.* New York: Hawthorne.

Weekes, C. (1976). *Simple, effective treatment of agoraphobia.* New York: Hawthorne.

Wellman, R. J. (1978). Fear of solo driving treated with sequentially arranged behavioral methods. *Behavior Therapy, 9,* 290-292.

Wiens, A. N., Montague, J. R., Manaugh, T. S., & English, C. J. (1976). Pharmacological aversive counterconditioning to alcohol in a private hospital: One year follow-up. *Journal of Studies on Alcohol, 37,* 1320-1324.

Wilder, J. (1950). The law of initial values. *Psychosomatic Medicine, 12,* 392-401.

Wildman, B. G., Erickson, M. T., & Kent, R. N. (1975). The effect of two training procedures on observer agreement and variability of behavior ratings. *Child Development, 46,* 520-524.

Williams, J. E. (1976). Self-monitoring of paranoid behavior. *Behavior Therapy, 7,* 562.

Wilson, G. T. (1981). Expectations and substance abuse: Does basic research benefit clinical assessment and therapy? *Addictive Behavior, 6,* 221-231.

Wilson, G. T., & Rachman, S. J. (1983). Meta-analysis and the evaluation of psychotherapy outcome limitations and liabilities. *Journal of Consulting and Clinical Psychology, 51,* 54-64.

Wincze, J. P., & Lange, J. D. (1981). Assessment of sexual behavior. In D. H. Barlow (Ed.), *Behavioral assessment of adult disorders.* New York: Guilford.

Wittenborn, J. R. (1955). *Wittenborn psychiatric rating scales.* New York: Psychological Corporation.

Wolf, M. M. (1978). Social validity: The case for subjective measurement or how applied behavior analysis is finding its heart. *Journal of Applied Behavior Analysis, 11,* 203-214.

Wolf, S. S., & Etzel, B. C. (1982). Reciprocity marital counseling: A replication and analysis. *Behaviour Research and Therapy, 20,* 407-410.

Wollersheim, J. P. (1974). Bewail the Vail, or love is not enough. *American Psychologist, 29,* 717-718.

Wolpe, J. (1958). *Psychotherapy by reciprocal inhibition.* Stanford: Stanford University Press.

Wolpe, J. (1969). *The practice of behavior therapy.* New York: Pergamon.

Wright, J., Perreault, R., & Mathieu, M. (1977). The treatment of sexual dysfunction: A review. *Archives of General Psychiatry, 34,* 881-890.

Wroblewski, P. F., Jacob, T., & Rehm, L. P. (1977). The contribution of relaxation to symbolic modeling in the modification of dental fears. *Behaviour Research and Therapy, 15,* 113-117.

Yeaton, W. H., & Sechrest, L. (1981). Critical dimensions in the choice and maintenance of successful treatments: Strength, integrity, and effectiveness. *Journal of Consulting and Clinical Psychology, 49,* 156-168.

Zamansky, H. (1958). An investigation of the psychoanalytic theory of paranoid ideations. *Journal of Personality, 26,* 410-425.

Zaro, J. S., Barach, R., Nedelmann, D. J., & Dreiblatt, I. S. (1977). *A guide for beginning psychotherapists.* Cambridge, England: Cambridge University Press.

Zilbergeld, B., & Evans, M. (1980). The inadequacy of Masters and Johnson. *Psychology Today, 14,* 28-43.

Zimmerman, J., Overpeck, C., Eisenberg, H., & Garlick, B. (1969). Operant conditioning in a sheltered workshop. *Rehabilitation Literature, 30,* 326-334.

Author Index

Subject Index

About the Authors

DAVID H. BARLOW received his Ph.D from the University of Vermont in 1969 and has published over 150 articles and chapters and seven books, mostly in the areas of anxiety disorders, sexual problems, and clinical research methodology. He is formerly Professor of Psychiatry at the University of Mississippi Medical Center and Professor of Psychiatry and Psychology at Brown University, and founded clinical psychology internships in both settings. Currently he is Professor in the Department of Psychology at the State University of New York at Albany and has been a consultant to the National Institute of Mental Health and the National Institutes of Health since 1973. He is Past President of the Association for Advancement of Behavior Therapy, past Associate Editor of the *Journal of Consulting and Clinical Psychology,* past Editor of the *Journal of Applied Behavior Analysis,* and currently Editor of *Behavior Therapy.* At the present he is also Director of the Phobia and Anxiety Disorders Clinic and the Sexuality Research Program at SUNY at Albany. He is a Diplomate in Clinical Psychology of the American Board of Professional Psychology and maintains a private practice.

STEVEN C. HAYES received his Ph.D. in clinical psychology from West Virginia University in 1977. He is past Associate Editor of the *Journal of Applied Behavior Analysis,* and is on the editorial boards of several psychology journals. He has authored two books and nearly 100 professional articles, and has lectured widely on the role of the clinician in the production and consumption of scientific knowledge. At present he is Associate Professor in the Department of Psychology at the University of North Carolina at Greensboro.

ROSEMERY O. NELSON is Professor of Psychology and Director of Clinical Training at the University of North Carolina at Greensboro and has published widely in the clinical literature. She was trained in clinical psychology at the Maudsley Hospital in London and at the State University of New York at Stony Brook. She is President of Division 25 of the American Psychological Association (Division for the Experimental Analysis of Behavior) and Past President of the Association for Advancement of Behavior Therapy. Her editorial duties have included being founding editor of *Behavioral Assessment,* and an associate editor of the *Journal of Applied Behavior Analysis.* Her chief professional interest is behavioral assessment, its techniques and theoretical basis.

359

Pergamon General Psychology Series

Editors: Arnold P. Goldstein, Syracuse University
Leonard Krasner, SUNY at Stony Brook